£1

CW00957414

PILTDOWN
MAN

PILTDOWN MAN

THE SECRET LIFE OF
CHARLES DAWSON
& THE WORLD'S GREATEST
ARCHAEOLOGICAL HOAX

MILES RUSSELL

TEMPUS

For Macsen
(who has known of nothing else)

Robert
(who once started something similar)

and Stella
(who sadly never saw the finished version)

Thank you all

First published 2003

Tempus Publishing Ltd
The Mill, Brimscombe Port
Stroud, Gloucestershire GL5 2QG
www.tempus-publishing.com

British Library Cataloguing in Publication Data.
A catalogue record for this book is available from the British Library.

ISBN 0 7524 2572 2

Typesetting and origination by Tempus Publishing.
Printed and bound in Great Britain.

CONTENTS

Acknowledgements 6

Preface 8

1 Introducing Dawson 10

2 Monsters in the Weald 28

3 Secrets of the dungeon 33

4 Sticks and stones 51

5 An Age of Iron 61

6 Antler, bronze and underwater forests 86

7 The Pevensey Bricks 97

8 The sincerest form of flattery? 108

9 Weird Nature 124

10 Time and space 141

11 Piltdown man I 149

12 Piltdown II and III 231

13 A brief history of crime 250

Postscript 266

Appendix I: The Lavant Caves 271

Appendix II: The Dawson Loans Collection 273

Bibliography 281

Index 285

ACKNOWLEDGEMENTS

All line drawings and photographs presented here are copyright of the Sussex Archaeological Society and have been reproduced (from their own photographic collection and also from that contained within the Robert Downes archive) with their permission, with the exception of figures 12, 36, 37, 38, 39, 40, 41, 42, 43, 44, 46, 47 and 99, which have been reproduced with the permission of Hastings Museum and Art Gallery, figure 66 which has been reproduced with the permission of the Booth Museum of Natural History in Brighton, and figures 6, 27, 58, 99, 101, 102, 103, 104, 105 and 106 which are copyright of the author. For allowing me access to these extensive archives I would especially like to thank Hannah Crowdy, Emma Young, Barbara Alcock, Helen Poole, Esme Evans, Cathy Wallings and Ed Jarzembowski. I would also like to thank Kate Bartlett, Anna Charlton and Dan Walker of BBC History and the Revd Scully of St John Sub Castro in Lewes for their help in locating both a number of allegedly 'missing' artefacts and also in the identification of the otherwise elusive grave plot of Charles and Helene Dawson.

During the course of this work I have benefited from lengthy conversations concerning Piltdown man with a large number of friends and colleagues and would particularly like to thank the following for their help, information, criticism and advice over the past two years: Kevin Andrews, Kate Bartlett, Mark Brisbane, Martin Brown, Chris Butler, Jeff Chartrand, Paul Cheetham, Margaret Cox, Tim Darvill, Roger Doonan, Mark Dover, John Gale, Ellen Hambleton, Iain Hewitt, Bettany Hughes, Alex Hunt, Glynis Laughlin, Mark Maltby, John Manley, Aubrey Manning, John Mills, Derek Russell, Jane Russell, Paul Sen, Helen Smith, Mark Taylor, Kate Welham and Andrew Woodcock. Thank you also to Peter Kemmis Betty, Emma Parkin and all at Tempus Publishing for their help, advice and faith that the finished version would one day be delivered (even after the first ten submission deadlines passed by without incident). A huge thank you to Linda Fransen and Louise Pearson for their support and much valued help (especially when my computer crashed taking all data with it to the IT graveyard) and to Rita Burr and Marie Dunning for their expert assistance in helping me manage (and spend) my Bournemouth University research budget.

My greatest debt of thanks, however, must be to Bronwen, Megan and Macsen who have had to endure *Eoanthropus dawsoni*, a largely uninvited house-guest, over the past two years. *Eoanthropus* has not been the best of visitors, leaving books and papers (not to say laundry and dirty dishes) everywhere and allowing rubbish to build up in almost every room of the house. Now that he has finally found somewhere else to go, the routine of 'normal' life may at last return. Macs has had a particularly raw deal, although he is at last coming to terms with the fact that he has a father. I would like to dedicate this book to him, as some poor recompense for the time that I should have spent playing in the park and not staring blankly at a computer screen, and also to my paternal grandmother Stella Russell, who read many of my very early (not to say rather tortuous) writings, but liked them all just the same.

I would also like to dedicate this work to someone I have never met: Robert L. Downes. Downes was a graduate student of Birmingham University at the time the Piltdown fraud was first revealed in 1953. As an undergraduate, he had made a study of the English iron industry, making much use of a particular discovery of Charles Dawson's: a cast-iron Roman statuette from Beauport Park near Hastings in East Sussex. Investigating the statuette more closely, Downes became aware that it was not all that it seemed. Probing Dawson's collection still further, Downes discovered a number of inconsistencies, most of which had never been fully discussed or even acknowledged. Much of this early work was used by Joseph Weiner for his book *The Piltdown Forgery* published in 1955. Afterwards, Downes endeavoured to write his own book on the subject, entitled *Charles Dawson on Trial (a study in archaeology)*. Unfortunately, the general feeling towards Piltdown man during the later years of the 1950s seems to have been one of acute embarrassment and most commercial publishers were rather unenthusiastic about prolonging the debate any further. Those to whom Downes approached with details of his proposal unanimously replied in polite but thoroughly dismissive terms. The manuscript wallowed in 'development hell' until the early 1960s, when Downes became tired of pursuing it any further. When in 1981 he died, aged only fifty-eight, his papers, documents and notes were passed to the Sussex Archaeological Society, where they remain to this day.

I first became aware of Downes' work whilst completing what I then believed to be the final stages of this particular book. Reading through the large collection of notes, letters, photographs and illustrations housed in the Sussex Archaeological Society's library at Barbican House in Lewes was a revelation. Downes had spent a not inconsiderable amount of his life researching, analysing and cataloguing Charles Dawson and his discoveries, ultimately to no avail. Integrating many of his comments into my book involved significant rewrites, not to say *rethinks*. Many new discoveries and reports were also revealed, and I have tried to acknowledge these throughout the course of my own revised study. Although my own ideas often differ from those expressed by Robert Downes, I hope that this version of the life and discoveries of Charles Dawson provides a suitable, if somewhat belated, tribute.

PREFACE

Piltdown. Even today the name sends a shiver down the collective spine of the scientific community, for this was the most dramatic and daring fraud ever perpetrated upon the world of science and academia and the fallout from it continues to affect us to this day.

The basics of the story are simple enough: between 1908 and 1912, a series of amazing discoveries relating to what appeared to be the earliest human were made close to the little village of Piltdown in Sussex. These remains belonged to the developmental 'missing link' between man and ape. The basic principles of evolution, first propounded by Charles Darwin in his thesis *On the Origin of Species* some fifty years before, now appeared as indisputable fact.

There then followed a frenzied bout of academic and media-related interest as the discovery was announced to the world in December 1912. The *Manchester Guardian* ran the first headline: 'THE EARLIEST MAN?: REMARKABLE DISCOVERY IN SUSSEX. A SKULL MILLIONS OF YEARS OLD' it screamed, adding that the find was 'one of the most important of our time'. The news spread quickly around the world, with anthropologists, geologists and archaeologists all voicing their eagerness to examine the find.

Few archaeological discoveries have the capacity to be front-page news twice over, but 'Piltdown man' (or *Eoanthropus dawsoni* to give him his proper scientific name) is a rare exception. Forty-one years after he first became famous, the 'Earliest Englishman' was again hot news. It was late November 1953, and the world was about to discover that Piltdown man had been a hoax. Not just any hoax mind, the London *Star* declared it to be 'THE BIGGEST SCIENTIFIC HOAX OF THE CENTURY'. There never had been a 'missing link' preserved in the gravels of Piltdown; the whole discovery had been part of an elaborate and complex archaeological forgery. The 'Earliest Englishman' was nothing more than a cheap fraud.

It has been fifty years since the full nature of the Piltdown 'discovery' was exposed and since then there have been many variations on the central question of 'who originally designed and perpetrated the fraud?' It is a question that seems no closer to resolution. Conspiracy and counter-conspiracy theories abound. Books, papers, Internet websites, television and radio programmes all regularly discuss, re-discuss and regurgitate the evidence, occasionally unearthing a nugget of new information, though more usually serving only to muddy the waters with new allegations, unfounded claims and increasingly wild supposition. Fifty years on it seems that pretty much anyone could have had legitimate reasons for having created the fraud:

> even the Piltdown milkman, or postman, falls into this 'guilty until proved innocent' category as do their wives, children, dogs, friends, relatives and acquaintances – in short anything animate in England in 1909, particularly to the south-eastern part of it.[1]

One name that continues to surface within any discussion of the hoax, however, is that of its finder, Charles Dawson FGS, FSA. Dawson was a solicitor and amateur antiquarian and palaeontologist of some considerable repute during the end of the nineteenth century and beginning of the twentieth. To him are credited a variety of finds, discoveries, theories and surveys which helped shape and mould an understanding of the earliest years of Sussex, the county in which he lived and worked. Some of Dawson's discoveries have, however, recently come under intense scrutiny and some archaeologists, anthropologists and researchers have openly accused him of a lifetime of deception if not downright fraud.

Unfortunately, to date no one has taken every one of Dawson's discoveries and investigated each on an individual, objective basis. No one has examined the recorded aspects, composition and circumstances of each discovery. No one has attempted to evade the supposition, hearsay and general string of allegations that anything (and anyone) associated with Piltdown will always possess. No one has put Dawson's career on trial nor his 'discoveries' under close archaeological examination.

In the chapters that follow, I hope to amend this situation by assessing each of Dawson's finds, from his earliest fossil discoveries at Hastings, to his claims to have discovered a new race of human, via an assortment of Roman statuettes and bricks, post-medieval maps and clocks, Neolithic axes, horseshoes, dog gates, dinosaurs and sea serpents, as well as the famous Piltdown assemblage itself, in an attempt to separate fact from fiction, supposition from evidence. For each find, the basic facts of discovery will be set out, as well as the claims made against them, and will conclude with a statement of the perceived authenticity and reliability of each.

A last chapter will pull all the assorted evidence together and come to a final conclusion as to the true identity and motive of 'Mr X': the real figure behind 'Piltdown man'.

Note: As a wealth of sources has been drawn upon for the purposes of this book, I have taken the opportunity of citing these in the Notes. It is hoped that these will make the checking of primary data and the process of continuing research a far easier task than it might normally have been.

1

INTRODUCING DAWSON

He is an enigmatic figure. Staring out from black and white photographs we see a slightly portly, if amiable-looking fellow, a balding head, jaunty moustache and twinkling eyes (**1**). People who knew Charles Dawson described him in positively glowing terms. Sir Arthur Smith Woodward called him 'a delightful colleague in scientific research, always cheerful, hopeful and overflowing with enthusiasm'.[1] His wife Helene was later to remember him as 'the best and kindest man who ever lived'.[2]

In his life he achieved recognition as a great, if not *the greatest*, British anti-quarian and amateur palaeontologist. Within the social circles of his home county, the extent and range of his amazing discoveries earned him the title 'the Wizard of Sussex'.[3] He was, in his professional capacity, also a well-respected solicitor, doing much to benefit his local community. Hard then to believe that this is the same man accused of being the mastermind behind the most infamous scientific fraud in history. Can this be the same Charles Dawson recently described as possessing a 'warped and unscrupulous mind', the perpe-trator of a 'despicable' and 'ugly trick' played out upon the innocent general public and unsuspecting scholars?[4]

How can these disparate perceptions of the man be reconciled? Did the outwardly genial 'Dr Jekyll' persona of Charles Dawson really, as some have suggested, mask an intrinsically evil and scheming 'Mr Hyde'? Can we ever understand what motivated the man, what drove him on and what, so to speak, made him tick? After so much time has passed, can we really be sure of ever knowing the *real* Charles Dawson?

Early days

J. Charles Dawson was born on 11 July 1864 at Fulkeith Hall in Lancashire[5] into a family made prosperous by the cotton-spinning industry of Preston. Dawson's father, Hugh, used part of his inherited wealth to fund his goal of becoming a barrister-at-law.[6] Ill-health, however, dogged Hugh Dawson and the family left Lancashire, whilst Charles was still a boy, moving to the healthier seaside air of St Leonards on Sea, then a new suburb of Hastings in Sussex. Of

Charles' early years we know very little, other than that he spent much of his time exploring cliffs and quarries in search of fossils and that he was enrolled into the Gosport Royal Academy to complete his education.[7]

Charles' younger brothers, Hugh Leyland and Arthur Trevor Dawson, both attended university, Hugh later pursuing a successful career with the Church, becoming vicar of Clandown (near Bath), whilst Trevor went to serve with the Royal Navy. Of all the brothers, perhaps it was Trevor who was the most successful, being knighted in 1909 and becoming the Managing Director and Superintendent of the Ordnance at Metro-Vickers and Maxims Ltd (one of the premier shipbuilding engineering and arms manufacturers of the early twentieth century). He attained the rank of Naval Commander during the First World War and was created a baronet in 1920.[8] He married Louise Grant, sister of Rear Admiral Noel Grant, a hero of the First World War, and the couple moved to Edgwarebury House in Elstree, London. Successful by any standards, Sir Trevor and Lady Dawson moved within an elite social circle, Trevor being in a position to introduce his elder brother Charles to King Edward VII in 1906.

Charles, in contrast, pursued a more modest early career path. He never went to university, opting instead, after leaving the Gosport Academy, to follow his father into the legal profession. In 1880, then aged sixteen, Charles began working for F.A. Langhams, a firm of solicitors based in London but

1 *Charles Dawson*

2 *Uckfield: the High Street in the early 1900s*

with a branch office close to the family home in Hastings.[9] By 1890 he was working with James Langham in Uckfield, a modest but steadily expanding East Sussex town (**2**), becoming a full partner and taking the practice over in 1900. In 1906, with George Hart as fellow partner, the firm became Dawson Hart & Co. Solicitors, a name that it retains to this day.[10]

In Uckfield, Dawson played a not inconsiderable part within civic affairs (**3**), being Clerk to the Urban District Council and Clerk to the Uckfield Justices for some twenty-two years. He was also appointed Secretary of the Uckfield Gas Co., Solicitor to the Uckfield Building Society and a Trustee of the Eastbourne Building Society.[11] In his professional capacity he further acted as Steward to a number of large and prosperous estates including the Manors of Barkham, Netherall and Camois.[12]

On 21 January 1905, then aged forty, Charles married Helene L.E. Postlethwaite, a widow with two grown children, Gladys and F.J.M. (later Captain) Postlethwaite. Helene, of Irish descent but born in Bordeaux,[13] may well have been introduced to Charles through his younger brother Trevor.[14] At the time of their engagement, she and her family were residents of Park Lane, Helene being a prominent member of Mayfair society. The wedding took place at Christ Church, Mayfair and was by all accounts a rather grand event, the bride being given away by Sir James Joicey MP, Dawson's best man being Basil Bagshot de la Bere of Buxted.[15] Following the wedding reception, held at Sir Trevor and Lady Dawson's Mayfair residence, Charles and his new wife honeymooned in Rome. Afterwards, Dawson made plans to return to Sussex and in 1907 the family moved into Castle Lodge,[16] a spacious, if rather eccentric town house set in the grounds of a Norman castle in the market town of Lewes.

Fossil hunting

From his earliest days, Charles Dawson possessed a keen interest in the natural world, collecting a variety of fossils from the coast, cliffs and quarries around Hastings.[17] In much of these searches he was encouraged by Samuel H. Beckles F.R.S., a distinguished geologist then in his twilight years.[18] Together with Beckles, Dawson amassed a considerable collection of reptilian and mammalian fossils, the prize piece being the 'finest extant example' of ganoid fish *Lepidotus mantelli*,[19] all of which he donated to the British Museum (Natural History) in 1884. The museum conferred upon him the title 'honorary collector' and in 1885, in recognition of his many discoveries, he was elected a fellow of the Geological Society,[20] quite an achievement for a man who was still only then aged twenty-one.

3 *Uckfield: the Urban District Council in 1897. Charles Dawson is standing third from the left in the central row. His partner in Dawson and Hart Solicitors, George Hart, is standing second from the right at the back*

He continued to add fossil discoveries to the British Museum's 'Dawson Collection' throughout the late 1880s, 1890s and early 1900s. Amongst the material forwarded were three new species of dinosaur, one of which was named *Iguanodon dawsoni* by the palaeontologist Richard Lydekker.[21] Later discoveries included the finding, in 1891, of teeth from a previously unknown species of Wealden mammal, later named *Plagiaulax dawsoni*. Dawson periodically continued his fossil-hunting activities up until 1911, at times working with Marie-Joseph Pierre Teilhard de Chardin, a young Jesuit priest and keen amateur geologist, discovering more unique remains, including a new species of mammal named *Dipriodon valdensis*, and two new forms of fossil plant, *Lycopidites teilhardi* and *Salaginella dawsoni*.[22]

In 1889 Dawson's connection with the antiquities of Hastings was strengthened when he co-founded the Hastings and St Leonards Museum Association, one of the first voluntary museum friends groups established in Britain.[23] The museum, which was established within the Brassey Institute (now Hastings Library), was eventually taken over by Hastings Corporation in 1905.[24] Dawson soon found himself, as a member of the Museum Committee, in charge of the acquisition of artefacts and historical documents. The museum itself proved to be the ideal display case for Dawson's own expanding antiquarian collection, which, by 1899, was to occupy a section all of its own.[25]

Whilst performing his legal role, Dawson found himself acting as solicitor to a number of prominent antiquarian collectors in the region and was in a good position to catalogue a variety of materials and artefacts bequeathed or donated to Hastings Museum throughout the 1890s and early 1900s.[26] By 1890, he was even conducting his own excavations in the town, most notably on and around Castle Hill. The work he conducted was reported to have produced a 'great haul' of artefacts,[27] though the full extent and nature of these discoveries unfortunately remains unknown.

The Great Antiquarian

By 1892, Dawson was increasingly turning his attention to matters archaeological, joining the Sussex Archaeological Society as honorary local secretary for Uckfield. The following year he was chosen, together with the Society's librarian and clerk, to represent the county-based organisation at the fifth Congress of Archaeological Societies in association with the prestigious London-based Society of Antiquaries.[28] The following year he was also co-directing, with John Lewis, excavation work at Hastings Castle and in the Lavant Caves near Chichester.[29] A paper on the examination of the Lavant Caves was presented to the annual general meeting of the Sussex Archaeological Society in August 1893.

It was about this time that Dawson's uncanny knack of making spectacular discoveries, as evidenced during the course of his geological exploits, came once again to the fore. In 1893 he presented the Keeper of Roman and Medieval antiquities at the British Museum, Augustus Wollaston Franks, with a Roman statuette made, uniquely for the period, of cast iron. This, he claimed, was found in a slag heap at Beauport Park, near Hastings.[30] The statuette was later displayed with much publicity before the Society of Antiquaries. Other discoveries followed, including a hafted Neolithic stone axe head and a well-preserved ancient timber boat, both of which were reported in the *Sussex Archaeological Collections* for 1894. In recognition of his many discoveries, theories and constant hard work in the field of antiquarian research, Dawson was elected a fellow of the Society of Antiquaries of London in 1895.[31] At the age of thirty-one, and without a university degree to his name, he was now Charles Dawson FGS., FSA.

In 1901 Dawson was present at the founding of the Sussex Record Society, a sister group to the Archaeological Society, itself originally established in 1846.[32] This new group was formed primarily to research, curate and publish historical documents relating to the county of Sussex. In April of 1902, by the time of the group's first annual general meeting, Dawson had become a full member of the Council.

At this point he began to write extensively on all aspects of Sussex history and archaeology, especially its ironwork, pottery[33] and glass.[34] He studied ancient quarries, mines and dene holes,[35] he reanalysed the Bayeux Tapestry[36] and produced the definite study of Hastings Castle.[37] He found evidence for the final phases on Roman military occupation of Britain at Pevensey Castle [38] and discovered a large supply of natural gas at Heathfield in East Sussex.[39] He took a great interest in the still relatively fledgling art of photography [40] and it was in this respect that he was invited on a number of archaeological expeditions, most notably in 1907 accompanying John Ray in the exhumation of prehistoric burials in Eastbourne.[41]

Later on, Charles Dawson started to investigate the more strange and unorthodox aspects of the natural world. Examples of the unnatural which caught his interest included a toad petrified inside a flint nodule (which he presented to Brighton Museum), sea serpents in the English Channel, 'incipient horns' found in cart horses, a new species of modern human and a strange cross between the goldfish and the carp.[42] It was even reported that in the latter years of his life, Dawson was experimenting with phosphorescent bullets as a deterrent to Zeppelin attacks on London.[43]

Archaeological societies

Charles Dawson's active involvement with the Sussex Archaeological Society unfortunately ended somewhat acrimoniously. In 1903 the Society was happily occupying Castle Lodge, a rather grand town house owned by the Marquess of Abergavenny, situated in a prominent position immediately to the north-west of the medieval barbican gate house (**4**), within the precincts of Lewes Castle. In the autumn of that year, however, the Council received some unexpected news, which they duly alerted Society members to via a notice in the 1904 edition of their annual journal:

> The Council [has] received an intimation that the Castle Lodge, which has been occupied by the Society since the year 1885, had been sold to Mr Dawson, and a notice to quit at midsummer 1904 had been served by him on the Secretary. This purchase by one of our own members, and its consequences, took the Council completely by surprise – as it understood that if the property was to be sold, the Society should have the option of acquiring it.[44]

The details surrounding the sale of the property to Dawson remain unclear, and unfortunately we possess only a one-sided version of the affair; that of the Sussex Archaeological Society, who were understandably rather aggrieved to have been evicted by one of their own members. Louis Salzman, a member of the Society in 1904 (and later president), believed that the purchase had not been wholly above board.[45] His accusation was that Dawson used both his official position as a solicitor and his connection to the Society (aided by his unauthorised use of Sussex Archaeological Society headed notepaper) to allow the vendors to assume that he was in some way acting in an official capacity for them.[46]

4 *Lewes: the medieval barbican gate in 2003 with Castle Lodge immediately to the left*

5 *Lewes: the High Street looking east, close to Barbican House, in the early 1900s*

Whatever the truth of the matter, Castle Lodge was eventually cleared of its tenants and in the spring of 1907 the Dawsons moved into their new home. Over the following years, the architectural features of Castle Lodge became increasingly elaborate, Dawson adding fake battlements, ornate windows and statuary, whilst also converting an abandoned wine cellar into a mock medieval dungeon complete with manacles and a stone bed.[47] Little is known about the interior of the Castle Lodge following Dawson's renovation though Marie-Joseph Pierre Teilhard de Chardin, a visitor to the property in May of 1912, observed that Charles' stepson F.J.M. Postlethwaite, then 'in the colonial army in the Sudan' was busy 'cluttering the house with antelope heads'.[48]

Having been removed from the Lodge, the Sussex Archaeological Society finally located a secure home in Barbican House, a three-storey town house on the eastern edge of Castle Precinct, directly opposite the Dawsons' new abode. Thus the relocation from Uckfield now meant that the Dawsons, as they sallied forth in to the Lewes High Street (**5**) from their family home, were to encounter 'the daily coolness of the recently evicted tenants'.[49] The move was eventually to prove beneficial for the Society, but their relationship with Dawson was never to recover. Even in the late 1940s, some thirty years after Dawson's death, feelings towards him still ran high, Louis Salzman commenting acerbically that 'his name was later given to the "Pilt Down Man" (*Eoanthropus dawsoni*), the lowest known form of human being, with the discovery of whose remains he was associated'.[50]

6 *Hastings: the Museum and Art Gallery in 2003*

Perhaps as a consequence of this new and rather awkward relationship with the county group, Dawson re-established his links with his boyhood town and joined the Hastings Natural History Society. Though both he and Helene were to remain fully paid-up members of the Sussex Archaeological Society until Charles' premature death in 1916, neither appears to have played any significant or active role within the organisation. Joining the Hastings Natural History Society may well have been a perfectly natural step for Dawson to have taken in any case, for he had already been a co-founder of the Hastings Museum Association and had an active interest in the town's castle. Following Dawson's death, much of his extensive collection of artefacts, both archaeological and geological, ultimately passed into the possession of Hastings Museum,[51] where it remains to this day (**6**).

Piltdown man

Charles Dawson's greatest claim to fame was the discovery, sometime before 1912, of remains of the missing link between ape and man. The find, which comprised parts of a human skull and a chinless ape-like jaw (**7**), came from just outside the quiet Sussex village of Piltdown. These pieces fitted the basic theory of evolution being propounded at the time for modern man had, it was argued, developed from the apes because of an expansion in brain capacity. The remains recovered from Piltdown confirmed this hypothesis, showing that it was the evolution of thought, and subsequent enlargement of the brain, that defined early humans (**8**). A huge media storm greeted the presentation of these remains to the Geological Society on 18 December 1912.[52] The finds were hailed as one of the most important archaeological discoveries *ever*, something that would irrevocably alter our perception of who we are and where we came from.

The press were ecstatic: 'REMARKABLE FIND IN SUSSEX' ran the headline of the *Manchester Guardian*, 'FIRST EVIDENCE OF A NEW HUMAN TYPE' trumpeted the London *Times*, whilst the New York *Times* noted that the 'PALAEOLITHIC SKULL IS MISSING LINK' adding that the discovery was 'FAR OLDER THAN CAVEMEN'. The best news of all, at least for those packed into the headquarters of the Geological Society at Burlington House to hear the first public report of the discoveries, was that the earliest known human was not French, German, Italian, Chinese or African, but British. This new species of human was, in recognition of its finder who had single-handedly elevated the world standing of British palaeontology, given the name *Eoanthropus dawsoni*, literally 'Dawson's man of the dawn'.

Discovery of *Eoanthropus dawsoni* at Piltdown appears to have done nothing to restore Dawson's former relationship with the Sussex Archaeological Society. In fact, as Weiner was later to note in his book *The Piltdown Forgery*,

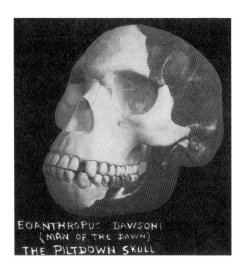

7 (Above) *Piltdown man:* Eoanthropus dawsoni *as reconstructed in 1914*

8 (Right) *Piltdown man: a lively recreation showing* Eoanthropus dawsoni *shaping an elephant bone with the aid of a flint 'eolith'*

The deliberate avoidance of the great Piltdown discovery in official local circles is quite undeniable. On my first visit of inquiry... I had fully expected to see much made of Piltdown in the local museums. The Borough Museum contained nothing but a small picture of an imaginary *Eoanthropus* presented by Dr S. Spokes and some Piltdown eoliths presented by Harry Morris.[53]

Further amazement followed when Weiner came to examine the pages of the *Sussex Archaeological Collections*:

I was not at all prepared to discover on reading through all these volumes of the years 1911 to 1916 – no mention of Piltdown at all! No meeting had ever been held, no address given by Dawson, by then their most famous member.[54]

However badly the relationship between the Uckfield solicitor and the county Society had deteriorated, it is clear that the Piltdown artefacts, combined with a similar range of finds from nearby Barcombe Mills (in 1913) and Sheffield Park (1915), finally established Charles Dawson as international antiquarian archaeologist *par excellence*. Unfortunately, just at the time of this his greatest achievement, and just when he appears to have been on the verge of reporting more exceptional discoveries, Dawson was taken gravely ill. The exact cause of his illness remains unknown, though it has been suggested he was suffering from pernicious anaemia.[55] Despite resting for a brief period at home in Lewes during the spring of 1916 and being put on a course of serum injections,[56] Dawson returned to work at Dawson and Hart in Uckfield. By June his condition had worsened significantly, and he was confined to bed throughout July. Early on 10 August 1916, aged only fifty-two, he died.

After Piltdown

Dawson's funeral, held on 12 August at the Church of St John Sub Castro in Lewes (**9**), was attended by over 100 mourners, the service being in part conducted by his brother, the Revd Hugh Leyland Dawson.[57] The eulogies and obituaries that followed were unanimous in their praise for the Sussex fossil hunter and antiquarian. His colleague and fellow excavator at Piltdown, Sir Arthur Smith Woodward, wrote in the *Geological Magazine*:

To a capacity for taking pains, with endless patience, he added a sharpness of sight that never overlooked anything of importance; and he was not only in close touch with all workmen in his district who might make accidental discoveries, but was also in constant friendly communication with a wide

9 *Lewes: the cemetery of St John Sub Castro in the early 1900s*

circle of professional scientific men who helped him make the best use of his material.[58]

Later in the same obituary Woodward adds:

> He had a restless mind, ever alert to note anything unusual; and he was never satisfied until he had exhausted all means to solve and understand any problem which presented itself... The premature loss of his inspiring and genial presence is indeed a great sorrow to his large circle of devoted friends.[59]

Sir Arthur Keith, in the *British Medical Journal*, observed that he had been:

> a splendid type of that great class of men who give the driving power to British science – the thinking, observant amateur. Without that class to serve as scientific scouts we could make little progress in our knowledge of the past.[60]

Judges in the magistrates court at Uckfield, where Dawson had been chief clerk, referred to him as:

> A quiet unassuming man with pleasantly smiling eyes gleaming through rather obtruding spectacles... He never gave an opinion, to his knowledge,

unless he was sure, he was never ashamed to look it up... If anyone had seen [him] issuing from the door of a matter-of-fact country lawyer's office they would not have realised what a man of romance he was.[61]

Twenty-two years later, on 22 July 1938, as a lasting tribute to both Dawson and his *Eoanthropus dawsoni*, a stone monolith, made from carboniferous sandstone, was erected at Piltdown on the approach road to Barkham Manor, close to where the first skull fragments had been discovered. The inscription read simply:

Here in the old river gravel Mr Charles Dawson FSA, found the fossil skull of Piltdown man 1912-13. The discovery was described by Mr Charles Dawson and Sir Arthur Smith Woodward in the quarterly journal of the Geological Society 1913-15.

Sir Arthur Keith and Sir Arthur Woodward (**10**) both made speeches during the unveiling of the monolith, Keith noting how:

Professional men took their hats off to the amateur, Mr Charles Dawson, solicitor and antiquarian. They did well to link his name with this picturesque corner of Sussex and the scene of the discovery.[62]

10 *Piltdown: the unveiling of a monolith, commemorating Dawson's discovery of Piltdown man, by Sir Arthur Smith Woodward in 1938*

In September 1950, the British Museum (Natural History) supervised the opening of a section of the gravel terrace within which most of the original Piltdown remains had been found. The edges of the excavation were, on completion, bricked up, two small glass window doors being set along the western edge to protect the site from flooding, but also to act as a permanent witness section.[63] In 1952 the area was designated as a Geological Reserve and National Monument by the Nature Conservancy.

A nagging doubt

There the story might have ended, were it not for some persistent and nagging doubts in the minds of certain anthropologists and palaeontologists, that there was 'something not quite right' about the Piltdown discoveries. There never had been full scientific agreement over what the remains found at Piltdown actually represented, nor how they could be satisfactorily reconstructed. A more pressing problem, as the 1920s and 1930s were played out, was exactly where to place *Eoanthropus dawsoni* within the tree of human evolution. When Dawson produced the first set of remains from Sussex, there was little comparative material with which to work. Few fossil remains of the early human or hominids had ever been found and there was a great deal of argument surrounding the way in which to interpret lines of descent.

As more fossil discoveries were made, especially during excavations conducted in China and Africa throughout the 1930s, it appeared that the aspects that best defined *Eoanthropus*, notably a human forehead and an ape-like jaw, were not present elsewhere. In fact the new fossil remains appeared to demonstrate that human-like teeth and jaw were a very early feature in human development, whereas the brain and forehead changed more gradually. The Piltdown skull had the features in reverse; it was an anomaly that scientists began to find increasingly embarrassing.

Analysis of the fluorine content of *Eoanthropus* undertaken in the late 1940s created more problems, for it suggested that the bones of 'Dawn man' could not be any more than 50,000 years old.[64] Such a comparatively recent date meant that Piltdown man could not have been an ancestor of the modern human, merely an archaic form; a strange sort of 'throwback' or mutant. Given all the concerns and issues raised by Piltdown, most scientists felt it easier to simply ignore the discovery completely. The situation was summed up by Joseph Weiner who, whilst attending a palaeolontological conference in London at the end of July 1953, commented that 'Piltdown man was not discussed. Not surprisingly. He had lost his place in polite society'.[65]

As the years passed, Dawson's last great archaeological discovery was coming under ever increasing scrutiny. In December 1953, the myth that *Eoanthropus dawsoni* had been a genuine archaeological discovery was exploded forever.

Joseph Weiner, Kenneth Oakley and Wilfred Le Gros Clark delivered their fatal blow in the pages of the *Bulletin of the British Museum (Natural History) Geology* for November 1953. Entitled simply 'The solution of the Piltdown problem', the article revealed that the jaw and teeth of Piltdown man had all been forged.

Suspecting Dawson

Since the exposure of Piltdown man as a scientific fraud, the main questions have been with regard to the identity of the perpetrator. Weiner, in his book *The Piltdown Forgery*, the first published work to deal explicitly with the hoax, was sure as to the identity of 'Mr X':

> It is not possible to maintain that Dawson could not have been the actual perpetrator; he had the ability, the experience, and, whatever we surmise may have been the motive, he was at all material times in a position to pursue the deception throughout its various phases.[66]

Weiner further alleged that, over a thirty-year period, Dawson had been implicated in a number of archaeological, geological and anthropological deceptions, some daring and some surprisingly low key, a series of cynical forgeries and incidents of blatant plagiarism; the suggestion ultimately being that all of his discoveries, theories and publications should be viewed with the deepest suspicion.

The backlash that followed seems, on the face of it, hardly surprising, for Dawson was a significant and well-liked figure within the worlds of palaeontology, anthropology and antiquarian archaeology. To attack Dawson meant an assault, not only upon all of his theories and findings, but also upon every single one of the scientific experts that had lined up to support him and help bolster his research.

Surviving members of his family were amongst the first to react, his stepson, Captain F.J.M. Postlethwaite, writing to the London *Times* in strident terms within days of the first press release surrounding the forgery:

> Charles Dawson was an unassuming and thoroughly honest man and very painstaking... His hobbies extended in many directions, but it is doubtful whether he could be described as a great expert in any single subject. Until the discovery of Piltdown he did not display any particular interest in skulls, human or otherwise, and so far as I know had none in his possession. To suggest that he had the knowledge and the skill to break an ape's jawbone in exactly the right place, to pare the teeth to ensure a perfect fit to the upper skull and to disguise the whole in such a manner as to deceive his partner, a scientist of international repute, would surely be absurd, and

personally I am doubtful whether he ever had the opportunity of doing so. No – Charles Dawson was at all times far too honest and faithful to his research to have been accessory to any faking whatsoever. He was himself duped, and from statements appearing in the Press such is evidently the opinion of those who knew him well.[67]

Postlethwaite, as others, noted Dawson's pedigree as antiquarian of no small repute, asking why he would have thought it necessary to fake the Piltdown skull. Francis Vere, in his 1955 book *The Piltdown Fantasy*, a speedy refutation of Weiner's accusations against Dawson, noted that:

Dawson, even if he had had the skill to do the faking, would never have dared. He had no guarantee against discovery. It would have been fatal to him. His reputation as an amateur archaeologist would have wilted; his reputation as a responsible lawyer would have suffered; he would have become an object of scorn.[68]

Others quickly followed Postlethwaite's central premise that Dawson was no more than the innocent victim of a cruel practical joke. Robert Essex, writing in the *Kent and Sussex Journal*, observed: 'I am certain Dawson suspected something, although at the time I had no idea what he suspected. He was not the man to broadcast suspicion'.[69] Essex saw the Piltdown discovery as a 'hoax that grew', a simple fraud targeted specifically at Dawson, but one to which the hoaxer would have been increasingly unwilling to confess to once the find itself had been made public:

When the first bait was swallowed and the hoaxer did not get the satisfaction of seeing the face of his victim when he realised he had been galled, he tried again and again and in the end all the hoaxer had was the knowledge that in the British Museum was his hybrid offspring which he cold not publicly claim.[70]

Since the mid-1950s the arguments have swung both for and against the possibility that Dawson, the discoverer of Piltdown man, could also have been its creator. Most of the discussions rely on the premise that Piltdown was a 'one off', a single, if rather elaborate hoax, designed to fool the scientific community, embarrass certain key figures of the establishment or to verify (or perhaps even to discredit) fledgling models of human evolution. Under such circumstances one of any number of people may plausibly be held responsible, though the most 'usual' of cited suspects are Charles Dawson, Arthur Smith Woodward (**11**), Pierre Teilhard de Chardin and Venus Hargreaves (all members of the original excavation team), as well as the writer Arthur Conan Doyle, the anatomist Arthur Keith, museum curator William Butterfield,

zoologist Martin Hinton, palaeontologist William Solas, neurologist Grafton
Elliot Smith, jeweller Lewis Abbott and chemists John Hewitt and Samuel
Woodhead. All have, at some time or another, come under suspicion of being
the real 'Mr X' of Piltdown.

Those who defend Dawson often cite his impressive credentials as solicitor,
amateur palaeontologist, much published antiquarian and learned member of
two Royal Societies. Vere, as we have already noticed, argued plausibly that
Dawson would not have wished to become embroiled with a hoax such as
Piltdown, for that would be tantamount to professional and academic suicide.[71]
Peter Costello has further argued that Dawson is unlikely to have been the
Piltdown forger as neither his field of experience nor career background would
support such a claim: 'A careful examination of his numerous investigations
and publications reveals the interesting fact that with one possible exception all
are honest and above board'.[72]

Interestingly, those who charge Dawson with complicity also cite his
extensive career as an amateur antiquarian as proof that only he could have
been the main forger at Piltdown. John Evangelist Walsh, in his book
Unravelling Piltdown, suggested that in the years prior to the discovery of
Eoanthropus dawsoni, 'Dawson perpetrated half a dozen or more frauds... all in
their own way ingenious'.[73] None of these forgeries, Walsh argued, were ever
conceived as a way of generating an alternative source of income, but as a way
of attaining much sought after academic credibility, each find being 'produced

11 *Piltdown: a postcard entitled 'Searching for the Piltdown Man' taken and produced by John Frisby, a
commercial photographer of Uckfield, and sold at the Lamb Inn (later 'The Piltdown Man'). Charles Dawson
is standing with hammer (and inset left) while Arthur Smith Woodward is seated with sieve (and inset right)*

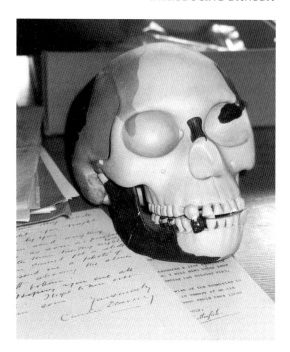

12 *Piltdown man: a reconstruction of* Eoanthropus dawsoni *and letter from Charles Dawson, indicating the circumstances of the original discovery, as preserved at Hastings Museum and Art Gallery*

with some definite effect or target in mind – impressing some highly placed museum official or an influential officer of some scientific body'.[74]

Is this strictly fair? Because Dawson was central to the discovery and initial reporting of Piltdown man (**12**), is it possible that, just as he is tarnished by the revelation of a fraud, so are all of his earlier finds, theories and discoveries? Is it true that because so many allegations of forgery have been so freely made, that the press has made up its own mind, conducting a savage witch-hunt in the process? As Robert Downes noted, way back in 1956 shortly after the hoax was first announced to the world, 'The crimes of which he [Dawson] has been accused are serious ones in the world of scholarship, and if the charges were not substantiated, they would call for heavy damages in a libel action'.[75]

Is Dawson guilty or is he innocent of all the charges put before him? Did he plan a significant number of antiquarian forgeries in intricate detail or was he duped by another? Was it all just an unfortunate set of coincidences? These are difficult questions to answer with any certainty, especially as so much time has elapsed since the discovery of Piltdown man and the first revelation of fraud. In order to address these awkward issues we must temporarily cease throwing accusations at all involved and go back to the primary evidence. We must trawl through Charles Dawson's extensive antiquarian back catalogue, objectively examining the information supplied on a case by case basis. We need, in short, to completely reassess the career of Charles Dawson, to say, once and for all, whether he was the shadowy 'Mr X'.

2

MONSTERS IN THE WEALD

Charles Dawson was an avid collector of fossils from a very early age. His friendship with Samuel H. Beckles FRS., then one of the country's most distinguished geologists, is well documented (e.g. Woodward 1916), the two men amassing an important collection of fossil remains, most of which were donated to the British Museum (Natural History). Dawson's prize discoveries during his many years searching the quarries and cliffs of the Hastings area were the ganoid fish *Lepidotus mantelli*, a new form of fossil plant *Salaginella dawsoni*, three new species of dinosaur, one of which was named *Iguanodon dawsoni*, and a new form of mammal known as *Plagiaulax dawsoni*.[1] There is nothing overtly suspicious about the majority of Dawson's early discoveries, in fact specimens such as *Lepidotus, Salaginella* and *Iguanodon* are exactly the sort of things that a determined amateur palaeontologist feverishly searching the quarries of his area would, during the latter years of the nineteenth century, be expected to find. One discovery, however, has caused concern, especially as it presents a worryingly familiar prelude to the discoveries later made at Piltdown.

Plagiaulax dawsoni

Late in November 1891, a young Assistant Curator at the British Museum (Natural History) presented a paper concerning an exciting new fossil discovery before the Zoological Society of London. The assistant curator was Arthur Smith Woodward and the fossil find a single tooth (**13**) which, although small, seemed to provide the first evidence of a 'European Cretaceous Mammal': an important missing link in the history of life on earth. The find had been made, Woodward reported 'by Mr Charles Dawson of Uckfield, in an irregular mass of communated fish and reptile bones, with scales and teeth, occurring in lenticular patches at one definite horizon in a quarry near Hastings'.[2] Woodward, undeterred that the exact location, date and circumstances of discovery were disappointingly vague, observed that the size of the tooth, when combined with the shape of the crown, suggested that it had derived from a wholly new species of the mammal order *Multituberculata*. This new species could, Woodward suggested, 'until the acquisition of further material... bear the provisional name of *Plagiaulax dawsoni*, in honour of its discoverer'.[3]

The order *Multituberculata* first appeared in the Jurassic period, between 206 and 144 million years ago, being at their most diverse and widespread during the late Cretaceous. Multituberculates do not belong to any of the groups of mammals alive today. They were small and hairy in appearance, their pelvic anatomy suggesting that they gave birth to tiny, marsupial-like young. The final lower premolars of most Multituberculates formed enlarged, serrated blades, such teeth often being described as 'plagiaulacoid' after the Mesozoic multituberculate genus *Plagiaulax*.

The tooth that Dawson had presented to Woodward was larger than any known example of the genus *Plagiaulax*. It was also far more abraded than was common, Woodward observing the 'extraordinary amount of wear to which the crown has been subjected', having lost all its enamel 'except quite at the border'.[4] It was the patterning of wear that most seemed to perplex the young geologist, especially as the abrasion had not been produced 'entirely by an upward and downward or antero-posterior motion, of which the jaws of the know *Multituberculata* seem have been alone capable'.[5] Any doubts concerning the antiquity of the abrasion were, however, dispelled by Woodward who noted that when he had first received it, the fossil had been so firmly embedded within its soil matrix that only long and diligent work by the technicians of the British Museum laboratory could satisfactorily detach it.

Assigning a new species on the basis of a single tooth was a potentially hazardous endeavour, though Woodward covered himself by acknowledging the need to acquire 'further material' to confirm the hypothesis.[6] Such confirmation did not occur for another twenty years when, in 1911, Charles Dawson together with Father Marie-Joseph Pierre Teilhard de Chardin and Father Felix Pelletier found three more mammalian teeth 'from the Ashdown Sands of the Fairlight Cliffs near Hastings'.[7] Woodward, after examining the pieces, observed that two of the three new finds, both of which had been discovered by Dawson, could be compared with *Plagiaulax*. Unfortunately, both teeth were 'very imperfect', though 'in one the crown is seen to be closely similar to that of the original tooth of *Pl. dawsoni*'.[8]

The third tooth (**14**), found by Teilhard de Chardin, was far better preserved, exhibiting the whole crown. The black shining enamel of this piece differed 'considerably in appearance from the paler coloured and faintly cracked enamel of the other Wealden teeth which have been provisionally referred to as *Plagiaulax*'.[9] On the basis of its shape and form, Woodward assigned Teilhard de Chardin's discovery to a species of mammal *Dipriodon*, 'recorded under the name *Dipriodon valdensis*'.[10]

No more examples of the species *Plagiaulax dawsoni* have ever come to light, though other early mammalian remains have sporadically appeared within the Ashdown Beds of the Hastings area.[11] Lack of additional remains has, understandably, created some uncertainty with the scientific community cornering the validity of the species originally identified by Woodward in 1891. Simpson,

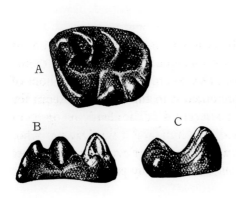

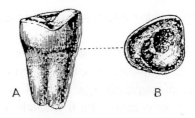

13 (Above) Plagiaulax dawsoni: *two views of the fossil tooth discovered by Charles Dawson in 1891*

14 (Left) Dipriodon valdensis: *three views of the fossil tooth discovered by Marie-Joseph Pierre Teilhard de Chardin in 1911*

whilst analysing Dawson's first tooth in the late 1920s, commented that the piece 'is probably plagiaulacid, although its generic and specific affinities are quite undeterminable'.[12]

Clemens, studying the remains of *Plagiaulax dawsoni* in the early 1960s, observed that 'the presence of a single pulp cavity in the root reduces the probability that the tooth is a plagiaulacid molar, which has two roots, and strongly suggests that it is not the tooth of a mammal'.[13] Clemens, ending his analysis of the Dawson's Wealden fossils, suggested that only the tooth recovered by Teilhard de Chardin and Pelletier was in any sense 'unquestionable', those pieces representing *Plagiaulax dawsoni* being of 'doubtful affinity'.[14]

In fact, careful examination of the first tooth of *Plagiaulax dawsoni* showed that the side-to-side abrasion that it has sustained, and which Woodward first noted as being otherwise unknown in the natural wear of this order of ancient mammal, is wholly artificial. Such damage, which effectively eroded the crown and much of the enamel, could only have occurred through a programme of extensive and prolonged post-mortem rubbing. Examination of the remaining plagiaulacoid teeth, recovered in 1911, shows that Woodward's initial comment that their crowns were 'closely similar to that of the original tooth',[15] was eerily prophetic for they too are the product of artificial abrasion. In short, *Plagiaulax dawsoni* is a fake.

Interestingly, the process and nature of the artificial scouring enacted upon the plagiaulacoid teeth mirrors the damage later observed upon the teeth of *Eoanthropus dawsoni* (Piltdown man) where microscopic examination 'revealed the presence of fine scratch marks on both the molars and canine which suggested the application of an abrasive'.[16] Similarly, the evidence that Woodward cites to reinforce the antiquity of the first plagiaulacoid molar, namely the firmness to which it adhered to the soil,[17] was also echoed at Piltdown, especially in the case of the beaver teeth and the elephant femur,[18] both points that we shall return to at a later date.

Plagiaulax dawsoni: conclusion

What can we make of this forgery with regards to its purpose and intended target? A number of possibilities as to the authorship of the fraud present themselves, the most obvious of which is Charles Dawson himself. It was Dawson, of course, who found the first tooth, and presented it to the British Museum for identification in 1891. It was Dawson who received full academic recognition for the discovery, having the species named after him, and it was Dawson who, following Woodward's hope of someday gathering 'further evidence' to support the tentative identification of *Plagiaulax dawsoni*,[19] dutifully produced two more teeth in 1911.

Other potential authors of the fraud include Arthur Smith Woodward, who was Assistant Curator of the British Museum (Natural History) when the first tooth was 'discovered'. Woodward made the first identification of the species, assigning it a name, and was the first to publish the results in *Proceedings of the Zoological Society of London*. He was also the first to comment on the second batch of plagiaulacoid teeth recovered in 1911, publishing the results in the pages of the *Quarterly Journal of the Geological Society*. Woodward was also, of course, more famously later involved in the recording and eventual publication of the Piltdown discoveries, so suspicion of his involvement in an earlier hoax may not, on the face of it, appear wholly unreasonable.

Woodward was not, however, involved in any way with the initial finding of *Plagiaulax dawsoni*, he was merely the conduit through which Dawson passed his discovery. If one was of a particularly suspicious mind, one could suggest that, even if he was not himself the forger, Woodward was in someway in league with the culprit, perhaps hoping that the discovery could somehow help boost his career. If this is true, however, it is not clear how a single mammal tooth from a quarry in Hastings could in any way have aided Woodward, who was by this time already extremely successful in his chosen vocation. It is also apparent that, although Woodward was willing to publish the results of the first discovery, he was reluctant to commit himself fully to the new identification. He was very keen to both acknowledge and praise Dawson, taking none of the credit for the discovery or analysis for himself. Even if he had been in some way involved in the first forgery, whilst still an assistant curator in 1891, it would appear strange that he would wish to instigate the second 'discovery' in 1911, by which time he was a full Keeper of Geology at the British Museum (Natural History).

Another name to consider at this point is that of Father Marie-Joseph Pierre Teilhard de Chardin, the young Jesuit priest who, together with Father Felix Pelletier, had been working with Dawson at the time of the 1911 discoveries. Teilhard de Chardin was later to work with Dawson and Woodward at Piltdown, and has been implicated by many in the forgery of *Eoanthropus dawsoni*.[20] Given the similarities of certain key aspects of the *Plagiaulax* and the

Eoanthropus cases, a link with Teilhard de Chardin may seem plausible. It is clear, however, that the priest was not involved in the discovery of the *Plagiaulax dawsoni* teeth in 1911, merely that of the mammal *Dipriodon valdensis* [21], though an argument *could* still be made for his having planted the teeth for Dawson to find. A rather more crucial argument against Teilhard de Chardin being the arch-forger here is that he was not actually present in Britain in 1891 at the time Dawson discovered the first tooth.

The finger of suspicion could of course be pointed towards a fourth, as yet unknown individual, hoping somehow to fool or ensnare Dawson; someone perhaps intending to discredit or publicly humiliate him before the academic and scientific community. Against this hypothesis we can argue the length of time between the 1891 and 1911 'discoveries', for who would instigate a hoax against Dawson and then wait twenty years for the second instalment, without ever fully revealing the punch line? Who would spend so much time grinding the teeth to shape, then plant the pieces somewhere in a large quarry in the vague hope that Dawson would find them and pass them directly on to Woodward? To do this successfully, a speculative forger would have to know precisely *where* Dawson was working and hope to plant the specimens well in advance, without invoking any form of suspicion.

Given all these considerations, Dawson would appear to be the most likely perpetrator of the *Plagiaulax* hoax, especially given the increased academic credibility the discovery provided for him at such a crucial stage in his antiquarian career. But where did the raw material for the hoax derive? Dawson was, as noted above, an enthusiastic collector of fossils since a very young age, [22] so the pre-abraded plagiaulacoid teeth could easily have derived from his own extensive private collection of fossils. Alternatively, given that Dawson had in his palaentological youth collected fossils with the famous geologist Samuel Beckles, it is possible a connection may be found there. Beckles collected many dinosaurian remains, having discovered a large number of the order *Multituberculata* from the Purbeck beds at Swanage in Dorset.[23] Woodward observed that, following Beckles' death in 1890, Dawson 'gave much help to the British Museum in labelling the collection of Wealden fossils which was acquired from that gentleman's executors'.[24]

How much access Dawson had to Beckles' private collection of specimens is not known, but as his colleague and fellow collector of many years it was probably not inconsiderable. Could it be that the enlarged, pre-abraded plagiocid tooth was originally one of Beckles' specimens? We shall never know for sure, but it is a tantalising possibility.

3

SECRETS OF THE DUNGEON

The earliest recorded pieces of archaeological fieldwork conducted by Charles Dawson involved the exploration and examination of a variety of subterranean passageways. The first to be investigated were the Lavant Caves near Chichester in 1893, followed soon after by the medieval castles of Lewes and Hastings.

The Lavant Caves

In 1916, Hadrian Allcroft wrote in damning terms about the investigation of a series of subterranean passages at Lavant, to the north of Chichester, by Charles Dawson and John Lewis:

> The skill of a north-country miner would have dealt easily with the matter at the outset, and enabled the whole area to be cleared, searched and planned. As it is, the Caves, it is to be feared, are now lost for all time, and their secrets with them, while even the few 'finds' are difficult of access to the majority.[1]

The main reason for Allcroft's displeasure was that, although the caves had been fully investigated in 1893, no official report had ever been published. To make matters worse, all artefacts recovered had apparently been dispersed whilst the caves themselves had been sealed, due to the threatened collapse of the roof, something which prevented any further investigation. Attempting to compile what little was known about the site for the pages of the *Sussex Archaeological Collections*, Allcroft complained that he had faced 'the greatest of difficulty in ascertaining something of the facts after the lapse of no more than twenty years'.[2]

Why should this have been so? The Lavant Caves represented Charles Dawson's first serious piece of archaeological investigation; so, surely he would have gone to extreme measures to ensure that everything was fully recorded and that all interested parties, especially the local antiquarians, were happy?

Unfortunately, there is little in the way of original documentation relating to the excavation of the cave site, what information we do have being filtered through secondary sources. Dawson himself appears to have officially discussed his work at Lavant only once, as a paper presented to a meeting of the Sussex Archaeological Society in August 1893.[3] Details of this lecture were reported shortly after in the *Sussex Daily News* and Dawson himself provided some detail to George Clinch who used it in his chapter on Early Man for volume 1 of the *Victoria County History of Sussex*.[4] What little we know about the caves today is therefore supplied from Clinch's chapter in the *VCH*, the sporadic observations of visitors to the 1893 excavation and from a variety of disparate sources compiled by Allcroft in 1916, shortly before Dawson's death.

The existence of a network of subterranean tunnels at Lavant had, according to Allcroft, for many years been suspected due to the refusal of livestock 'to draw the ploughs over the thin roof of chalk which concealed the caves'.[5] Confirmation of the presence of a significant area of underground workings came in around 1890 when an unnamed shepherd lost two hurdles he had been carrying through an opening in the roof of the buried feature.[6] Realising the potential significance of the find, the landowner, the sixth Duke of Richmond, having first forced a brick and mortar stairway into the caves (**15**), commissioned two members of the Sussex Archaeological Society, Charles Dawson and John Lewis, to conduct further investigation.

Quite how and why Dawson got the commission, especially as his work to date had been primarily examining the geology of the Hastings area, is unclear. Dawson was, by 1893, the Honorary Secretary of the Sussex Archaeological Society for Uckfield and he had already represented the organisation at the fifth Congress of Archaeological Societies.[7] Perhaps, therefore, as one of the up-and-coming new members of the Society, he was simply the logical (or most available) choice. John Sawyer, commenting on the excavation of the caves in the July 1893 edition of *The Antiquary*, notes enigmatically that Dawson had a '*penchant* for explorations of this kind', whilst Lewis had apparently 'done some good work in the same line, especially in India'.[8]

Having gained access to the caves via the new staircase, Dawson and Lewis set about examining the subterranean workings. Dawson busied himself with the investigation of floor debris, whilst Lewis began recording the nature and extent of all tunnels. Information supplied to Clinch by Dawson and the inked

15 *Lavant Caves: the backfilled and partially collapsed brick arch entranceway into the caves as constructed by the Duke of Richmond in 1893 (photographed in 1955)*

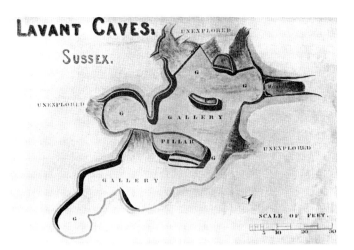

16 *Lavant Caves: a plan of the subterranean passages as compiled by John Lewis*

plan compiled by Lewis (which appeared as a plate facing page 326 in the *Victoria County History*) (**16**) suggest that 'whilst the supporting pillars occupy a comparatively small space, the galleries, or chambers, are large, indicating that the excavation was made for the sake of chalk or flint'.[9]

The original entrance to the caves could not be found, the Duke of Richmond's staircase, which provided the only point of access for the excavation team, having been inserted through the collapsed roof of the main domed chamber. John Sawyer, Clerk of the Sussex Archaeological Society, who visited the caves during the course of 1893, observed that:

> Entrance was obtained into a gallery about 100ft long, 5ft in depth and, as I judge, 4 to 6ft wide, but in parts widening out to form a series of chambers. The largest of these chambers found as yet, connected with another gallery, is 18ft in diameter, from the gallery first cleared others radiate, nor is it easy to say how extensive the excavations may be, since all the passages are, for the most part, nearly choked with loose chalk, all of which it may be hoped will eventually be cleared away.[10]

Unfortunately Sawyer's comments contradict Lewis' published plan, which seems to show 'a vast chamber, 70ft long by some 30ft wide with three large chalk pillars left in the centre to support the roof'.[11]

There seems to be little way of reconciling these two very different accounts, though it must be noted that Sawyer's version was based on observations made whilst negotiating the partially cleared caves, when the scope for disorientation was high. Given that his statement was part of a generalised account of the caves, and not an objective piece of archaeological recording, it would appear safer to accept the Lewis plan as the definitive version.

A total of five irregular galleries or interconnecting tunnels and three domed chambers were partially cleared during the 1893 season. The maximum height of the galleries were noted as being between 4 and 5ft.[12] The full size of the chambers was unfortunately not recorded, though Mary Wyndham, daughter of the 2nd Lord Leconfield, who visited the site in 1893, noted 'the cave consists of a tunnel 30 yards long, down which you walk doubled up, till you reach a small chamber in which you can stand upright'.[13]

Analysis of Dawson's original comments as compiled by Clinch, Allcroft and the *Sussex Daily News*, led Robert Downes to hypothesise that, given the recorded depth of compressed chalk rubble, the overall height of the galleries 'may have been about 7ft'.[14] Something akin to 5ft (1.5m) of rubble had built up across the main floor of the cave, Dawson, via Allcroft, noting that this comprised two main layers:

> the lower, upwards of 2ft in thickness, was of finely crumbled and compacted chalk, probably trodden to powder by the feet of those who used the Caves; the upper stratum consisted of larger and looser fragments of chalk, the accumulation of later falls from the roof at a time when the Caves were no longer frequented.[15]

This is quite a mass of debris, and could indicate that the roof of the caves was extremely unstable. Alternatively, the majority of compacted chalk rubble could relate to the deliberate infilling of a redundant workspace by those engaged in the original quarrying. In a number of Neolithic flint mines, for instance, redundant galleries often completely filled with rubble derived from excavations in other areas of the shaft. Such infilling would suggest that the Neolithic miners deliberately packed abandoned tunnels with debris excavated from new areas in order to avoid hauling all material out to the surface.

The lower layer of chalk rubble in the Lavant Caves, as recorded by Dawson, contained the bulk of the cultural and datable material. All artefacts retrieved from this level were formally presented to the Duke of Richmond on completion of the work, and stored at Goodwood House. By the 1950s the whole collection had been transferred to Chichester Museum where it was later examined by Robert Downes and H. Dixon Hewitt. It is fair to say that the assemblage was diverse, containing a mass of disparate materials including pieces of Roman mosaic, bronze ware and pottery (including high-status Samian and table lamps), sixteenth-century metalwork, a possible Georgian halfpenny, human teeth, some prehistoric worked flints, a miner's 'chalk lamp', a red deer antler and objects of amber, lead and silver. To get an idea of the problems surrounding the collection, the complete finds catalogue, as generated by Downes and Hewitt in 1955, is reproduced here as Appendix 1.

Unfortunately, there exists no independent verification as to the context of the finds, the nature of their discovery, or indeed *who* exactly found them. It appears clear that Dawson and Lewis did not do all the work themselves, and that, as with many large excavations of their day, much of the basic shifting of soil was conducted by a local labour force, possibly a team drafted in by the Duke of Richmond. Only two of the team are specifically named on the list of artefact labels recorded from Goodwood House (Appendix 1): a Mr Lawrence and 'Workman Hammond', but there were undoubtedly more.

The first and perhaps most obvious problem surrounding the Lavant Caves finds assemblage is the lack of coherency or affiliation to any one specific time period. In fact the overall feeling is of 'the sweepings of rubbish thrown out of some antiquarian's collection. There is hardly anything of value and nothing tells a clear story in such a motley collection'.[16] The prehistoric artefacts recovered from the Lavant Caves, namely the flint, antler and worked chalk, have at times been used to propose that the site was originally a Neolithic flint mine.[17] Flint mines were, by the end of the nineteenth century, hot news as early archaeologists struggled to expose the full antiquity of human endeavour. Between 1868 and 1870, Cannon William Greenwell oversaw the first full excavation of a flint mineshaft in Britain, at Grimes Graves in Norfolk, to a depth of some 12m. Three horizontal seams of subterranean flint, named by Greenwell as the 'topstone', 'wallstone' and 'floorstone', had been severed by this shaft. The 'floorstone' deposits represented the good quality flint that was so extensively exploited by Neolithic miners through the cutting of galleries radiating out from the base of the shaft.

Greenwell's work kindled huge interest in prehistoric mine sites, especially of those detected in Sussex. In 1873 Ernest Willett began work at Cissbury, to the north of modern day Worthing, where he traced another Neolithic shaft to its full depth of 4.2m. After Willett came Plumpton Tindall, Colonel Augustus Lane Fox, J. Park Harrison, Professor George Rolleston and Sir Alexander Gordon, all of whom opened new areas across the chalk hill of Cissbury between 1873 and 1878.

Grimes Graves and Cissbury had a massive impact upon antiquarian and early archaeological thinking, for they appeared to suggest that pretty much any hole in the ground could potentially represent the remains of a substantial prehistoric flint mine. For a while, shafts of all shape and size, together with a variety of marl pits, chalk quarries, dene holes, wells and natural solution pipes, were grouped together with genuine prehistoric mines, as early archaeologists attempted to define and understand this new class of field monument.

Looking at the Lavant Caves, however, it is clear that they do not fall into the category of prehistoric flint mine: the most serious concern being that they do not cut through any major seam of subterranean flint. The shape and scale of the galleries also do not conform to the standard type of Neolithic shaft, which usually possesses cramped tunnels and restricted areas of extraction. Last, but by no means least, the so-called 'prehistoric artefacts', although initially convincing, do not bear any form of scrutiny. The worked flint assemblage is very poor, especially for a Neolithic mine, comprising only a single core, a flake, three worked pieces and a scraper. Examples of all such material could, as Downes and Hewitt noted in their 1955 reassessment, be easily located on the modern ground surface around the site 'within a few yards of the Caves'. The 'red deer antler' is little more than a single brow tine (hardly convincing as a prehistoric pick), whilst the antler 'scoop' resembles 'a modern potato-peeler'.[18] The single chalk 'lamp' recorded from the caves does not compare at all well with any known example of Neolithic worked chalk retrieved from mine sites in Norfolk, Sussex or Wiltshire.

If the caves are not prehistoric then perhaps the artefacts suggest a period of later use? The Roman finds, including the mosaic cubes, pottery and metalwork, although they do indicate a presence here in the second to fourth century, are also unfortunately neither uniform nor convincing. If the cave had been a place of Roman activity, it is surprising that the people who left 'these numerous bronze ornaments left nothing substantial in the way of human comforts, as traces of their permanent habitation or temporary refuge'.[19] The cave could of course have possessed some religious significance, the Romano-British population perhaps using it as a place of ritual deposition. This could in part explain the metalwork recorded, though in this case the clear absence of coins would require some explanation. The post-medieval artefacts pointed to a yet later period of utilisation. In conclusion, Allcroft elected for a compromise, suggesting that the cave may well have had its origins in the Neolithic, having been reused and extended on numerous occasions thereafter 'by any population frequenting the vicinity, as for example by Romano-British refugees fleeing from the Saxons, and centuries later by Down sheep-farmers, who found the place convenient for storing wool'.[20]

This interpretation was later supported by Elliot Curwen who noted that the surface area around the excavated cave was covered in hollows or other filled-in shafts (**17**), suggesting a potentially extensive area of prehistoric flint extraction.[21] Surface examination of the Lavant Caves site by the Royal Commission on the Historical Monuments of England in 1995, however, has suggested that the site is perhaps more comparable with known areas of post-medieval chalk extraction, rather than being a prehistoric or flint mine or Roman quarry.[22]

The poor levels of site recording at Lavant and the absence of a definitive publication, when combined with the diverse and disparate nature of the artefact assemblage (not to mention Dawson's apparent reticence in discussing it) has led some to suggest the possibility of fraud. That the cave itself existed, there can be no doubt, but there remains a significant question mark over the finds that Dawson and Lewis claimed to have made there. Following his 1955 examination of assemblage, Robert Downes, in a letter to H. Dixon Hewitt, confided that the artefacts 'have only one thing in common – their size. They could all have been smuggled into the Caves in somebody's pocket and planted in the soft chalk debris by a person with free access to the Caves.'[23] Downes was adamant that the only person with the means, motive and opportunity to 'salt the mine' at Lavant was no other than the director of excavations, Charles Dawson himself.

17 *Lavant Caves: the surface area around the main cave as photographed in 1955 showing the craters formed by additional backfilled shafts*

The Lavant Caves: conclusion

There is, of course, no way of conclusively proving fraud at the Lavant Cave site, there being nothing inherently obvious within the finds collection that could point towards a forgery. There are, however, a number of discrepancies in the assemblage which are worth pointing out.

The earliest datable artefacts, the worked flint, are certainly Neolithic or Early Bronze Age, and would be compatible with the cave being a prehistoric flint mine. Unfortunately, as already noted, the recorded form of the cave is in direct contrast to every known example of a Neolithic flint mine, and the fact that no subterranean seams of flint were detected during the cutting of the shaft would seem to argue conclusively that this was not its primary function. We must ask, therefore, if the cave is not prehistoric, then how did the worked flint arrive within accumulated floor debris? The flint could of course have been residual: ancient finds accidentally incorporated within the fill of a much later shaft. It could have fallen through fissures in the roof of the cave. It could have been brought in deliberately by an unscrupulous member of the 1893 excavation team, hoping to push back the date of the site by a couple of millennia.

Given the small size of the artefacts recovered, any piece *could* easily have been smuggled in and planted. The question here is whether such material would have been brought in to fool the site director Charles Dawson, site recorder John Lewis, or one of their largely anonymous workforce (of which only 'Hammond' and 'Lawrence' are specifically mentioned by name: see Appendix 1). But, one has to ask, why would anyone actually want to do this? What would be the point of fabricating the artefactual evidence of the Lavant Caves? Who would hope to benefit from such a convoluted deception?

When one studies the early history of flint mine exploration, it quickly becomes apparent that the story is curiously littered with a large quantity of frauds. This may be due to the way in which some sites were investigated: by teams of paid labourers not always working under very close supervision. Labourers were sometimes paid by the quality of the finds made, something which could easily have generated a desire to create more interesting (and thus more financially rewarding) discoveries. This is not to suggest that at Lavant the workforce were up to no good, and we certainty have no record as to how Dawson or the Duke of Richmond reimbursed them for their trouble, but it could conceivably supply a motive for the planting of finds. The problem here is that in order to place artefacts in the caves, one would require both access to specialist dealers in antiquities as well as the necessary hard cash to pay for them. Alternatively one would need an extensive private collection of artefacts, built up over many years, in order to supply the demand for a range of finds of different time periods. Both counts would appear to rule out the workmen employed by Dawson and Lewis, who would probably possess neither the disposable wealth necessary to buy from a dealer, nor the time to build up a private collection (especially if that collection was later to be dispersed among the local museums).

Perhaps the suspect artefacts could have been deposited by an illicit visitor to the caves, someone who was not officially part of the excavation team. As both Dawson and Lewis had full-time employment commitments at the other end of the county, it is likely that any on-site work was conducted on an episodic basis, possibly at weekends or on occasional weekdays. In the absence of rigorous security or a permanent presence at the caves, access was probably relatively easy, the prevention of unauthorised visitors never being fully guaranteed. If an illicit visitor was indeed 'salting the mine', then we have to ask to what purpose? Neither Dawson nor Lewis was ever 'outed' or exposed by any accusation of fraud, and neither was the site ever fully questioned by local archaeologists, though many may have entertained doubts as to the reliability of the evidence.[24] If an outside agent was planting dubious material in the cave, they never appeared to have materially gained from the deception, in fact quite the reverse: they would have lost the greater part of their collection to the storerooms of Goodwood House.

A case could be made against the sixth Duke of Richmond, or someone working for him, hoping to make the caves appear more interesting by seeding them with a range of materials that suggested occupation in the prehistoric, Roman and late medieval periods. This is a distinct, if ultimately unprovable, possibility. As the landowner, the duke would have gained in prestige over the ownership of such an interesting site, and, as he would be entitled to all the finds at the end of the excavation, he would not have lost any of the artefacts placed in the cave for Dawson or Lewis to find. Certainly the duke was keen to have the site explored, to the point of having a staircase built into the main chamber, but if he gained in any way from the publicity, we shall never know. Absence of a final report from either of the two key investigators would, in such an instance, probably have been extremely galling.

A far more convincing case can be built up against the chief archaeological investigators of the Lavant Caves, Charles Dawson and John Lewis. Both would have benefited from an impressive site, well stocked with artefacts. Both would have had easy and unfettered access to the caves. Neither would be under suspicion on behalf of the landowner, from any visiting Archaeological Society members or from the general public. From their point of view, a 'few worked flints', a simple 'chalk cup' and a piece of deer antler would help to establish a Neolithic date for the Lavant site, placing it with the discoveries made less than twenty years before by Cannon Greenwell at Grimes Graves (1870) and Colonel Lane Fox at Cissbury (1869, 1875). Other, later artefacts from the caves would have provided additional finer detail, demonstrating that their 'flint mine' possessed greater currency than the shafts examined by Lane Fox *et al.*, having been re-used in the Roman period and again in the sixteenth century.[25] The chronological depth provided by the artefactual assemblage made the Lavant Caves appear extremely interesting; certainly more than a mere post-medieval chalk quarry which is what, in reality, the caves appear to have been.

Either one of Dawson and Lewis could be held accountable for any such deception. They could both have worked together, though collaboration on such 'projects' could bring many complications, not least of which was the threat of exposure or blackmail. Dawson certainly had the means (being the owner off an extensive private collection of ancient artefacts), the motive (public acclaim and the recognition of both the Duke of Richmond and the Society of Antiquaries) and the opportunity (as director of the excavations, no one would question what he was doing on the site). Of all the suspects in the case, Dawson would, therefore, appear to have gained the most from any potential sabotage. His reticence in publishing the details of his work at Lavant could thus be easily explained. The site was an 'important' discovery which was much heralded in the pages of the local press and amongst national archaeological societies such as the Society of Antiquaries. All this helped establish Dawson as an antiquarian of some repute, but it would not have been a site that he would have wanted to dwell on for long. Publication would certainly have required interpretation of the results, perhaps drawing attention to any inconsistencies, errors or shortcomings in the original data set.

Hastings Castle

On 10 October 1894, the Sussex Archaeological Society made a formal visit to Hastings Castle, where they were greeted by Charles Dawson and John Lewis. Both men had recently overseen the clearance and recording of an extensive tunnel underneath the castle (**19**), and Dawson was understandably keen to disseminate the results. The existence of tunnels or 'dungeons' beneath Hastings Castle had long been known, tours having formed a major part of any visit to the medieval fortifications (**18**). In 1872 Dawson himself, then aged eight, explored part of the subterranean chambers in the company of 'a former custodian', whilst a brief description of the tunnel had been made in 1877 by the Revd E. Marshall of St Leonards on Sea in the pages of the *Sussex Archaeological Collections*.[26] So popular had visits to the 'dungeons' become that in 1878 'the door to this excavation was strictly closed upon the public, the custodian becoming tired of taking people over; the atmosphere was bad and the steps then dangerous'.[27]

All this changed in 1894 when Dawson and Lewis persuaded Lord Chichester, who owned the site, to be allowed to reopen and clear the passage (**20**). Having got through the first door, Dawson and Lewis were confronted by two further doorways leading to passages running in a north-east and south-easterly direction. The north-east passage descended almost immediately via a series of eight steps (**21**), 'hewn out of the sandstone rock, which are worn to such an extent that they can only be descended with great difficulty'.[28] Having constructed a wooden staircase over the badly eroded original, the investigation team followed the tunnel as it veered to the south-east, via a small vestibule or chamber (**22**). Along the western edge of this south-facing chamber, the basic outline of a 'round-headed arched passage or door' had at some date been cut, presumably, Dawson and Lewis speculated, with the intention of connecting with the southern passage.[29] From the vestibule, an archway led through to another passage (**23**) running in an east-north-easterly direction.

> This passage is formed in a singular and skilful manner; the arched roof is on the curve; the left side wall is concave; the right convex, giving the whole a semi-circular trend. The floor at this point inclines sharply upwards for some distance. The walls of the passage are smooth, the original pick marks being obliterated.[30]

18 *Hastings Castle: a popular destination for late nineteenth-century visitors, as shown in this print of 1860*

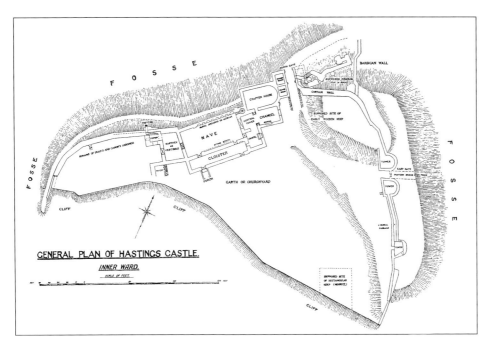

19 *Hastings Castle: a plan of the main buildings as compiled by John Lewis. Note the presence of the subterranean passageway (here marked as 'supposed dungeon') in the top right-hand corner*

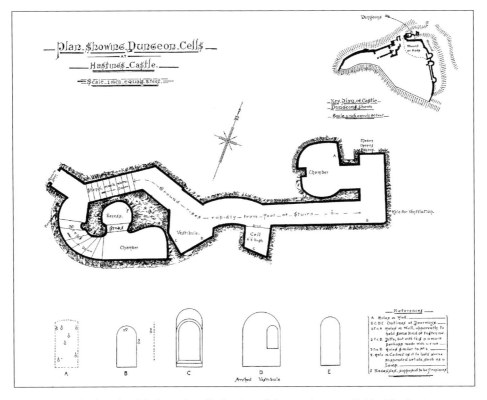

20 *Hastings Castle: a detailed plan and profile drawings of the tunnels as compiled by John Lewis*

21 (Above left) *Hastings Castle: a photograph taken by Charles Dawson showing the heavily worn 'rock-hewn' steps descending into the tunnels from below*

22 (Above centre) *Hastings Castle: a photograph taken by Charles Dawson showing 'the vestibule' of the northern tunnel from the west*

23 (Above right) *Hastings Castle: a photograph taken by Charles Dawson showing the 'curved passage' connecting the vestibule to the main gallery of the northern tunnel*

24 (Left) *Hastings Castle: a photograph taken by Charles Dawson showing the 'rock-hewn fire places' of the main chamber in the northern tunnel*

Passing a small arched recess, which was interpreted as a second abortive attempt to drive a gallery south, Dawson and Lewis entered what they described as 'the main gallery'. This measured 17ft (5.18m) in length, 4ft (1.22m) in width and was 9ft (2.74m) high. At the north-eastern end of the gallery, a short section of tunnel led first to the north, then finally west, connecting to a 'peculiarly domed chamber' measuring 7ft (2.13m) high. Two small recessed areas 'like fire-places' (**24**) were noted in the southern wall of this final chamber.[31]

Following the second tunnel from the south-east of the main entrance door, Dawson and Lewis observed that the steps were not as heavily worn as those in the northern passage, a large quantity of debris, presumably derived from roof collapse, having blocked all access. Finds within the debris included both human and animal bone together with 'a small fragment of carved white marble'.[32] Unfortunately, the extent, quality and final destination of finds retrieved during the course of the clearance of the Hastings tunnels, remains unknown.

The continued instability of the overhanging rock meant that Dawson and Lewis were:

compelled to sink a kind of coffer dam through the loose earth, between the wooden palings on the Castle mount and the curtain wall. The first attempt proved unsuccessful, for when the excavations were nearly completed bad weather came and the dam collapsed, the workmen narrowly escaping with their lives.[33]

Having expended all this effort, the excavators were no doubt greatly disappointed to discover that the second tunnel had never been completed: it terminated 12ft (3.66m) from the stairwell.

Analysing the results of their explorations within the subterranean tunnels, Dawson and Lewis were critical of earlier evaluations that stressed a dungeon or prison interpretation:

> At the outset we can but regard the suggestion of the steps having been worn away by a chain attached to the leg of a prisoner as highly fanciful, for all we could discover was that the steps had been very much worn by ordinary and constant usage. The remark as to the prisoner being fettered in the first small chamber or vestibule... is obviously conjectural, as also the question of its use as a guard room. With regard to the holes in the walls, said to be used for staples, we have carefully examined them and have come to the conclusion that only one or two out of the many could possibly have held staples strong enough for holding a prisoner; for the most part they are the merest cavities.[34]

Only one aspect of the dungeon theory appeared somewhat inexplicable to Dawson and Lewis, and this concerned two areas of rock face discoloration on the southern wall of the main gallery in the north-eastern tunnel. This discoloration or staining 'resembled two shadows of human bodies on the wall, falling side by side between the so-called staple holes'.[35] The sketch which accompanied the article (**25**) shows the peculiar humanoid markings in some detail, suggesting that they were indeed caused by the placement of bodies against the side wall of the underground chamber. Dawson himself compiled this sketch as the report clearly notes that 'this discoloration... was certainly plainly visible when Mr Dawson first saw the cavern, in 1872, especially when a light was held in a particular position near the wall'.[36] By the time of the 1894 clearance however, the images appear to have faded, Dawson and Lewis commenting that 'strange to say, in our many recent visits to the dungeons, we have never yet again observed this phenomenon, and it now appears entirely lost.[37]

As to what may have caused the staining, Dawson and Lewis reiterated Marshall's view that they may have been generated by 'exudation' or decay of substances in the body, though they add a singular note of caution:

> We have suspicions that it might easily be simulated by applying oily substances to the wall. It is difficult to believe that such marks, if caused as

Diagram No 5.

DIAGRAM OF ORIGINAL PORTION OF SUPPOSED OCTAGONAL BASTION,
WITH DOORWAYS TO DUNGEONS. (THE MODERN MASONRY IS OMITTED.)

Diagram No 6.

PECULIAR MARKINGS, LIKE SHADOWS, FORMERLY ON THE SOUTH WALL
OF THE MAIN GALLERY.

25 *Hastings Castle: a sketch by Charles Dawson showing the entrances to the 'dungeons' (top) and the shadow markings of the southern wall of the main gallery in the northern tunnel (bottom)*

suggested in Mr Marshall's note, after having existed from medieval times up to twenty years ago, should by now have utterly disappeared.[38]

Hastings Castle: conclusions

Although the 1894 exploration of the tunnels had not added a huge amount of detail to the history of Hastings Castle, the task of clearance had evidently not been easy, involving much hard work for both Dawson and Lewis as well as their team of unnamed workmen. The record produced by Dawson and Lewis was, however, totally new; John Lewis' inked drawings which accompanied the 1896 report (and later in Dawson's *History of Hastings Castle*), adding significant detail to aid the understanding of the feature. Dawson's own photographs of the subterranean workings, taken 'with the magnesium light'[39] have furthermore greatly aided tunnel interpretation, although the absence of a detailed finds report is of course regrettable. In short, there would appear to be nothing inherently untoward or devious about the work undertaken by Lewis and Dawson within the Hastings Castle tunnels, in fact, given the time and conditions in which they were explored, the work appears exemplary.

One aspect of the survey which does, however, cause a certain amount of concern are the so-called 'shadow-markings' discovered on the walls of the main gallery. Dawson, as already noted, provided an informative (if not wholly objective) sketch of the stains, showing their clear humanoid shape. Lewis comments that the images had been 'plainly visible' in 1872, when Dawson was taken on a guided tour of the tunnels by the then custodian.[40] The problem with this sketch is that the shadow-markings themselves had vanished by the time that Lewis explored the tunnels in 1896. Presumably, as no other illustration of the features is known to be in existence, Dawson's drawing must have been compiled from memory. Dawson was, however, a mere eight years old when he had seen the shadows for the first (and last) time, this being at least some twenty years *before* he finally published the drawing. He could, of course, have sketched the figures during, or shortly after, 1872, though it must be said that the illustration does not appear to be the work of a young boy.

This brings us to an interesting conundrum, for the published article plays down the significance of the shadow-markings, even going so far as to imply that they may have been crude forgeries (generated by 'applying oily substances to the wall'), whilst the illustration which accompanies it conclusively favours their existence. We could of course infer some form of foul play: perhaps the markings were generated by Dawson and Lewis to support the prison hypothesis. This would seem plausible were it not for the fact that the published report so vigorously attacks any suggestion that the tunnels had been used for such a purpose.

It is worth noting here that although the discoloration of the main gallery wall had been first observed by the Revd E. Marshall in 1872,[41] Marshall himself made no attempt to define or describe the shape of these 'shadows', other than to note their possible origin (from 'exuding' corpses). It is, in fact, Dawson who created the first, and to date only, image of the 'shadows' as two discrete individual humans, apparently held securely in place by metal staples. Of course we have no way of assessing the validity of Dawson's sketch, as it would appear to have been drawn entirely from memory. Perhaps, then, it is Lewis – who did not see the original staining in 1872 and was unable to see it in 1894 – who is the voice of caution in the final published report, even going so far as to suggest that the figures may have been faked. Dawson, who was only eight at the time, is unlikely to have generated such a hoax, but it is conceivable that in 1894 he *created* the images through the subjective interpretation of a series of amorphous stains seen some twenty-one years previously. We have, after all, only Dawson's word that the areas of discoloration ever looked anything like the images that he dutifully sketched.

The drawing could, therefore, be viewed (in an unfavourable light) as a hoax perpetrated by Dawson upon the antiquarian community. Alternatively, and perhaps more favourably, the sketch may be viewed as the end product of Dawson's highly subjective memory. Perhaps Dawson actually 'remembered' more detail than was initially present; a man who wanted others to see the outline of two poor unfortunates, manacled to the wall of the subterranean tunnel, when the reality was far more prosaic. Such an explanation could explain Lewis' scepticism, and the final inconclusive nature of this part of the published report.

Castle Lodge, Lewes

At the start of 1904 the Sussex Archaeological Society was based in Castle Lodge, a grand town house nestled at the base of Lewes Castle (**26** & **27**). The Lodge itself was owned by the Marquess of Abergavenny whose agents had agreed with the Society that if the decision was ever made to put the property on the market 'the Society should have the option of acquiring it'.[42] When notice to quit the property arrived on midsummer's day 1904, it was, therefore, a bolt from the blue. The house was no longer in the hands of the marquess, it had been sold and the new owner wanted the Society and all its possessions out.

To elaborate on the facts relayed earlier, the exact details surrounding the sale of the property are unclear, but it is safe to say that the board of the Sussex Archaeological Society felt rather aggrieved. What made matters far worse, in their eyes, was the fact that the eviction was taking place due to the actions of one of their own members, Mr Charles Dawson. Louis Salzman, who later became president of the Society, described how in his view the purchase of Castle Lodge had not been wholly above board.[43] The central thrust to his accusations was that Dawson had misused both his official position as a solicitor and his connections with the Sussex Archaeological Society to imply that he was buying the property *on their behalf*.[44] In 1954, Joseph Weiner interviewed Ernest Clarke, apparently a friend of the Dawsons, who recalled some of the events surrounding the Castle Lodge incident. According to Clarke, a Mr Arthur Huggins, agent of the Marquess of Abergavenny, had related to him that 'the vendors too, were taken aback, for they had not realised until the last stages of the sale what Dawson had been about'.[45]

Of course, because we do not have Dawson's side of the story here, only the recollections of those who may not have been all that well disposed towards him and his family, we do not know whether he bought the property in good faith, assuming that the Sussex Archaeological Society were looking for new premises anyway. He may well have believed that the move would not have so greatly inconvenienced the Society, although the whole affair seems to have left him 'virtually ostracised' within the antiquarian circles of the county.[46] If Dawson did play on his connections to the Sussex Society (as secretary for Uckfield) as well as the (unauthorised) use of Sussex Archaeological headed notepaper to conduct his private correspondence, then these would both be serious charges; a gross breach of professional conduct. As it stands, however, no charges were ever formally made and so the accusation remains unfounded.

26 *Lewes: an aerial photograph of the medieval castle (centre) and barbican gate (centre right) taken in 1972. Castle Lodge is visible between the castle mound and the barbican, whilst Barbican House lies to the bottom right of the gate tower, fronting the High Street*

27 *Lewes: Castle Lodge, flanked by the mound of Lewes Castle and the masonry of the barbican gate, seen from the High Street in 2003*

Having purchased Castle Lodge, Dawson quickly set about renovating and adapting his property, clearing out the last vestiges of the Sussex Archaeological Society and turning the place into a family home. It is during the course of this renovation that, it has been alleged, Dawson attempted to play a somewhat bizarre trick upon the local antiquarian and archaeological community. Clearing the back garden of Castle Lodge, Dawson encountered a 'disused and long-forgotten wine cellar'.[47] Robert Downes related how a Mr R.A. Niedermayer of Hailsham, at the time one of Dawson's articled clerks, sometimes visited the Lodge and provided him with details as to how the basic structure of the cellar was carefully altered.

> Dawson found a long stone slab near Uckfield, and brought it to Lewes. There he treated it with cow dung to give it an ancient and mossy appearance, and put it in the cellar. He cemented a staple into the wall, from which dangled a set of old iron manacles... When his preparations were

complete, Dawson invited fellow archaeologists to inspect his old dungeon, furnished with fetters and a stone bed for the prisoner. He attended meetings and listened to papers on this supposed dungeon in the castle precincts without a smile on his face.[48]

This account was, in Downes' opinion, 'the undoubted evidence of a reliable witness who testifies that he saw Dawson in the act of perpetrating one of his hoaxes'.[49] Of all the accusations levelled against the solicitor from Uckfield, this was the one that Downes felt really 'nails him down' as a forger of antiquities *par excellence*.[50]

Castle Lodge: conclusions

There is nothing specific about the Castle Lodge incident, nor the renovation of the building's wine cellar, that conclusively demonstrates that Dawson was up to no good. As noted above, the allegations surrounding the sale of the Lodge and the subsequent eviction of the Sussex Archaeological Society are all ultimately unsubstantiated. Dawson's attitude towards the Society during the purchase of the house was, it must be admitted, at best ambivalent and, though there is some suspicion surrounding the exact nature of his dealings with the vendors, there is no clear proof of professional misconduct.

With regard to the modification of the Castle Lodge wine cellar, though a case could be made for attempting to defraud certain members of the Sussex Archaeological Society, possibly as a result of having been publicly ostracised, the creation of a mock dungeon would seem an unlikely way of exacting revenge. Neither could Dawson have believed that the creation of a gothic-style prison would have fooled anyone; the masonry of the cellar structure and the sheer incongruity of the manacles and stone 'bed' were clearly not designed as clever pieces of forgery. More likely these were attempts to imitate a *feeling* of the past; the sort of 'Do It Yourself' period imitations that are more common-place today.

We do not have any record of whom exactly Dawson invited round to inspect his handiwork; more likely it was friends and work colleagues (such as Niedermayer) rather than members of the archaeological establishment. If Dawson had been attempting an elaborate hoax, it is unlikely that he would in any case have invited one of his own articled clerks to see the 'work in progress', nor would he have confided all the secrets to him. It simply does not make sense, for Dawson would have placed himself in a position where he could at any time be exposed or blackmailed. Revelation that the old wine cellar of Castle Lodge was altered so as to appear like a medieval dungeon suggests nothing more serious than a piece of Gothic fantasy; a romantic piece of home improvement. It is not the 'smoking gun' that proves that Dawson was a fraudster.

4

STICKS AND STONES

In 1894, less than two years after joining the Sussex Archaeological Society, Charles Dawson was publishing the results of his antiquarian investigations across the county. The first articles to see the light of day were concerned with two unusual discoveries, a Neolithic hafted axe head from East Dean and a wooden boat from the coast at Bexhill. Both finds were not made by Dawson himself, but by others, Dawson's role here being to interpret the discoveries and bring them to the greater attention of the academic world.

Blackmore's Stone Axe

In 1893, the newly founded Committee of the Hastings Museum Association began to acquire collections from various local antiquarian collectors. One such collection examined at this time comprised an extensive quantity of prehistoric worked flint assembled by Stephen Blackmore, resident of Frost Hill Cottage, East Dean, near Eastbourne. Charles Dawson, who inspected the material, judged it to be 'one of the finest collections of Neolithic flint implements in private hands in England'.[1]

Whilst discussing the nature of the collection and terms for which the Hastings Museum would be allowed to purchase elements for their Loan Collection, Dawson recorded that his eye was taken by 'a drawing of a haft bearing an implement *in situ*'.[2] As evidence of how prehistoric flint tools were originally hafted was extremely rare, certainly in the latter years of the nineteenth century, Dawson was intrigued and asked Blackmore about the history of the drawing. Dawson later transcribed Blackmore's comments surrounding the discovery of the piece in his article for the *Sussex Archaeological Collections*:

> Some years ago Mr Blackmore was trenching, not far from the edge of the cliff, at Mitchdean, East Dean, that he had the good fortune to find several flint implements, namely a flint arrow head, along pick-shaped worked flint, a peculiarly worked flint, much curved, bearing a notch at one end, rather resembling a netting needle, and a long polished stone, probably for honing or polishing purposes. It was close to these, about three feet below

the surface, Mr Blackmore discovered a flint implement lying in its wooden haft. The haft was perfectly carbonised and crumbled at the touch, and all attempts to save it proved futile.[3]

The non-availability of the artefact, it having 'crumbled at the touch', was unfortunate, but luckily Blackmore 'was able to make a drawing of this most interesting discovery, from which the accompanying illustration is taken'.[4]

It is important to note here that the figure accompanying Dawson's article (**28**) was *not* the drawing by Blackmore that first caught Dawson's attention at Frost Hill Cottage; rather it was an interpretation of that first (and as yet unpublished) illustration. Worse, the drawing published by Dawson does not actually appear to be by Dawson himself (nor Blackmore for that matter), for a comparison with the illustration accompanying Dawson's second article in the *Sussex Archaeological Collections* for 1894 (on the Bexhill Boat: see below) shows that 'both were redrawn by a single commercial artist, and thus that neither directly exhibits the handiwork of its original draughtsman'.[5] It is probable that here the 'commercial artist' was none other than Dawson's colleague at both the Lavant Caves and Hastings Castle excavations: John Lewis.

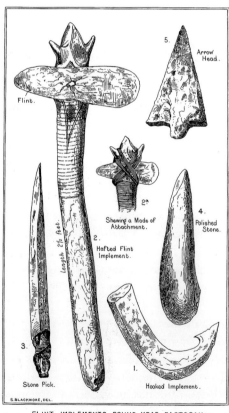

28 *Blackmore's stone axe: a drawing of the main pieces in Blackmore's collection as illustrated by John Lewis*

How close to the original drawing, or indeed for that matter the original find from the Mitchdean cliffs, Dawson's version was, we shall unfortunately never know. The same note of caution may also be added with regard to the other flint implements appearing in the figure accompanying Dawson's article, most of which do not appear to have any parallel with the known Neolithic tool types recorded from southern Britain. Blackmore was an experienced collector of artefacts, but Dawson was the wide-ranging antiquarian and so we may expect that in this instance 'he suggested or added a touch here and there to Blackmore's drawing... small touches, no doubt, but transforming in their effect'.[6]

In discussion with Blackmore, Dawson was able to supply a significant amount of detail concerning the hafted tool, noting that:

> the implement was received in a horizontal groove and on one side of the shaft near the head. Above it, in the head of the haft, appeared two small stumps, apparently where small shoots had been trimmed off the wood. Below the implement were a number of grooved rings running around the haft. The object of the stumps above the implement and the grooves beneath appear to leave no doubt that they were made to receive the cross lashings which secured the implement in its groove in the haft. The blade of the implement itself was inclined slightly downwards, and the haft curved back slightly in the centre.[7]

Such detailed observations and comments would appear plausible enough, especially if the haft in question had actually survived as a complete artefact. Unfortunately, as we have already noted, the object had not survived at all, having been destroyed at the very moment of its discovery. Dawson's record is, therefore, based entirely upon Blackmore's memory, of events conducted 'some years ago'. John Evans raised this point shortly after the publication of the axe head in his book *Ancient Stone Implements* where he noted that 'neither the description nor the drawings of this... are such to inspire confidence'.[8] Veryan Heal expressed similar misgivings, some eighty years later, when she re-examined the evidence for Blackmore's hafted axe head and observed that 'given the reported condition of the piece, the details and reconstruction are quite remarkable'.[9] Still, we do not possess Stephen Blackmore's side of the story and so cannot assume that any elements of misinterpretation or 'wishful thinking' apparent in Dawson's account were entirely due to the Uckfield solicitor.

What is surprising, however, is the recorded *condition* of the hafted flint, given its provenance, within the well-drained chalk soils of East Sussex. Had the soils that Blackmore is supposed to have disturbed been in any way waterlogged, creating the anaerobic (or oxygen-lacking) conditions that normally reduce the composition rate of organics, then the discovery of such an item would not appear out of the ordinary. Dawson does note that the wooden haft was 'carbonised', suggesting that direct contact with fire had in someway preserved it, but unfortunately fails to elaborate on how such a fire could have left the head and surrounding area strangely unburnt. Given the circumstances (and date) of the artefact's initial excavation, Blackmore's skill at exposing and recording the item must be greatly admired.

Since the reporting of Blackmore's axe, a number of well-preserved hafted axe heads have come to light from waterlogged prehistoric contexts across northern Europe and from these it is possible to more closely examine the evidence from Mitchdean. In addition, the increase in experimental techniques in archaeological research means that there have been a number of modern attempts to use prehistoric tools in a variety of alternative fittings. Given all this new information it is worth noting that:

> it is questionable whether Dawson's reconstruction would have been of much practical use; experience suggests that if an axe head were to be lashed into a lateral groove the binding would loosen in use and the head would drop (or fly) out.[10]

Looking at the details of Blackmore's hafted axe in retrospect, Downes concluded that 'we are faced with an unlikely method of hafting supposed to have been discovered in unlikely circumstances accompanied by unusual types of alleged Neolithic flint implements'.[11]

Blackmore's Stone Axe: conclusion

The evidence supplied by Dawson to account for Blackmore's hafted stone axe is not at all convincing. Given the circumstances of the artefact's discovery and eventual reporting, through an interpretation of a memory of an artefact found 'some years ago', then this is perhaps not surprising. An objective account of what was really found on the cliffs at Mitchdean is unlikely ever to be forthcoming, and the version that we possess (provided by Dawson) could easily have been distorted, garbled or inflated at any stage in its recounting. It is worth reiterating however that we only possess Dawson's account of both the artefact and the events surrounding its discovery. That Stephen Blackmore existed, there is no doubt, but the items credited to him by Dawson (and illustrated for the *Sussex Archaeological Collections*) have never been seen since Dawson described them. The objects in question never appeared in the Hastings Museum Loan Collection (to be fair Dawson did not state that he was successful in purchasing them for the museum), and neither did they turn up within Dawson's own private collection. Given the total absence of information in this particular case, all we can do is observe that the hafted axe itself, as well as its reconstruction by Dawson and style of preservation at the time of recovery, are all highly dubious. If one were of a particularly suspicious mind one could argue that the 'find' itself was a complete fabrication.

The Bexhill Boat

The second article by Dawson to grace the pages of the *Sussex Archaeological Collections* for 1894 concerned the discovery and interpretation of an 'ancient boat'. This particular sea-going vessel had, Dawson related, first been discovered 'about thirty years ago, embedded in the blue Wealden clay or 'blue slipper' on the sea shore, 100 yards east of the site of the old No. 48 Martello Tower, west of Bexhill'.[12] The boat had apparently been first exposed in the 1860s, during a particularly violent storm. Following this dramatic natural event, a coastguard walking the stretch of the shore, saw the boat together with:

> some bones, a perfect skull of a horse of small size, and a mass of debris, consisting of decayed leaves, hazel nuts and pieces of wood derived from the Ancient ('Submarine') Forest, which originally formed part of the great forest of Andred, but has now been submerged beneath the sea.[13]

The horse skull proved an interesting find, for its small size suggested an early date whilst its spatial association with the boat could indicate that both were contemporary. Unfortunately, the boat was subsequently covered again by the shifting coastal sand, whilst the unnamed coastguard sold the horse's skull to 'a gentleman (unknown) at Hastings for seven and sixpence'.[14] Dawson observed that the ancient boat had been periodically revealed and submerged until the winter of 1887, when a massive 'displacement of sand' exposed it almost entirely. At that point the vessel:

> was noticed by Mr Jessie Young, a boatbuilder, of Bexhill, who felt much interested in this ancient relic of his craft and immediately took steps to excavate it. The work was undertaken on a bitterly cold night and with the sea almost at their heels, with the dreaded sand, the men dug out the boat.[15]

The details and circumstances surrounding the removal of the vessel (date, associated finds, names of individuals involved), though undeniably dramatic (with the sea threatening to overcome the team at any moment), are unfortunately vague and insubstantial. Even the exact position of the find, which could easily have been noted from witness statements, is left unrecorded. Also, quite why it was thought necessary to extract the ancient boat at night, is never fully explained; conducting the operation during a low tide in daylight hours would presumably have had a better chance of a successful outcome. Perhaps Young and his team simply did not wish to be observed during their undertaking. Sadly, the speed at which the vessel was removed from the sand only complicated matters, Dawson observing that 'owing to the rottenness of the wood, the tenacity of the clay, the darkness of the night, and the haste with which the work was necessarily conducted, the boat was very much broken'.[16]

Having extracted the vessel, presumably at no small cost to himself, Young appears to have lost all interest in the project. When Dawson first saw the boat, 'a short time afterwards' it had been left to quietly decay 'on the grass outside Mr Young's workshop... the wood had already begun to shrink rapidly, and an attempt to preserve some of the least decayed portions by soaking in a strong solution of alum yielded no satisfactory results'.[17] Dawson instantly recognised the object for what it was, and understanding its potential significance, he 'made a careful note of all details' and with Young's assistance 'placed the pieces in juxtaposition and so made the sketch or restoration figured in the illustration' which accompanied his article.

Dawson's illustration is undeniably impressive (**29**), though it appears to indicate a very well preserved vessel, with none of the evident decay ascribed to it. This of course implies that Dawson's sketch was more than just a 'restoration', more a speculative recreation of various jumbled pieces. That no record

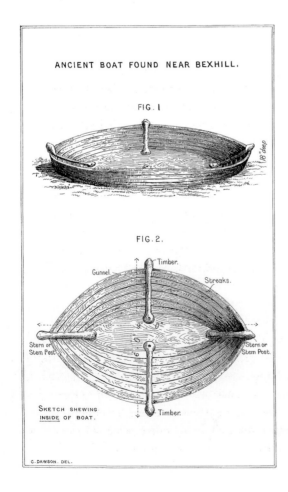

29 *The Bexhill Boat: Dawson's interpretation of the boat as illustrated by John Lewis*

of the broken fragments found outside Young's workshop was made, is to be regretted, for now it is impossible to provide an objective statement as to the validity of the finished reconstruction. Dawson, however, was convinced he had understood the complexities of the boat, which to him appeared to 'furnish an interesting link in the history of boatbuilding'.[18]

At this point it is worth quoting Dawson's observations concerning the Bexhill Boat in full, for the detail that he managed to extract from so many fragmentary pieces is quite remarkable.

The general outline of the boat had a very coracle-shaped aspect. It was flat-bottomed and double-bowed, being nine feet long, six feet broad, eighteen inches deep, and built entirely of oak, which was perfectly black throughout. The flat keel was of one piece, of a long oval shape, narrowing at each end, about eighteen inches broad in the centre, the wood two inches thick. The stem posts were cut to the shape of the boat and were about three feet three inches long and two and a half inches square, their heads rounded and their bases broadened and riveted to the inner side of the keel with large wooden rivets. The timbers on each side were similarly formed, but were not quite so long. The streaks (or planks) were irregular and consisted of six on either side of the boat, about six to eight inches broad and their length according to their position in the boat. They were not bent artificially, but were apparently chosen from naturally bent boughs and roughly trimmed up. Considerable skill was shown in the mode of putting them together. The keel above mentioned was bevelled upwards along the edge, to receive the first streak which was riveted with wooden pegs to the keel. All the succeeding streaks were bevelled and overlapped in a style known as Clinker building (or weather boarding). Strange to say, their ends did not meet on the stern or stem posts, but were pieced and pinned together at their ends in a manner most laborious. The stern or stem posts on the inside were again pinned to them with wooden pegs and the streaks pinned to the timbers in the centre. A gunwale ran around the edge of the boat two inches by two inches and unlike the streaks were made up of several distinct pieces pegged on. Speaking generally upon the construction, the work must have been a laborious task. All the oak bore evidence of having been cleaved into shape with an axe and left without any other finishing. The assumed want of knowledge of the proper uses of stern and stem posts to fasten the streaks at either end, the selection of suitable and curved timber, and then the riveting and fitting, must have proved formidable work... there is no evidence as to its mode of propulsion, though an oar may have been fastened, rowlock-like, to either the timber or stem posts in a manner resorted to by other primitive races. Owing, however, to the state of the wood, this could not be clearly made out. There was no attachment for a mast or seat.[19]

The description and interpretation is impressive, and no doubt would have enhanced Dawson's antiquarian and academic standing greatly. His interest in boats and boatbuilding is not evident prior to the writing of this particular article (it may have been a private hobby), but we can certainly infer that he received much enthusiastic help from Young and his colleagues. The finished version, although somewhat ungainly, was, Dawson reassured his audience, 'in the opinion of expert boatbuilders' certainly seaworthy 'owing to its wide beam'.[20] Dawson further hypothesised that the sinking of the vessel had, in all likelihood, been due to a failed attempt to negotiate the cross-Channel transportation of a horse (presumably the same one whose skull had been found in the 1860s) for 'the landing of a horse tethered in such a boat on the open sea or in deep water must have proved a venturesome experiment'.[21]

How much of the general description of the Bexhill Boat is guesswork, we will never know for, as with the illustration already noted, an absence of any objective statement concerning the survival and general appearance of the vessel prior to Dawson's reconstruction was never compiled. Given Dawson's brief statement reflecting on the shrinkage of timbers and broken nature of the whole, it is probable that in reality any number of plausible recreations could have been made by the simple repositioning of stray fragments. Also unfortunate is the delay between the extraction of the boat from the sand and the publication of the article in the *Sussex Archaeological Collections*: possibly as much as seven years. After all this time, should anyone have wanted to re-inspect the vessel to check the validity of Dawson's recreation, they would undoubtedly have found little left to examine.

Dawson remained guarded as to the date and purpose of the small boat. Its basic form, he conceded, appeared to indicate 'a link between the coracle and "burnt out" boat' of popular ancient British tradition, with 'the more modern type depicted in the Bayeux Tapestry'.[22] Its importance then was increased as a transitional form, or 'missing link' in the whole history of British and northern European boatbuilding traditions.

Only one curious element of the whole Bexhill Boat story remains. On 21 January 1888, some six years before the appearance of Dawson's article in the *Sussex Archaeological Collections*, the *Southern Weekly News* reported a strangely similar discovery of a wooden boat preserved in the sands of Bexhill. The *Southern Weekly* article, however, identified the finder as Mr Webb, foreman of a construction gang at work nearby.[23] Intrigued as to the nature of the find, Webb instructed his team to remove the object 'with pick-axe and spade', a digging technique which resulted in the boat being extracted in 'detached pieces'. Attempting to later juxtapose these rotting fragments of timber proved impossible 'even if the ingenuity of a carpenter would have been equal to the task' observed the reporter for the *Southern Weekly*. The only element of the boat on which it was possible to venture an opinion was the constructional form, which was noted as being 'entirely of oak, the side planks being all pegged together with wood'.[24]

John Evangelist Walsh, though, considered that there was no real proof that Webb's boat was the same as the jumble of timber later found outside Young's workshop, for 'it would be a heavy strain on coincidence to have two such ancient vessels found at about the same time buried in the same place on the same stretch of beach'.[25] A coincidence surely, but not an altogether impossible one. Walsh believed that it was Webb's boat that somehow ended up outside Young's workshop, but if this were so it would imply that either Young lied as to the circumstances surrounding the recovery of the boat, or that Dawson later elaborated the tale, making it more dramatic in the process. It is, however, just conceivable that Young had originally been involved in Webb's attempt at boat retrieval, for the report appearing in the *Southern Weekly News* gives no indication as to whether the extraction occurred during the day or night.

The Bexhill Boat: conclusion

The evidence supplied by Dawson for the Bexhill Boat is, as with that surrounding Blackmore's hafted stone axe, not at all convincing. A lack of any statement regarding the state of preservation of the boat prior to any attempt at reconstruction at once destroys the validity of Dawson's arguments, leaving the reader unsure as to whether Dawson is *inferring* the survival of specific features or accurately recording their presence. Given the circumstances of the boat's initial discovery, extraction, storage and subsequent decay, any interpretation of its original form was probably as valid as any other. The long delay in Dawson's assessment of the vessel and his reporting of it in the pages of the *Sussex Archaeological Collections* would have further clouded the matter as, by 1894, there was probably little of the boat left to inspect. As we are not in possession of any alternative witness statement as to the nature, survival and basic form of the boat, between its finding in 1887 and its publication in 1894, it is possible that the story could once again have become distorted, inflated or irrevocably garbled.

It is also worth reiterating we only possess Dawson's account of both the boat and the events surrounding its discovery and extraction from the Bexhill sands. That at least one boat did indeed exist, being found in 1888 and reported in the pages of the *Southern Weekly News*, there can be no doubt, but certainty evaporates when we attempt to link that discovery with the one described by Dawson. The circumstances surrounding the finding and retrieval of both boats is surprisingly similar, as is their reported condition following their removal from the beach. Dawson's boat appears to have been found first, in 1887, and had certainly been widely known about since the 1860s, though Dawson's reporting of it postdated the reporting of Webb's boat by six years. It is possible that the two boats were in fact the same, Young being involved somehow in the original recovery of the vessel from the beach and later becoming the recipient of the remains once

Webb had decided that it was not worth keeping. It is also possible that Young misremembered certain details of the recovery, telling Dawson that it had occurred in 1887, rather than in the third week of 1888. It is possible that he neglected to inform Dawson of Webb's role in the affair. It is also possible that the story is a complete fabrication.

Dawson could have used the tale of the 1888 boat, as found by Webb and his workers, as the basis of his article. Carefully he removed details which could implicate him in fraudulent reporting, replacing 'Webb' with 'Young' and keeping the details of the discovery vague, but intimating that it had a long history stretching back to the 1860s. The inclusion of an unnamed 'coastguard' and the details of the horse skull (since lost) and 'decayed leaves, hazel nuts and pieces of wood' adds further detail (and authenticity), indicating that Dawson had privileged information concerning the findspot. Use of the dates 1887 and 'the 1860s' would also have given Dawson's boat precedence over Webb's. Should anyone challenge Dawson's version of events, he could always claim later that he had been supplied with faulty information. He had not, after all, actually claimed that he discovered the boat, only that he had been able to interpret it when all others, including at least one boatbuilder, had singularly failed. If anyone had ever mentioned Webb's boat, Dawson could have legitimately claimed that the two were indeed one and the same (after all his description of both its recovery and eventual deposition outside Young's workshop are so vague that they could easily accommodate the alternative find).

Ultimately, given the total absence of objective information in this case, all that can be said is that a boat was found at Bexhill in 1888 (not '87 as Dawson stated – though he was only out by three weeks), and that it was removed by Webb, possibly with the aid of Young. The boat, having been discarded by Webb, could easily have found its way to the nearest boatbuilder's workshop (in this case belonging to Young) where it was later spied by Dawson. So much can be surmised with no intimation of fraudulent activity. Interestingly, however, as with Dawson's article on Blackmore's hafted stone axe, which accompanied the Bexhill Boat in the 1894 edition of the *Sussex Archaeological Collections*, the boat paper also deals with an object made of timber which is badly decayed and requires Dawson's expert eye in order to reconstruct its original form. In neither case was there a real, fully quantifiable object which anyone else could examine and provide an alternative interpretation.

5

AN AGE OF IRON

Dawson's loan collection, bequeathed to Hastings Museum, contained a variety of diverse iron objects such as a 'hippo-sandal', the tied-on footwear of the Roman packhorse, which he purchased from a Mr E. Newman of Chichester (and which was supposedly derived from a grave in the town),[1] a variety of nails, and a mass of material from Hastings Castle including 'keys, knives and spears'.[2] Much of this material would probably have formed part of the many displays and exhibitions that Dawson organised on Sussex ironwork and metalworking, such as the 'home-made' spear used for 'arming the peasantry' and the 'pair of tobacco tongs' that appeared in the Sussex Archaeological Society exhibition of 1903.[3] Few of these strange and rather intriguing artefacts were ever individually reported upon by Dawson. A number of iron objects are, however, examined in some detail here as either their basic form or provenance has at times been called into question.

The Beauport Park Statuette

Early in 1893, Augustus Wollaston Franks, Keeper of British and Medieval Antiquities at the British Museum and President of the Society of Antiquaries, was presented with an unusual artefact: a small and rather corroded iron statuette (**30**). The statuette was clearly Roman in style, and appeared to represent a miniature copy of a horseman from the Quirinal in Rome.[4] The owner of the piece, Charles Dawson, confirmed to Franks that the object had been found beneath a slag heap from the Roman ironworking site of Beauport Park in East Sussex by a workman digging for material to surface a local road.[5] Dawson's evident excitement concerning the statuette was that, in his view, it was made of cast iron and not the more usual wrought (or hammered) form.

In the late years of the nineteenth century, it was believed that highly carbonised or cast iron had not been produced in Europe before the end of the fourteenth century, and had certainly not appeared in the British Isles until at least the end of the fifteenth. Such iron was used primarily for making castings, but in its finished form was quite hard and brittle and could, therefore, not be welded or forged. In order to produce cast iron by melting the iron in iron ore,

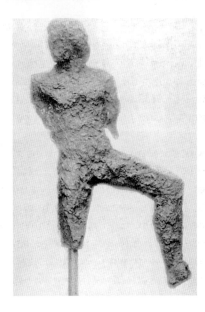

30 *The Beauport Park Statuette: photographed by Charles Dawson in 1893*

a metalworker would have to generate a temperature of around 1,200°C; something which was considered impossible before the advent of high-blast furnaces. Before the blast furnace, iron was smelted in 'bloomery hearths' (usually attaining temperatures of just over 900°C) which reduced the material 'to a pasty mass of sponge iron'.[6] 'Bloom' iron, containing about less than 1 per cent of carbon, is tough and malleable and can easily be worked in a blacksmith's forge, where it is referred to as 'wrought iron'. Any iron worked in the Roman period *ought* to be of the wrought variety.

> Of course, there was always the possibility that bloomery-hearths might have reached such high temperatures that they melted the iron accidentally and produced cast iron. Historians have also had in mind the possibility that the Romans, with their technical skill, might have produced cast iron deliberately from their bloomeries, but no certain evidence has been found to suggest that the Romans possessed this art.[7]

James Rock, who observed the destruction of the Roman ironworking site at Beauport Park in the 1870s, certainly believed that the Romano British iron-workers had the capability to generate cast iron, for, in his description of the site published in the *Sussex Archaeological Collections* for 1879, he observed that:

> The process of ironmaking used here seems to have been simply to form a mound of earth, then to cover it with charcoal; upon this to place the ironstone or ore, and to cover the whole with clay, probably with some arrangement for the passage of air, to secure the combustion of the charcoal when ignited; the molten iron running off from the ore to the bottom of the mound.[8]

Molten iron can only mean that the Roman ironworkers in East Sussex had indeed attained temperatures in excess of 1,200°C and had been able to liquefy iron for use in moulds. Later observers of the Beauport Park site doubted that free-flowing iron was ever produced in Britain during the Roman occupation[9], and that Rock had simply got his facts wrong. If Dawson's statuette had indeed been cast, then the whole history of ironworking in Europe would be turned on its head.

In order to determine whether the Beauport statuette had been cast in a mould, or whether it had been hammered into shape, the specimen was submitted to W.C. Roberts-Austen, Professor of Metallurgy at the Royal School of Mines and assayer to the Royal Mint.[10] A small sample of the figure (6.77 grains) was taken and dissolved by Roberts-Austen, who observed that, because of the minute quantity of carbon recorded, he had 'no hesitation in saying that the figure was not made of cast iron, but was of wrought, malleable iron, a steel-like iron, such as was manufactured in early times by a direct reduction process from iron ore'.[11]

When, on 18 May 1893, Dawson's statuette was exhibited at a London meeting of the Society of Antiquaries, it was described as being made of 'wrought iron', presumably in the light of Roberts-Austen's analysis. Dawson attended the meeting with his object, but could not speak in its defence, as he had yet to be elected a fellow of the Society (this honour not occurring until two years afterwards in 1895). Presumably, however, Dawson supplied Charles Hercules Read, Deputy Keeper of British and Medieval Antiquities at the British Museum, who introduced the artefact to the meeting, with all the necessary details concerning its original discovery and perceived antiquity. Read stated that the piece had been discovered by an unnamed labourer, employed to quarry material from the Roman site, 'at a depth of 27 feet' into a slag heap.[12] The work of Roberts-Austen implied that the statuette had been manufactured 'by hammering and chiselling', such a slow process apparently making it 'inconceivable that it can have been done at a time when the casting of iron was practised'.[13] To Read, this observation appeared to confirm that the artefact was of Roman date, rather than having been made at any later time.

The questions and comments that followed Read's presentation were not overly enthusiastic. A.H. Smith displayed a small bronze statuette to the assembled meeting, which was of the same basic design as Dawson's exhibit. This figure of a horseman had, Smith noted, only recently been purchased in Orange, southern France, in the belief that is was a genuine Roman artefact. Following a close inspection of the figure however, Smith was of the opinion that it was in reality a modern replica, possibly manufactured as a souvenir of Rome.[14] A.S. Murray, Keeper of the Department of Greek and Roman Antiquities at the British Museum, noted that the 'fine modelling' evident in Dawson's iron statuette, combined with the observation that it appeared to be a reproduction of a genuine Roman piece, were strong arguments against its authenticity.[15] Sir John Evans noted the great similarities between Dawson's iron figure and the 'modern' replica belonging to Smith, adding that 'suspicion might be aroused as to their belonging to the same category'.[16]

Dawson's reaction to this overtly negative response is not recorded, though four months later, on 13 September 1893, he wrote to W.V. Crake, then Secretary of the Hastings Museum Association, that 'they rather disputed my iron-statuette at the Society of Antiquaries so they put me on my mettle a bit'.[17] Also contained in the letter to Crake is a more explicit reference to the circumstances surrounding the initial discovery of the iron figure which had not previously been circulated:

> On Sunday I managed to collect evidence at Westfield about my little cast iron statuette. I found the labourer who dug it up and who says it was with coins of Hadrian's time. The coins found their way into the collection of Mr Rock – late Rock and Hawkins – White Rock. Do you think you could discover him? I believe he had many losses after retiring. I should be very much indebted if you could – and perhaps he has other local specimens he would cede to the Hastings Museum.[18]

This letter is interesting for a number of reasons. First it suggests that an issue arising from the London meeting of the Society of Antiquaries had been the exact provenance of the statuette. The details provided to Read had been vague, possibly fuelling the suspicion that the piece was somehow fraudulent. If Dawson could obtain a sworn testimony as to the circumstances of the discovery, as well as the precise location of the spoil heap in which it had been buried, then there was a good chance the piece may be accepted as a genuine Roman artefact. Secondly, the observation that the statuette had been found 'with coins of Hadrian's time', was something that could be directly linked with an earlier, authenticated Roman discovery made by James Rock in the 1870s. In an article entitled 'Ancient Cinder-Heaps in East Sussex', published in the 1879 edition of the *Sussex Archaeological Collections*, Rock had observed:

> I have in my possession two coins of bronze, which were also found among the cinders – one of Trajan, the other of Hadrian. Both are in good preservation, especially the latter. These would seem to fix the date of the cinder-heap at a somewhat early period of the Roman occupation.[19]

Rock also mentions, in his description of artefacts recovered from Beauport Park, a bronze ring, a bronze spoon found 'at the bottom of the cinder-heap' and numerous fragments of pottery, including fine red Samian ware.[20] Quite why the statuette, surely the most prized find from Beauport Park, was not mentioned is unclear. Perhaps Rock was not aware of its existence as the workman who found it simply did not pass it on to the collector. Perhaps the coins and figurine, though found in the same spoil heap, were discovered at different times or by completely different labourers (Dawson's account does not specifically state that it was *the same* workman that made both discoveries). Had the coins and statuette been found at broadly the same time (in the 1870s), however, it would be strange that the workman or men in question did not attempt to sell the piece on (as most were paid extra for any interesting discoveries). Why did the as yet still unnamed workman hold on to the artefact until the 1880s, before selling it to Dawson? This was an anomaly that was to remain unexplained.

Also of note in Dawson's letter of 13 September 1893 to Crake is that the solicitor remained convinced, despite the analysis of Roberts-Austen, that the Beauport Park figurine was in reality made from cast iron, not wrought as had been suggested. One last piece of evidence was, Dawson commented, now available to him which could change the accepted view of the Society of Antiquaries:

> Fortunately and almost wonderfully, an iron spearhead cast in a mould as in the Bronze Age, has been found in an ancient iron pit in the west of England and is now on its way to me. The question is had the ancients the knowledge of casting iron? I hope it will be a knockdown blow.[21]

Nothing more was ever heard of this mysterious iron spearhead. Either Dawson never received it, or it proved not to be the 'knockdown blow' that he had hoped.

The Beauport Park Statuette disappeared from public view until the 1903 exhibition of Sussex ironwork which Dawson organised in Lewes on behalf of the Sussex Archaeological Society. In the publication that followed the exhibition, published in the *Sussex Archaeological Collections*, Dawson provided the most detailed account to date of the discovery of the iron figurine:

> The specimen referred to was found by one of the workmen employed in digging the iron slag for road-metal about the year 1877. His name is William Merritt, and he lives at King Street, Seddlescombe Road, Westfield. All the workmen engaged in digging were in the habit of picking up any of the more important specimens... such as Mr Rock describes, and keeping them for certain people who were interested in the discoveries at the time. The work extended over many years, and the principal slag heaps were disposed of. The author, who had been recommended in the year 1883 to see Mr Merritt about some geological specimens, procured from him, with other specimens, a small, much corroded statuette, all of which he stated that he had dug up in the slag heaps of Beauport... The author, as far as possible, took considerable trouble to settle the bona fides of the discovery, and received from Mr Merritt a written account authenticating it.[22]

The 'written account' to which Dawson alludes, must presumably have been obtained from the 1893 meeting with the labourer from Westfield which the solicitor mentioned in his letter to Crake. Why he had waited until 1903 to 'go public' with these details, especially as they seemed so important to him ten years before, is unclear. Sadly, Merritt's written account authenticating the find has not survived.

Dawson continued to describe the Beauport Park figure in some detail, it representing one of the finest (and most ancient) of materials in his exhibition of Sussex ironwork. He related the fallout of the 1893 Society of Antiquaries meeting, noting the 'modern bronze specimen' produced by Smith, adding that Read considered the iron figurine to be 'greatly superior'.[23] Dawson also related the questions that arose as to whether the statuette was really cast iron:

> the late Sir W.C. Roberts-Austen, of the Mint, examined it, and gave as his opinion that it was of steel-like iron, such as was manufactured in early times by a direct-reduction process from iron-ores. It was afterwards examined by several different experts with great diversity of opinion, some stating that it could not be Roman, because the Romans had no tools capable of producing it in wrought-iron, others dismissing the matter by stating that if it was of cast-iron it could not be Roman. Wishing to decide the question definitely the author sent the statuette to Dr Kelner, of the Royal Arsenal, Woolwich, who has, of course, great experience in the analysis of iron, for his determination on analysis. A portion of the metal was removed from the interior of one of the leg stumps. The Arsenal workman who bored it stated that it cut like cast-iron. Dr Kelner reported that there was not the slightest doubt as to its being of cast-iron. Under these circumstances, and in the absence of further evidence, the author is disposed to claim that this little statuette is Roman, or Anglo-Roman, and the earliest known example of cast-iron in Europe at least.[24]

Thus Dawson was finally able to proclaim that he had indeed located the earliest example of cast iron in Europe, proving that not only did the Roman state possess far greater technological capabilities than had previously been supposed, but also that the 'missing link in the history of the iron industry', between primitive methods of hammering and the more advanced use of blast furnaces, had been found in Sussex.[25] Not everyone was so convinced.

Writing in the early 1930s, Ernest Straker, in his book *Wealden Iron*, the definitive study of the iron industry of south-eastern England, commented that:

> Notwithstanding Mr Dawson's belief in the authenticity of this find, there are some doubts on the matter. The sale of the objects found was a valuable

source of income to the diggers, and it is possible that deception may have been practised. From the context it is evident that similar bronze figures have been produced, and a replica in modern cast iron would not be difficult to cast and corrode by burial.[26]

Part of the doubt expressed by Straker may have derived from the observation that workmen removing the Roman slag heaps of Sussex were frequently paid for any archaeological finds that they made. Payment could easily have induced certain labourers to create more interesting discoveries; certainly Hastings Museum and Art Gallery possesses a number of dubious, 'Roman-looking' bronze objects supposedly recovered from the slag heaps around Beauport Park.[27] Such 'finds' would certainly have increased the meagre salary of the slag heap labourers, though the fabrication of metal artefacts must surely have been a drain on both the time and resources of the average workman.

In the early 1950s, following the revelation of the Piltdown hoax, Robert Downes, then having just completed a study of the English Iron Industry at Birmingham University, decided to investigate the Beauport Park Statuette more closely.

> A thin slice was taken from the fractured right leg of the statuette, just above the knee, and examined under the microscope. The research manager H. Morrogh, reported that the material was a grey cast iron. There was nothing in the structure to suggest any date, and it could have been made at any period during which the manufacture of cast iron was possible. The carbon and silicon contents were fairly high, consistent with the material being produced deliberately as cast iron, and not accidentally. Mr Morrogh said the amount of sulphur present was significant [0.05 − 0.1 per cent] and might indicate that the statuette was produced from a furnace using coke as fuel. If this were the case, the statuette could not have been made before the eighteenth century and not in Sussex at any date.[28]

As to the perceived antiquity of the figurine, as gauged by the level of corrosion it had suffered, Morrogh concluded that the rusting 'could indicate burial for many hundreds of years, but [it] was equally consistent with burial for one year at a suitable site'.[29] Whatever Dawson's figurine was, it did not appear to be either Roman or indeed a product of the Wealden iron industry.

The Beauport Park Statuette: conclusion

That the Beauport Park Statuette is not a genuine Roman object appears clear enough, but there is sufficient doubt concerning its provenance (not to say the exact nature of its discovery) to cloud whether it can be classed as a deliberate fraud designed to fool the scientific community or a minor piece of deception generated to increase the pay of a particular labourer. If suspicion falls upon William Merritt, of 'King Street, Seddlescombe Road, Westfield', then one must ask where he first obtained the piece. Despite Straker's conviction that a cast-iron figurine, copied from a bronze replica of a genuine Roman statue, 'would not be difficult to cast and corrode by burial',[30] one must ask where Merritt (or any other labourer) would have obtained either the bronze replica or the time (and resources) necessary to create a mound, produce cast iron and fabricate the artefact in the first place. Surely the effort required in generating such a fraud would have vastly outweighed any financial gain derived from the sale of the piece?

Also, if Merritt had, as Dawson claimed, found the statuette in 1877, together with some coins of Hadrian, why did he wait six years before selling it to Dawson? Surely, if he had been in possession of both the coins and the statuette, he would have sold them all to James Rock, rather than keeping the more valuable object back? The apparent contradiction in Merritt's actions were not commented upon until 1996, when John Evangelist Walsh observed that the workman had twice acted:

> against his own interests by withholding critical information: when selling the coins to Rock he kept silent about the statuette, and when selling the statuette to Dawson [in 1883] he kept silent about the coins. Any worker accustomed to digging in British soil would have understood that selling statue and coins together would have brought the best return.[31]

Of course, it is possible that Merritt did not have the statuette when the coins were sold to Rock. If the piece had actually been made by Merritt, perhaps inspired by the financial reward he had received for the coins, then it is possible that it was either not ready in time, or that Rock, being suspicious of its origin, declined to purchase it. Such information would, of course, have been withheld from Dawson, for Merritt would have been keen to avoid generating any suspicion concerning the authenticity of his 'find'. It has to be said, however, that, when one considers Dawson's actions in the case of the Beauport Park Statuette, the idea that Merritt was solely responsible for the fraud does not appear a convincing one.

Dawson supposedly bought the statuette from Merritt in 1883, aged only nineteen, but then neglected to report it for a further ten years until finally presenting it to Augustus Wollaston Franks in 1893. Why did Dawson wait so long before reporting his discovery? Perhaps his new job with F.A. Langhams took up all of his time, whilst whatever free time he had was consumed with his fossil discoveries (which by 1883 had earned him a fellowship in the

Geological Society). Perhaps he was unaware of the true significance of the Beauport Park find (though why then had he bought it in the first place?). Perhaps the time delay was crucial if the iron figurine was to be accepted as being authentic.

In 1956 Robert Downes noted that the lapse in reporting the artefact was an important one, for:

> We know that a Highway Surveyor began to excavate the cinder heap at Beauport Park about 1870 and used large amounts for road metal every year. When Rock visited Beauport Park in 1878, he estimated that the supply would be exhausted in another ten years. The discovery had therefore to be placed between the years 1870 and 1880 if it was going to appear genuine.[32]

A time lapse of ten years since Dawson's retrieval of the artefact and sixteen years since its first discovery would also prove useful in order to cloud the specific details of both provenance and recovery. Sixteen years after the event, it would be likely that few involved in the discovery would be able to *precisely* recall how and when it first came to light. Furthermore, William Merritt, even if he did exist (and there was never any independent verification that this was so) would have been a difficult man to track down in 1903, when Dawson first publicly announced his name. An added bonus would be that the slag heap from which the statuette was supposed to have come would, by 1903, have been totally obliterated, making re-excavation or re-examination impossible.

If we accept that Dawson was aware that the cast-iron figurine was fraudulent, then many of the curious aspects of the whole Beauport Park case simply disappear. The time lapse between discovery and reporting has already been explained, but of course if Dawson had generated the find in the first place, then it was never in the ground for Merritt or anyone else to have found it. The inconsistencies in Dawson's story between 1893 and 1903 may further be explained by a change in strategy following the lukewarm reception at the Society of Antiquaries meeting, for now Dawson had to verify the provenance if the find was to be taken seriously. The association with James Rock and the coins described in 1879 served furthermore to increase the perceived authenticity of the find (even though the inconsistencies in the way that the coins and the statuette were then treated could not adequately be explained).

Dawson was, of course, the one character in the story who benefited most from the discovery of the Beauport iron figurine. He had attracted the attention of Augustus Wollaston Franks and Charles Hercules Read, who, apart from their positions in the British Museum, were respectively the President and Secretary of the Society of Antiquaries. He even had his prized exhibit presented before the Antiquaries, quite an honour for an amateur anti-quarian. Although the artefact was not totally accepted by all members of the Society, it was one of a number of exiting discoveries that, two years later, helped Dawson to be elected as a fellow of the Society of Antiquaries. Dawson was also able to use the iron figurine in many of his later displays, most notably the 1903 Lewes exhibition, and publications where it was exulted as the earliest example of cast iron in Europe.

The Uckfield Horseshoe

In 1903 Dawson supplied an apparently unique horseshoe for the Lewes exhibition on Sussex ironwork. The object was illustrated and briefly discussed by Dawson in his article accompanying the exhibition, entitled 'Sussex Ironwork and Pottery', which was published in the *Sussex Archaeological Collections* for 1903 (**31**). Here, the artefact was described as being:

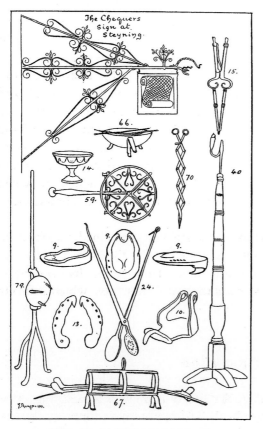

SPECIMENS OF SUSSEX WROUGHT IRON

31 (Left) *The Uckfield Horseshoe: numbered as specimen 9 in this illustration for the 1903 Lewes exhibition. Note the appearance of a Roman hippo-sandal from Chichester here numbered as specimen 10*

32 (Above) *The Uckfield Horseshoe: a drawing of the shoe which accompanied Sidney Hollands' 1896 article on the Sussex iron industry (where it originally appeared upside down)* a somewhat heavy slipper-form, the plate slightly moulded to the frog of the foot of the horse, and the front edge perforated with nail holes somewhat in the manner of a modern shoe. The back centre of the plate was flanged upward, the flange terminating in a hook-shaped piece as if used to strap the hinder part of the shoe to the horse's hoof.[33]

In other words the object seemed to represent an intermediary stage between the slipper or hippo-sandal, a temporary shoe often tied directly onto the hoof of an unshod horse, and the more usual nailed variety. The sketches provided by Dawson for the purposes of the publication are unfortunately lacking in detail, making an objective assessment of the piece rather difficult. The same object appears however to have featured in an article authored by Sidney Hollands on the Sussex iron industry published in 1896 (32). Unfortunately, here again, the oversimplified style of drawing makes interpretation of form almost impossible. The main reasons for assuming that the horseshoe illustrated in Dawson's article of 1903 was the same as that appearing in Holland's piece of 1896, are not only that Dawson was the supplier of both drawings, but also the derivation for both pieces is given as the 'river Ouse at Uckfield'.[34] The exact context of discovery is never established, though Dawson observes that it had originally been found by person or persons unnamed 'associated with the piles of an ancient bridge... which had been superseded by another wooden bridge time out of mind'.[35]

Dawson presented the find to Sir Wollaston Franks of the British Museum for identification at some date before 1896 (Franks died in 1897),[36] and reported that the scholar 'was disposed to regard it as a development of the type of the 'Roman shoe' or 'hippo-sandal'[37] Robert Downes, who examined the evidence for the Uckfield Horseshoe in the mid-1950s, was extremely sceptical, noting that 'even in the existing state of knowledge, such a 'missing link' must have appeared superfluous... An alleged horseshoe which was nailed at the front and tied on at the back would combine mutually contradictory principles in it as it flapped about'.[38]

The artefact itself has unfortunately since been confined to oblivion. Holland's article notes that, in 1896, the shoe was 'in the British Museum', presumably a temporary affair whilst it awaited identification. Its last appearance was as part of Dawson's 1903 exhibition at Lewes, after which it finally disappeared from view.

The Uckfield Horseshoe: conclusion

As with a number of Dawson's finds, the lack of context as regards the nature of discovery, makes interpretation difficult. We do not know, for instance, who exactly found the shoe, where they found it and how, if at all, it related to the timbers of the 'ancient bridge'. It is possible that Dawson himself was the original discoverer, the findspot being not far from his Uckfield office, or that someone who knew him brought the artefact to his attention. It is also possible that he purchased the horseshoe from a dealer in antiquities, for a number of objects in his collection were derived from just such a source. It is also possible that it is a hoax.

As Downes observed in 1956, there is no real need for an intermediary stage between the tied-on Roman hippo-sandal and the more conventional nailed shoe. The possibility of there being a half nailed, half-tied horseshoe does, on the face of it, appear ludicrous. Alternatively the 'horseshoe' may perhaps have been used for an entirely different purpose; perhaps it was not Roman at all (certainly no more have come to light in the years following 1903); perhaps it was a one-off, made by someone for a specific purpose that is now lost to us. In short, it is not possible to prove that the Uckfield Horseshoe is fraudulent; merely that it is unusual and that it was found under circumstances that were not fully recorded by Dawson or anyone else.

The Herstmonceux Fireback

The 1903 exhibition of Sussex ironwork, organised by Charles Dawson, contained a number of firebacks recovered from a variety of sources across the county. Dawson notes that in his experience,

> specimens of firebacks in Sussex are well-nigh endless, and this is hardly to be wondered at, considering their durability when used in a wood-fire, the number of years during which they were executed, the constant changes of fashion, and the fact that every homestead and cottage up and down the country possessed at least one plate.[39]

Most of those displayed in the exhibition belonged to the Sussex Archaeological Society,[40] but two – an example from 'The Rocks, Buxted' and one from Herstmonceux Castle – stand out as being 'in the author's possession'.[41] Dawson notes that the Herstmonceux example was a 'class II' fireback (**33**), that is to say one made from a single-piece mould possessing either 'armorial bearings' or 'allegorical subjects'.[42] The 'private armorial bearings' were in this instance interpreted as being 'the Dacre Crest'.[43]Francis, third Lord Dacre of the family of Lennard, was on the Parliamentary side during the English Civil War, and was chosen by Oliver Cromwell as a member of the House of Commons in 1654. Following the restoration of the Stuart monarchy in 1660, Francis' wife Elizabeth was made countess of the island of Sheppey in Kent by Charles II. Their son Thomas, fourth Lord Dacre, married Anne, daughter of King Charles (by the Duchess of Cumberland), and was created earl of the county of Sussex in 1674.

33 *The Herstmonceux Fireback*

In 1926, some twenty-three years after the exhibition, Charles Beetlestone examined the Herstmonceux Fireback in the course of his studying of the heraldry of Kent. Looking at the artefact in detail, Beetlestone wondered 'how such a description was written is a puzzle, as the crest is not Dacre, nor is there a single Dacre coat among the twenty-two quarterings'.[44] The crest displayed could only, in Beetlestone's mind, represent that of the Trevor family.[45]

The Herstmonceux Fireback: conclusion

The case of the Herstmonceux Fireback need not detain us long. The details provided by Dawson are clearly incorrect, but this could be due to a simple misidentification of the original crest, rather than to any attempt on his behalf to deliberately deceive. Given the number and sheer variety of iron objects assembled for the purposes of the 1903 exhibition, it is quite possible to believe that Dawson could have made errors in specific interpretation or identification. Although no information is supplied as to how the object came to be in his private collection, the artefact itself would otherwise appear wholly genuine.

The Chiddingly Dog Gate

In his article on 'Sussex Iron Work' accompanying an exhibition held by the Sussex Archaeological Society (and published in the *Sussex Archaeological Collections* for 1903), Charles Dawson drew attention to a 'Sussex dog gate' which he illustrated as figure 1 (**34**). In the catalogue at the end of the article, Dawson comments:

> Iron dog gate from Chiddingly (temp. Elizabethan), mounted as a fire screen (the standards modern). These gates were formerly used to keep the dogs from wandering upstairs and were fixed at the foot of the staircase in the main hall.[46]

The gate itself was not directly referred to within the main text of Dawson's article, other than to note 'it is surprising that so handsome an addition as a dog gate to a staircase has been allowed to fall into disuse'.[47] A similar ornamental iron gate had earlier featured in an article entitled 'The extinct Iron industry of the Weald of Sussex', written by Sidney Holland and published in the July 1896 edition of *Antiquary* magazine (**35**). The caption accompanying the Holland illustration provides a little more detail concerning the deviation of the piece, noting that it comprised 'a grille formed from an iron gate made by Fuller, of Heathfield forge'.[48]

The gate appearing in Holland's article is very similar to that depicted by Dawson in basic form and style. There are, however, a number of key differences in construction, which should be noted. First, a series of ornamental loops or scrolls, which in Holland's 1896 illustration run the whole length of

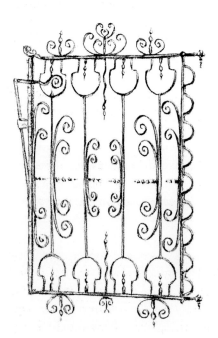

34 *The Chiddingly Dog Gate: sketched by Charles Dawson in 1903*

35 *The Chiddingly Dog Gate: a drawing accompanying Sidney Hollands' article of 1896*

both sides of the gate, are, in Dawson's illustration of 1903, missing from the left-hand side where a single latch is clearly indicated. Secondly, the ornamental fretwork on the top and bottom right of Dawson's illustration is far more intricate and decorative than that appearing in Holland's. Holland's gate is also set within its own (ornamental?) stand, whilst Dawson's appears to have been free-standing (though the catalogue refers to a set of modern stands).[49] Despite these differences, it would appear that the two illustrations were, in all probability, of the same piece, especially as Dawson is expressly thanked in the acknowledgements to Holland's article, presumably for providing certain illustrations. How then can we explain such anomalies in depiction?

Robert Downes, who examined the gate in 1953, observed that the differences could only have occurred if the decorative scrolls had been forcibly removed and the original gate, as depicted in Holland's article of 1896, had then been 'taken out of its stands and laid flat on a covered floor; the latch must have been laid loose in position; and the photograph must have been taken from above'.[50] Unfortunately for this theory, neither illustration is actually a *photograph* of the gate, rather they are sketches which depict the main features and which have been photographically reproduced for the purposes of publication. Any differences in minor form could, therefore, be explained by the misinterpretation of surviving detail by the artist or from a subjective form of artistic licence in the final rendering. At no point are we ever provided with an objective assessment of the condition or survival of the iron gate, so any missing, damaged or corroded areas could simply have been imaginatively reconstructed for the finished articles. In any case, in the seven years between Holland's and Dawson's publications, the gate could easily have been modified, the scrollwork along one side of the piece having been removed to make way for the addition of a latch.

Downes, however, maintained his suspicions concerning the derivation of the gate, observing that the caption which accompanied the illustration in Holland's article,

> could not possibly be true. Such ornamental gates are wrought iron, made at a blacksmith's forge. But the Fuller's of Waldron were not blacksmiths, but a wealthy landed family who built the 'New Furnace' in Heathfield near the end of the seventeenth century.[51]

Downes was also keen to note that the historical records relating to the New Forge at Heathfield showed that its chief products were 'pig iron and cannon'; the absence of a refining forge meaning that the wrought-iron dog gate could not possibly have been created there.[51] Such an erroneous description could, in Downes' mind, mean only one thing: 'that Dawson attributed a false and impossible origin to one of his specimens and then changed it to suit his whim'.[53]

The Chiddingly Dog Gate: conclusions

Suspicions concerning the nature and origin of the dog gate attributed to 'Fuller, of Heathfield forge' appear, on the face of it, largely unfounded. Downes' intimation that the gate had been in some way photographically altered by Dawson so as to appear different in his article of 1903 are ground-less, for, as already noted, the figures accompanying both Holland's and Dawson's publications are no more than sketches designed to show basic struc-tural detail. Any anomalies or inconsistencies in the depiction of the gate could, therefore, be easily explained by a lack of objectivity on behalf of the artist, rather than as part of a deliberate attempt to deceive. Furthermore, we cannot be sure whether it was Dawson himself who drew the gate in both instances, there being no signature accompanying either illustration. If the figures *can* be treated as an objective record of the iron gate as it appeared before 1896 and before 1903, we may assume that any minor differences apparent were due to the modification of the original gate possibly to suit new owners, a new location or a new use.

Downes' accusation that Dawson 'attributed a false and impossible origin' which he arbitrarily changed 'to suit his whim', also does not stand up to close scrutiny, for once again we have no positive proof that Dawson was in any way involved with the compilation of captions in Holland's 1893 article. It may well have been Holland himself who suggested that the gate had been made by Fuller of Heathfield forge, a derivation which Dawson later realised could not be correct and which he altered for his own article on Sussex ironwork. All we can really say about the Chiddingly Dog Gate is that there was a lack of objectivity in its recording, making a definitive statement as to its original derivation and form difficult. There is no evidence here of fraudulent activity.

The Lewes Prick Spur

In June 1908, Charles Dawson brought three iron objects to a meeting of the Society of Antiquaries in London. Two were described by Dawson as 'prick spurs' from Hastings Castle whilst the third (**36**) was simply categorised as 'an iron object from Lewes Castle'.[54] Dawson never supplied any additional information as to the

36 *The Lewes Prick Spur: as photographed in 2003*

exact circumstances under which these pieces were recovered, though we may presume that the Hastings Castle artefacts were derived from one of the many investigations conducted there by Dawson and Lewis prior to 1900. The object from Lewes Castle is less easy to provenance, though given the date of the London exhibition it is possible that it had been found in the back garden of Castle Lodge, the Lewes town house that Dawson and his family had moved into during the spring of 1907. The extent of clearance enacted by Dawson at the back of Castle Lodge between 1907 and 1908 is unknown, though the discovery of a 'disused and long-forgotten wine cellar' is certainly well documented.[55]

The key point of interest surrounding the Lewes Castle object is its identification and interpretation. When Dawson exhibited the piece at the meeting of the Society of Antiquaries, it is clear that only the accompanying objects from Hastings Castle had by then been securely identified as spurs, being 'of the same form as those worn by Norman knights as figured in the Bayeux Tapestry'.[56] When the object from Lewes was displayed by Hastings Museum in 1909, it too appears to have been identified as 'a prick spur'.[57]

Spurs, designed primarily to control a horse through the digging of something sharp into its flanks, made their first widespread appearance in Britain at the time of the Norman Conquest, though certain Roman cavalry units may have made use of them earlier. The first recognisable form of spur is the prick spur; a simple immovable point fastened to the heels of the rider. Over time the form of the spur developed and evolved, whilst the object itself became a sign of prestige, not only in the ownership of horses (with all its implied status), but also as a sign of chivalry, later references to becoming a knight being described as 'winning one's spurs'.

The Lewes Castle 'prick spur' is made of wrought iron, measures 13cm in length and possesses a rather lethal-looking sharpened point where it contacted with the horse. Robert Downes, as part of his investigation into the ironwork of Charles Dawson, forwarded the piece to Rupert Bruce-Mitford, then Keeper of the Department of Romano British and Medieval Antiquities at the British Museum, in September 1954, in the hope of obtaining a view as to its function. Bruce-Mitford wrote back that 'the object is certainly not a prick spur and is nothing we can recognise. I am sorry we cannot be more precise'.[58] Looking at the piece again, Downes observed that, if it were in fact a spur 'it would have gored rather badly any poor horse to which it was applied'.[59]

As to what the iron object may actually have been, Downes postulated that:

> Perhaps the specimen was a clumsy attempt to represent an imaginary early prototype of the Norman prick spur. It might have been supposed that in the course of evolution the neck grew thinner and the point sharper. But, in fact, Roman bronze prick spurs had much shorter necks than iron ones. The difference was no doubt to the nature of the material as the point in wrought iron had to be hammered into shape.[60]

It was clear in Downes' mind that the Lewes Prick Spur was a fake, though he fell short of actually accusing anyone, noting that 'we do not know who was responsible for manufacturing this... but we may write it off as a failure'.[61]

The Lewes Prick Spur: conclusions

The Lewes Castle 'prick spur', as noted above, does not conform to any known example of medieval spur identified yet in Britain. This observation does not, however, automatically imply that the piece is fraudulent, merely unique. It could just as easily be a genuine, albeit unusual, piece of medieval equestrian kit as it could a hoax designed to fool the archaeological establishment. The real problem with regard to the interpretation of the 'spur', as with a number of Dawson's artefacts, is provenance: where and how exactly did Dawson come to acquire the piece? If we could securely answer this we would be nearer to understanding its meaning.

It is possible that the artefact was found at Castle Lodge during renovations and excavations conducted informally by Dawson in the late spring and summer of 1907. Such a discovery then would have provided him with ample time to present the piece before the Society of Antiquaries (London) in 1908, but possibly not enough time to adequately conduct research (hence the artefact is first exhibited without any form of interpretation). By the time an exhibition was organised in Hastings the following year (1909), Dawson had investigated the artefact more closely and was able to confidently assert that it was a form of medieval prick spur.

Given that we know nothing concerning the context of Dawson's discovery, however, it is just as possible that the piece is a modern forgery, created by Dawson either to add credence to his medieval-style dungeon at Castle Lodge or simply as just the sort of artefact that one would expect to find so close to the Castle tilting ground (a space now occupied by Lewes bowls club). Alternatively the iron find could have been purchased by Dawson from a local collector of antiquities (who supplied a dubious provenance) or passed to him by a friend or local workman. Given the total absence of data concerning the artefact, anything is possible.

The Bermondsey Abbey Curfew

At the Hastings Exhibition of 1909, Charles Dawson displayed a fireguard or 'curfew', said to have originated from Bermondsey Abbey in Surrey (**37** & **38**). The word 'curfew' itself is derived from the Norman French term *couvre feu* meaning 'to cover a fire' and relates specifically to a solid iron or brass guard, sometimes in the shape of a quarter sphere, which was placed directly over a

37 *The Bermondsey Abbey Curfew: from the front in 2003*

38 *The Bermondsey Abbey Curfew: from the rear in 2003*

hearth at night in order to prevent accidental fires. The example from Bermondsey Abbey was described as being 'of Latten brass, embossed; used for muffling the fire in the open hearth when the Curfew bell was rung'.[62]

Robert Downes was particularly taken by this description, noting that:

> Latten was a vague term for copper alloys in the Middle Ages. From the sixteenth century the strict meaning of brass was a particular alloy of copper and zinc. But the strict signification of the two words together is brass rolled into thin plate, a process dating from the late seventeenth century. The words used to describe this kind of fireguard were 'curfew' and 'cover-fire'. The Oxford Dictionary has one example of their use in the seventeenth century, and more in the eighteenth. The design of this particular specimen would agree with such a late date.[63]

If the curfew is originally of late seventeenth- or early eighteenth-century date, however, then certain problems arise, not least that the area around London was, by the end of the seventeenth century, becoming increasingly reliant on Newcastle mineral (or 'sea') coal, rather than the more expensive timber option. Downes comments that, in his opinion 'we would not expect the family residing on the site of Bermondsey Abbey in the eighteenth century still to be burning wood'.[64] This could, of course, make the Bermondsey fireguard something of an anachronism. Perhaps, Downes speculated, the 'curfew' had not originated from Bermondsey Abbey at all, but from somewhere entirely different, only being credited to the abbey (which was at that time undergoing something of an antiquarian renaissance) by Dawson in order to make it appear 'more interesting'.[65]

The Bermondsey Abbey Curfew: conclusions

There is nothing intrinsically fraudulent about the curfew credited by Dawson to Bermondsey Abbey. Such items were certainly very popular in the sixteenth and seventeenth century and, though Dawson never specifically supplied a date for the piece, it is possible, given the constant risk of overnight fires, that such items remained in active use well into the nineteenth century, despite the common use of fuels other than wood. The fact that sea coal was becoming more popular around London in the eighteenth century cannot really be used as proof that the curfew was redundant or anachronistic. With no clear evidence concerning the provenance of the curfew, it is just as likely to have derived from Bermondsey Abbey as anywhere else. True, the caption that accompanied the artefact at the Hastings Exhibition of 1909 may not have been correct in all of its detail, but this does not prove deception.

The Hastings Mace

Also appearing alongside the Lewes Prick Spur and the Bermondsey Abbey Curfew in the Hastings Exhibition of 1909 was a short tipstaff derived from the Dawson Loan Collection. Dawson himself claimed to have found the artefact in a pawnbroker's shop 'somewhere in Kent'.[66] The staff was composed predominantly of ivory and silver, terminating in a small silver oar, and bore both the Hastings coat of arms and a hallmark dating to the year 1833. The exhibition catalogue described the object as a 'mace of Hastings water-bailiff; called the 'oar'-mace; formerly used in making arrests on the neighbouring seas'.[67]

Mainwairing Baines, Curator of Hastings Museum, examined the artefact in the early 1950s, subsequently reporting to Robert Downes that:

> it is true that there was an official called the water-bailiff at Hastings. But far from having magisterial duties of making arrests on the high seas, his humble and sanitary employment was to keep clean a stream which ran through the town.[68]

To make matters worse, the office itself was abolished in 1825, eight years before, if we are to believe the hallmark, the staff itself had actually been made. All the evidence, Baines concluded, suggested that the staff, in its basic form, had originated from:

> the manor of Grange, in North Kent, which enjoyed the privileges of the Cinque Ports in return for contributing two oars towards the Hastings quota of the Cinque Ports fleet.[69]

The 'Cinque Ports' was a term that covered a confederation of the five premier medieval ports of the south-eastern English coast. The fishing fleets of the south-east had, for a considerable period throughout the Middle Ages, represented the military frontline, regularly being pressed into service in order to convey troops across the English Channel as well as bearing the brunt of pirate activity. In return for their service to the Crown, the five major ports of Hastings, Romney, Hythe, Dover and Sandwich were together granted significant privileges, which included freedom to trade, freedom from tolls and customs duties and the right to hold their own judicial courts.

The Hastings Mace: conclusions

It would appear that the Hastings Mace is a simple case of misidentification. Mainwairing Baines, who presumably had more information to hand than Dawson, was able to place a more secure attribution to the artefact than the solicitor from Uckfield, who had erroneously linked it to the office of the Hastings water-bailiff (possibly misconstruing the duties of that office in the process). There is nothing with regard to the captioning of the mace for the purposes of the 1909 Hastings Exhibition which suggests deliberate intent to deceive. With regard to the original provenance of the artefact, however, it is unfortunate that Dawson was unable to identify the Kentish pawnbrokers, nor relate any details surrounding its placement there. Such vagueness unfortunately serves only to cloud the background of the piece, making it difficult, if not impossible, to research its origins further.

The 'Arabic' Anvil

A small blacksmith's anvil, stamped with the date '1515', appears in the Dawson loan of Hastings Museum (**39**). The object, which was never commented directly upon by Charles Dawson, did, however, feature in a number of local exhibitions though its provenance, circumstances and date of discovery all remain unknown. Robert Downes examined the artefact in the mid-1950s, observing that the 1515 inscription:

> is very clumsy. The figure 5's all look like capital letter S's. The intervals between the figures increase progressively from a quarter inch to one inch. The grooves of the incised figures are extremely shallow and rounded in section.[70]

The position of the inscription, along one of the least inconspicuous sides of the anvil, suggested to Downes that this was not the product of the original

39 *The 'Arabic' Anvil: from the side in 2003*

manufacturer, who would presumably have made 'a more legible inscription in a more readable position'.[71] The form taken by the inscription also raises potential problems, for the date is presented using Arabic numbers, rather than the then more usual Roman numerals.

> At that time the use of Arabic numerals was only just being introduced in manuscripts in this country and not until the middle of the century did they begin to be used for monumental inscriptions.[72]

What we know today as 'Arabic numerals' were in all probability developed in India, possibly as early as the sixth century AD, being transmitted to the West through the Arabic worlds of North Africa and Spain. This new number system (using combinations of the symbols 0, 1, 2, 3, 4, 5, 6, 7, 8 and 9) was far more efficient than the long-established Latin/Roman system which was calculated using a combination of only seven basic symbols, each with its own specific numerical value (I for 1, V for 5, X for 10, L for 50, C for 100, D for 500 and M for 1,000). Use of Arabic numerals greatly eased all forms of calculation and computation, not least of all because, unlike the Roman system, the Arabic possessed a point zero. It is not known exactly when these numerals were first introduced to Europe, although the oldest-dated European manuscript containing such a system is probably the *Codex Vigilanus*, copied in Spain around AD 976. In Britain, the first recorded use of the Arabic numbers is from a series of thirteenth-century statues preserved at Wells Cathedral in Somerset.

The date '1515', (and not 'MDXV') would, therefore, not have been wholly out of place in early sixteenth-century Britain, but its application to a small iron anvil (rather than say a more monumental inscription or statue) is admittedly rather curious. Perhaps the ironmonger originally in possession of the anvil was rather forward thinking, or had travelled further afield to the Arabic world, where conversion to the radical new way of counting had occurred.

There is another possible explanation for the appearance of the date '1515' upon a small common anvil. When Dawson set out his display of Sussex iron as part of the 1901-3 exhibition at Lewes, there included within it a cast-iron anvil 'loaned by Mr E. Newman of East Street, Chichester'. This particular artefact was itself not especially interesting, other than it bore the moulded inscription of '1616' as the date of manufacture. This, suggested Robert Downes, had likely been Dawson's inspiration for the fraud of the 'Arabic anvil' for 'to inscribe 1515 on a small common anvil is to go 101 [years] better'.[73]

The 'Arabic' Anvil: Conclusions

It is possible that everyone has been reading the inscription incorrectly. Downes has already observed that both 5's do look more akin to 'capital letter S's',[74] something which would in turn generate, not suggest, not a date ('1515'), but a name: 'ISIS' (**40**).

Isis was the sister and wife of Osiris, the Egyptian god of the dead, and mother of the falcon-headed god Horus. Like Osiris, Isis was closely associated with concepts of life, rebirth, fertility and the endless cycles of nature. She was venerated throughout the Roman Empire, some elements of her worship being assimilated into the early Christian Church (her relationship with Horus arguably having acted as a model for that of Mary and Jesus). The application of the name of such a prominent ancient deity to an object as seemingly mundane as an anvil may seem to us bizarre, but metalworking as a process was far more mystical an experience in the past than the heavily mechanised industry it has become today. Association with the exotic Egyptian goddess of rebirth and recycling may not have seemed at all strange, even within a late medieval and supposedly Christian context.

Alternatively the name 'Isis', in this instance, could have related to a personal, business or street name or even a specific geographical location such as the upper course of the River Thames around Oxford which still bears the name 'Isis'. Unfortunately, because the inscription was generated upon the piece with a red hot iron, its application could belong to any period from the

40 *The 'Arabic' Anvil: detail of the '1515' or 'ISIS' inscription in 2003*

medieval to the modern day, there certainly being no guarantee that it related in any way to the original use or function of the artefact.

What use Dawson actually made of the anvil, other than as part of his extensive loans collection stored in Hastings Museum, is not entirely clear; the date and circumstances of its discovery have never been satisfactorily resolved. The anvil itself is fairly nondescript, it being just as possibly a product of the sixteenth century as it is of the seventeenth, eighteenth or nineteenth. The inscription causes some concern with regard to its style and supposed date, but, given that we know nothing about where the object was supposedly found, when or by whom, we cannot securely state that this was the product of fraudulent activity on the part of Charles Dawson.

The Beauport Park Axe

The collection of artefacts purchased from Helene Dawson by Hastings Corporation in 1917 contains a 'A small iron axe head found in a slag-heap at Beauport Park'.[75] A minor amendment to this description was made (possibly by Mainwairing Baines, curator of the museum at the time of the Piltdown exposure) by the deliberate erasure of the word 'Park'. No further details exist as to the provenance of the piece, its supposed interpretation or how it ended up in Dawson's collection. It could have derived from the collection of William Merritt, a workman at Beauport Park, for Dawson notes that when he purchased the statuette from Merritt in 1883, he also acquired 'other specimens'.[76] If these 'other specimens' had indeed included the axe head, it would however seem strange that Dawson never produced it in support of his theories concerning Roman ironwork. If he had come into possession of the piece at the same time as the statuette, it would also appear strange that he failed to exhibit it either at the Society of Antiquaries meeting of 1893, or the Sussex Archaeological exhibition of Sussex ironwork in 1903. As with the 'Arabic' Anvil already described, the Beauport Park Axe does not appear to have been an object that Dawson ever publicly acknowledged or discussed in print, though it could conceivably have formed part of the display which had been on loan to Hastings Museum.

The artefact, which measures 8.9cm in overall length and possesses a cutting edge 3.4cm long, is heavily corroded, much like the Roman statuette that Dawson claimed was recovered from Beauport Park in 1877. Unlike the statuette, however, there is no dispute that the axe head is of wrought (or hammered) iron, rather than being cast. With regard to the date of the axe, it is important to remember that Dawson never voiced an opinion on this. The implication must, of course, be that it was Roman, especially if it had been retrieved from 'a slag heap' within the Roman ironworking site at Beauport Park. It could, however, easily have been an intrusive find or a later piece of casual or accidental loss.

In September 1954, as part of his re-analysis of the Beauport Park ironwork, Robert Downes passed the axe head on to Rupert Bruce-Mitford, Keeper of the Department of Romano British and Medieval Antiquities at the British Museum, for identification. Working on the assumption that the artefact was thought to be of Roman date, Bruce-Mitford observed that 'the miniature axe is of Medieval shape, but we do not know of another so small'.[77] To Downes, this was a clear indication of fraudulent activity, for 'it is rather puzzling to know what an axe head, Medieval in shape, was doing in a Roman cinder heap'.[78] The size of the piece was also a potential problem, Downes wondering why iron, an expensive material at any time, had been used to manufacture an object that was apparently 'ornamental rather than utilitarian'. In conclusion, Downes felt sure that the Beauport Park axe head was 'another doubtful specimen' from the Dawson archive.[79]

The Beauport Park Axe: conclusions

The axe head supposedly recovered from Beauport Park is certainly unusual, but this, in itself, does not constitute grounds for believing it to be a hoax. Dawson, as already noted, provides us with no clear indication as to the interpretation or derivation of the piece, and it could just as easily be a unique form of Roman axe as it could a medieval axe, accidentally dropped or deposited within an existing slag heap. The fact that the piece was small, when compared to other medieval axes of similar form, certainly makes it atypical but we may find parallel in the miniature flint axes manufactured in the British Neolithic or the miniature bronze forms of the Roman period. As we do not know why the artefact was made in the first place (it may, for example, have been a specialist wood or leatherworking tool), no firm statement concerning its validity as a secure archaeological artefact may here be made.

6

ANTLER, BRONZE AND UNDERWATER FORESTS

Charles Dawson's collection of archaeological discoveries was not just restricted to iron. During his lengthy career as an amateur antiquarian he collected a variety of curious artefacts of bronze, antler and bone from across south-east England. Some of this material he collected himself, during the course of field examination, other pieces he procured from antiquarian collectors, labourers, antique shops and pawnbrokers.

The Bulverhythe Hammer

In 1905, George Clinch, writing in the 'Early Man' section of the *Victoria County History of Sussex* (volume 1), recorded a number of 'curious objects of deer-horn' preserved in the Dawson Loan Collection of the Brassey Institute in Hastings.[1] One piece, '11 inches long, pierced in the middle by a nearly square hole' is described and photographed in particular detail (**41**), Clinch noting that 'it is said to have been found in the submarine forest at Bulverhythe, halfway between St Leonards and Bexhill'.[2]

Dawson had, for the purposes of the Brassey Institute accessions register, identified the artefact as 'a hammer', though, as Clinch observed, as a hammer 'it does not seem to be particularly fitted'.[3] This would seem clear enough for, though the central squared hole could easily have been where the item was hafted, the absence of a clear flattened head, or signs of obvious impact, would seem to rule out Dawson's interpretation as a hammer or instrument of percussion.

As the object was both unstratified and unassociated with any other datable material other than the submerged forest, a landscape of oak, alder and hazel tree stumps drowned when the sea levels rose towards the end of the Mesolithic some 6,000 years ago, Clinch was unable to assign the object to any time period. As a consequence the curious item appeared under the heading of 'miscellaneous antiquities', though assumption was that it was probably either of Neolithic or Bronze Age date.

Finding a parallel for the antler 'hammer' proved difficult, Clinch commenting that:

it seems rather closely related to those objects made of the tines and beams of the red deer antlers which, it has been suggested, were used as the cheek-pieces of bridle bits, and of which examples have been found in the river Thames; in Heathery Burn Cave, Durham; and in the Bronze Age lake dwellings of Switzerland.[4]

Antler cheekpieces, which served as a form of toggle connecting a horse's reigns to a rope or sinew mouthpiece, have been found from different periods and from various sites across Europe. The Bulverhythe antler, although similar in broad form to these examples, 'is clearly too long for such a purpose'.[5] Robert Downes, examining the artefact in the early 1950s, noted the lack of obvious parallels and interpretations, adding that 'it can hardly have been a "shaft straightener" for straightening wooden shafts, when the hole in the centre was nearly a square'.[6]

Both Clinch and Dawson appear to have favoured a prehistoric date, based upon the fact that the item was made from red deer antler (a favoured raw material during the Mesolithic, Neolithic and Bronze Age) but also as it had been found within the remains of the Mesolithic submerged forest (though the details of association were not totally clear). Neither, however, considered the central 'hafting' hole which seemed to represent an insoluble puzzle (certainly as to the object's function), but which on close inspection actually holds the key as to its date.

Two aspects of the cut require attention here. The first is that the hole is both rectangular and straight edged, suggesting that the bone was already quite old, almost fossilised and not freshly discarded, when worked. The second is that 'the almost perfectly rectangular shape suggests it was made with a sharp instrument, such as a steel chisel'.[7] In fact the cut marks made by such a steel implement are still clearly visible in the corners of the squared central hole (**42**). No

41 *The Bulverhythe Hammer: the reverse side photographed in 2003 showing Charles Dawson's original label*

42 *The Bulverhythe Hammer: the front as photographed in 1905 showing cut marks made by a steel knife around the edge of the central perforation*

prehistoric implement of flint, stone, copper alloy, bronze or iron could have created such a sharp and clear cut within the fragment of antler. The object, however it was originally intended to be used, was clearly not prehistoric. The antler itself may be ancient, but the rectangular hole could not have been made before the eighteenth century AD.

The Bulverhythe Hammer: conclusions

All this brings us to the thorny question of whether the Bulverhythe Hammer can strictly be classed as a forgery. It is clearly neither a hammer nor a cheekpiece and it is certainly not prehistoric, but was it ever designed to fool the scientific community into believing it was a genuine archaeological artefact?

If we take Dawson at his word, then the object was retrieved, presumably at low tide, from amidst the fossilised tree stumps of a submerged forest. Dawson himself supplies no extra detail as the circumstances of discovery, nor of whether the object was lying on the surface when discovered or (at least partially) embedded within sediments. What is clear, however, is that the condition of the piece suggests that it had not been exposed to a marine environment for any length of time; the edges of the cut hole are too sharp and there is no evidence of salt-water damage or tidal battering. Perhaps the artefact had only recently been discarded and washed up, in the way that quantities of disused material dumped from seagoing vessels regularly appears on the Sussex coast today. Perhaps it had been freshly dislocated from a secure and sealed environment, such as a pit, posthole or ditch eroded out of the cliffs. Perhaps it was new when Dawson found it.

The details surrounding the artefact do not help us very much here. The original note in the Brassey Institute records simply *where* the 'hammer' was found, not by whom or in what context. We cannot even be sure that it was Dawson who originally made the discovery. If the 'hammer' was indeed an isolated, unstratified object lying on the tidal sands off Bulverhythe, then it could just as easily be found by him as anyone scanning the county with an eye for the unusual. Dawson was renowned as an avid collector of antiquarian curiosities, so it could plausibly have passed into his hands through a colleague, associate or dealer, rather than having been the product of his own keen eye.

Despite being able to assert that the central hole in the antler piece could only have been produced *after* the advent of the Industrial Revolution, it has, to date, been impossible to find a parallel for the artefact within a post-medieval context. This in itself should not necessarily pose a problem, many objects recovered from any given period may be classed as 'unique', being the product of a bored mind or created to fulfil a specific requirement and manufactured from materials that were readily available. The fact that it simply 'looks a bit like' a cheekpiece for a prehistoric horse, does not prove that this was the type of object that it was intended to mimic.

One point is, however, worth noting here. The squared cut into the antler almost exactly matches the type of cut mark recorded from the elephant femur recovered in 1914 in association with the discoveries from Piltdown 1. At the time of its initial discovery, the femur was considered to represent a genuine piece of Palaeolithic workmanship. Only later, in 1949, did a close analysis of the piece by Kenneth Oakley reveal that the worked facets could not have been made by a flint knife,

> for this produced only scratchy marks. In fact, it proved impossible to cut, in the sense of whittling, a fresh or recently dried bone, which could only be worked by flaking, scraping, sawing or grinding... the Piltdown bone was already fossilised when it was worked and... the shaping must have been done by a metal knife.[8]

The Bulverhythe Hammer, though unproven as a forgery, contains many elements (including its uncertain derivation, unique appearance and clear signs of modern shaping) that were to be repeated at Piltdown; points we shall return to at a later date.

The St Leonards Bronze Hoard

Recorded alongside the 'Bulverhythe Hammer' in the pages of the *Victoria County History of Sussex*, were a number of Bronze Age axes or palstaves both 'whole and broken'.[9] No specific details as to the circumstances of their discovery or coherency as a single group are provided by George Clinch, author of the *Victoria County History* chapter on 'Early Man', other than to note that they were derived from St Leonards on Sea and 'are now in the possession of Mr Charles Dawson FSA'.[10]

Palstaves represent one of the most common and recognisable artefacts of the British Later Bronze Age (conventionally 1400–600 BC). The term 'palstave' itself is usually applied by modern archaeologists to a form of bronze axe with a flared, curving edge and distinct shoulders. The metal head often possessed a stop-ridge to hold a wooden axe haft in place and occasionally this was supplemented by a metal loop so the blade could be tied directly to the haft with the help of leather strips or twine. Palstaves were gradually super-seded in the Bronze Age by socketed axes, a hollow axe head which allowed the direct insertion of the haft.

Both socketed axes and palstaves commonly occur archaeologically in discrete groups or hoards. A hoard is a collection of related metal objects that were buried together at one particular time. Quite why the original depositor of the hoard never returned to claim the material is a question that archaeology itself cannot answer, though a number of possible interpretations are often cited. Perhaps the metal within a discrete group or hoard represented scrap collected by an itinerant smith or metal worker (founder's hoard); perhaps they were quality items kept for later exchange or sale (merchant's hoard); possibly they were acquired as the spoils of war (loot hoard); or represent a range of private affects hidden at a time of civil unrest (personal hoard). They may even represent a form of ritual or religious offering which accompanied the remains of the dead (votive hoard).

Two objects from the tentatively identified 'St Leonards on Sea hoard' were illustrated in the *Victoria County History*: a corroded bronze palstave (**43**), slightly chipped along its cutting edge, and an unusual 'bronze socketed object' in slightly better condition (**44**). Clinch describes the socketed object as 'evidently only a part of a larger implement and ending in a reversed shield'.[11] Unfortunately neither artefact is discussed in any detail, though the caption that accompanies the socketed object notes a slightly more specific provenance than the palstaves, namely 'the marina' at St Leonards on Sea.[12] This, together with the differing states of artefact preservation, may cast some doubt as to whether the two pieces were originally found at the same time or whether they formed part of the same group or hoard.

Dawson himself first mentions the bronze material in his 1909 book the *History of Hastings Castle*, when outlining the extent of prehistoric activity in the immediate area of the town. It is worth quoting his comments here in full, as they represent the closest we ever get to a full description of the nature and circumstances of the initial discovery.

43 *The St Leonards bronze hoard: a corroded palstave as photographed in 1905*

44 *The St Leonards bronze hoard: the 'socketed object' as photographed in 1905*

The author knows of few instances of the discovery of implements of the Bronze Age near Hastings. One discovery of bronze axes occurred many years ago in forming the Seddlescombe Road, on the north side of Battle... Another was in a fall of the cliff behind the houses at West Marina, St Leonards on Sea, which took place about the year 1869. Three whole axe heads and a portion of a fourth were found, together with a piece of bronze, technically called a 'runner', left over from the mould in casting. Hence it is probable that all these implements formed [a] portion of a 'founders hoard'. They are of ordinary type, with two lateral grooves for hafting.[13]

Dawson does not mention the strange 'socketed object', earlier illustrated in the *VCH*, as being part of the hoard, only the palstaves (complete and fragmentary) and a 'runner' or piece of casting debris.

Leslie Grinsell, in his 1930s study of 'Sussex in the Bronze Age', noted the strange socketed object, interpreting it as a 'bronze mount (? for standard)', a similar example 'with part of wooden shaft remaining' having been discovered in Tower Street, London in 1883.[14] The St Leonards object compares favourably in size, scale and form of manufacture with the London object, as well as with a third example unearthed at Longstone, Derbyshire in 1910.[15]

Despite there being no independent verification of the fact, the article appearing in the 1935 edition of the *Antiquaries Journal* restated the belief that the St Leonards on Sea artefact originally formed part of a hoard together with 'a chisel and palstaves'.[16] Unfortunately, as has already been observed, neither the socketed object, nor the narrow-bladed chisel were specifically noted by Dawson as having been in any way associated with the palstaves. Also absent from Dawson's initial description of the hoard was a small anvil, displayed with the palstaves and originally described in the accessions register of the Brassey Institute as a 'wedge-shaped lump of bronze'.[17] This particular artefact could, however, have been the 'runner' or piece of casting debris (and originally misidentified by Dawson).

Robert Downes, writing in the mid-1950s, was deeply suspicious of the socketed bronze object, noting that 'its purpose appears uncertain'[18] and that no clear parallel could be found for it amidst the Bronze Age collections of Britain. This is not strictly true, for at least two closely similar forms to the St Leonards item had, as already noted, been found in Britain prior to 1910,[19] although their interpretation remained unclear. Downes was also sceptical of the circumstances of the initial hoard discovery, observing that:

equally surprising is the fact that the cliff fall at Marina which exposed these implements happened in 1869, when Dawson was five years old. When did these objects come into his possession?[20]

The date does not, it must be admitted, cause any significant concerns surrounding the authenticity of the find. Dawson had not only been a resident of St Leonards since a boy, where he could easily have heard of the find, but also as a keen antiquarian collector he could at any time have purchased or obtained the bronzes from the original discoverer prior to the publication of the *Victoria County History* in 1905. The crucial point is that although the *exact* circumstances surrounding the 1869 discovery are never fully provided, Dawson never claimed to have actually *found* the bronzes himself, only that he was later in possession of them.

The St Leonards Bronze Hoard: conclusions

The full extent, nature and original context of the St Leonards on Sea 'hoard' is unknown (if not unknowable) as indeed, are the exact associations of the pieces credited to it. Dawson refers only to the palstaves and the 'runner', probably the small anvil later identified by Rowlands.[21] The chisel and 'socketed object' or standard mount do not appear, contrary to later reports, to have originally formed part of this hoard, otherwise Dawson would certainly have mentioned them in his *History of Hastings Castle*, published some four years after the *Victoria County History*. The differential surface form of the standard mount, when compared to the more heavily corroded palstaves, would also appear to argue that the mount was not originally part of the hoard, as, perhaps, would the way in which Clinch separately referred to them within the pages of the *VCH*.

If one were of a particularly suspicious mind, one could perhaps argue that the standard mount came into the hands of Dawson, either as direct purchase or as a donation, in the form of an unprovenanced artefact, Dawson later supplying a location to add a degree of authenticity. St Leonards on Sea would provide a useful provenance for such an object, for, not only did Dawson possess close associations with the place, but also because a hoard of Bronze Age materials (notably palstaves) had already been located there. Given that the original discovery of the hoard had been made some forty years earlier, and given also that Dawson is decidedly non-specific as to where in 'the marina' the material had been located, it is possible he realised that, even if someone had wished to check the validity of his statements, this would not be possible. Perhaps he even made up the details of the hoard, for we have only his word that it ever existed. He could easily have compiled or conflated a whole variety of Bronze Age artefacts from other sources.

This is, of course, all speculation. Although it would not appear likely that the standard mount and palstaves were ever archaeologically connected, there is no clear evidence here of intent to deceive, defraud or lie. All the recorded artefacts appear genuine and independent verification as to the authenticity of the curious socketed standard mount has been made from unassociated discoveries in London and Bakewell. Unusual it may be, but the object itself does not appear to be specifically fraudulent.

Sussex Loops

In 1901 Dawson presented 'two bronze bracelets' (**45**) to a meeting of the Society of Antiquaries of London. The bracelets were in fact examples of a distinctive class of Later Bronze Age dress ornament known as the 'Sussex' or 'Brighton Loop'. Sussex Loops comprise a single, thick rod of bronze which has been twisted, bent and hooked over itself to form a single bracelet or arm ring. The distribution of this distinctive form of ornament has, to date, been restricted to the immediate area surrounding the Brighton Downs. They are usually found in groups of two or three, significant hoards having been found at Blackrock, Hollingbury and Falmer Hill in Brighton and Stump Bottom near Worthing and may originally have been worn in pairs as a form of status-defining Bronze Age jewellery.

Rather unusually for Dawson, he provides precise information as to the circumstances surrounding the discovery of the Loops; 'William Berry, a workman, found them lying 18 inches apart five feet below the surface of the Downs at a spot now occupied by the centre of the lower main wall of the house numbered 133 Bonchurch Road, Brighton'.[22] The find had apparently been made around 1896, some five years before Dawson's presentation, though, as with a number of Dawson's 'discoveries', he makes no reference as

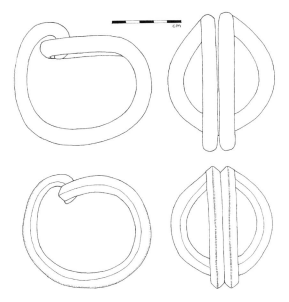

45 *The Sussex Loops: redrawn from Rowlands 1976 (plate 18)*

to how he actually came by the material. Given the date, it is *conceivable* that Dawson was in the general area at the time the find was made, though it is probably more likely that, as a noted antiquarian collector, he was contacted by the workman or one of his associates, shortly afterwards. That the finds could have come directly to the Uckfield solicitor from the workman William Berry seems by far the more likely scenario for, as Arthur Woodward was later to note, Dawson was 'in close touch with all workmen in his district who might make accidental discoveries'.[23] Both Loops were eventually presented by Dawson to the British Museum in 1903.

Sussex Loops: conclusion

Although the exact context in which the two Sussex Loops were found is unknown (they may have been part of a burial, a hoard, or from a settlement), there is no real suggestion of any underhand dealing here. Many important artefacts of prehistoric date have been retrieved from the area now covered by Brighton and Hove, the rapid development of housing throughout the nineteenth and early twentieth century having obliterated many significant archaeological sites. Large numbers of Neolithic, Bronze Age, Iron Age and Roman objects today housed in Brighton and Lewes Museums are sadly unstratified, having been recovered from the town during archaeologically unrecorded drain cutting, house building or general landscaping activities. By these standards, the information surrounding the Sussex Loops from 133 Bonchurch Road is positively colossal.

Neither can there be any doubt as to the authenticity of the finds. These are genuine prehistoric objects of a category found solely within the Brighton area. They do not represent an exotic or alien class of archaeological artefact and neither does their appearance in this part of Britain at this period of prehistory appear in any way incongruous. There is, in short, no reason to doubt either the Sussex Loops nor the details provided by Dawson as to their nature and circumstances of discovery.

The Chinese Vase

In or around 1886, Charles Dawson presented the British Museum with a rather curious find; a Chinese bronze bowl which he claimed to have found at Dover, in Kent.[24] Sadly the precise circumstances of the discovery were never elucidated, though both the artefact and its unusual context were both mirrored by a slightly earlier presentation (in 1885) of a Chinese *hu* or bronze ritual vessel which was given to the museum by Henry Willett. Willett claimed to have discovered his vessel 'in the Dane John (donjon) at Canterbury'.[25]

Unfortunately there are no recorded archaeological investigations within the medieval 'Dane John' of Canterbury in the later decades of the nineteenth century, so how the bronze was first found, and how Willett came into possession of the artefact, are unlikely to be satisfactorily explained.

Doubts surrounding the authenticity of Willett's bronze arise when the various time periods are considered, for the vessel dates from the fourth or third century BC, whilst the influx of Chinese vessels into the Northern European market only occurred after the seventeenth century AD 'when trade with China had brought not only porcelain but textiles and curios of every kind to the west'.[26] The date of Willett's *hu* would, therefore, appear to be at odds with its alleged context, making it somewhat unlikely (though not altogether impossible) that the artefact was found within a medieval feature inside a Kentish town. Robert Downes has suggested that it could have been brought from China by an antiquarian collector,[27] though how it could then have materialised in the Canterbury Dane John remains unclear (unless of course either Willett was lying or had perhaps been fooled as to its provenance by a dealer in antiquities). In this respect, Dawson's vessel appears to be more suspect than Willett's, for Dawson supplies no context or circumstances of discovery other than the rather vague comment that it had originated 'from Dover'.[28]

Dawson's bowl measures 33cm (13 inches) in diameter, being decorated in the style of the former (Western) Han dynasty, which lasted from 206 BC to AD 25. A circular panel in the centre of the dish contains two fish set either side of an inscription which may be translated as 'May you have sons and grandsons'.[29] Robert Downes, a metallurgist by training, and William Watson, then Assistant Keeper of the Department of Oriental Antiquities at the British Museum, examined the bowl in the mid-1950s. Both men were intrigued by the bowl's surface patination, comprising 'a dull olive green... with a rich incrustation... resembling malachite in places'.[30] Watson observed that such patination 'certainly looks strange' for a vessel of its supposed date, noting in addition that 'the metal has been beaten, which is not the technique usually found in Han dynasty metal vessels'.[31] In conclusion, Watson stated that 'I do not, however, think that it is a fake, though it may be a copy of some age made in China'.[32]

The Chinese Vase: conclusion

It is apparent from the way in which Dawson's bowl had been manufactured, as well as the nature of surface patination, that it is more likely to have been created within the last few hundred years, rather than the two thousand it first appeared. This is not unusual for the art of copying or mimicking early forms of metal and ceramic artefacts, textiles and texts for economic gain has a long and established history in China, certain 'archaic' bronze forms having been forged at least from the eleventh century AD. The great period of Chinese frauds was, however, between the sixteenth and early seventeenth century when there was a huge increase in the manufacture of such artefacts 'to feed a market larger than could be satisfied by the limited supply of genuine items'.[33] Dawson's piece probably fits within such a category.

Although not a clear 'forgery', in the sense of having been created specifically to dupe the scientific community, one must ask what a post-sixteenth-century Chinese bronze is doing in late nineteenth-century Dover. The suggestion made by Downes, that it was brought to Kent by an antiquarian collector, seems plausible, but the question of Dawson's complicity to deceive remains. Did he know that this was a relatively modern import, even if he was unaware that it was a sixteenth- or seventeenth-century copy of an ancient piece? Did his enthusiasm to present the piece to the British Museum outweigh his duty to fully investigate the true nature and provenance of the artefact? Did he attempt to pass it off to the British Museum as a genuine discovery, perhaps in emulation of his colleague Henry Willett? Was he alternatively duped by a dealer in antiquities who claimed to have received it from a reliable source somewhere in Dover? This latter suggestion could explain the somewhat vague circumstances of its discovery and context and would, if taken at face value, further imply that Dawson was the innocent victim of an unscrupulous salesperson or dealer in antiquities, rather than the actual instigator of a cynical hoax.

Willett's *hu* must, under these circumstances, also be considered, for, although there is no clear evidence that this piece is a forgery, its 'discovery' in a medieval context in Kent seems, in the light of it, similarly dubious.[34] Perhaps Willett too had been deceived by an unscrupulous dealer, who claimed to have details of its provenance to add an air of authenticity to the object. Possibly he himself bought the piece and attempted to pass it off as a genuine discovery to make it appear more interesting. Perhaps he and Dawson were in on the charade. We can never be sure of the exact circumstances surrounding the 'discovery' of two Chinese bronzes in such unusual conditions within a year of each other in the same British county, but here it is just as possible that Dawson (and Willett for that matter) were the innocent parties, having been led to believe that the artefacts had genuinely been retrieved from Kent, rather than being the perpetrators of a cruel hoax upon the scientific establishment.

7

THE PEVENSEY BRICKS

On Thursday 11 April 1907, Charles Dawson addressed a meeting of the Society of Antiquaries in London with a brand new, exciting Roman discovery:

> I have the honour to exhibit to the Society certain impressed or stamped bricks and tiles, discovered by me in the Roman Castra at Pevensey, which have a bearing upon the date of the building of its walls.[1]

Here Dawson was being rather modest. The pieces of brick and tile that he displayed to the society (**46**), were stamped with the Latin text:

HON AVG ANDRIA

which may be translated as 'Honorius Augustus Anderida' (**47**). These bricks not only had a bearing on the date of the Roman fortress at Pevensey (**48**), but also for the whole chronology of Roman Britain, for they appeared to indicate nothing less than the last official building project authorised by the Roman state within the province of *Britannia*.

Flavius Honorius Augustus was emperor of the western half of the Roman Empire between AD 395 and 423 (his brother Arcadius ruling jointly in the East from Constantinople). It is widely acknowledged that his reign was not altogether successful, his rather uninspired form of leadership during the invasion of Italy by the Visigoths and subsequent sacking of Rome in AD 410 seriously destabilising the western half of the Mediterranean world. Crucially, from the point of view of Roman Britain, it was Honorius who finally severed all official links with the province, following a series of rebellions there between AD 406 and 409. The discovery of tiles with his name on from a Roman fortress in Britain would therefore suggest a final piece of officially sanctioned garrison strengthening (**49** & **50**), prior to the first revolt against his rule in AD 406. No other inscription recovered from Britain had been made so late in the island's Roman history and certainly no other official text made such a strong link with the last legitimate Roman emperor to rule over the province. This piece marked nothing less than the transition from Roman Britain to Saxon England.

46 *The Pevensey Bricks: a cast of the brick recovered by Charles Dawson in 1902 in Hastings Museum as photographed in 2003 (the original is in the British Museum)*

47 *The Pevensey Bricks: detail of the complete inscription as photographed by Charles Dawson in 1907*

What made things even more exciting, certainly from the perspective of the wider academic community, was that Dawson's brick could actually be related to an established historical event. In AD 396 the central government of the emperor Honorius finally turned its attention towards the deteriorating military situation in Britain and an expedition to the province was planned. The general put in charge of the campaign to Britain was Honorius' chief of staff, Flavius Stilicho. Frustratingly we do not possess a full and detailed account of the expedition, the only literary sources for it being the rather syco-phantic verses of the Roman court poet Claudian who, in AD 398, notes, 'with the Saxons subjugated the sea is now more peaceful, with the Picts broken Britain is secure'.[2] Later, in AD 400, Claudian records that Britannia 'when on the point of death at the hands of neighbouring tribes, found in Stilicho protection'.[3] Both references, though vague, would appear to refer to a successful campaign around Britain's coastline, at some point between AD 398 and 400. Dawson's brick would easily fit within such a period of intense military activity.

Although the HON AVG part of the inscription was easy enough to translate, the term ANDRIA was more tricky. Dawson, however, confidently asserted that 'it suggests *Anderida, Anderesium* or *Andredes-ceaster*, names already identified with the *Castra* of Pevensey.[4] The brick therefore provided, in three short abbreviated words, an approximate date, an imperial sponsor and a name for the fort. There was no doubt about it: the bricks that Dawson had found at Pevensey were a major find, probably the most important ever found from within Roman Britain.

The brick bearing the most complete inscription, Dawson noted, had been found 'beneath the arch' of the northern postern gate of the Roman wall (**51**) 'in the year 1902'.[5] No one at the time seemed all that concerned that it had taken Dawson some five years to formally report the find, despite its clear importance. In retrospect, nondisclosure appears all the more puzzling

48 (Above) *Pevensey Castle: an aerial photograph taken in 1972 showing the inner medieval castle (top left) and the curving outer circuit wall of the Roman fortress. The postern gate, where Charles Dawson found the stamped brick, is in the section of Roman wall at the bottom of the shot covered by trees*

49 (Left) *Pevensey Castle: a projecting tower on the north-eastern circuit of the Roman wall as photographed at the time of the Sussex Archaeological Society excavations in 1907*

50 (Below) *Pevensey Castle: the imposing west gate of the Roman fort as photographed at the time of the Sussex Archaeological Society excavations in 1907*

considering that Pevensey had, shortly after Dawson made his find, been the target of some considerable archaeological excavation, directed by Louis Salzman and co-ordinated by the *Sussex Archaeological Society* (**52** & **53**). These discrepancies were unfortunately never explained.

The brick from the northern postern had, Dawson believed, 'fallen down with other pieces from the roof of the arch, where similarly burnt bricks are to be seen'.[6] Close examination of the remaining *in situ* pieces did not, however, reveal any further examples either of the same fabric or bearing any similar form of inscribed stamp.[7] In a footnote to the published article, however, Dawson noted that 'I have also found portions of red brick from the eastern part of the wall bearing the mutilated outline of the same stamp'.[8] Sadly these pieces were never mentioned again and their exact location within the eastern wall of the fortress has never been ascertained.

A third discovery, albeit fragmentary, of the same form of stamped tile came to light within the finds assemblage recovered during the course of the 1906 excavations at Pevensey. Unfortunately the chief director, Louis Salzman, did not give any indication as to where within his excavations, which were conducted to the immediate south of the postern gate, the tile had originally been located.[9] The only record of the piece was that relating to its inscription which read:

$$\text{...ON AVG ...NDR...}$$

At the time of the discovery of the fragmentary tile in 1906, Salzman's team was unaware that Dawson had a more complete version of the same stamp in his possession. Without the full version, Salzman did not venture an interpretation and the nature of the text appears to have stumped all who examined it; that is, however, until a comparison with the better-preserved example in Dawson's care was made, and a full translation became possible.

The possibility that a fourth stamped tile had originally been recovered from Pevensey was first raised by David Peacock in 1973. Peacock observed that the initial reports on the Pevensey Brick[10] and subsequent reproduction in volume 3 of the *Victoria County History of Sussex*, showed a stamp with 'a chip removed in the bottom right-hand corner'.[11] The chipped example resurfaced in the British Museum in the late 1960s, Peacock noting that:

> it is certainly not the mutilated specimen referred to in Dawson's footnote for it is grey-black, not red, in colour. Thus three stamped bricks are specifically mentioned by Dawson while the existence of a fourth is implied by his illustration.[12]

Unfortunately, the matter is not totally clear. The absence of a detailed description or illustration of the 1902-7 finds, by either Dawson or Salzman,

51 (Above) *Pevensey Castle: the surviving Roman brickwork of the northern postern gate as photographed in 2003*

53 (Left) *Pevensey Castle: the area of the Roman postern gate under excavation in 1907*

52 (Below) *Pevensey Castle: a plan of the Roman fortress (in solid black) compiled by Louis Salzman for his report on the 1906-7 excavations*

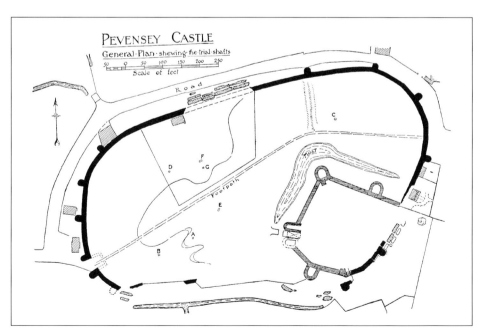

obscures the exact nature and number of artefacts originally located. In the absence of any clear resolution, it seems sensible to assume that the example held by the British Museum is the piece that Dawson claimed to have found in 1902, whilst the fragmentary pieces currently stored in the museum of the Sussex Archaeological Society in Lewes are those recovered during the Salzman excavations of 1906. The whereabouts of the 'portions of a red brick' that Dawson noted as originating from the eastern part of the Roman fortress wall [13] remain unknown.

The significance of the Honorius tiles was not lost upon the archaeological community and the pieces were referred to in pretty much all of the major discussions concerning Roman Britain (all reports except, that is, those of the 1906-7 site director of Pevensey, Louis Salzman, who strangely only ever referred to them once).[14] Doubts concerning the provenance and authenticity of the Pevensey Bricks began to surface throughout the late 1960s. The biggest worries surrounded the 'spidery' nature of the lettering, a style most unusual for official military Roman stamps, whilst the fabric of the bricks, 'fine quartz grains... set in a matrix of grey optically isotropic clay' did not match with any of those still preserved within the walls of the Roman fort.[15] These doubts were expressed by John Mainwaring Baines, Curator of Hastings Museum, to David Peacock of Southampton University early in the 1970s. 'I've not hard evidence one way or the other,' Baines said, 'only the indisputable fact that both have passed through the hands of Charles Dawson'.[16] Intrigued, Peacock decided to subject the bricks to a new form of scientific dating, namely thermoluminescence.

Thermoluminescence (or TL) is a method of dating geological samples, such as lava flows and meteorite impact craters, and archaeological materials, such as bricks, ceramics, hearths, kilns and all forms of heat-processed material (especially the residue of pyrotechnological or industrial activity). At its core is the principle that minerals, when artificially heated, emit a flash of light, the intensity of which is proportional to the amount of radiation the sample has been exposed to as well as the length of time since the sample itself was last significantly heated. For thermoluminescence dating, the so-called mineral 'clock-resetting event' which will provide an estimate of when the ceramic brick or tile in question was originally fired, is heating to a temperature above 400°C. Needless to say, TL is a relatively new dating technique, one that was certainly not available in the early years of the twentieth century when discoveries such as the Pevensey Bricks were first reported.

When the results of the TL dating of the Pevensey Bricks were returned, the dates were startling. Dr S.J. Fleming of the Research Laboratory for Archaeology and the History of Art at the University of Oxford confidently calculated that the bricks possessed a 'firing date of no earlier than between AD 1900-1940'. [17] Retests and recalibrations were conducted: even the possibility that the wood glue that held the fragmentary Lewes example together and may have affected the date, was assessed. The results, however, remained stubbornly unchanging: the tiles were no older than the date at which they were first uncovered. This fact, observed Peacock, when considered:

> alongside the anomalies in fabric and style there are very strong grounds for suggesting that the bricks are twentieth-century forgeries and that the piece from Salzman's excavations was planted to strengthen the case for their acceptance as genuine.[18]

Peacock was in no doubt of the fact that the forgeries had to be associated with Charles Dawson.

The Pevensey Bricks: conclusion

There is no doubt that the Pevensey Bricks were created in the early years of the twentieth century in order not only to confirm the name for the Roman fort at Pevensey, but also to supply a date for the final phase of reconstruction there, placing it in the twilight years of Roman rule in Britain. The question is though, who in the field of antiquarian research, so desperately required such evidence that they were prepared to fabricate it and what would such forgery have achieved? The two foremost suspects in this case have to be those who claimed to have 'discovered' the finds in the first place, namely Louis Salzman and Charles Dawson.

Salzman, as one of the main directors of excavations at Pevensey, is a clear and obvious suspect. The first fragmentary stamped brick was, of course, found in one of his trenches, whilst the actual circumstances of its discovery are kept annoyingly vague (Salzman never supplying even an approximate indication of *where* within the excavations it was found). This may seem somewhat bizarre, for given the general absence of inscribed material recorded from Pevensey (or indeed from any of the Late Roman shore forts of Britain), the artefact was clearly of major significance. Surely Salzman would have been keen to tie the discovery down to a particular area of the fort interior, say a pit, hearth or other archaeological feature, or, if not, to note that it had been turned up unstratified within topsoil? Unfortunately he does not, the published discussion of the brick [19] concentrating solely upon the problems of translation and not provenance.

We should not, however, take any vagueness on the part of Salzman as indication of his complicity in the hoax. The 1906-7 season at Pevensey was no different to most pieces of early antiquarian fieldwork in that little attention was placed to the context of archaeological discoveries. Any artefacts recovered were of course recorded, some in elaborate detail, but usually in the form of a general discussion placed at the end of the final published report. Few excavation reports of the late nineteenth and early twentieth century ever gave consideration as to exactly *where* on site specific materials had been unearthed, for few antiquarians gave any thought as to the understanding of discrete phases or sequences in building activity. That is not to say that Salzman's excavations were in any way below standard, far from it; in fact the detailed plans (**54**), wall elevations, excavated sections and black and white photographs (**55**) reproduced in the final published report are, for their time, exemplary. It is just that from a modern perspective, the Pevensey text left crucial details of phasing and sequence frustratingly intangible.

Salzman, therefore, is not being deliberately unhelpful when he introduces the artefactual discussion with the words 'during the progress of the work great

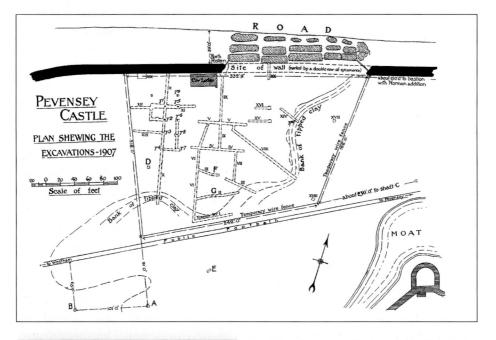

54 (Above) *Pevensey Castle: a plan of the 1907 excavations compiled by Louis Salzman showing the confusing mass of internal structures and the northern postern*

55 (Left) *Pevensey Castle: a photograph of a Roman tiled hearth within the fortress as taken in 1907*

quantities of objects belonging to various periods were unearthed'.[20] Neither is he attempting subterfuge when he lists some of the coins retrieved, covering the date range of AD 254-375, with no clear indication of where on site these were found or how they originally related to one another. It does, however, leave us with a major problem, for without a clear idea of the circumstances of discovery for the '…ON AVG …NDR…' tile, we cannot be sure of where or how it was originally planted, let alone of who the culprit could have been.

There is no doubt, however, that the Honorius tile was the major find of the 1906-7 excavations. It was just the sort of thing that Salzman must have hoped to discover, something that provided a date for at least one of the major building phases at Pevensey and which tied the site into a major historical event: the abandonment of Britain by the Roman state. We may, therefore, be excused for immediately pointing the finger of suspicion towards Salzman and accusing him, or at least one of his team, of generating the artefact in order to add a spectacular element to what was, in all honesty, a rather unexceptional list of discoveries.

For this explanation to work, however, we have to ask why Salzman did not make more of the brick in his excavation report. Given its importance, which Salzman himself acknowledges,[21] the piece does not receive the attention that we would perhaps expect, being buried deep in the text, close to the very end of the report and sandwiched between a discussion of the coins, pottery and 'miscellaneous relics'. Furthermore, if Salzman *had* manufactured the find, why did he plant only a very broken example within his excavation trench, allowing Dawson to claim the better, more complete prize? Also, if he did create the stamped brick intending it to be found at Pevensey, why did he plant the first example, as found by Dawson, some five years *before* his own excavation took place? It is conceivable that Salzman, having planned the hoax, required independent verification of the stamp. Therefore in order to corroborate the find, he ensured there was a second discovery, made at a different date by someone wholly unconnected to the main excavation team. If this was the case, Salzman must have been deeply aggrieved that Dawson, having found the brick in the northern postern, made no immediate mention of his find. With no public disclosure from Dawson, Salzman would have to go ahead with his investigation of Pevensey, hoping that the recovery of a second, more corrupted version of the stamp, would at last force the Uckfield solicitor to bring his find out into the open.

As chief hoaxer, Salzman does not appear to have made very much of his brick. In fact his thunder was totally stolen by Dawson, who published his own article on the importance of the stamp in the pages of the internationally renowned *Proceedings of the Society of Antiquaries* for 1907, at least a year before Salzman's article was to appear in the *Sussex Archaeological Collections*. Perhaps this explains Salzman's cursory treatment of the artefact in his report where he notes, in hindsight almost grudgingly, that the translation of his find was only made possible through a 'comparison with a perfect example from the same stamp, in the possession of Mr Charles Dawson'.[22]

What then of the other potential forger, Charles Dawson? Dawson, of course, supplies us with far more detail as to the whereabouts and context of his discoveries. His first example of the stamped brick, he tells us, was found within the area of the collapsed northern postern gate where it had apparently fallen 'with other pieces from the roof of the arch'.[23] Dawson's claim that additional examples of brick 'bearing the mutilated outline of the same stamp' are clearly visible in the eastern circuit of the Roman wall,[24] though why it took him a full five years to report the discovery – given its clear importance – is never fully explained (and indeed never queried by members of the Society of Antiquaries to whom Dawson first presented the artefact).

Perhaps, though the Pevensey Brick was clearly of national significance, Dawson required time to consider its importance, research its background and be thoroughly convinced of the translation, before making any form of public presentation. Perhaps he was just too busy to make any public acknowledgement of his find; the years 1902 to 1907 being ones where, as well as coping with the intricacies of his legal practice (which became Dawson Hart & Co. in 1906) and various civic duties, Dawson was also wooing (and in 1905 marrying) Helene Postlethwaite, researching Sussex ironwork, pottery and glass, reanalysing the Bayeux Tapestry and attempting to produce the first definite study of Hastings Castle. He was also engaged in the tricky business of moving his family and all their possessions from their home in Uckfield to Castle Lodge in Lewes, evicting the Sussex Archaeological Society in the process. Small wonder, therefore, if during this time the small stamped brick from Pevensey Castle took up very little of his time. Perhaps it was the notification of Salzman's excavation of 1906 that triggered Dawson's memory and brought the brick out of obscurity and into the public domain.

As innocents duped by the hoax of another, it could be argued that both Dawson and Salzman were the intended targets. In such a scenario, however, the forger would not only have to have been an extremely patient individual, waiting some five years between Dawson's 1902 discovery and that made by Salzman in 1907, but also very determined, embedding further examples of the brick within the solid matrix of the eastern circuit of the Roman wall. If this was the case, it is not entirely clear what the motive for the forgery was, as no one was discredited and no one's career appears to have been damaged by the sudden revelation of a hoax.

It could, of course, be argued that Salzman, a fully paid-up member of the Sussex Society at the time of the Castle Lodge affair, was seeking some form of retribution upon the Uckfield solicitor, by planning an obvious fraud for him to find. This elaborate theory does not, however, tally with the dates, for Dawson claims to have made his find in 1902 and the notice of eviction that he served upon the Society did not occur until the autumn of 1904. Neither does the 'retribution' theory makes sense when one considers that Salzman was to find pieces of the same tile in 1907, which he duly reported without comment, in the pages of the *Sussex Archaeological Collections*, publication of which would have been the ideal opportunity to expose Dawson to ridicule.

Let us rethink the nature of the discovery. The Honorius tile was a find that was clearly exceptional. For such a well-preserved piece to be discovered purely by chance on the ground surface would not be impossible, but it could elicit a certain degree of surprise. If such a piece were to be discovered by Charles Dawson, already known within local circles as the 'Wizard of Sussex' on account of his amazing archaeological and geological discoveries, surprise may turn to scepticism. If, however, independent verification of this 'discovery' was made by another, then any suspicion surrounding the reliability of the artefact would be likely to dissipate. As John Baines has recently observed:

> the most difficult part would be to create an atmosphere where no suspicion would arise... So the first thing would be to arrange for something to be in existence already. Two complete stamps would be too much to hope for, so obviously one must be only a part of the complete stamp but a recognisable part.[25]

Dawson is, therefore, in possession of the complete tile, but does not report it until the incomplete fragments of the second are found during the course of an archaeological excavation. The director of that excavation, who has no links to Dawson (and who by 1904 had good reason to dislike him), circulates reports of the discovery but is unable to interpret it fully until Dawson brings forward his tile which he claims to have discovered half a decade before.

> The first would authenticate the second and what is really more important from our point of view, the second would now certify the first. In other words a sort of inverse camouflage.[26]

Dawson is now in an excellent position to make a formal presentation of both bricks, his complete example and the fragmentary remains of the one found by Salzman, to the Society of Antiquaries in London.

It is Dawson then, who, given the facts of the case, makes the more convincing candidate forger. It is he who claims to have found the well-preserved tile in 1902. It is he who, when Salzman's excavations reveal a similar fragmentary stamped brick, unveils the first and resolves the inscription. It is he who further substantiates the discoveries by claiming to have seen further examples preserved within the eastern wall of Pevensey. It is he who makes the most of the discoveries, receiving the praise of a learned and well respected society. It is he, therefore, who gains most from the whole affair.

8

THE SINCEREST FORM
OF FLATTERY?

Charles Dawson was elected a fellow of the Society of Antiquaries of London in the autumn of 1895 following the remarkable range of archaeological discoveries, surveys, reports and pieces of fieldwork that he had conducted since 1892, when he had first joined the Sussex Archaeological Society as honorary local secretary for Uckfield. After this, Dawson began to expand his *curriculum vitae* by diversifying his interests into new areas. His publication record to date had been rather poor, two short articles in the *Sussex Archaeological Collections* for 1894 and a few scattered references within other people's work. This was something that the Uckfield solicitor instantly set out to rectify. Over the next few years Dawson's research and subsequent output was prodigious, especially when one considers that archaeology and history represented no more than a hobby, a distraction from his 'bread and butter' job in the legal profession.

The works examined in this chapter represent Dawson's main academic publishing achievements between the years 1898 and 1911, prior to the big discovery of Piltdown man. Because the accusations that have been made against these publications are essentially the same (i.e. plagiarism), each will be considered in turn with a single concluding section at the end of the chapter.

Dene Holes

In 1898 Charles Dawson published a lengthy article entitled 'Ancient and Modern "Dene Holes" and their Makers' in the *Geological Magazine*. The term 'dene holes' was one which, in the late nineteenth century, was used to cover a multitude of subterranean passages, tunnels and caverns found in the chalk of southern England. Few were well understood or dated and many were confused with Neolithic flint mines, medieval quarries and a host of natural fissures or sinkholes. Dawson observed that, though a variety of suggestions concerning their origin had been made, there appeared little consensus as to function or purpose.

Dawson set out to resolve the many issues surrounding dene holes, 'by simple comparison... with excavations of exactly similar character and design' still being worked across England.[1] He had, in fact, managed to explore 'two very fine' dene holes in Brighton together with John Lewis at some unspecified time in the past. Lewis was the ideal partner to accompany Dawson on such an exploration, for he was a civil engineer who had previously been involved in underground construction work in India.[2] Unfortunately, unlike his work at either the Lavant Caves or Hastings Castle, Lewis does not appear to have made a drawing of the subterranean workings beneath Brighton, or, if he did, these have not survived. He does, however, supply a section of a bell pit from Brightling in Sussex (**56**), together with examples taken from Kent and Essex, for the main plate accompanying Dawson's article, so there may have been some confusion at the editorial stage of the report as to which site was actually being described.

Dawson gives us very little detail concerning the shape or form of the Brighton/Brightling dene holes other than to note that one had been:

> incomplete with respect to depth. In the floor were excavated two or three steps. The workmen seemed to have been excavating the chalk laterally from these steps and thus lowering the floor.[3]

Removal of spoil from the subterranean tunnels appears to have been difficult, Dawson recording that larger blocks of rubble were hauled to the surface by a man operating 'a windlass of very primitive description' with a distinctively curved wooden handle. A sketch of this 'primitive' windlass appears in

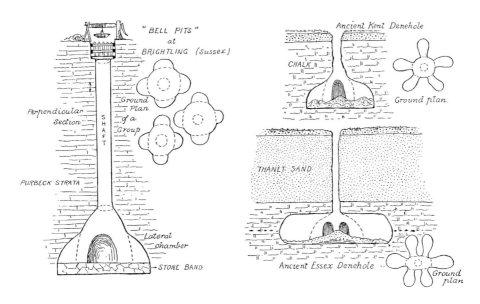

56 *Dene Holes: cross sections of three shafts, from Kent, Essex and Brightling in Sussex, as compiled by John Lewis*

57 *Dene Holes: a sketch of the shaft mouth showing 'primitive windlass and trug-basket' as drawn by John Lewis*

Dawson's article (**57**), and though its authorship is uncredited, it possesses the clear and distinctive style of John Lewis, presumably having been sketched at the time the two men made their exploration. The rope wound around the windlass was fixed to a Sussex basket, known as a 'trug', into which looser rubble from the workings below could be dumped, larger pieces being 'tied by the cord and hauled separately'.[4] It was via this windlass device that Dawson and Lewis made their initial descent into the shaft, a feat performed by:

> placing the toe on the hook of the cord and holding the rope above, the windlass being carefully unwound by the man at the surface. With a frayed rope not an inch in diameter this may seem dangerous; but few accidents have been known to occur.[5]

The rest of Dawson's article is concerned with his own personal observations of the Sussex dene holes, together with the results of interviews conducted with those involved in their digging, and a lengthy description, compiled from other writers, of the dene holes of Hertfordshire and Kent 'made over a century ago'.[6] In conclusion, Dawson notes that:

> no mystery exists with respect to the 'dene holes' in Essex. The whole class of these excavations have their origin and inception of design in the very ancient custom of 'bell pit' mining... the balance of probability in favour of their having been merely chalk-pits is overwhelming.[7]

Shortly after its publication, a comment by Essex geologist T.V. Holmes on the possible origin of dene holes appeared in the *Geological Magazine*. Holmes was concerned that a report made by the Essex Field Club some ten years before had not been acknowledged in Dawson's article; unfortunate as some of the conclusions reached by Dawson had already been reached in a number of earlier publications. Holmes noted that the views of the Field Club:

> do not appear to be injuriously affected by Mr Dawson's remarks, yet as the dene report is now more than ten years old it is probable that few of the

readers of the Geological Magazine have both seen and remember it. And the impression that the reader would derive from Mr Dawson's article is that his bell-pit hypothesis is something quite new, and therefore uninvoked by us, whereas it was an old view before the report was written, having been forwarded by the late Mr Treave Smith in the Gentleman's Magazine in 1867; and an account of working for chalk of the kind described by Mr Dawson, written by Mr F.J. Bennett, of the Geological Survey, is appended.[8]

Sussex iron, pottery and glass

In 1903, Charles Dawson organised and co-ordinated a major exhibition in Lewes focusing upon the iron and pottery of Sussex. To accompany this he wrote a detailed article simply entitled 'Sussex Ironwork and Pottery' (**58**) which was published in the *Sussex Archaeological Collections* for that year,[9] together with a lengthy catalogue listing all objects displayed (**59**).[10] A summary of Dawson's views on Sussex pottery was later published in *Antiquary*, entitled 'Sussex Pottery: a new classification', it ended by urging that:

> all who are interested should take an early opportunity of visiting the Lewes collection, since these specimens on loan must soon be dispersed and returned to their owners, perhaps never to be seen together again.[11]

A second article by Dawson appeared in *Antiquary* two years later. This time, entitled 'Old Sussex Glass: its Origin and Decline', it purported to continue Dawson's research 'into the ancient industries of Sussex' whilst simultaneously hoping that additional material on the subject may be forthcoming.[12]

58 Sussex Iron: the Pevensey Castle cannon, an object of major interest to Charles Dawson, as photographed in 2003

Dawson's article on 'Sussex Ironwork and Pottery' appears to be a weighty examination of both ancient Sussex industries, combining Dawson's own views with a sizeable section compiling the observations of earlier writers. One of the lengthier extracts quoted in support of Dawson's arguments (a piece from Dr Lardner's *Cabinet Cyclopaedia; Manufactures in Metal* of 1831) was supplied by the solicitor's colleague at Hastings Castle and the Lavant Caves, John Lewis.[13] Lewis also provided 'a working drawing' or reconstruction of a hammer forge as shown in a 1772 painting by the artist Joseph Wright (**60**). The publication was viewed by many as both the culmination of Dawson's extensive work into the subject area and a suitable tribute to the excellent exhibition organised and co-ordinated by him for the Sussex Archaeological Society. The ironworking section in particular was considered a major and notable contribution to the study of the defunct Wealden industry.[14]

In 1953, following the revelation of the Piltdown hoax, Robert Downes, a graduate of Birmingham University who had made a study of the English iron industry, re-read Dawson's work in the *Sussex Archaeological Collections* with a view to assessing whether it was wholly original. Having minutely examined the work,

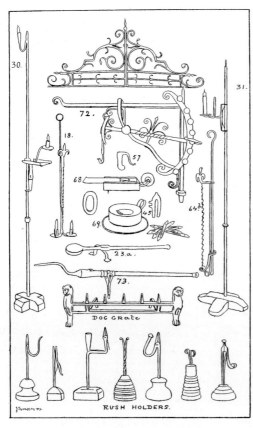

SPECIMENS OF SUSSEX WROUGHT IRON.

59 *Sussex Iron: specimens of Sussex wrought iron as compiled by J. Thompson for the 1903 Lewes exhibition*

60 *Sussex Iron: a reconstruction of a hammer forge drawn by John Lewis and inspired by a painting of 1772 by Joseph Wright*

Downes concluded that 'three quarters of the article has been plagiarised, having been taken directly from at least ten published sources, but mostly from William Topley's *Memoir on the Geology of the Weald*.[15] This observation was picked up by Joseph Weiner, to whom Downes passed his conclusions, who used it in his book, *The Piltdown Forgery*, noting that Topley's work had been shamelessly used 'almost word for word without acknowledgement'.[16] John Walsh later summarised the lengthier observations of Downes [17] in his book *Unravelling Piltdown*:

> all the usual tricks of the accomplished plagiarist were readily discovered. There were specific acknowledgements to a fact or two, when in reality whole sections had been lifted from the cited work. There was the breaking up and paraphrasing of longer passages taken bodily from the source, with a subtle weaving together of facts and phrases from different texts. There were incomplete or deliberately inaccurate acknowledgements. Dawson's own contribution to this melange amounted to a few simple comments, some personal observations, and transitional material.[18]

The Bayeux Tapestry

In 1907 Dawson published an article entitled 'The Bayeux Tapestry in the Hands of the Restorers' in the *Antiquary*. The report, which critically assessed the nature and contribution of 'successive "restorations"', was prefaced by a note from Dawson which stated that the his article:

> represents a 'by-product' of a critical study of the Tapestry and its literature, undertaken for a larger work dealing, in part, with the early phases of the Norman Conquest of England.[19]

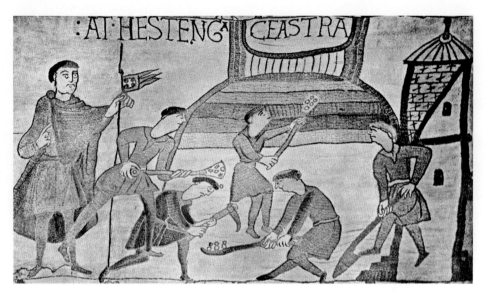

61 *Bayeux Tapestry: a section depicting the construction of Hastings Castle as photographed by Charles Dawson in 1903*

As Dawson never published a 'larger work' specifically on 'the early years of the Norman Conquest', it is assumed that he was actually referring to his two-volume analysis of Hastings Castle which finally appeared in 1910 (**61**). No specific claims concerning the report's perceived authenticity (or lack of it) have ever been made, though Walsh, in his book *Piltdown Unravelled* makes the comment:

> for many years this article was cited in tapestry literature as an important contribution, and since no study of possible sources has yet been made, nothing can be ventured here about its origins. It may in fact represent that extremely scarce commodity, original, underived work by Dawson. After all, there seems no good reason why a forger and plagiarist might not, now and then, have a genuine flash of inspiration. Still, common sense counsels otherwise.[20]

The history of Hastings Castle

In 1910, Dawson's *magnum opus*, the *History of Hastings Castle: the Castlery, Rape and Battle of Hastings, to which is added a History of the Collegiate Church within the Castle, and its Prebends*, was finally published in two volumes by Constable & Co. Ltd of London. The work was supposed to have appeared a year earlier, indeed the title pages of both volumes still show the publication date as 1909, but some unspecified delay seems to have prevented this.[21]

The two-volume *History* appears to represent a major academic endeavour, every piece of data concerning the fortress and its surroundings (**62**, **63** & **64**) having been assembled, collated and compiled. In the Preface to the work Dawson sets his reasons for having commenced such an obviously time-consuming study:

> Concerning Hastings Castle a recently-published Hastings guidebook informs its readers that 'one of the charms of this venerable ruin is, that no authentic record of its history exists'. It is, therefore, with some diffidence that the author intrudes upon this state of bliss by presenting to the public a connected series of records, unrivalled in local history, relating to this castle... The plan of the present work at the outset was an ambitious one, namely, to take as a type an English Castle and Barony, the details of the history of which were almost unknown; to search out its records in the British and foreign depositories, public and private; and finally to arrange them in chronological order, interspersed with extracts from contemporary chronicles, in such a manner that the whole collection may tell its own story.[22]

The contemporary works which Dawson set out to use in order that the Castle may tell its 'own story', were, of course, set down in a variety of different forms,

62 *Hastings Castle: an aerial photograph taken in 1970 looking north-east*

63 *Hastings Castle: a 'fish-eye' perspective photograph of the castle taken by Charles Dawson in 1909*

64 *Hastings Castle: copy of 'an original tinted drawing' (c. 1750) in Charles Dawson's possession showing the eroded cliff line and the 'ancient harbour', used as the frontispiece to the History of Hastings Castle*

utilising different languages and modes of speech, across a broad span of time. Dawson conceded that, given the 'lack of special knowledge and opportunities' provided for students of history, any attempt to reproduce the early documents in their original form would serve only to make reading impossible. Therefore:

> The author believes that the average reader will prefer to read their ancient records and chronicles, in the same way as most persons read their Bibles, that is, by means of a translation, and he has provided accordingly. For the rest, it is hoped that the references given to the original documents will prove sufficient.[23]

In such a way Dawson hoped that he could:

> present to the reader the most reliable data obtainable, retaining to a great extent all the vigour and beauty of the original draughtsmanship, freed from and untrammelled by former conclusions, and in such a manner that he may be enabled to picture for himself the true history, as nearly as possible, at first hand.[24]

A large number of sources were specifically cited by Dawson in his Preface to volume 1 of the *History*. These included volume 3 of Francis Grose's *Antiquities of England and Wales*, 1773-87, (which Dawson noted 'may be considered the first important printed topographical reference'), William Herbert's 1824 'letter-press' to 'Moss's *History of Hastings*' (**65**: noted as 'the first serious attempt to unravel the history of the Castle') and G.T. Clarke's *Medieval Military Architecture of England*, 1884, ('an excellent if brief description of the architectural details of the Castle and Chapel').[25] Other materials used for the compilation of Dawson's *History* were:

> almost entirely the result of private researches in the records compiled by the Royal Historical Commissioners and the Public Record Office; some, however, are derived from France, and others from diocesan records in England and from private sources.[26]

Despite having lived, worked and researched in Hastings since a boy, Dawson found it difficult to locate details of the 1820s excavations conducted within the castle bounds until at last he:

> discovered some drafts in manuscript of such a description in the Guildhall Library, where Mr Herbert, above mentioned, was formerly the librarian... Mr Herbert... noted and planned almost every detail that was discovered, and subsequently prepared in handsome form a fair copy of his work, which he delivered to Lord Chichester. Upon hearing of the present author's researches Lord Chichester (the fourth Earl) in 1897 most generously presented him with this invaluable record.[27]

The location of Herbert's manuscript was a godsend, containing as it did many observations on important architectural features, some since lost.

> Mr Herbert's work is executed in a fine neat hand, and the text is illustrated by maps and drawings plotted out by an artist named B. Howlett. Some of these drawings, executed in black and white wash are originals, and others are copied from certain eighteenth-century drawings by James Lambert of Lewes and S.H. Grimm, now in the British Museum and in the Bodleian

Library, at Oxford. The author in the compilation of the present work has made free use of this magnificent record.[28]

At the conclusion of his Preface, Dawson appended a short, and rather vague, acknowledgement:

> the author must express his grateful acknowledgement to the many experts, both living and dead, who have personally or by their writings contributed assistance to him in the production of these volumes. For those manifold errors and omissions inevitable in a work of this character, so easily over-looked and yet so vexatious, to a conscientious writer, the author can but crave the indulgence of the reader.[29]

The *History of Hastings Castle* soon became a standard work [30] and is still regularly cited today. At the time of its publication, however, not everyone appeared so enthusiastic; one reviewer for the *Sussex Archaeological Collections* commenting that:

> The author has displayed much industry in collecting material, but little judgement in its selection and arrangement. Apart from errors of transla-tion, the misreadings are extremely numerous. It is difficult to say how far these are due to carelessness, inaccuracy and neglect of proof-reading and how far reliance on second-hand authorities, as references are frequently omitted or given unintelligible form. In many cases where matter is taken, mistakes and all, from earlier writings, no acknowledgement of the source is made.[31]

Of course, by 1909 Charles Dawson had few friends in the Sussex Archaeological Society, his purchase of Castle Lodge (and subsequent eviction of the county-based group) in 1904 being an all too recent, not to say unpleasant, memory. In 1953, John Mainwaring Baines, then Curator of Hastings Museum, came across a copy of William Herbert's unpublished 1824 manuscript, which Dawson claimed he had 'made free use of', in a local book-seller.[32] Baines later related to a reporter from the London *Times* that he 'found the manuscript and Dawson's *History* 'to be almost identical, although re-arranged and with a lot of extraneous matter added".[33] Later he reiterated his views to Joseph Weiner, adding more forcefully that Dawson's two volumes of the *History of Hastings Castle* had been 'copied unblushingly from Herbert's manuscript'; the remainder he accused of being 'gross padding'.[34]

Following the revelation of the Piltdown hoax, Robert Downes reviewed the *History of Hastings Castle*, to see if the 'inaccuracy and neglect' cited in the *Sussex Archaeological Collection* was actually evidence of a more fraudulent kind of activity. In a damning indictment of the two volumes, Downes concluded that the bulk of Dawson's work had been plagiarised from a variety of sources, the main one being Herbert's unpublished manuscript of 1824:

> The preface implies that the Herbert manuscript consisted of a description of the excavations at the Castle in 1824. The 54 references in the 54 pages of Part V, 9 per cent of the book, appear to confirm this. But apart from the conclusive evidence in Mr Baines possession, we have deduced our own reasons for supposing that Herbert wrote much of Parts II, III, and IV. Yet in this 76 per cent of the book, Herbert's name is mentioned only 5 times. And not one of these references really suggests that Dawson was indebted to him for more than a sentence or two... [Dawson] does not state specifically that he has done all the research himself, but he implies as much in his Preface. The absence of acknowledgements to the sources from which he took his material is scandalous.[35]

Others felt less comfortable with the charges of outright plagiarism. In his book *The Piltdown Inquest*, Charles Blinderman critically assessed the Preface to Dawson's *History of Hastings Castle*, noting that the solicitor had repeatedly stressed his desire to present original information in an unedited and unmodified form in order that it retained 'all the vigour and beauty of the original':

> He not only does not claim originality; he specifically denies that he aims to be original. He carries out his scheme of compilation through anthologising records: registers, letters, appointments, declarations, petitions, confirmations, titles, grants, charters, decrees, and inquisitions. He alludes throughout to William Herbert, noting in one place: 'the author in the compilation of the present work has made free use of this magnificent record'. The accusation of plagiarism stands as not proven.[36]

There the arguments surrounding the perceived authenticity of the two-volume *History* remained; a stalemate which looked unlikely to be broken. Then, in the early 1990s, brand new evidence came to light which presented an alternative take on Dawson's scholarship. In 1994, Peter Miles published an article in the journal *Studies in Bibliography* in which he reported the finding of 'a small cache of books' that had been recovered 'more than twenty years ago' in builders waste derived from 'an Uckfield store-room with a remote association with Dawson'.[37] The books, which seemed to have once formed part of Dawson's own library, were a fortunate discovery, for it was on record that all paperwork relating to the solicitor had either been destroyed [38] or 'cleared out during the war for salvage'.[39] The volumes represent background research (comprising 'ten nineteenth-century texts') and working papers for the *History of Hastings Castle*, one book in particular being a 'provisional printer's copy'.[40]

A number of the primary texts recovered from Uckfield contained marginal annotations and pencilled comments in Dawson's hand. In the *Chronicle of Henry of Huntingdon* (edited and translated by Thomas Forester in 1853), Miles observed that:

> the opening of the chronicler's paragraph-long entry for AD 490 is marked with two horizontal lines in pencil and the word 'Begin', while the paragraph closes with similar marks and the word 'End'. The marked lines are quoted to precisely these boundaries in *Hastings Castle* (Vol. I, p.12, note 2). However, they are also quoted a little too fully. Forrester's edition of the Chronicle of Henry of Huntingdon has a footnote to the sixth line of the quoted passage; curiously, Dawson's footnote reproduces not only the passage but also Forrester's related footnote of approximately fifty words. It does so quite without acknowledgement, interpolating Forrester's words by breaking the quotation of the text at a point where the original note was keyed in. Effectively this is plagiarism.[41]

The notes 'Begin' and 'End' at certain points in the primary text could, in the absence of a photocopier, have been notes to Dawson himself, but, Miles conceded, they are more likely to have been directed to a secretary who could 'transcribe (or set up in type) the passage for use in *Hastings Castle*'.[42] A lengthier sequence in the *Chronicle of Henry of Huntingdon*, outlining the Battle of Hastings, is also edged by the words 'Begin' and 'End', Miles observing that this 'represents the exact span of Henry of Huntingdon's account quoted by Dawson in his battle sheets'.[43] In conclusion, Miles felt that the many and varied forms of annotation visible in the Uckfield cache:

> testify to a certain energy if also a limitation in the depth of Dawson's methods of working, and so to some problems caused, arguably, by over-ambition and loose scholarly method. While they suggest no fraud on the scale of Piltdown, they do perhaps suggest a man not afraid of taking a short cut or two.[44]

The Red Hills of Essex

> The so-called 'Red Hills' of the Essex Marshes and 'Saltings' have been ranked, like the 'Dene Holes' among the archaeological mysteries of the county.[45]

So wrote Charles Dawson at the start of his five-page analysis of the curious mounds of red clay in Essex as published in the pages of *Antiquary*. The clay deposits in question measured 'from 3 to 6 feet deep', occurred in 'large patches or low mounds, often... a few acres in extent', and were usually found along the old tidal margins of the Essex salt marshes 'locally called 'Saltings''.[46] As with his earlier works, Dawson confided that much had already been written concerning these hills, the best information being thanks to 'the patient and skilful researches of the 'Red Hills' Exploration Committee'. Published sources that Dawson consulted for the purposes of his paper are cited as Henry Laver's article in the *Transactions of the Society of Antiquaries* for 1880 as well as the reports by J.C. Atkinson and H. Stopes appearing in the *Archaeological Journal*.[47]

The mounds or 'Red Hills' themselves comprised burnt earth, wood, ash and slag or vitrified material. They appeared to represent the debris caused by a 'great extinct industry', Dawson mused, but what exactly?

> There is one possible explanation which appears not to have been considered, and yet it is perhaps the most obvious, in the light of comparison and deduction – namely these 'Red Hill' are ballast-hills, the result of pottery rubbish carried and discharged as ballast by ships sailing from some one or more great pottery centres (probably distant) during a considerable period of time, the return cargoes being clay for use at the potteries.[48]

In the remainder of the article, Dawson assessed the various pieces of evidence available for Late Iron Age ('Late Celtic' as he calls it),[49] both literary and archaeological, finally concluding that his work was no more than 'a preliminary notice of a theory' to explain the possible origin of the famous red hills: 'it behoves one to hold one's theories on the subject with a light hand, since further evidence may, and probably will, be discovered by which time this interesting subject will finally be determined'.[50] Almost immediately a response to the article, by the Red Hills Exploration Committee, published in the *Antiquary*, commented that the summary of evidence was 'largely a repetition of what has already appeared in the reports',[51] accusations that are curiously similar to those made by the Essex Field Club, following the publication of their article on dene holes which appeared in the *Geological Museum*.

Dawson's publications: conclusion

Accusations of literary theft are often made against Dawson for the articles written between 1898 and 1911, but is there really evidence that he was indeed an accomplished plagiarist? Certainly claims of 'naïve referencing' could be made for a great deal of Dawson's work, especially publications where he loosely attributes his source or quotes whole chunks of another's text without accurately citing the derivation of materials used. In publishing, it is fair to say you will be accused of plagiarism if it can be demonstrated that you have taken

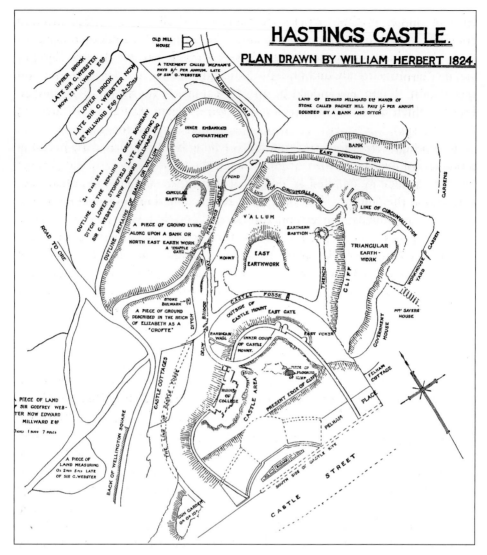

65 *Hastings Castle: a plan of the castle and its immediate environs compiled by William Herbert in 1824 and used by Dawson in his* History of Hastings Castle

or copied another person's writings (whether published or not), thoughts, ideas or inventions and presented them as your own. Plagiarising may further be defined as the failure to *properly reference or attribute* pieces of work or quotations appearing in your work which have been directly taken from an article, book or unpublished manuscript that is not your own.

When we examine Dawson's articles on 'Sussex Ironwork and Pottery', 'Dene Holes' and the 'Red Hills of Essex', we can see that they do all contain a large amount of other people's work, but it must be noted that these elements *are* referenced (albeit sometimes rather vaguely). All the direct, and somewhat lengthy, quotes in these articles are sourced and all appear within inverted commas, something which helps distance them from Dawson's own perspective. The accusations made against Dawson's article on the Bayeux Tapestry are, furthermore, totally unfounded, amounting to little more than hearsay and speculation. There *may* indeed be an original article (or group of articles) in French which cover the tapestry's restoration in detail (Dawson was fluent in that language), but to date no evidence has been supplied for this.

In hindsight then, the articles noted as having been plagiarised are in reality more acts of *compilation* than original theses. As such, Dawson should perhaps be more accurately credited as 'editor' of them than simply (and rather inaccurately) as the 'author'. A poor style of referencing does undermine some of Dawson's arguments concerning the Sussex iron industry, especially when attempting to attribute specific ideas to their source, but it must be said that for the accusation of plagiarism to stick, it would have to be shown that Dawson avoided referencing other authors and regularly passed significant chunks of their work off as his own and this is something that he specifically does not do.

The *History of Hastings Castle* represents Dawson's greatest act of compilation, for here he has amassed an incredible wealth of primary data, secondary references and miscellanea, most inaccessible to the ordinary interested reader, and republished them with comments and overall thoughts and conclusions. Downes is correct in stating that a large quantity of the *History* Parts II, III and IV was taken directly from Herbert's unpublished manuscript, but allowing the records to tell their own story is of course something which Dawson carefully and expressly cites as an aim of the *History*.[52] Perhaps again, if Dawson had been credited as *editor* or compiler, rather than author, then the issue of plagiarism would never have arisen. As it is, the most serious accusation that may be brought against the solicitor in the case of his major publications is that, as Miles observed, he was 'not afraid of taking a short cut or two'. The *History of Hastings Castle* may have been hastily compiled, but it is not the devious piece of literary theft that some have claimed.

9

WEIRD NATURE

Charles Dawson's interests continued to diversify following his election to the prestigious Society of Antiquaries in 1895. Throughout the early years of the twentieth century he became increasingly involved in the exploration of strange and unusual natural phenomena. He used his photographic talents to experiment with the recording of lightning.[1] He discovered unusual forms of fish in local ponds (which he dutifully forwarded to his friend Arthur Smith Woodward),[2] and examined genetic abnormalities in cart horses.[3] He lectured at length about the discovery and properties of natural gas beneath the Sussex town of Heathfield. He observed toads preserved inside solid nodules of flint and discovered a 'new race' of humans from the icy lands of the Arctic Circle. He revived his earlier interests in fossil hunting, recovering additional evidence for *Plagiaulax dawsoni* (see chapter 2) and retrieving remains of *Iguanodon* and *Lepidotus* from Roar Quarry near Hastings, for the British Museum (Natural History) collection.[4] He even managed to record a rare sighting of the English Channel Sea Serpent, a creature that had arrogantly defied the British public throughout the nineteenth and twentieth centuries.

All these discoveries and experiments, a testament to the 'restless mind, ever alert to note anything unusual',[5] demonstrated Dawson's unparalleled knowledge and ever-increasing expertise in a variety of diverse scientific fields. At the same time these amazing observations were being made, Dawson appears to have craved election to the Royal Society, something that would have marked the pinnacle of academic recognition. His first candidacy certificate for the fellowship was filed on 19 December 1913, and was renewed every year, without success, until his death in 1916.[6]

Natural gas at Heathfield

The first indication of the presence of 'inflammable natural gas' in Sussex is credited by Charles Dawson to Henry Willett. Willett had, in 1875, observed an explosion in a geological bore hole, and recorded the subsequent oscillation in the water table, following the lowering of a light.[7] Twenty years later, in 1895, a foreman in charge of an artesian bore hole being sunk close to the London to

Brighton railway, noticed that water that had been poured down the narrow shaft to 'assist the working of the tools' was boiling. As the foreman, inadvisably, proceeded to light a candle in order to inspect the cause of this rise in temperature, the gas ignited 'and burnt to about the height of a man'.[8] Subsequently, Dawson noted, the gas was ignited from a safer distance of 15 yards.

A third discovery of gas occurred in August 1896, in the railway cutting at the north-eastern end of Heathfield railway, whilst boring for water. This time a strong smell of gas occurred 'for nearly a month' before someone applied a match whereupon 'a flame immediately sprang up to the height of 15 or 16 feet, and burned with great fury until it was put out by means of damped cloths being thrown on to the top of the tube'.[9]

How Dawson got involved in the reporting of the gas at Heathfield is not known. It is possible that he learnt of it via the 1875 reports of Henry Willett, or from his colleague at the Lavant Caves and Hastings Castle excavations, the civil engineer John Lewis (he expressly thanks Lewis for providing plans of the boring).[10] In his report to the Geological Society, Dawson notes vaguely that he first 'made enquiries' concerning the gas after hearing about it from unnamed eyewitnesses.[11]

Having examined the borings for himself, Dawson submitted samples of the gas to Samuel Allinson Woodhead, County Analyst for East Sussex. Woodhead stated that the gas was probably 'derived from petroleum',[12] exciting news for it suggested that there was an untapped source of oil beneath the Sussex/Surrey Weald. Once in receipt of Woodward's preliminary report, Dawson swiftly submitted a paper to the journal *Nature*, which was published in late December 1897. In the report Dawson conjectured that:

> There appears to be at present an ample supply of gas for the lighting of a town if the necessary plant were erected in connection with the tube, and there seems to be, as far as one can judge, a constant supply. How long it may continue is, of course, a matter of conjecture; but having already run to waste so long without any decrease in force, I think that the supply might be made use of with reasonable prospects of lengthy continuance.[13]

In early January 1898, Dawson again called upon Samuel Woodhead, who this time fitted a makeshift laboratory at the site of the borings. Woodhead's more detailed analysis confirmed his earlier observations that the gas was a 'petroleum-derivative'.[14] This news was relayed to the public via papers presented to the Southeast Union of Scientific Societies in Brighton and the Geological Society in London during the summer of 1898. The presentation to the Geological Society was dramatically enhanced by the burning of gas 'brought in cylinders from Heathfield'.[15]

Not everyone agreed with Dawson's conclusions however. John Hewitt, Professor of Chemistry at Queen Mary College, London University, had, at the request of the London, Brighton & South Coast Railway Co., conducted his own analysis and, in the discussion that followed Dawson's presentation, concluded that he had detected only methane gas derived from decayed vegetable matter; there was no evidence of petroleum.[16] Dawson responded that, if Hewitt was right, then the gas 'must vary considerably', though he was unaware of it ever having been to such an extent.[17]

Despite the public excitement generated by Dawson's reports, no oil was ever found in the Weald and the gas discovered close to Heathfield Station was never fully exploited. In late March 1909, Dawson wrote exasperatedly to Arthur Smith Woodward that 'the natural gas site goes on undiminished... but no one has yet attempted to fathom its source and the Company which took it up did a bad turn and now, beyond the station lamps being lit by it, it is allowed to waste'.[18]

Natural gas at Heathfield: conclusion

Although the initial conclusions of Dawson and Woodhead concerning the petroleum content of the gas at Heathfield were criticised by some, no one can dispute the 'burning properties' of the gas itself, which for many years served to illuminate Heathfield railway station. Dawson certainly never claimed to have 'discovered' the gas in the first place, though he does appear to have been the first to realise its potential significance and to arrange for proper scientific analysis (conducted by Samuel Woodhead). His involvement in this particular story may at first appear strange, but Dawson's experience as an amateur geologist and fossil hunter of many years was to prove extremely useful in his consideration of the possible origins and properties of the gas. His fellowship of the Geological Society allowed him free range to report the discovery, with a certain degree of dramatic flourish, at a London meeting of the group, and he certainly received the full credit and academic recognition for the find. Despite claims that there was '*something* peculiar' about the affair,[19] there is no trace here of any fraudulent activity.

Toad in a Hole

One of the strangest of Charles Dawson's natural discoveries was that of the so-called 'Toad in a Hole' (**66**) presented before the Brighton and Hove Natural History and Philosophical Society on 18 April 1901. The artefact itself comprised an apparently mummified toad preserved within a hollow nodule of flint. The 'curiously light' lemon-shaped flint had, according to Dawson, been broken apart by two Lewes workmen, Joseph Isted and Thomas Nye, in the summer of 1898, and had been examined *in situ* by a Dr J. Burbridge 'who

66 *Toad in a Hole: a photograph of the mummified toad preserved inside a flint nodule taken in 1979*

testified to the integrity of Nye'.[20] Quite how the artefact arrived in Dawson's hands is never established, though this could again be explained by contact Dawson kept 'with all workmen in his district who might make accidental discoveries'.[21] At the time of the presentation, the Lewes 'Toad in a Hole' caused quite a stir amongst the scientific community and caught the popular imagination, lengthy reports appearing in a number of papers including the *Illustrated London News*.[22] Eventually the artefact was passed on to Brighton's Booth Museum of Natural History, through the agency of Dawson's anti-quarian colleague Henry Willett.[23]

The 'Toad in a Hole' puzzled Joseph Weiner who observed that 'no one has claimed that this is a true fossil; the toad when young must have got into the nodule through a small hole and found enough insects to enable it to grow until it became too large to get out again'.[24] True, this was an unusual discovery, though it was something that was not entirely without precedent. In 1811, the Derbyshire geologist White Watson reported that Dr Jack Treagus of Manchester University had, in 1795, broken a block of limestone calculated to weigh 'a ton and a half in weight' only to discover a toad 'alive in the centre'.[25] In 1825, intrigued by the possibility that amphibians could survive for long periods within inhospitable environments, the naturalist Dr William Buckland conducted, certainly by today's standards, a not altogether ethical experiment by taking twenty-four toads, placing them in 'sealed cells' and burying them in solid and porous limestone for just over a year. When the toads were exhumed, on 10 December 1826, Buckland noted, with some surprise, that only those fortunate enough to have been sealed within porous limestone had survived the experience.[26]

Though other cases of frogs and toads entombed in solid rock have from time to time been reported, the only firm example which today 'proves that there is a basis for reports of the phenomenon'[27] is Dawson's example in the Booth Museum. Since its presentation to the museum, in 1901, the supposedly mummified toad has shrunk considerably 'indicating that it cannot have been very old at the time of discovery'.[28] Though no one has ever specifically said as much, the intimation is that the 'Toad in a Hole' was an obvious scientific hoax perpetrated by Charles Dawson.

Toad in a Hole: conclusion

The 'Toad in a Hole' is certainly a curious discovery, but that in itself does not constitute firm evidence for a fraud. That there are precedents for frogs and toads preserved within hollow rocks, is clear enough, though much of the evidence to date unfortunately appears to be little more than hearsay. The Lewes Toad would therefore, if genuine, constitute a rather important discovery in the history of this particular natural phenomenon. Dawson's involvement in the matter, however, makes accepting the find without reservation rather difficult.

Dawson does not claim to have actually found the 'Toad in a Hole', nor inspected it *in situ*, and he certainly does not appear to have discussed the discovery in detail with the Lewes workmen Joseph Isted and Thomas Nye. His role in the affair was merely to exhibit the find and make a report to the Brighton and Hove Natural History and Philosophical Society. That it took Dawson some three years between the discovery (in 1898) and the exhibition (in 1901) is, furthermore, not an unequivocal admission of guilt, for we do not know how long Isted and Nye, or even the mysterious Dr Burbridge, held on to the piece before handing it over. We do not even know the mechanics of how it was eventually passed on to Charles Dawson. As for the toad itself, the British Museum reported that it was clearly 'not very old' at the time Isted and Nye first freed it,[29] something which may cast doubt as to its authenticity. Dawson does not, however, claim that the amphibian was ancient or in any way fossilised, so its age at exhumation should not cause any consternation.

If the 'Toad in a Hole' *was* a fraud, and it is important to note that there is no clear evidence that this is the case, then any number of perpetrators may be 'put in the frame'. Isted and Nye, if they had wished to supplement their meagre pay as workmen, could perhaps have generated an interesting find, secure in the knowledge that Dawson, or someone like him, would readily stump up the cash necessary to purchase it. Perhaps someone in local antiquarian or geological circles wished to provide the evidence necessary to confirm a hypothesis concerning amphibian survival in solid rock. Perhaps someone was playing a practical joke. Perhaps Dawson was indeed enacting a scientific hoax. Certainly the solicitor from Uckfield received all the credit for making the discovery public and, although he never formally published his conclusions, his name was attached to the find in both the local and national press. Beyond that, all is speculation.

Sea Serpents in the English Channel

Five years after his reporting of the 'Toad in a Hole', Charles Dawson encountered a second mystery of nature, this time a monster from the deep. Writing to Arthur Woodward on 7 October 1907, Dawson related that, whilst travelling on board the steamer SS *Manche*, on what was otherwise a fairly a routine journey from Newhaven to Dieppe, Dawson spotted something through his binoculars:

> It was some two miles away right ahead of the ship. While trying to focus on the object as sharply as possible I heard two men (passengers) talking about it. One said, 'Hallo! What's that coming, the sea-serpent or what is it?' The object had then shifted its course and instead of coming at us had turned on a side track of about 45 degrees from our port side, but offered a more extended and less complicated view. I could not see any head or tail but a series of very rounded arched loops like the most conventional old sea-serpent you could imagine, and the progressive motion was very smart and serpentine for when one loop was up is neighbour was down. I could see no detail except the long black arched line, dipping into the water at either end... The loops were fully 8 feet out of the water, and the length 60 to 70 feet at the smallest computation... I watched it receding from the vessel in an oblique direction until it entered the path of the sun's rays upon the water until [I] finally lost it.[30]

Fortunately, as well as his binoculars, Dawson also had his camera, a small Kodak, with him, and was able to take 'several shots' of the beast as it came about. Sadly the developed film showed no sea serpent or 'detail of the sea beyond a few yards'.[31] Undeterred by his lack of evidence, Dawson told Woodward that he had discussed the sighting with a number of his fellow passengers, exchanging cards with 'several' in the hope of bringing forth witness statements if required. There is no evidence that either Dawson or Woodward ever followed up these witnesses to collect formal statements. Furthermore there is no evidence that Woodward ever questioned his friend over *why* it had taken him so long to report the sighting. Dawson wrote to Woodward on 7 October 1907, but the sea serpent was allegedly sighted on Good Friday 1906, a whole eighteen months *before* Dawson finally put pen to paper.

Strange as it may seem today, the possible existence of sea serpents was, in the later half of the nineteenth century, quite a popular topic of conversation. Sea monsters are, of course, present in the mythology of most ancient cultures, and, despite the more extensive exploration of the world's oceans in the last century, they remain a potent symbol of 'the great unknown'. The majority of monster sightings through the eighteenth and nineteenth century were, however, largely unsubstantiated or related by those considered to be wholly unreliable. All this changed for the great British public in 1848 when Peter M'Quhae, captain of Her Majesty's frigate HMS *Daedalus*, reported a monster sighting to the Admiralty. M'Quhae claimed that, between the Cape of Good Hope and St Helena, *Daedalus* had for some twenty minutes been accompanied by a large sea creature which 'held at the pace of twelve to fifteen miles per hour, apparently on some determined purpose'.[32] The head of the beast, which M'Quhae claimed resembled that of a snake but with the mane of a horse, was raised some 4ft (1.2m) above the water, the creature as a whole measuring at least 60ft (18.3m) in length.

When Captain M'Quhae's report was published in the London *Times*, it caused a sensation. The somewhat unsettling feeling that there might be similar creatures skulking in British coastal waters sparked a flurry of worried letters to the national press and generated a sense of mild hysteria for those communities facing the English Channel. A sense of the palpable unease caused by the *Daedalus* incident is reflected in the experience of HMS *St Vincent*, which, in the summer of 1848, only weeks after M'Quhae's report had been leaked to the press, was lying at Spithead anchorage, off Portsmouth in Hampshire. W. Gore Jones, then attached to the crew of the *St Vincent* later recalled that one evening at about 6pm:

> just as the officers were sitting down to dinner, the midshipman of the watch ran into the wardroom and reported that a sea serpent was passing rapidly between the ship and the Isle of Wight... We all got our glasses and went on deck, and there, sure enough, about a mile off, was a large monster, with a head and shaggy mane, about 100 feet long, and tapering towards the tail; it was going with the tide, and had a rapid, undulating motion. Two or three boats were manned, and some officers got their guns and went in pursuit. We watched them from the ship; they gradually got close, and guns were raised and levelled at the creature's head; but just as we thought the sport was about to begin, down went the guns, and from their gestures we saw something very laughable had occurred. On their return we found that the supposed serpent was a long line of soot. Some steamer in the Southampton Waters had evidently swept her dirty flues, and the soot from tubes or flues is always of a very sticky nature, and as it was pitched overboard it went away with the tide, sticking together, and gradually forming into the shape of a long serpent, the wave motion giving it an undulating life-like appearance.[33]

Despite this wholly explicable 'creature' incident, sightings of sea serpents in the English Channel were to remain a regular fixture in the national press, letters to *The Times* continuing until the early 1890s.[34]

How does Dawson's sighting fit into all this? Admittedly, the observations of the Uckfield solicitor (and subsequent letter to Woodward) were amongst the last in a long line of documented creature 'sightings', but were they genuine? John Evangelist Walsh, when examining the case of the English Channel Sea Serpent, was particularly damning, interpreting the whole incident as a piece of 'clownish ephemera' which demonstrated Dawson's 'unlimited power to deceive',[35] but is this strictly fair? Given the context of public hysteria generated by past encounters, the Good Friday 1906 sighting from the SS *Manche* does not after all appear wholly ludicrous, but it leaves us uncertain as to whether Dawson really did see *something* as he looked out to sea (and if he did, whether others saw it too). If the encounter was wholly fabricated, as some suggest, what could have been Dawson's motive for it?

Sea Serpents in the English Channel: conclusion

The case of the English Channel Sea Serpent is a particularly strange one. Dawson makes no public acknowledgement of his sighting, other than in the context of a private letter to his friend Woodward and this a full year and a half after the event. Unfortunately, Woodward's response to the whole affair is lost to us. Was he intrigued by the details supplied by Dawson or, as an expert on marine palaeontology, did he laugh the incident off as the misidentification of something else in the water? Even if Woodward had been interested enough to attempt to follow-up potential witness statements, the lengthy gap between sighting and reporting it (Woodward does not hear about the serpent until early October 1907) may well have proved difficult in locating Dawson's travelling companions, let alone extracting a convincing report from them.

Perhaps, given the nature of the evidence, a lack of confidence on Dawson's part may well not be surprising for, even today, those who claim to have witnessed unnatural events or mysterious creatures often find themselves outcasts from polite society. Dawson may have felt that his 'sea serpent' was, without the evidence of his camera, something that would not be taken seriously by either the media or the wider scientific community. Perhaps he was not sure himself about what he and his fellow passengers had actually seen that day. Perhaps they had seen a line of soot, similar to that encountered by HMS *St Vincent* in 1848, or other form of Channel pollutant. Perhaps he made the whole story up.

What is interesting here is the form taken by Dawson's creature. His description of 'very rounded arched loops' does not sound like either the *Daedalus* or *St Vincent* sea serpents, but it does fit perfectly with the late nineteenth- and early twentieth-century view of what it was felt a lake serpent, such as that often ascribed to Loch Ness in Scotland, *ought* to look like. Up until the late 1960s, the Loch Ness Monster (or 'Nessie') was often described or drawn (especially by countless schoolchildren) as a collection of coils and humps emerging from the surface of the loch. From the 1970s, however, the general form of 'Nessie', and indeed of all sightings relating to her, have changed. This is due in no small part to the work of Dr Robert Rines at the loch between 1971 and '75.[36] Rines claimed to have photographed a great beast with a long neck, wide body and diamond-shape flippers: in short a plesiosaur. Plesiosaurs were a type of marine reptile that inhabited freshwater and marine environments of the Triassic to the Cretaceous periods, feeding mainly on fish and other small water creatures such as ammonites. Since the publication of Rines' rather startling photographs of 'Nessie', people have only seen plesiosaurs.

Dawson's observations of the alleged serpent were clearly 'of their time' and, given the general lack of sightings through the twentieth century, it does seem somewhat unlikely that anything quite as large as the creature that Dawson claimed to have seen could really be out in the English Channel. It has been shown that, when it comes to unexplained phenomena, people often see what they want to see. That is not to doubt that, in the case of the world's oceans, there is not something large and wholly unknown still lurking in the depths (in fact given how little of the seabed has been adequately mapped, it would be surprising if there was not), but a large number of 'monster sightings' at somewhere like Loch Ness can be attributed to the human mind telling the eyes what really *ought* to be there: a plesiosaur rather than, say, a piece of wood, an otter, a rock or a piece of loch debris.

This still begs the question: 'did Dawson *really* see something in the waters of the Channel?' Was he genuinely convinced that the SS *Manche* had had a close encounter with a large aquatic beast or was he playing a bizarre trick on his colleague Arthur Woodward? Surely, if he were attempting to fool Woodward, there would appear to have been little to gain from such a deceit? Perhaps it is the context of the alleged sighting that is important here, for in the early years of the twentieth century Dawson's interests appear to have been shifting away from matters historical and archaeological, and more towards those of the natural world. Part of this shift in interest may have been due to his election in 1895 to the Society of Antiquaries, in much the same way that his passion for geology seems to have declined following his election to the Geological Society in 1885. Having achieved such goals, Dawson may have felt that to continue in such fields would be akin to merely 'treading water' whilst diversifying would prove an altogether more challenging experience. Perhaps the increasingly poor reception that his work was receiving from Sussex antiquarians, or indeed the major falling out with the Sussex Archaeological Society following the Castle Lodge incident of 1904, helped convince him that his research should be directed elsewhere. We will never be entirely sure, but it is to this period that the more unorthodox aspects of the natural world, such as the Toad in a Hole, the 'incipient horns' of cart horses, the goldfish/carp cross and wholly new species of human really began to dominate his time.[37]

The Thirteenth Dorsal Vertebra

On 12 May 1912, barely a month after Dawson first alerted Arthur Smith Woodward to the first discovery of what was to become Piltdown man, Dawson was again writing to Woodward, this time about an entirely new race of human:

> Since I saw you I have been writing on the subject of 'The Thirteenth Dorsal Vertebra' in certain human skeletons, which I believe is a new subject. I send you the result and if you think well enough of it I should be very much obliged if you would introduce the paper for me at the Royal Society. I am very anxious to get it placed at once because I have had to work the photographs under the nose of Keith and his assistant. I gather from the later person that Keith is rather puzzled as to what to make of it all, and I want to secure the priority to which I am entitled.[38]

The original draft of Dawson's report, alluded to in this letter, is preserved in the Library of Palaeontology at the Natural History Museum in London.[39] The paper, entitled 'On the persistence of a Thirteenth Dorsal Vertebra in Certain Human Races', is accompanied by a number of photographs of human skeletal remains, apparently taken of 'skeletons displayed in glass cabinets in the museum exhibition halls of the Royal College of Surgeons' where Arthur Keith worked as conservator.[40] The photographs appear to have been taken somewhat hastily, some being 'marred by the glare of the flash', which may support Dawson's comment that they were taken 'under the nose of Keith and his assistant'.

The basics of the report deal with the observation that, though the normal number of vertebrae in a human skeleton is twelve, certain Inuit skeletons in the Royal College of Surgeons appeared to possess thirteen. An extra vertebra is common enough in apes and the loss of this during the process of human evolution was often ascribed to the development of an upright walking posture. Human skeletons retaining that 'Thirteenth Dorsal Vertebra' were therefore an anomaly, one that Dawson appeared keen to explain.

Dawson obviously felt that his discovery was of sufficient importance to be reported to the Royal Society, though, as he had not been elected to a fellowship, Dawson could not himself speak directly to the group. In 1912, however, Arthur Smith Woodward was already a fellow (rising to be a member of its Council the following year), and was, therefore, in an excellent position to introduce his friend's paper. The urgency with which Dawson asks Woodward to press ahead with his draft paper appears, in the letter of 12 May, to stem from his belief that the idea will be stolen from him once Keith or his assistant realise the significance of the discovery (quite why they had not noticed it before, especially in the skeletons on display in their own college, is never explained).

It is plain from Dawson's letter that he believed the find to be entirely new. To some extent this is true, though the Uckfield solicitor had been pre-empted by the recent publication (in February 1912) of a book by the French anatomist A.F. Le Double entitled *Variations de la colonne vertébrale de l'homme, et leur signification au point de vue de l'anthropologie zoologique*, which covered the same themes as those propounded by Dawson. Arthur Keith had been forwarded a copy of Le Double's book early in 1912 and had been asked by the Royal Anthropological Institute to write a review. This he singularly failed to do for nearly three years until the journal *Man* published a short comment praising the work.[41] Perhaps because of this, the wider dissemination of Le Double's book, or a sense of disinterest from Woodward himself, Dawson's own paper never saw the light of day. Joseph Weiner was later to record that, as he was told, the newspapers ran the story 'as the discovery of a new race by the discoverer of Piltdown',[42] but the academic impact of Dawson's unpublished article was ultimately negligible.

The Thirteenth Dorsal Vertebra: conclusions

Frank Spencer thought that Arthur Keith's delay in producing a review for Le Double's book *Variations de la colonne vertébrale de l'homme, et leur signification au point de vue de l'anthropologie zoologique* masked something more sinister:

> Why had Keith taken so long to write a ten-line (!) review of such a 'valuable work'? was there really a connection between Le Double's book and Dawson's paper? Had Dawson really expected to communicate this paper to the Royal Society and had he really hoped that Woodward might use his authority to push a paper through? Or was the paper merely a camouflage? But to hide what? [43]

At this point Spencer unfolds a conspiracy of devious complexity, attempting to link Dawson's paper 'On the persistence of a Thirteenth Dorsal Vertebra in Certain Human Races' with the creation of the Piltdown man hoax. The paper was, in Spencer's view, nothing more than a smokescreen allowing Dawson and Keith to secretly meet in London in order to plan the greater fraud, without arousing suspicion. This conspiracy theory falls badly awry, however, when the facts of the accusation are objectively considered. For example why did the two men not meet somewhere else? Why was it important to meet in Keith's office at all? Why, if this was all intended merely as a camouflage to secretly meet with Keith, did Dawson photograph and examine the skeletons in the Royal College of Surgeons when Keith was not even in the country (something Spencer notes but fails to elaborate upon? [44] Keith's failure to quickly publish a review of Le Double's book merely reflects the pressures of time that many in the academic community then felt (and indeed continue to feel today). It does not hide something sinister. Spencer's hypothesis sadly rests upon supposition, guesswork and a host of unfounded claims ad it is an unfortunate end to his otherwise exhaustive and authoritarian study of the Piltdown man forgery.

A simpler solution presents itself. By May 1912, when Dawson first alerted Woodward to his new find, Le Double's book, although published in France, had yet to receive a full English translation. Dawson was, as has previously been observed, fluent in French, and may therefore have been aware of both the existence of the book and its content before many of his scientific associates. His sense of urgency to 'secure the priority' to which he felt entitled, may therefore reflect the very real worry that Woodward, Keith, or any other member of the Royal Society, might hear of Le Double's research first.[45] Certainly the announcement of Dawson's 'discovery', coming so soon *after* the publication of Le Double's book (which itself took years to fully compile), casts severe doubt over the reliability of the solicitor's research.

The Hastings Rarities

The case of the Hastings Rarities is a curious one, and its link to Charles Dawson remains unproven. The basics of the case are simple enough: between 1892 and 1930, a large number of exotic birds were reported (i.e. shot) from a restricted area on the south-east coast of Sussex (**67** & **68**). To put this 'number' into better perspective, the journal *British Birds* reported in 1962 that:

> Of the 520 forms (representing 424 species) [of bird] described in 1941 in the *Handbook of British Birds*, 301 were residents, summer visitors, regular winter visitors and passage migrants or occasional breeders. The rest, the

67 *The Hastings Rarities: a group of eleven terns, shot at Rye by 'John Saunders' in 1912 and stuffed by George Bristow*

68 *The Hastings Rarities: a thick-billed nutcracker shot at Guestling in 1909 and stuffed by George Bristow*

occasional and irregular visitors, were a large class of very varied status... yet of this remaining 219, no fewer than 28 – just over one eighth – owed their inclusion solely to occurrences reported during 1903-1919 from a small area in East Sussex and West Kent, within roughly a twenty-mile radius round Hastings.[46]

After 1919, the same area produced only two new additions, this despite the fact that the number of observers (as opposed to shooters) rose steadily after both World Wars. In short, the Hastings 'Rarities', as they were known, were frauds, part of a large-scale forgery that duped the world of ornithology for generations. The majority of the rare and exotic birds, it transpired, had probably been shot abroad and imported into the British Isles in a frozen condition so that they appeared to represent 'fresh kills'.[47]

Two main questions arose from the revelation of fraud: who had perpetrated the forgery and what had they hoped to gain from it? The second question is the easiest to answer, for the deception appears to have been undertaken purely for financial reasons. In the latter half of the nineteenth century and early part of the twentieth, the science of ornithology was less concerned about *observing* birds as proving their presence, and what better way to prove the presence of a specific species than to have them shot, stuffed and displayed? The records of those who merely *watched* birds were frequently dismissed as irrelevant or inac- curate, the oft quoted maxim of the early ornithologist being: 'What's hit's history, what's missed's mystery'.[48] Furthermore, the record of the sharp- shooting ornithologist was not only useful from a scientific point of view, it also carried with it significant financial rewards: 'the trinity of the casual gunner, the busy taxidermist and the wealthy collector still formed the backbone of the system by which additions were made to lists of local, county or national rarities, and the nexus between them was cash'.[49]

When the full extent of the Hastings Rarities case was revealed, the press and ornithologists alike began their search for the likely perpetrator. Throughout the whole history of the discovery, reporting and subsequent sale of the rarities, one name stood out: George Bristow. Bristow was a taxidermist and gunsmith operating from a small shop at 15 Silchester Road in St Leonards on Sea. He had died in 1947, untarnished by any suspicion of fraud, but as the investigation into the hoax continued apace, realisation dawned that he had been the one constant force throughout: 'it was to him that the Hastings Rarities were brought, and by him that they were usually first shown to the various local ornithologists who were able to place them on record in *British Birds* or by exhibition at the British Ornithologists' Club'.[50]

Once Bristow's name began to be circulated as the most likely candidate for the imposture, there were howls of protest and vehement letters in his defence from friends and surviving family members. Echoing the feelings of Dawson's family following the disclosure of the Piltdown hoax in 1953, one of George Bristow's daughters wrote to the *Daily Telegraph* to state that:

> I am distressed at suggestions that my father may have been in some racket over imported birds, and that he could be suspected of being responsible for a hoax. Nothing could be further from the truth. He was not that kind of person who would try to mislead anybody. I can only assume that he may have been mislead by someone else.[51]

The 11 August edition of *The Times* added that both daughters remained convinced that 'he would never have been party to any dishonesty or deception'.[52]

The main problem with attempting to disassociate Bristow from the fraud was that he appeared to have deliberately concealed the source of the rarities brought to him. Many of the collectors and shooters who brought their catches to Bristow's taxidermist shop appear to have been reticent about recording their identity. Many of the records were deliberately vague, later researchers noting the repeated occurrence of unspecific references to birds simply being 'shot' or 'picked up' without reference to who was actually doing the shooting. When there was mention of a collector, it was usually no more than 'the man who shot the bird'.[53] Of the 542 specimens analysed in 1962, only seventy had any sort of name attached to them; 'eleven of these are M.J. Nicholl and four G. Bristow, but only 13 of the remainder have more than a surname and most of those are such common and untraceable ones as Sargeant, Clarke, Mills and Miller'.[54]

Try as they might, the investigation team could not interview or even locate any of the named individuals cited by Bristow as having shot or otherwise found rare species from the Hastings area. In their exasperation, Nicholson and Ferguson-Lees concluded:

it would not be an exaggeration to say that we have yet to find any evidence that most of the men implicitly credited with finding and collecting the majority of the Hastings Rarities ever existed. If they did, they must have been remarkably modest and self-effacing to obtain all these difficult birds which the most skilled ornithologists have been unable to discover either at the time or since, and to forgo all the credit and interest and much even of the commercial profit of their astonishing harvest.[55]

Bristow, it seems, was the only person who it could be shown was not only 'in on the hoax', but had also profited directly from it. He had the means, the motive and the opportunity. He even admitted that, on at least one occasion, he had received '4 Albatrosses, a Gannet, a Cape Pigeon and a Hoopoe' from a Captain of the Natal Line of Steamers who had caught the birds on his ship and placed them 'in the refrigerator' for the return journey to England.[56]

All very interesting perhaps, but what have Bristow and the Hastings Rarities to do with Charles Dawson FGS, FSA? First, the main phase of the ornithological hoax was conducted around the Hastings area between 1903 and 1916,[57] exactly the same time that Dawson was actively involved in the creation and establishment of the Dawson Loans Collection in Hastings Museum. Second, Bristow lived and worked in Silchester Road, St Leonards on Sea, inheriting the business (and the shop) from his father, at the same time that Charles Dawson was growing up a few streets away in Warrior Square. Third, and perhaps most damningly, Dawson and Bristow *were acquainted*.[58]

The nature of Dawson's acquaintance with Bristow was quickly seized upon by the press as confirmation of Bristow's guilt; the Piltdown hoax further tarnishing Bristow's already tattered reputation. Harrison, in his strident rebuttal of the accusations made against Bristow (which is strikingly similar in tone to the defence of Charles Dawson by Francis Vere (aka Francis Bannister) in 1955), Harrison rejected the idea that Bristow's perceived guilt was in any way confirmed by his association with the Uckfield solicitor: 'here again is an example of the use of purely circumstantial evidence to condemn a man, evidence which is inadmissible and which should carry no weight whatsoever with fair-minded people'.[59]

Yet the fact that two elaborate hoaxes, albeit ones with using different materials and with ultimately different objectives, were conducted *at the same time* in the same part of Sussex seems a huge coincidence. The fact that the chief suspects in both cases were well acquainted, spending much of their time *in the same town*, makes it appear more remarkable if there had *not* been a connection between them. Of this, Rex Marchant was convinced, noting that 'when one looks at the many points of contact between the... men, not least the shared connection with the Hastings museum, and then adds to that the fact that they had regular social meetings... the idea of coincidence no longer becomes tenable'.[60]

The Hastings Rarities: conclusion

Rex Marchant has recently propounded the theory that Dawson and Bristow, together with Lewis Abbott, a jeweller, amateur antiquarian and (ultimately) a rival of Dawson's, designed their respective frauds in order 'to see who could achieve the greatest success in fooling the experts'.[61] This scenario, however plausible it may at first appear, is something which unfortunately makes both the Piltdown fraud and that of the Hastings Rarities appear nothing more than light-hearted pranks. The truth is that both 'pranks' were in reality far more calculating and devious.

That Bristow was intimately involved in the Hastings Rarities seems clear enough. Even if he was unaware that the birds in question had been shot abroad and brought into Britain in a frozen state, he certainly gained substantial rewards from the sale of the specimens, which, together with his failure to ultimately divulge their source, makes him the prime candidate for the entire deception. But did he have an accomplice and, if he did, is it possible to infer that this unnamed partner in crime was the Uckfield solicitor Charles Dawson?

At first glance, the Hastings Rarities appear to be a world away from the many discoveries that punctuated Dawson's great antiquarian career. Here a great many bird specimens were shot, captured and collected over a long period of time, apparently with no motive other than financial. Bristow did not claim academic recognition for his 'discoveries' and he never attempted to describe, publish or otherwise disseminate his findings. In fact, throughout the whole history of the affair, Bristow appeared solely as the conduit through which other peoples discoveries flowed. Though he failed to name or identify his sources, he only claimed credit for four of the 542 rare specimens that passed through his shop.

Dawson, furthermore, never claimed to have found, collected, identified, spotted or shot rare birds at any stage in his antiquarian career. Ornithology is one science that he appears to have, publicly at least, taken little interest in. If he had, in any way, been involved in the Hastings Rarities fraud, he would surely have attempted to lecture on or otherwise publish his 'findings'. Some of the rare specimens in Bristow's care were, it is true, allegedly shot in places such as Beauport Park, Bulverhythe, Pevensey, Bexhill and Beachy Head,[62] areas where Dawson himself regularly worked, but this is not proof of complicity. The fact that the number of rarities reported dramatically tailed off after 1916, the year of Dawson's death, is further not necessarily evidence of his involvement in the fraud, as rare birds continued to be 'found', albeit in smaller numbers, until 1930. Furthermore, the passing on of objects (be they archaeological, geological or palaeontological) for financial gain does not seem to have been a part of Dawson's character; in fact, if anything, he appears to have nearly bankrupted himself in the *acquisition* of rare and unusual items.[63] If one was of a suspicious mind however, one may point to all these traits as evidence of complicity in the Hastings Rarities deception for, if Dawson and Bristow *had* together intended to deceive bird collectors into parting with their hard earned cash, they would hardly have advertised their association. For Bristow, Dawson would have provided a means of supplying rare specimens for his taxidermy; for Dawson, Bristow's craft and assured silence would have ensured a valued source of extra income to help fund his ever diversifying (and no doubt expensive) antiquarian interests.

On present evidence, it must be admitted, there is no conclusive evidence to link George Bristow, the main suspect in the Hastings Rarities hoax, with Charles Dawson, the main suspect in the Piltdown hoax, other than to note they lived and worked in the same general area, at the same time and that they were aware of one another's existence. Beyond that, all is speculation.

10

TIME AND SPACE

There remain two further anomalous 'discoveries' credited to Charles Dawson that require serious consideration here: the Maresfield Map and the Ashburnham Clock Dial. Neither was ever referred to by Dawson during his life, though both have been cited as providing clear evidence of Dawson's involvement in fraudulent activity.

The Maresfield Map

The so-called 'Maresfield Map' first appeared as an illustration in the 1912 volume of the *Sussex Archaeological Collections*.[1] The map (**69**), which has been accepted as a copy, made by Charles Dawson, of a genuine eighteenth-century artefact,[2] has more recently been described as a cheap fake; something which is 'wholly fictitious and of no value as evidence for anything depicted at any period'.[3] Philip Howard, writing in the New York *Times*, was more explicit; noting that the map was akin to a 'smoking gun' which proved that Dawson was an accomplished, habitual forger:

> The circumstantial evidence suggests that Dawson's chief scientific talents were deception and hoaxing, distraction and long derision. The missing link in the evidence so far has been any direct connection positively identifying Dawson's hand in a forgery. That missing link has now been supplied by a map made and signed by Dawson in 1912, the very year of Piltdown man.[4]

The 'smoking gun' is, on closer inspection, far less damning than Howard enthusiastically suggests. There is no doubt concerning the map's lack of authenticity, but its connection to Charles Dawson is, as we shall see, somewhat ambiguous.

The first issue to deal with is that of legitimacy. There is no doubt that the illustration that accompanied the 1912 article 'A notice of Maresfield Forge in 1608' is a forgery, and a crude one at that. In 1974, Lieutenant-Colonel P.B.S. Andrews managed to compile a detailed list of errors, mistakes and incongruities contained within the map and which counted against genuineness of the article.

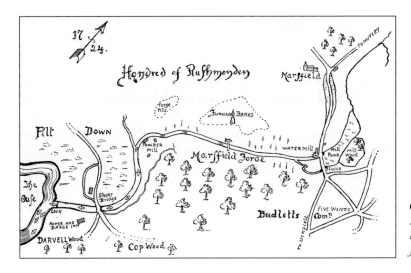

69 *The Maresfield Map: as drawn by John Lewis*

For a start, there was no provenance or title given for the map and the scale employed was hugely distorted, the left side of the map being compressed to one quarter of that on the right. The scripts used were anachronistic and inconsistently applied, Andrews noting particularly the spelling 'Hondred' as a 'pseudo-archaism' for Hundred, whilst certain nineteenth-century anachronisms were set out in 'small Roman capitals of nineteenth-twentieth-century type'.

A number of named places cited on the map were also hopelessly incorrect, 'Five Wents' for example, actually having been 'Six Wents' at the time the map was supposed to have been compiled. The River Ouse, shown as navigable in the map, was only cleared and opened after 1790, whilst roads shown on the 1724 map actually post-dated 1830. The position of a cutting on the road to the south of Maresfield dated from the time of the 1752 turnpike. The Mill Pond, which was shown to exactly the same dimensions as in the 6 inch Ordnance Survey map of 1900, used early twentieth-century map conventions for a marsh. The Powder Mill as shown was not actually attested until 1852. The depiction of the stream above Maresfield Forge 'explicitly denies [the] existence of [a] hammer pond', something which would make the forge itself unusable, whilst a furnace is depicted on the highest hill with no direct access to water.[5] All these observations, Andrews concluded, served 'to demonstrate the total absurdity of the map and its uselessness as evidence for anything historical'.[6]

The Maresfield Map: conclusions

To whom then may we credit authorship of the Maresfield Map? Andrews held short of actually naming names, other than to note that the map was supposedly 'made by C. Dawson FSA', as stated in the original caption of 1912.

Howard, as we have already noted, was less vague, stating that: 'For the first time Dawson has been caught red-handed'.[7] Later re-examination of the map, however, shows that things are not quite that clear cut.

Although Dawson's name is appended to the figure in the final publication,[8] there is nothing about the illustration that explicitly suggests that he had a hand in its manufacture. In fact an analysis of the drawing's form and style strongly suggests authorship by another, in this case by sometime Dawson collaborator John Lewis.[9] There is nothing about the illustration that irrefutably demonstrates the handiwork of Charles Dawson, only that the version of it appearing in Crake's article of 1912 had been *made* by him. Combridge takes this as implying that the map, drawn by Lewis, had merely been 'copied photographically by Dawson in circumstances unknown, and later published by the editor of *SAC* to illustrate an independently written article'.[10]

This observation is worth examining in greater detail for a number of reasons. First, though Dawson was indeed an accomplished photographer, there is no reason as to why, in 1912, he should be photographically copying anything for inclusion in the *Sussex Archaeological Collections*, especially when, according to certain accounts, he had dramatically fallen out with the Sussex Society in or around 1904 (ostensibly over the sale of Castle Lodge in Lewes).[11] Dawson and the Society certainly seem to have severed all active links by 1912, the Sussex solicitor preferring at this time to work only with the Hastings Natural History Society and Hastings Museum.

Secondly, and perhaps more tellingly, there is no reason as to why the illustration should *appear at all* with Crake's article of 1912 as there is no explicit reference to it nor any other figure in the published text, the article having been written as if it were intended to be unillustrated.[12] Why then, if both text and illustration are not linked, the article standing well on its own without any appended figures, did anyone feel it necessary to include the map in the first place? Furthermore, why, if Dawson only *made a copy* of a drawing made by Lewis of an original map of 1724, is Lewis himself not credited?

A clue to all this may be found in the involvement of John Lewis. Lewis was a fellow of the Society of Antiquaries and a member of the Sussex Archaeological Society from 1892 to 1907. He appears to have been a more than competent draftsman, collaborating with Dawson on a number of archaeological projects, including the examination of the Lavant Caves in 1893[13] and the dungeons of Hastings Castle in 1894.[14] Relations between the two seem to have deteriorated, however, Weiner noting that in 1911 'a serious quarrel' resulted in the effective termination of their friendship.[15] The causes of the quarrel remain unknown, though Combridge has inferred that the dispute could have supplied a motive for Lewis to perpetrate a number of hoaxes upon Dawson as a way of perhaps undermining his academic credibility.[16]

Certainly as a forgery, the Maresfield Map does not appear very good. It is lacking in technical ability and contains so many typological, cartographic and chronological errors that it is surprising that it took as long as the early 1970s to be exposed. It is almost as if, by including so many obvious anachronisms and blatant mistakes, the forger actually wanted to be discovered. This misspelling of the word 'Hundred', for example, appears to have been deliberately highlighted by the positioning of an arrow-like blot, directly pointing to the mistake. All the nineteenth-century anachronisms identified by Andrews[17] were set out in 'small Roman capitals of nineteenth-twentieth century type', something which only served to illuminate them and emphasise their untrustworthiness. This is something which may also be inferred by the date of 1724 given to the map for this was also the year of the original 6 inch to one mile map twelve of the county made by Budgen, something which Howard suggests may have been 'a strident warning... to recall Budgen's well-known genuine map of Sussex of that date and compare them'.[18]

This is not then the work of an adept and clever hoaxer hoping to gain significant 'academic points' for its apparent discovery and detailed analysis. Dawson certainly never appears to have publicly acknowledged the map or discussed it in any shape or form. If his name had not appeared so prominently within the caption appended to the map in the 1912 article, we probably would not make any such link with Dawson at all. Admittedly there is no record of him ever denying his involvement with the illustration, or that he had ever photographically copied it for inclusion within the *Sussex Archaeological Collections*, but even if he had made such a public statement, it is unlikely that the Society would have published an apology or retraction given the state of affairs in the months following Castle Lodge and the later discovery of Piltdown man.[19] Whatever the interpretation of the blatant forgery that is the Maresfield Map, and this will be discussed in greater detail later in the final conclusions, it is worth reiterating that there is nothing about the map that can directly associate it with the name of Charles Dawson.

The Ashburnham Dial

In 1912, Arthur Hayden, in his charmingly titled book *Chats on Cottage and Farmhouse Furniture*, published a picture of a brass clock dial engraved with a variety of scenes supposedly depicting ironworking at the Sussex site of Ashburnham (**70**). The caption accompanying the image did little to explain the piece, other than to note that it was probably late seventeenth century and had derived from 'the collection of Charles Dawson, Esq., FSA'.[20] Dawson himself does not appear to have ever commented on the artefact, either privately or in print. After his death in 1916, the clock dial was sold at auction, presumably by surviving members of the family, to an unnamed 'Sussex resident'.[21]

Through the 1920s, the piece aroused not insignificant attention[22] especially as few seventeenth- or eighteenth-century scenes of Sussex ironworking,

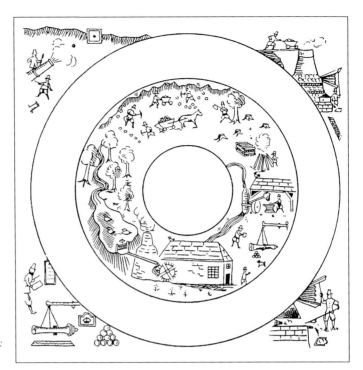

70 *The Asburnham Dial:
as drawn by John Lewis*

an industry that was largely defunct by the twentieth century, appeared to exist. By 1953, the dial resurfaced in the collection of the Colonial Williamsburg Foundation in Virginia, USA,[23] where it continued to be viewed as an authentic Georgian artefact. Certain doubts concerning the authenticity of the piece began to surface following the exposure of the Piltdown fraud in 1953 and subsequent questions surrounding any material associated with the late Charles Dawson.[24]

Robert Downes, an expert on the Sussex iron industry, examined the piece in the mid-1950s and noted 'three major errors' in the composition of the clock face drawing. These he believed would not have been made by anyone conversant with Wealden iron.

> Piles of wood are being burnt into charcoal without a covering of turf to slow down combustion, the blast furnace is shaped more like a large pottery kiln than an iron furnace, and the idea of the man in the bottom right-hand corner tapping the furnace to release the molten metal with a lance in his left hand, whilst he works the enormous bellows, with a kind of lavatory chain in his right hand is simply ludicrous.[25]

It is possible, however, that any of these errors could relate more to the original artist's unfamiliarity with the ironworking activities that he or she was attempting to record, rather than any deliberate attempt by a later individual to deceive. The piece could, on the nature of composition alone, still therefore be considered to be genuine, albeit with certain reservations.

Rather more serious are a number of curious chronological issues which generate suspicion concerning a supposed seventeenth- or eighteenth-century date for the drawing. First, as John Combridge has observed, the royal crown appearing at the bottom left of the dial is anachronistic, for it possesses 'the Imperial form which was given to the heraldic crown by making the two arches semi-circular [in] about 1880 after Queen Victoria became Empress of India [and] which continued in use to the end of King George VI's reign'.[26] Secondly, the headgear of the workmen shown engaged in ironworking do not possess the flat or slightly rounded forms more typical of the period.

> Instead, their tops are indented in the anachronistic style of the 'Homberg' hat which was popularised by the Prince of Wales, later King Edward VII, after his first stay at Bad Homberg in 1889, and of its derivative the 'trilby' hat, named after the heroine of G. du Maurier's novel Trilby, 1894.[27]

These lapses are, in Combridge's view, of sufficient seriousness to question the entire credibility of the piece.

Though the images do not appear to be genuine examples of Georgian art, the clock plate itself does appear to be authentic, Combridge noting that the basic dimensions of the piece were suitable for a 'wall time-piece-with-alarum'. The struck circles and numbers appearing on the dial are furthermore representative of pieces made between 1810 and 1830 [28] whilst the maker's name 'Beeching' and place of manufacture ('Ashburnham') are also set out in typically early nineteenth-century style. The Beeching family were prominent nineteenth-century clockmakers, working in East Sussex and Kent, and Combridge has suggested [29] that the original, unillustrated dial could have been the product of one Thomas Beeching working in Ashburnham in or around 1820. Unfortunately, with the disc plate having been removed, the remainder of the clock and case are lost to history.

The engraving recorded from Dawson's Beeching/Ashburnham clock dial does not, therefore, appear to be an authentic piece of early nineteenth-century art, having been added to a genuine disc plate, removed from an original 'pull-up-winding thirty-hour wall timepiece'[30] at some point in the late nineteenth or early twentieth century.

The Ashburnham Dial: conclusions

This of course brings us to two crucial questions, namely: 'who created the images?' and 'what would they have hoped to achieve with them?'. Since the mid-1950s, the Ashburnham Dial has been treated as an obvious fraud; a forgery designed to fool people into believing it to be a seventeenth- or cigh-teenth-century depiction of the Sussex iron industry. The fact that the piece originated from Charles Dawson's own private collection has served, in most minds, to confirm that the dial was just another of his many 'fraudulent objects', manufactured to increase his own standing as an antiquarian.[31]

Dawson, however, as has already been noted, never seems to have made use of the artefact; never displaying it, describing it in print nor discussing it within any of the local antiquarian circles. He never, as far as it is possible to ascertain, even appears to have acknowledged the existence of the piece; which seems strange if he had originally manufactured the item, presumably at no small personal cost, with the intent to deceive and defraud. The only certain connection that we have between the clock face and Dawson is that it was derived from his own private collection, but was not one of the objects passed over to Hastings Museum following his death in 1916. The fact that the item was in Dawson's possession is, of course, no certain guarantee of fraud, for here it could be just as likely that he was the hoaxer as the victim of a hoax.

A clue as to the origin and possible significance of the engraving is provided by a detailed analysis of its pictographic style. John Combridge, in his analysis of the piece, identified a number of key artistic flourishes which strongly suggest that the original artist was not Dawson, but his erstwhile collaborator at Hastings Castle and the Lavant Caves, John Lewis. Comparing the clock dial with drawings known to be the work of Dawson's colleague, Combridge observes that:

> Confirmatory evidence supporting the suggestion that John Lewis was himself the designer of the engraved scenes is afforded by their markedly map-like appearance, the result of the use not only of shifting bird's eye viewpoints, but also of the map-makers' conventions for the depiction of water and trees.[32]

Many of the scenes depicted on the dial seem to have been directly copied, with some minor alterations, from a mezzotint engraving of 1773 by Richard Earlom which itself was derived from a 1772 painting by Joseph Wright of Derby, entitled *The Iron Forge*[33] reproduced by Dawson in his published article 'Sussex Ironwork and Pottery'.[34]

Lewis, as has already been noted in the case of the Maresfield Map, quarrelled with Dawson at some point in 1911, at which point their friendship ended. Some have suggested that the dispute *could* have provided a motive for Lewis or his friends to perpetrate hoaxes upon Dawson in order to somehow undermine his academic credibility.[35] This is a possibility and the fact that Dawson acquired the dial but did not make a report on it, could further hint that he suspected the piece to be not altogether genuine. If we assume Dawson to have been involved in the significant manufacture of fraudulent objects, the dial could perhaps have been one such hoax, designed by Lewis at Dawson's direction, which was finally discarded (as a possible source of blackmail) when the two fell out in 1911.

Alternatively, the origins of the engraved dial could be far more innocent. For example, the piece could plausibly have been created as a gift for Dawson's birthday, a memento of past work or even perhaps 'on the occasion of his marriage in 1905'.[36] It is unfortunate that we cannot gauge exactly when the engraving was made, for this could help provide a potential motive for its creation. As a personal gift, however, Dawson would certainly not have included the dial in his collection of antiquities, something which could explain its later absence from the material bequeathed to Hastings Museum.

This is of course all rampant supposition, for although we can state that the dial was in Dawson's possession and that it appears to have been designed from a drawing made by John Lewis, there is no proof of any deliberate attempt at fraud by either party. Allegations of forgery only came from those later writers who assumed that the clock dial had originally been passed off as a genuine early eighteenth-century artefact, and for that we have no evidence whatsoever.

11

PILTDOWN MAN I

On the morning of Tuesday 15 February 1912, Arthur Woodward, Keeper of Geology of the British Museum (Natural History), opened the morning mail from his office desk little realising that one of the letters in his hand would change the course of his life forever. The letter, from his friend and colleague, the Uckfield solicitor and amateur antiquarian Charles Dawson, was in part a reply to a query from Woodward about expenses incurred during a recent fieldtrip to a Hastings quarry. In his earlier correspondence, Woodward had also asked Dawson whether he had heard anything about the new novel that Arthur Conan Doyle, creator of Sherlock Holmes, was writing. Doyle, then a resident of Crowborough, a small town to the north-east of Uckfield, was familiar to Woodward and Dawson, having corresponded with both men over the nature of potential fossil remains in the Sussex Weald.

Dawson's reply seemed, on the face of it, fairly innocuous. He related that, though he had 'not kept account of the expenditure' of the field visit to the Hastings quarry, it did not, in all probability, amount to very much. Yes, he had heard about the book currently being finished by Conan Doyle, entitled *The Lost World*, which featured a secret South American valley filled with prehistoric flora and fauna and visited by 'the usual "professor"'. Meanwhile work in the solicitors office had been 'very busy', whilst recent fossil-hunting activities had temporarily been curtailed due to the fact that one of his colleagues, the French Jesuit Felix Pelletier, had 'gone to Jersey'.[1]

Halfway through this otherwise pedestrian letter, Dawson dropped in an observation that must have instantly grabbed Woodward's attention:

> I have come across a very old Pleistocene (?) bed overlying the Hastings bed between Uckfield and Crowborough which I think is going to be interesting. It has a lot of iron-stained flints in it, so I suppose it is the oldest known flint gravel in the Weald. I portion [sic] of a human skull which will rival H. Heidelbergensis in solidity.[2]

The phrasing appeared somewhat garbled, possibly due to Dawson's obvious enthusiasm, but in essence Dawson appeared to be saying that he had *found* part of an early human skull contained *in situ* within an ancient deposit of gravel.

Eoanthropus dawsoni: the first reports

Dawson's comparison of his find to '*H. Heidelbergensis*' was intriguing for, in 1912 *Homo heidelbergensis*, or 'Heidelberg man', represented one of the earliest of human ancestors so far recovered from Europe. Found in a quarry on the banks of the River Neckar near the village of Mauer (halfway between Heidelberg and Mannheim in Germany), Heidelberg man comprised a single, robust, ape-like jaw, lacking a prominent chin. The jaw possessed all its teeth, which were quite human in appearance, along its right side, together with the first and second incisor, canine and third molar on the left. The bone had been recovered from a deeply buried layer of sand and gravel and had been associated with a variety of fossilised mammal remains. Despite the poor survival of the data set, Otto Schettensack, a palaeontologist from the University of Heidelberg, confidently asserted that the remains represented the best evidence to date for an ape-like ancestor of the human race, a predecessor of both modern *Homo sapiens* and the Neanderthals.

Dawson had, at some time prior to 1912, examined a cast of the famous Heidelberg jaw for himself. The exact date and circumstances of this examination are not recorded, though Dawson later related in the pages of the *Hastings and East Sussex Naturalist* that 'the massive appearance of the two pieces of cranium from Piltdown made it seem likely that they had belonged to an individual allied to the original possessor of the Heidelberg jaw'.[3]

If the skull fragments that Dawson claimed to have in his possession were in any way comparable to the 1907 Heidelberg find, then this would prove to be an explosive discovery. Up to 1912, it is fair to say that British palaeontology had been skulking around in the doldrums. French and German scientists had, throughout the nineteenth century, produced a range of well-preserved Palaeolithic deposits including skeletal remains such as *Homo neanderthalensis* (Neanderthal man) and a wealth of worked flint assemblages, each helping to identify specific 'cultures' such as the Acheulean, Magdalenian, Levaloisian and Mousterian. In comparison, very little had been recovered from Britain, despite the best efforts of many capable palaeontologists, geologists and antiquarian researchers. To make matters worse, what meagre remains of the period had been recorded from British contexts provided some French palaeontologists with a rather derogatory term for their British counterparts: 'chasseurs de cailloux' or 'pebble hunters'.[4]

However eager Woodward may have been to examine Dawson's find, the nature of both men's work appears to have prevented an immediate inspection.[5] On 24 March 1912, Dawson wrote to Woodward explaining that 'our visit to the gravel bed will depend on the weather, at present the roads leading to it are impassable and excavation is out of the question'.[6] Despite any problems associated with the weather, Dawson was able to forward two of his gravel bed discoveries to Woodward on 26 March together with a brief note which read 'will you very kindly identify enclosed for me. I think the larger one is hippo?'.[7] Almost by return of post Woodward had replied with the note '28th Premolar of Hippopotamus and a piece of sandstone concretion'.[8]

His appetite whetted by Dawson's description of the human remains, their context and possible association with ancient mammalian remains, Woodward seems to have counselled the Uckfield solicitor to some form of secrecy until the exact nature of the discovery could be ascertained, for on 28 March Dawson wrote:

> I will of course take care that no one sees the pieces of skull who has any knowledge of the subject and leave all to you. On second thoughts I have decided to wait until you and I can go over by ourselves to look at the bed of gravel. It is not far to walk from Uckfield and it will do us good![9]

Evidently Dawson's enthusiasm eventually got the better of him and, despite his insistence to Woodward, he began to show the skull fragment to people who clearly possessed 'knowledge of the subject'. On 20 April, Dawson visited his friend the Jesuit priest Marie-Joseph Pierre Teilhard de Chardin, then living in Hastings. Writing shortly after to his parents, Teilhard commented that Dawson:

> brought me some prehistoric remains (silex [flint], elephant and hippopotamus, and especially, a very thick, well-preserved human skull) which he had found in the alluvium deposits not far from here; he did this in order to stir me up to some similar expeditions; but I hardly have time for that anymore.[10]

Other people to whom Dawson showed his prized skull fragment appear also to have included Samuel Allinson Woodhead, then a chemistry instructor at Uckfield Agricultural College, Henry Sargent, a former Curator of Bexhill Museum and Ernest Victor Clarke, a close personal friend.[11] Perhaps the length of time it was taking for Woodward to visit the site was proving unbearable, or perhaps Dawson was simply trying, in Teilhard's words, 'to stir' people up in the hope of gathering together a team of experts or helpers for any future expedition to the gravel bed. Finally, on Friday 24 May 1912, the paths of Dawson and Woodward finally crossed, the solicitor walking into the Keeper of Geology's South Kensington office and revealing the pieces of ancient skull with the remark 'How's that for Heidelberg?'.[12] Woodward's reaction is unfortunately lost to us, but the find was evidently far greater than he could ever have expected.

Having established the true nature of Dawson's find, Woodward then needed to establish the provenance and exact circumstances of discovery. One of the earliest (and most detailed) accounts of the initial discovery was provided by Dawson in the *Hastings and East Sussex Naturalist* for 1913, and it is worth repeating his comments here in full:

> Many years ago, I think just at the end of the last century, business led me to Piltdown, which is situated on the Hastings Beds and some four or five miles north of the line where the last of the flint-bearing gravels were recorded to occur. It was a Court Baron of the Manor of Barkham at which I was presiding, and when business was over and the customary dinner to the tenants of the Manor was awaited, I went for a stroll on the road outside the Manor House. My attention was soon attracted by some iron-stained flints not usual in the district and reminding me of some Tertiary gravel I had seen in Kent. Being curious as to the use of the gravel in so remote a spot, I enquired at dinner of the chief tenant of the Manor where he obtained it. Having in remembrance the usually accepted views of geologists above mentioned, I was very much surprised when I was informed that the flint gravel was dug on the farm and that some men were then actually digging it to be put on the farm roads, that this had been going on so far as living memory extended, and that a former Lord of the Manor had the gravel dug and carried some miles north into the country for his coach drive at 'Searles'. I was glad to get the dinner over and visit the gravel pit, where, sure enough, two farm hands were at work digging in a shallow pit three or four feet deep, close to the house. The gravel is an old river-bed gravel chiefly composed of hand-rolled Wealden iron-sandstone with occasional sub-angular flints. The men informed me that they had never noticed any fossils or bones in the gravel. As I surmised that any fossils found in the gravel would probably be interesting and might lead to fixing the date of the deposit, I specially charged the men to keep a look out.
>
> Subsequently I made occasional visits, but found that the pit was only intermittently worked for a few weeks in the year, according to the requirements of the farm roads. On one of my visits, one of the labourers handed to me a small piece of a bone which I recognised as being a portion of human cranium (part of a left parietal) but beyond the fact that it was of immense thickness, there was little else of which to take notice. I at once made a long search, but could find nothing more, and I soon afterwards made a whole day's search in company with Mr A. Woodhead MSc, but the bed appeared to be unfossiliferous. There were many pieces of dark brown ironstone closely resembling the piece of skull, and the season being wet, any fossil would have been difficult to see. I still paid occasional visits to the pit, but it was not until several years later that, when having a look over the rain-washed spoil heaps, I lighted on a larger piece of the same skull which included a portion of the left supra-orbital border. Shortly afterwards I found a piece of hippopotamus tooth.[13]

Dawson presented a more compressed version of the *Hastings and East Sussex Naturalist* story to the Geological Society on 18 December 1912 as part of his presentation, later published in the *Quarterly Journal of the Geological Society London* (117-151). In this account the formal dinner of the tenants of Barkham Manor is omitted,[14] as is the 'whole day's search in company with Mr A. Woodhead'. The essential details of the discovery, namely the observation of flints in the road leading to the discovery of two labourers extracting gravel, remains the same, as does Dawson's request to 'preserve anything that they might find'.[15] One useful addition to the Geological Society report, however, is the approximate date of Dawson's discovery of a second 'larger piece of the same skull' which is cited as having occurred 'in the autumn of 1911'.[16]

Although Dawson is vague as to exactly when he first encountered the gravel digging at Barkham Manor, other than to note it was probably 'just at the end of the last century', given that the discovery occurred during a meeting of the Court Baron of the Manor, it should be possible to supply a more accurate date. Dawson, in a letter to Woodward dated 22 May 1915, enclosed 'a notice of our four-yearly meeting at Piltdown which led years ago to the discovery of the gravel bed'.[17] As the meeting of the Court Baron to which Dawson draws Woodward's attention to was scheduled to occur on 'Thursday, the 10th day of June, 1915 at 12 noon', it must follow that there had been previous meetings in 1911, 1907, 1903 and 1899. Joseph Weiner, who examined the records of the Barkham Manor Estates in the early 1950s, observed that Dawson had assumed Stewardship in 1898, presiding over his first court on 27 July 1899.[18] Such a date would fit perfectly with Dawson's statement that he had investigated the gravel digging 'at the end of the last century',[19] although Dawson's own (rather vague) observation to the Geological Society in December 1912, that the first discovery of the gravel occurred 'several years ago', would seem to fit more with a meeting in either 1907 or 1904 (the four-yearly meeting scheduled for 1903 was, for some reason, postponed until 3 October 1904).[20]

Unfortunately, attempts to pin down the date of Dawson's subsequent visit, where he was handed the 'small piece of a bone' by the farm labourers, does not appear in any official report. If Dawson was not tied to visiting the site during meetings of the Court Baron, which occurred on 3 October 1904, 10 May 1907 and 4 August 1911,[21] he could have picked up the artefact at any time between 1899 and his 1911, when we know he found the second 'larger' fragment. A report appearing in *The Times* the day after Dawson and Woodward's presentation to the Geological Society was, however, rather more explicit concerning the date of the first discovery of skull which it states occurred 'four years ago'.[22] If Dawson had been quoted correctly as inferring that the first piece of skull was handed to him in 1908, it seems odd that this rather crucial fact escaped mention in either the official or subsequent reports. Most writers on the Piltdown discoveries accept the suggestion that 1908 was indeed the year that Dawson was first handed a piece of skull.[23]

Whatever the *exact* date that the first piece of skull was found, it is clear, from Dawson's own account that there was a gap of 'several years' before the larger piece preserving the 'left supra-orbital border' was finally located in 1911.[24] What Arthur Woodward does not appear to have picked up on, either on receipt of Dawson's letter of 15 February 1912 (where he first informed him of the finding of the skull) or at any subsequent time (and especially after the presentation to the Geological Society in 1912), was the lengthy time gap between Dawson's first discovery and his reporting of the find. If the first skull fragment had indeed been made 'several years' before the second (and possibly as early as 1899), Woodward ought to have questioned why Dawson had not mentioned it to him before. It is possible that the solicitor, having found the first piece, may have wished to hold back from alerting his friend, perhaps hoping either to make further discoveries or to be able to conduct more research into the nature of the piece. It has to be said, however, that the letter to Woodward supplies no additional information beyond the bare fact of the discovery, something which Dawson could conceivably have written to Woodward about as early as 1908. Furthermore, as both Dawson and Woodward had in 1912 only just examined a quarry near Hastings together (as set out in the opening paragraph of Dawson's letter of 15 February), why did Dawson not present or even discuss the find with Woodward then? Surely the fieldtrip would have been the perfect opportunity to show the artefact and gauge Woodward's opinion. A visit to Piltdown itself could even have been arranged in order to inspect the gravel at first hand. No explanation for this curious oversight on Woodward's behalf, nor indeed of Dawson's curiously long delay in reporting the find, is ever provided by either man.

Here we encounter another problem with Dawson's story, for if, as Dawson implies, the first meeting with the farm labourers excavating the gravel at Barkham Manor occurred in 1899, it follows that his request for them to 'keep a look out' for interesting finds did not bear fruit until around 1908. This point, left unremarked upon by Woodward, was picked by Weiner who observed that 'the two labourers must have kept Dawson's request in mind, or been reminded of it, over a period of *some eight or nine years* before 'one of the men (and the context makes clear, one of the *same* men) at last alighted on a piece of cranium.'[25] Is it really conceivable that Dawson's request was recalled by the workmen after such a lengthy time lag and with no artefacts recovered in the meantime?

In his book *The Earliest Englishman*, published after his death in 1948, Arthur Woodward presented a slight variant on the story of the discovery. In this account, the workmen charged with extracting the gravel, after several unsuccessful visits to the area by Dawson,

> dug up what they thought was a coco-nut, and felt sure that this was the
> kind of thing which would please their curious and presumably generous

friend. They could scarcely doubt that it was a coco-nut because it was rounded and brown and of the right thickness, with the inside marked in the usual way by branching lines and grooves. It seemed a familiar and common object, but, as it was a little bulky to keep, they broke it with a shovel and threw away all but one piece, which they put in a waistcoat pocket to show Mr Dawson on the first opportunity. When he came round again, the men produced their find and described to him the 'coco-nut' from which they had broken it. They showed him the place where they had found it, and told him that the pieces which they had thrown away were in the heaps of rubbish around. Mr Dawson recognised at once that the supposed coco-nut was really a human skull of unusual thickness and texture, which had been hardened and stained brown by oxide of iron in the gravel. He did not show any excitement or concern about the misfortune that had happened to the unique fossil, but he patiently waited for a favourable occasion to examine the pit and see whether the labourers' story was true.

Time after time Mr Dawson visited the spot and searched the rain-washed heaps of gravel, but it was not until a few years had elapsed that he found a second piece of the skull, which fitted exactly one broken edge of the fragment which the men had given to him. Renewed search eventually unearthed a third piece which fitted the other two, and then came two more separated pieces which certainly belonged to the same skull. The men's story was thus confirmed, and it was evidently desirable to dig up and sift all the gravel which remained in and around the pit.[26]

Where did this particular version of the story originate? Dawson's original statements concerning the discovery of Piltdown man describe the primary find as a single 'small piece of a bone' discovered in, or around, 1908. Nowhere does Dawson himself relate a story, at least in print, recounting the unearthing of a more complete skull which was deliberately smashed in the misguided belief that it was a coconut, and yet Woodward appears quite positive in his belief that this was how it actually happened. The origins of the 'coco-nut' story can only have lain with Dawson himself, for no one ever claims to have interviewed the two anonymous farmhands, who could have verified the statement, and Woodward does not appear to have spoken in detail with any of Dawson's early colleagues, such as Samuel Allinson Woodhead.

Walsh suggests that the incident was concocted by Dawson as a way of lending colour to the story of how the piece was first found, but that Dawson 'used it only in conversation', never intending to put it into the permanency of the printed word.[27] This may well be true, for certainly William Lewis Abbott, jeweller and amateur geologist, related a similar story in February 1913,[28] whilst *The Times*, relating the details of Dawson's presentation to the Geological Society in December 1912, commented that one of the labourers originally gave Dawson 'a fragment of a human skull which they had just discovered and had evidently broken up and thrown away'.[29]

No mention of a coconut, but a similar idea, albeit different to the account provided by Dawson in the official reports of 1913. The version of the story published in the *Quarterly Journal of the Geological Society* for that year does suggest why so many cranial fragments of the same individual had been found scattered across various spoil heaps, 'apparently the whole or greater portion of the human skull had been shattered by the workmen, who had thrown away the pieces unnoticed'.[30] But this is very different to the deliberate breaking up and discarding of a 'coco-nut' for here the labourers were not aware of their actions. Woodward does not appear to question the obvious divergence in accounts, and neither does he comment upon the strange idea that two labourers, having specifically been asked to look out for unusual artefacts, managed to deliberately destroy the only interesting thing that they had seen in eight years of digging.

> Glaringly obvious is the inanity of the claim that the men kept only one piece of what they found as of possible interest to Dawson while throwing the greater part away. If there was a chance for financial reward... why throw away any portion of the object before they had Dawson's reaction? Why keep only a single piece? The men had only to drop the whole thing on a shelf in a shed awaiting their man's next visit. Once dwelt on, the second contradiction is even more blatant. The men, supposedly, broke up the skull because they thought it was only a worthless coconut. But did they really expect that a bit of coconut shell would be of interest to an antiquarian? [31]

There is one final, rather important problem with the various accounts supplied by both Dawson and Woodward which explain the initial discovery of Piltdown man: namely the supposed location of the gravel extraction pit (**71**). Dawson says that, having seen 'iron-stained flints' in the road outside the Manor House, he was surprised to hear that not only were the flints derived from the farm, but that 'some men were then actually digging it.'[32] Why should the location of the extraction pit and the fact that two men were at present working it have surprised Dawson? In order to have gained access to Barkham Manor so as to attend the meeting, Dawson would have to have passed directly in front of the gravel pit. Why, given his recorded interest in the sort of artefacts accidentally unearthed by labourers, did he not pause on his way in to the meeting to inquire what had been found? Why did he not remember the pit when told by the chief tenant of the Manor where the unusual flints had been obtained? Once again, Woodward does not question the discrepancy in Dawson's account, nor wonder why the published version describing the location of the pit was so obviously misleading.

71 *Piltdown I: the Barkham Manor gravel pit 'in flood' during the winter of 1913. The manor house may be seen in the background*

Eoanthropus dawsoni: 1912

Arthur Woodward's analysis of the first skull fragments from Piltdown that Dawson presented to him on 24 May 1912, left him in no doubt as to the potential significance of the find. Woodward was later to recall that, in the discussion that followed the preliminary examination, he and Dawson decided to commence work in the gravel pit almost immediately in the hope of retrieving more remains: 'we felt a little impatient because we had to wait until the end of May before the pit was dry enough for us to dig to the bottom of the gravel'.[33]

Dawson swiftly obtained permission for work from the landowner, George Maryon-Wilson and the tenant farmer, Robert Kenward, both of whom he knew quite well (**72**). The secrecy that Woodward first impressed upon Dawson back in March 1912,[34] when he first became aware of the potential significance of the find, appears to have been retained, for Dawson did not reveal the true motive for the excavation, merely expressing 'interest in the brown flints there'.[35] Dawson had by this time recruited his old fossil-hunting companion Father Marie-Joseph Pierre Teilhard de Chardin, and a date for the initial phase of examination at Piltdown was set for 2 June.[36] Teilhard, in a letter to his parents, observed that much of the morning of the 2nd was spent preparing for the excursion.

72 *Piltdown I: posing by the gravel pit (visible to the left of shot), on the drive to Barkham Manor during the summer of 1912. The individuals pictured are, from right to left, Robert Kenward and his dog, Charles Dawson, Arthur Smith Woodward, 'Chipper' the goose and Venus Hargreaves*

> Around 10 o'clock, we were in Uckfield where professor Woodward joined us... At three o'clock, armed with all the makings of a picnic, we started off in the car.[37]

The greater part of the day had, therefore, been lost by the time the team of Dawson, Teilhard and Woodward arrived at the Barkham Manor gravel pit. Fortunately 'a man was there to help us dig'.[38] Though not specifically mentioned at the time, it is probable that this unnamed workman was one Venus Hargreaves (**73**), who appears to have been the sole labourer employed throughout 1912 and 1913. The strategy of the first day's investigation would appear simple enough: Dawson, Teilhard and Woodward were first to inspect all existing spoil heaps surrounding the area of recent gravel extraction, whilst Hargreaves generated more spoil through the enlargement of the pit.

The work was at first painstakingly slow, 'for every spade-full had to be carefully sifted and examined'[39], so as not to miss the even smallest of artefacts (**74**). Agonising though this must have been, especially for Dawson who had been keen to examine the pit for some considerable time, Woodward observed that it was:

> probably an advantage to work only at intervals for short periods, because the discovery of bones and teeth, all stained brown, in a dark-coloured gravel, which was full of bits of ironstone and brown flints, needed very

73 *Piltdown I: a posed shot of the main excavation team of 1912 comprising Arthur Smith Woodward (extreme right), Venus Hargreaves (centre) and Charles Dawson (seated with shovel). Robert Kenward Jnr is standing to the extreme left of the shot, whilst 'Chipper' the goose protects the pit from unwelcome visitors*

74 *Piltdown I: Charles Dawson (extreme left) and Arthur Smith Woodward examine freshly excavated spoil in the sieve whilst Venus Hargreaves stands with pickaxe in the main trench during the summer of 1913*

close and slow examination of every fragment. We could not employ more than one labourer to do the heavy work of digging because every spade full had to be watched, and generally passed through a sieve. It was necessary also to crawl over the spoil heaps each time that the rain washed the particles of gravel and made them more easy to examine. We spread the gravel as much as possible, so that, if there were rain between our visits, it could be well washed in readiness for our return.[40]

At this point there is some confusion over the exact sequence of events. Dawson, in his presentation to the Geological Society, is unspecific as to when material was first unearthed, noting only that:

We accordingly gave up as much time as we could spare since last spring (1912), and completely turned over and sifted what spoil-material remained. We also dug up and sifted such portions of the gravel as had been left undisturbed by the workmen.[41]

The fieldwork at Barkham Manor continued sporadically throughout June, July and August 1912, and, in the absence of specific dates, any of the finds generated could conceivably have been recovered at any point within this broad time bracket. Unfortunately neither Woodward nor Dawson appears to have kept a notebook in order to chronicle the events as they unfolded (or if they did, such a work has not survived). In fact, the only time that a key date may plausibly be cited for the 1912-3 season is when a visitor to the excavation, such as Teilhard, makes note of it in their own diary or personal correspondence. The closest that Arthur Woodward himself comes to recording the sporadic nature of the gravel pit examination is when he observes, in *The Earliest Englishman*, that 'we were both well occupied with ordinary duties during the week, so we could devote only our weekends and occasional holidays to the task'.[42]

Dawson's summary account for the pages of the *Quarterly Journal of the Geological Society* notes the discovery of unspecified numbers of cranial fragments from the spoil heaps, the 'right half of a human mandible' and a 'small portion of the occipital bone' from the 'undisturbed gravel', teeth of elephant, mastodon, beaver, horse and hippopotamus, as well as a red deer antler, a deer metatarsal and a number of worked flints.[43] The implication must be that these were found throughout the 1912 season. Woodward's later account, in *The Earliest Englishman*, is unfortunately no real help here as it conflates all elements of the fieldwork into a few short sentences.[44] Perhaps, by the time Woodward came to compile the book (which, although not published until 1948, appears to have commenced no later than 1915),[45] he had become unclear as to the *exact* order that material had been found. Re-reading Dawson's comments on the 1912 dig cannot have helped.

In the account of the excavation supplied to the *Hastings and East Sussex Naturalist* in 1913, Dawson is slightly more specific, observing that the first stage of investigation at Barkham Manor did not go terribly well for, 'there were many days of most unpromising work.'[46]

Teilhard, in a letter to his parents on 3 June 1912, however, commented that, despite not having arrived on site for the first day's digging until after 3pm, the team:

worked for several hours and finally had success. Dawson discovered a new fragment of the famous human skull; he already had three pieces of it, and I myself put a hand on a fragment of elephant's molar; this made me really worth something in Woodward's eyes. He jumped on the pieces with an enthusiasm of a youth and all the fire that his apparent coldness covered came out. To meet my train, I had to leave before the other two were to abandon their search.[47]

Of course the crucial aspect here is that Teilhard was recalling the events of the first day not less than *twenty-four hours after they had occurred*. The initial hours at Barkham Manor had, therefore, proved to be highly successful, with strong indications that, not only were more pieces of the human skull in evidence, but that more was undoubtedly to come. Quite why Dawson (and much later Woodward), provided such a downbeat account of the excavations 'unpromising' beginning, remains a mystery. Perhaps neither man could remember the exact order in which things were discovered or perhaps both were embarrassed that spectacular finds were retrieved within a very short time of work having got underway.

As the work progressed over the following weeks, more exciting discoveries came to light, Woodward noting later that:

in one heap of soft material rejected by the workmen we found three pieces of the right parietal bone of the human skull – one piece on each of three successive days. These fragments fitted together perfectly, and so had evidently not been disturbed since they were thrown away.[48]

At some point in late June,[49] Dawson found the crucial fragment of skeleton which could at last be used to compare the Piltdown specimen with that of *Homo heidelbergensis*: a jaw (**75**). The piece was recovered from:

a somewhat deeper depression of the undisturbed gravel... so far as I could judge, guiding myself by the position of a tree 3 or 4 yards away, the spot was identical with that upon which the men were at work when the first portion of the cranium was found several years ago.[50]

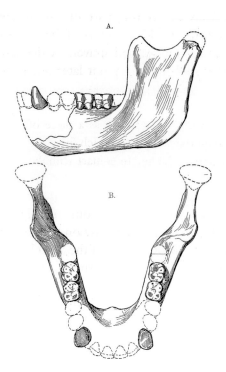

75 *Piltdown I: a 1913 restoration of the jaw of* Eoanthropus dawsoni *showing the left side and view from above*

Aside from its scientific value, the jaw was an important piece of evidence for, as it derived from a patch of *undisturbed* gravel, it was the first *in situ* discovery from the entire investigation of the pit. It demonstrated that, not only was this indeed the correct place to dig (and that the earlier cranial fragments had not merely been introduced from somewhere else) but also that the activities of the earlier farm labourers had not completely eradicated all trace of their early ancestor. In an alternative account of the dig, Dawson relates the circumstances of his priceless discovery 'I struck part of the lowest stratum of the gravel with my pick, and out flew a portion of the lower jaw from the iron-bound gravel'.[51]

Dawson was not the only one to find human remains at this stage in the excavations, for:

> Dr Woodward also dug up a small portion of the occipital bone of the skull from within a yard of the point where the jaw was discovered, and at precisely the same level. The jaw appeared to have been broken at the symphysis and abraded, perhaps when it lay fixed in the gravel, and before its complete deposition. The fragments of cranium show little or no sign of rolling or other abrasion, save an incision at the back of the parietal, probably caused by a workman's pick.[52]

Contrary to the impression given by Dawson in this part of the article appearing in the *Quarterly Journal of the Geological Society*, the 'small portion of the occipital bone' was not 'dug up' from undisturbed gravel, as the jaw appeared to have been, but from a nearby spoil heap, a point later noted by Woodward himself:

> After much inspection, which prevented my discarding it as a piece of ironstone, I found in another heap an important fragment which fitted the broken edge of the occipital bone and gave us the line to contact with the left parietal bone.[53]

The bone in question had therefore *already been removed* from its original context before Woodward discovered it. It is possible that Dawson had meant to say that his colleague had 'dug the bone up from the top of the spoil heap', a relatively minor mistake in phrasing perhaps, but a rather crucial difference from finding the piece *in situ* (as the jaw had apparently been).

Human bone was not the only thing recovered during this first investigation at Barkham Manor, a small but diverse collection of faunal remains being assembled. In their report to the Geological Society, Dawson and Woodward recorded that:

> we found two small broken pieces of a molar tooth of a rather early Pliocene type of elephant, also a much-rolled... molar of Mastodon, portions of two teeth of Hippopotamus, and two molar teeth of a Pleistocene beaver. In the adjacent field to the west, on the surface close to the hedge dividing it from the gravel bed, we found portions of a red deer's antler and the tooth of a Pleistocene horse. These may have been thrown away by the workmen, or may have been turned up by a plough which traversed the upper strata of the continuation of this gravel-bed. Among the fragments of bone found in the spoil-heaps occurred part of a deer's metatarsal, split longitudinally. This bone bears upon its surface certain small cuts and scratches, which appear to have been made by man. All the specimens are highly mineralised with iron oxide.[54]

Apart from the bone assemblages, a number of apparently worked flints (**76**) were also retrieved during the course of the 1912 excavations. Of course it was flint material in the trackways around Barkham Manor that had drawn Dawson to the gravel pit in the first place. The discovery of humanly worked, or 'knapped', flint at Piltdown would prove a significant boost to the excavations, demonstrating the presence of early prehistoric activity. It was even possible that the flint tools themselves could have been generated by the ape-like human that the team was in the process of investigating. The first flints recovered were generally brown in colour, Dawson observing that they:

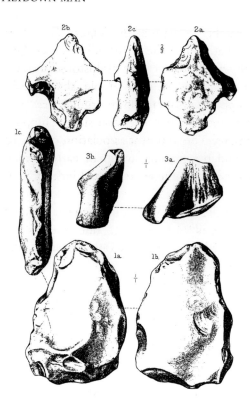

76 *Piltdown I: artefacts from the 1913 investigations at Barkham Manor comprising a 'flaked flint' (1a, b and c), an 'eolith' (2a, b and c) and a premolar of a rhinoceros (3a and b)*

appear to be in every way similar to the plateau flints of Ightham (Kent), and generally to those of the High-Plateau gravels of the North and South Downs. There is the same appearance of tabular and prismatic structure, 'frost fractures', thick iron-stained patina, and often the same tendency to assume the well-known 'Eolithic' forms. There also occur more occasionally certain brilliantly-coloured iron-red flints, presumably more highly oxidised than the prevailing flints... Among the flints we found several undoubted flint-implements, 9 besides numerous 'Eoliths'. The workmanship of the former is similar to that of the Chellean or pre-Chellean stage 10; but in the majority of the Piltdown specimens the work appears chiefly on one face of the implements. They have been very slightly rolled or worn, and, although iron-stained, their patina is not so strong and thick as that of the other flints in the bed. Their form is thick, and the flaking is broad and sparing, the original 'bark', or surface, of the flint frequently remaining at the grasp, the whole implement thus having a very rude and massive form.[55]

During the late nineteenth and early twentieth century 'eoliths', or 'stones of the dawn', were a popular subject of sometimes heated debate. These crudely broken flints were considered by some to represent the first human tools, though others viewed them less charitably as natural breakages. The main problem with these 'dawn stones' was that, unlike the beautifully worked flint axes, scrapers, projectile points and digging tools of later prehistoric periods, the typical eolith often comprised no more than a simple sharp edge, sometimes with signs of battering. Supporters of the eolith argued that frost shattering or riverbed tumble would not produce the one-sided chipping clearly evident on a number of specimens. The apparent association of eoliths with the bones of extinct mammals and the possible traces of early human activity appeared to increase the likelihood that these stones had indeed been deliberately created.

Dawson was, of course, well aware of the controversy that then surrounded eoliths, noting that 'it is necessary to speak of them with due reserve and caution'.[56] This caution was further explained in Dawson's paper to the *Hastings and East Sussex Naturalist*:

> If these specimens are subsequently proved to be 'artefacts' they must belong to the early dawn of the formation of implements by man. But much work remains to be done, both as to this and other branches of the subject relating to the earliest history of Man, including the correlation of implements and the strata which contain them, and perhaps at no time before the present was the subject so extended and complicated.[57]

If the eoliths were to be accepted as genuine products of early human endeavour, then it was vital that an accurate provenance be obtained. Unfortunately Dawson was vague as to exactly *where* the material had origi-nated, noting only that 'they occur both in the gravel-bed and on the surface of the plough-lands, and are found in both a rolled and an unrolled (or very slightly rolled) condition'.[58]

On completion of the first season at Piltdown, Dawson and Woodward compiled the data and set about preparing for a formal announcement to their fellow academics and the world's press. Dawson was understandably keen, before he made any pronouncements on his find, to ensure that the pieces of human skull recovered were indeed fossilised. For this reason he submitted 'a small fragment of the skull' to Samuel Allinson Woodhead 'Public Analyst for East Sussex & Hove, and Agricultural Analyst for East Sussex'.[59] Dawson had of course worked with Woodhead before, successfully utilising his knowledge of chemistry in relation to the nature of the Heathfield gas and in his article on dene holes. Woodhead reported back that:

> the specific gravity of the bone (powdered) is 2.115 (water at 5°C. as standard). No gelatin or organic material is present. There is a large proportion of phosphates (originally present in the bone) and a considerable proportion of iron. Silica is absent.[60]

The skull fragment tested was, therefore, seen to be almost completely fossilised. Unfortunately the jaw was not examined at this or at any other time, in order to determine whether it was similarly fossilised. Such a test would have established straight away whether the skull and jaw were in any way related. This curious oversight was never picked up or questioned by Arthur Woodward or any of the scientists to whom the remains were later presented.

Within weeks of the completion of the fieldwork in August 1912, rumours were starting to circulate about the startling nature of the Piltdown discoveries. On Thursday 21 November the *Manchester Guardian* printed a story leaked by an anonymous informant. Under the headline 'THE EARLIEST MAN? REMARKABLE DISCOVERY IN SUSSEX', the paper observed that:

> One of the most important prehistoric finds of our time has been made in Sussex. In spite of the extreme secrecy of the authorities who are in posses-sion of the relic the news is leaking out and is causing great excitement among scientists, although there are very few even among geologists and anthropologists who have any first-hand information. The facts are that a few weeks ago men quarrying in a deep gravel pit turned up a human skull. It was in fragments, but there was enough of it for the experts to form a conclusive judgement. It turns out to be the skull of a Palaeolithic man, and is by far the earliest trace of mankind that has yet been found in England... The theory of evolution applied to man suggest that he had a common origin with the apes, and since Darwin's theory gained acceptance the need has been felt for discovering 'the missing link' between the highest apes and the lowest men. The gulf between the two has not yet been bridged, though we must wait for the judgement of the experts to know how much it has been narrowed by the discovery in Sussex.[61]

Woodward was unimpressed. Full disclosure of the Piltdown remains was not due to take place for another month, giving himself and Dawson more time to prepare their statements and complete the first reconstruction. His exasper-ation was increased when a number of reporters descended upon his office at the British Museum (Natural History) and demanded to know whether the leak was true. Woodward confirmed the story, but provided only circumstan-tial detail, asking the journalists to be patient.[62]

Annoyed though he may have been that the story had been leaked, press speculation over the nature of the find certainly helped excite both public and academic interest. As a consequence, the numbers descending upon London's Burlington House, where the Geological Society's meeting was to take place, was unprecedented, one reporter observing that 'never has the meeting room been so crowded'.[63] The presentation began at 8pm, with Dawson providing a summary of the events leading up to the initial discovery, the geological background and the preliminary results of the first season's excavation.

Woodward's presentation focussed upon the interpretation of the Piltdown skull and the technical nature of its reconstruction (**77** & **78**). There could be no doubt, he stated, concerning the perceived humanity of the skeletal remains.

> While the skull, indeed, is essentially human, only approaching a lower grade in certain characters of the brain, in the attachment for the neck, the extent of the temporal muscles, and in the probably large size of the face, the mandible appears to be almost precisely that of an ape, with nothing human except the molar teeth.[64]

In conclusion, Woodward noted that the characteristics of the Piltdown skull thus outlined presented the question of:

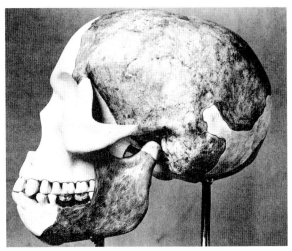

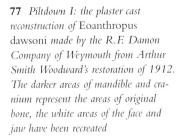

77 *Piltdown I: the plaster cast reconstruction of* Eoanthropus dawsoni *made by the R.F. Damon Company of Weymouth from Arthur Smith Woodward's restoration of 1912. The darker areas of mandible and cranium represent the areas of original bone, the white areas of the face and jaw have been recreated*

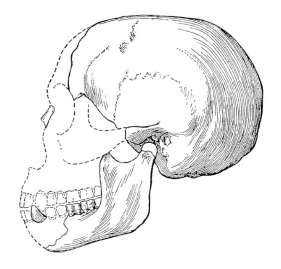

78 *Piltdown I: Arthur Smith Woodward's speculative reconstruction based upon the surviving pieces of* Eoanthropus dawsoni *recovered up to 1913*

whether it shall be referred to a new species of *Homo* itself, or whether it shall be considered as indicating a hitherto unknown genus. The brain-case alone, though specifically distinguished from all known human crania of equally low brain-capacity, by the characters of its supra-orbital border, and the upward extension of its temporal muscles, could scarcely be removed from the genus *Homo*; the bone of the mandible so far as preserved, however, is so completely distinct from that of *Homo* in the shape of the symphysis and the parallelism of the molar-premolar series on the two sides, that the facial parts of the skull almost certainly differed in fundamental characters from those of any typically human skull. I therefore propose that the Piltdown specimen be regarded as the type of a new genus of the family *Hominidae* to be named *Eoanthropus* and defined by its ape-like mandibular symphysis, parallel molar-premolar series, and narrow lower molars which do not decrease in size backwards; to which diagnostic characters may probably be added the steep frontal eminence and slight development of brow-ridges. The species of which the skull and mandible have now been described in detail may be named *Eoanthropus dawsoni*, in honour of its discoverer.[65]

The third presentation that evening, by Grafton Elliot Smith, Professor of Anatomy at Manchester University, provided details on the brain of *Eoanthropus dawsoni*. Having taken a cast of the braincase and studying the endocranial markings preserved, Smith observed that there was:

> a very prominent elliptical swelling, the summing of which... is raised more than a centimetre above the level of the surrounding cortex... This peculiar conformation assumes quite a special interest when it is remembered that this obviously expanding area occupies the position where in the modern human brain is developed the territory which recent clinical research leads us to associate with the power of spontaneous elaboration of speech and the ability to recall names.[66]

In the lively discussion that followed the presentations, most seemed to agree with Dawson, Woodward and Smith concerning the importance of the find, but many took exception to the proposed age of the early human. Dawson and Woodward had made the case that the 'stratified gravel at Piltdown is of Pleistocene age' (**79** & **80**), but noted, as a word of caution, that its lower levels contained animal bone 'derived from some destroyed Pliocene deposit' close by.[67]

'Pliocene' and 'Pleistocene' are geological terms which, at the time the Piltdown remains were discovered in the early years of the twentieth century, possessed relatively elastic qualities. Today we interpret the Pliocene as the fifth epoch of the Cenozoic (or era of 'recent life'). The Pliocene, which spanned

79 *Piltdown I: a section cut through the edge of the Barkham Manor gravel pit in order to show the relationship of the Tunbridge Wells sand (lowest layer in the section) and the artefact bearing gravels above, taken by John Frisby in 1912. The partially visable boy standing on the ground surface at the edge of the pit is Arthur Smith Woodward's son Cyril*

the period between 5.2 million and 1.6 million years ago (being preceded by the Palaeocene, Eocene, Oligocene and Miocene), was an epoch of geological change in which the continent of Africa collided into Europe, creating the Mediterranean Sea, and South America impacted with the North. The Pleistocene, which followed the Pliocene, is often referred to the 'Great Ice Age'. In fact it was a time of at least nine major periods of glacial advance, when ice sheets covered anything up to between 20 and 30 per cent of the world's surface. At the maximum point of glacial advance, during a period known as the Anglian (which began approximately 478,000 years ago and ended around 423,000), the ice sheet over Britain extended as far south as northern Cornwall, following a line towards Bristol, north London and out towards Essex. The Holocene, or modern epoch, began at the end of the last ice age around 10,000 years ago. Quite when, where and how the earliest humans fit into this, remain popular topics of sometimes quite heated debate. The present consensus, disputed by some, is that early humans, or 'hominids', first entered the north-western European peninsula around 500,000 years ago, before the Anglian glacial. The 'British Isles' simply did not exist at this time, the area of modern-day Britain being joined to the rest of continental Europe (the waters that separate them today being locked up in an immense ice sheet covering the North Sea).

In 1912, though the basic processes of geologic change were understood, the antiquity of human endeavour was not. The question of where *Eoanthropus*

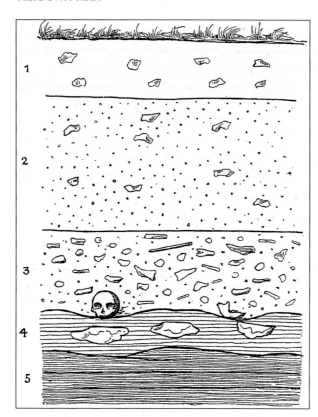

80 *Piltdown I: a sketch section drawn by Charles Dawson to illustrate the nature of stratigraphy at Barkham Manor – 1 represents surface soil; 2 is a pale yellow sandy loam containing a single 'Palaeolithic worked flint'; 3 is the dark brown gravel containing the bulk of the artefact assemblage; 4 is a pale yellow clay and sand; 5 is the undisturbed bed of Tunbridge Wells sand*

dawsoni fit within 'earth time' was, therefore, crucial if the processes of Darwin's evolutionary model was to be fully understood. Dawson and Woodward suggested that their 'Man of the Dawn' had probably existed in an early phase of the Pleistocene (probably 'during a warm cycle'),[68] an epoch that was then estimated to be 'certainly one hundred thousand years ago, perhaps as much as five times this sum'.[69] William Boyd Dawkins, a retired Professor of Geology at Manchester University, agreed with Dawson and Woodward's view that the gravel deposit, and, therefore, by implication the human remains and flint tools contained in it, was undoubtedly Pleistocene, all '*Pliocene mammalia*' recovered therein being residual.[70] Clement Reid, a geologist attached to the National Geological Survey, disagreed with this, observing that, in his view, the gravel deposits found by the Piltdown team were 'not pre-Glacial or even early Pleistocene – they belong to an epoch long after the first cold period had passed away'.[71]

The anatomist Arthur Keith raised an objection to both Dawson and Woodward's hypothesis, as well as that of Reid, which suggested a more recent date for the gravel. The 'very simian characters' of the Piltdown jaw, Keith noted, together with the 'large anterior teeth' and 'primitive characters of the skull' suggested that *Eoanthropus dawsoni* had existed much earlier, possibly as far back as the Pliocene.[72] This view was confirmed by the palaeontologist Edwin Newton who pointed out the 'highly-mineralised condition of the specimens', commenting that this did indeed suggest a 'Pliocene rather than... Pleistocene age'.[73] In reply to the, by now raging, debate, Dawson stated that he was:

> quite prepared, from an anthropological point of view, to accept an earlier date for the origin of the human remains, and Dr Woodward and he had perhaps erred on the side of caution in placing the date as early Pleistocene. However, the stratigraphical aspect of the occurrence, as at present understood, compelled them to suggest the comparatively later date for the human remains.[74]

One further objection to the Dawson/Woodward hypothesis was recorded on the night of the Geological Society presentation, this time concerning the proposed reconstruction. Arthur Keith voiced his concern that 'the chin-region of the mandible and the form of the incisor canine, and premolar teeth' of *Eoanthropus* was incorrect.[75] Another anatomist, David Waterson, was more forthright in pointing out that the cranium was 'human in practically all its essential characters' whilst the mandible resembled that of a chimpanzee. With these considerations in mind, Waterson concluded, it was 'very difficult to believe that the two specimens could have come from the same individual'.[76]

Eoanthropus dawsoni: 1913

The secrecy with which Dawson obtained permission to dig at Barkham Manor, when he told the landowner, George Maryon-Wilson that he was interested merely 'in the brown flints there',[77] backfired rather spectacularly on the Uckfield solicitor early in 1913. On 5 February, the British Museum (Natural History) received a letter from Maryon-Wilson, who, it transpired, had only heard about the significance of the discoveries on his land through reports appearing in the national press. As the owner of Barkham Manor, Maryon-Wilson felt obliged to point out that the Piltdown skull:

> is unquestionably my property (as there can be no question of 'treasure trove' in the matter) and I must formally claim the ownership of it and the other fossils which were found at the same time and further request you to kindly take care that they are not removed by Mr Dawson or any other person, without my permission.[78]

As any continued analysis of the Piltdown remains, not to say the opportunity of conducting further work at the site of the gravel pit, depended on the goodwill of the landowner, the museum urged Dawson to resolve the situation quickly. The very same day (5 February), Dawson replied to Maryon–Wilson regretting that the landowner 'should conceive the slightest cause for complaint', noting that he was in no way responsible for the 'newspaper accounts', but would endeavour to forward copies of the 'official account (illustrated)' to be authored by Woodward and himself when it was published, probably in March.[79] The official report would, Dawson further assured Maryon–Wilson, be 'acknowledging your kindness in granting me permission', something he had to date avoided in the hope of limiting trouble from trespassers. In a final paragraph, Dawson reasserts his legal training, noting:

> In accordance with my practice for nearly 30 years past I have given the pieces of skull to the British Museum where they will be properly guarded and treated. If I had [not] gone to the trouble and expense of making this exploration, the specimen might have fallen into other hands and been utterly lost to Science or the Nation, for it is well-established law that no right of property exists in human remains.[80]

Six days later the situation was resolved, and with Maryon–Wilson's concerns regarding the ownership of the artefacts finally being eased, he authorised Arthur Woodward to 'offer to the Trustees of the Museum... the Piltdown skull and other fossils'.[81]

Towards the end of April 1913, the first plaster casts of *Eoanthropus dawsoni* became widely available, being made to order (price £9 17s) by the Damon Company of Weymouth. One of the first to purchase a copy of the skull, as well as the disassembled cranium and mandible, was Arthur Keith, anatomist and conservator of the Hunterian Museum, Royal College of Surgeons.[82] Keith believed that the reconstruction proposed by Woodward was not totally correct. The current model was too ape-like for his liking.

Keith's main objection to Woodward's interpretation was with regard to cranial capacity. Reconfiguring the surviving fragments of skull, Keith was able to heighten the brain chamber 'by nearly half an inch',[83] making the overall brain capacity nearly 1500cc, as opposed to the 1070cc proposed by Woodward (**81**). Central to Keith's reassessment of *Eoanthropus* was the reconstructed jaw, especially the enlarged canine which, he felt, was fundamentally flawed: 'all the evidence was against a big canine tooth... the joint for the lower jaw was exactly as in modern man and the mechanism of that joint was incompatible with a projecting canine'.[84]

For the purposes of an exhibition held at the Royal College of Surgeons, Keith renamed his modified reconstruction of the Piltdown skull as *Homo piltdownensis*. This apparently simple reclassification from 'Dawson's man of the dawn' to 'man of Piltdown', was in actual fact quite a radical alteration, for Keith was suggesting that Dawson's discovery was actually a new species of

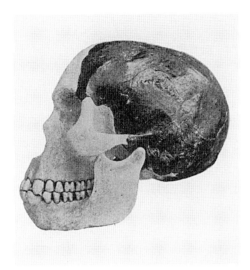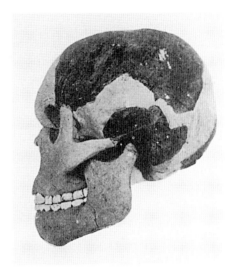

81 *Piltdown I: two alternative interpretations of* Eoanthropus dawsoni *– the preferred model of Arthur Smith Woodward (left) and that of Arthur Keith, which, it should be noted, is missing Woodward's hypothetical projecting canine (right)*

human, rather than a completely new genus. He qualified this change in nomenclature in a letter to *The Times*, following protests from a number of scientists at the British Museum (Natural History): 'The generic name *Homo* cannot be withheld from an individual in whom the brain and skull are human in every essential feature save one – the chin'.[85]

Keith was keen to explain that this was not, in his view, intended as a slight on Charles Dawson, or even on Arthur Woodward, for without either the remains would certainly have not been so well recorded and without Dawson's first observations the find would almost certainly 'have been ground to dust' by vehicles 'lumbering to market'. The name change was, however, important as scientists had tended to name fossil humans 'according to the place in which their remains were first found'. If this habit was junked so that each new discovery was named after its discoverer, then 'matters will become very complex for our descendants'.[86]

Dawson's first reaction to Keith's behaviour can only be guessed. When contacted by the *Daily Express* for a suitable comment, he deferred, but 'telephoned a letter' which was published the following day under the pseudonym 'EOANTHROPUS DAWSONI'.[87]

> I am told that Dr Arthur Keith and Dr Bather are disputing in The Times as to what is my right name. Permit me to say that I have not the slightest objection to Dr Keith naming his plaster reconstruction Homo keithii, if he will only leave me at rest, but I do not think it right he should discuss a lady's age.[88]

Sometime in late May, Woodward and Dawson recommenced their excavation of the Barkham Manor gravels. As in the previous season, much of the heavy earth-moving activity was conducted by Venus Hargreaves, whilst Dawson and Woodward sifted through the spoil. First job was to clear all soil overlying the gravel close to where the mandible and occipital bone of 1912 were discovered.[89] Here the team observed:

> that the floor was full of depressions, often measuring 2 to 7 feet across and 1 to 2 feet in depth. Into these depressions had been drifted the dark ferruginous gravel, and in places there yet remained small undisturbed patches... Following a small rift or channel in the floor which was yet filled with undisturbed gravel we discovered another fragment of a tooth of Stegodon bearing three cusps. This specimen was worked out very carefully, and preserved in the gravel matrix. It seems probable, from its general appearance and condition, that this fragment is a portion of the same molar as that to which the two fragments found last year belonged: like them, it is shattered, and shows little sign of rolling. If so, it must have been broken before its original deposition, and not by the workmen.[90]

In another 'depression', close to where the jaw had been recovered the previous year 'was found what appears to be a flint-flake roughly worked on one face and stained dark brown; also a triangular flint of Palaeolithic outline, but having 'Eolithic' 'edge-chipping' about the apex, the colour and patination resembling those of the 'Eolithic' forms found in the pit generally'.[91] Another roughly worked flint was recovered from the 'disturbed gravel' by Arthur Woodward, whilst an incisor and jaw fragment of a beaver 'occurred in the dark gravel'.[92]

As with the previous year the excavation and examination of the gravel was conducted on a methodical, if painfully slow, basis, Dawson recording that:

> we found it impossible to employ more shall one labourer, for the actual excavation had to be closely watched, and each spade full carefully examined. The gravel was then either washed with a sieve, or strewn on specially-prepared ground for the rain to wash it; after which the layer thus spread was mapped out in squares, and minutely examined section by section.[93]

On the weekend of the 9-10 August, the team were joined by Teilhard de Chardin, just recently returned from France, and Maude Woodward, Arthur Woodward's wife.[94] It was on the Saturday, a point confirmed in a letter from Teilhard to his parents (dated 15 August 1913)[95] that a small but important discovery was made by Dawson:

> While our labourer was digging the disturbed gravel within 2 or 3 feet from the spot where the mandible was found, I saw two human nasal bones lying

together with the remains of a turbinated bone beneath them in situ. The turbinal, however, was in such bad condition that it fell apart on being touched, and had to be recovered in fragments by the sieve; but it has been pieced together satisfactorily by Mrs Smith Woodward.[96]

The fragile nasal bones fitted Woodward's reconstruction of *Eoanthropus* perfectly (**82**). The team were, however, no closer to ascertaining whether Woodward's or Keith's interpretation was closer to the reality of the Piltdown remains. What they really needed to clinch the matter were more pieces from the fragmentary jaw; preferably the canine. What happened next was therefore extremely fortuitous.

we continued to work without much success until Saturday, August 30th, when we were accompanied by Father Teilhard. For some time we had been making an intensive search for the missing teeth of the lower jaw round the spot where the half of this jaw was found. We had washed and sieved much of the gravel, and had spread it for examination after washing by rain. We were then excavating a rather deep and hot trench in which Father Teilhard, in black clothing, was especially energetic; and, as we thought he seemed a little exhausted, we suggested that he should leave us to do the hard labour for a time while he had comparative rest in searching the rain-washed spread gravel. Very soon he exclaimed that he had picked up the missing canine tooth, but we were incredulous, and told him we had already seen several bits of ironstone, which looked like teeth, on the spot where he stood. He insisted, however, that he was not deceived, so we both

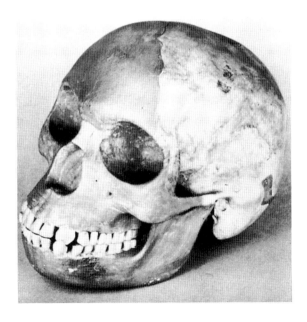

82 *Piltdown I: Woodward's reconstruction of* Eoanthropus dawsoni *complete with turbinal*

left our digging to go and verify his discovery. There could be no doubt about it, and we all spent the rest of that day until dusk crawling over the gravel in the vain quest for more.[97]

Woodward must have been jubilant, for this was exactly the type of find necessary in order to destroy Keith's model of *Homo piltdownensis* once and for all (**83**). Woodward's interpretation of *Eoanthropus*, which had been considered contentious by some, was now totally vindicated. Later, in a letter to his parents written on 10 September, Teilhard recorded his feelings concerning the discovery:

> This time we were lucky: in the earth dug up from previous excavations and now washed by rain I found the canine tooth from the jaw of the

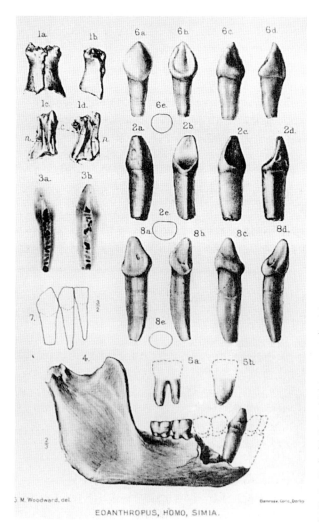

EOANTHROPUS, HOMO, SIMIA.

83 *Piltdown I: a comparison of* Eoanthropus dawsoni *with selected pieces of human and chimpanzee as made by Arthur Smith Woodward in 1914 – nasal bones of* Eoanthropus *(1a-d); right lower canine of* Eoanthropus *(2a-e); radiograph of* Eoanthropus *canine (3a-b); mandible of* Eoanthropus *with canine (4); root cavity impression of* Eoanthropus *lower molar 3 with crown restored in outline (5a-b); right lower milk canine of* Homo sapiens *(6a-d); right lower milk canine and incisors of* Homo sapiens *(7); right lower milk canine of* Simia satyrus famous Piltdown man – an important piece of evidence for Dr Woodward's reconstruction plan: it was a very exciting experience![98]

Teilhard returned to Hastings that evening 'with a light heart'. A few weeks later he left the Hastings seminary and, via a short stay in London, where he visited the Woodwards, he returned to France. He was never to return to Piltdown.

The canine tooth provided an incredible finale to the 1913 season. Woodward, though ecstatic over the find, planned to hold back from a public announcement until the September meeting of the British Academy in Birmingham. Unfortunately for him, history was to repeat itself. On Tuesday 2 September the story was leaked to the press, this time to the *Daily Express*. Almost grudgingly, Woodward confirmed the next day to a reporter from the *Express* that a find of 'tremendous importance' had indeed been made, one that may 'serve to clear up the question whether its owner was simian shape',[99] but the exact details he left vague, presumably in order to keep something back for the meeting in Birmingham. On seeing the first report, Dawson wrote immediately to Woodward noting his anger over the leak:

> I am sure you will be disgusted as I am that someone has let out about the tooth to the Express. The worst of it is that I have no doubt it was done by someone here who ought to have known better. It is a great pity and undermines things in more ways than one and I am very annoyed about it.[100]

Nevertheless, the story in the *Daily Express* served, as with the earlier tip-off to the *Manchester Guardian*, to heighten public interest in Piltdown, ensuring a packed audience for Woodward's later presentation to the British Association. In this he now confidently asserted that the new canine proved beyond a doubt that *Eoanthropus* was a 'genus distinct from *Homo*'.[101] Keith, however, was not convinced.

Eoanthropus dawsoni: 1914

Arguments over the correct interpretation of Piltdown man raged on in the pages of various academic journals well into 1914,[102] becoming increasing acrimonious in the process. The battle lines between supporters of *Eoanthropus* and *Homo* gradually coalesced around Arthur Keith and Elliot Grafton Smith, then Professor of Anatomy at Manchester University. Matters came to a head at a meeting of the Royal Society in February, Smith recalling to a friend that:

> I had to speak straight because so many British anatomists have been content to dance to Keith's rag-time, without thinking for themselves; and foreign anthropologists think therefore that all the anatomists are

supporting him... For years I have stood up to Keith, at times at the peril of my own reputation and sanity, in the hope of restraining him from too wild excesses. I hoped the F.R.S. would have made him regard his utterances more seriously. But this disgusting mess is the result.[103]

The consequences of the very heated public exchange between the two academics that February were later remembered by Keith in his autobiography:

I did not mince my words in pointing out the glaring errors in the reconstructed brain-case he exhibited to the meeting. It was a crowded meeting, and so it happened that he and I filed out side by side. I shall never forget the angry look he gave me. Such was the end of a long friendship.[104]

One other controversial element in the Piltdown debate was noted by William King Gregory, vertebrate palaeontologist at the American Museum of Natural History in an article entitled 'The Dawn Man of Piltdown' published in the *American Museum Journal*. On the second page of the article, Gregory observes that, in relation to the bones of *Eoanthropus dawsoni*:

it has been suspected by some that they are not old at all; that they may even represent a deliberate hoax, a Negro or Australian skull and an ape jaw, artificially fossilised and 'planted' in the gravel-bed to fool the scientists.[105]

This is the first intimation of any underhand dealing at the Barkham Manor site, though Gregory appears keen, perhaps naturally, to distance himself from the suggestion of fraud, later adding 'none of the experts who have scrutinised the specimens and the gravel pit and its surroundings has doubted the genuineness of the discovery'.[106] Unfortunately the American palaeontologist did not elaborate on the identity of the 'some' of whom he claimed suspected a hoax. It is conceivable that he was referring, at least in part, to Harry Morris, a bank clerk and amateur archaeologist from Sussex who, by 1912 at the earliest, was in possession of a flint from Piltdown which he claimed was fraudulent (see below). Whatever the origin of the rumours noted by Gregory, they did not publicly surface again for nearly forty years.

As the anthropological debate intensified in Britain, the storm clouds of war were gathering over Europe: the summer of 1914 proved to be the last official season of archaeological investigation at the Barkham Manor gravel pit. To begin with, things did not look promising for the team, Woodward noting that:

as we worked further from the original spot, discoveries became fewer. I found another piece of molar tooth of a mastodon, and Dr Davidson Black, of Perkin, who was with us one day, picked up part of the upper molar tooth of a rhinoceros.[107]

No additional human remains were forthcoming, but then, in late June, came a sensational discovery that would rival anything that had been found before: unique proof that *Eoanthropus dawsoni* had been a thinking, rational being. The circumstances of this new discovery were later outlined by Woodward in his book *The Earliest Englishman*:

> I was watching the workman, who was using a broad pick (or mattock), when I saw some small splinters of bone scattered by a blow. I stopped his work, and searching the spot with my hands, pulled out a heavy blade of bone of which he had damaged the end. It was much covered up with very sticky yellow clay, and was so large as to excite our curiosity. We therefore washed it at once, and were surprised to find that the damaged end had been shaped by man and looked rather like the end of a cricket-bat; we also noticed that the other end had been broken across, and we thought it must have been cracked by the weight of the gravel under which it was originally buried. Mr Dawson accordingly grubbed with his fingers in the earth around the spot where the broken end had lain, and soon pulled out the rest of the bone, which was still more surprising. This piece was also covered with sticky yellow clay, but when we had washed it we found that it had been trimmed by sharp cuts to a wedge-shaped point.[108]

More precise contextual detail concerning the artefact was supplied by Dawson and Woodward in their December 1914 presentation to the Geological Society:

> This bone implement was found about a foot below the surface, in dark vegetable soil, beneath the hedge which bounds the gravel-pit, and within 3 or 4 feet of the spoil-heap whence we obtained the right parietal bone of the human skull. On being washed away, the soil left not the slightest stain on the specimen, which was covered with firmly-adherent pale-yellow sandy clay, closely similar to that of the flint-bearing layer at the bottom of the gravel. The bone, therefore, cannot have lain buried in the soil for any long period, and was almost certainly thrown there by the workmen with the other useless debris when they were digging gravel from the adjacent hole.[109]

The piece had, therefore, not been lying *in situ* when 'the workman' (presumably Venus Hargreaves) had struck it with his mattock, Dawson and Woodward noting that it lay in soil redeposited during a recent period of gravel extraction. The overall condition of the 'implement' (**84**) was described as being 'much mineralised with oxide or iron, at least on the surface', the 'cut facets being slightly darker than the rest'.[110] In basic shape the bone had been made:

> into a useful tool by trimming it at both ends and straightening the inner edge. The tool thus made measures 40.5 cm. (16 inches) in length and

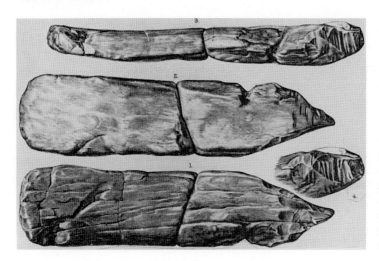

84 *Piltdown I: the worked bone implement showing the outer surface (1), inner surface (2), outer edge (3), and a detail of the cut facets (4)*

10 cm. (4 inches) in width, and its thickness varies from 2.5 to 5 cm. (1 to 2 inches). Its outer face is nearly smooth... The other face of the bone shows the spongy structure of the wall of the marrow cavity of the thigh bone. The thinner end of the tool is gently and regularly rounded by three rows of small cuts, of which the middle row is terminal and the two bordering rows are inclined towards it. The thicker end, which is wedge-shaped... is trimmed on the outer face by several broad cuts, some at least 14 mm. (over half an inch) in width; here and on the opposite face the flatting is broad because it is in the direction of the fibres of the bone. On the side faces of the wedge, where the cuts are across the fibres, they are more numerous and irregular, as might be expected, being merely little chips. On one edge of the bone near the pointed end there is a small smooth, round groove in an irregular hollow. This groove seems to be part of a round hole originally bored through the bone, and the outer side must have been accidentally broken away, as shown by the peculiar colour of the bone at the spot. A small pit close by, on the inner face of the bone, suggests that the owner of the tool started to make another hole, which was never finished.[111]

The implement therefore appeared to have been manufactured and shaped 'entirely by cutting', examination of the cut facets leaving no doubt in the mind of the team that working of the bone had been undertaken whilst 'it was in a comparatively fresh state'.[112] The raw material for the implement had, in all probability, derived from an elephant (**85**), whale bone being briefly considered, only to be disregarded as being insufficiently compact.[113] The piece could only have been supplied by the striking of the elephant thighbone on the outer edge, perhaps indicating that *Eoanthropus* 'may, indeed, have been breaking up the bone to feast on the marrow, and saved this flake because it suited a purpose which he had in mind'.[114]

Quite what this mysterious 'purpose' was, neither Dawson nor Woodward could elaborate. The terminal ends of the artefact provided 'no marks of grinding or rubbing', which could provide a clue to how the piece had originally been used, only 'a slight battering at the point'.[115] 'Its shape is unique', the presentation rather lamely stated 'and an instrument with a point would be serviceable for many purposes'.[116] Later, when compiling data for his book *The Earliest Englishman*, Woodward seemed no closer to resolving how *Eoanthropus* may have used the bone tool:

> The rounded end seems to have been the handle, and the heavy wedge-shaped end would be the working part. Whether the round hole was needed during use, or whether it was merely to be threaded for convenience of carrying, is uncertain, but it is clearly worn smooth by a thong, which may have been a strip of skin or a sinew. The fact that the tool is scarcely worn may mean that the hole was important, and that when it was broken the tool became useless. On the whole, it suggests a digging stick, and may have been used for grubbing up roots for food![117]

Function aside, the retrieval of a tool manufactured from a large elephant bone at Piltdown had significant implications as to the perceived date of *Eoanthropus dawsoni*, the excavation team suggesting that:

> the individual who made the implement was contemporary with an elephant bigger than the Mammoth (*Elephas primigenius*). Such gigantic elephants are only known to have lived in Western Europe at the end of the Pliocene and the beginning of the Pleistocene Period. The nature of the implement itself thus confirms our conclusion based on its mineral condition, that it originally occurred in the lowest layer of the Piltdown section. This layer sometimes passes imperceptibly into the overlying gravel in which the skull of Eoanthropus was found, and there is no reason to suppose that it is substantially older than the latter. Like the evidence previously described, the discovery therefore seems to suggest that the deposits date back at least to the beginning of the Pleistocene Period.[118]

In the discussion that followed the presentation of the elephant bone artefact, many suggestions as to its use were proposed from members of the audience.

85 *Piltdown I: an outline of the left femur of* Elephas meridionalis *showing the area from which the implement was removed*

'A club' suggested G.F. Lawrence; whilst S.H. Warren suggested it was more akin to a 'hacking tool'.[119] S.H. Warren thought a club-type weapon was an appropriate suggestion, adding that the grip could have been improved by use of 'a thong' originally threaded through the perforated hole.[120] Other comments from the floor concerning the antiquity of the bone artefact were less helpful, W. Dale, for example, pointing out that the 'tool marks' recorded 'appeared to have been made, not with a flint flake, but with some stronger cutting or chopping implement.[121]

A.S. Kennard observed that the difference between the 'natural surface' of the bone and the 'cut portion' seemed to imply that 'the bone was not in a fresh state when cut'.[122] F.P. Mennell added that, in his experience 'in countries where elephants were still plentiful', their bones tended to 'weather rapidly as soon as the flesh had decayed away'. As a consequence there was 'no difficulty in detaching pieces from such bones, but they were usually so splintery and even friable, that they were unsuitable for any kind of serviceable implement'.[123] Reginald Smith noted that if authentic, the bone tool 'would rank as by far the oldest undoubted work of man in bone', though he added the proviso that:

> The possibility of the bone having been found and whittled in recent times must be considered; and, if it were not shaped in its fossil state, it had evidently never been used for any purpose such as grubbing for roots, as the cuts were unscratched, and must have been made with an even-edged chopper.[124]

Experimental work could, Smith continued, demonstrate how the object had been manufactured and for what purpose it had been made, though he admitted that he 'could not imagine any use for an implement that looked like part of a cricket-bat'.[125] Having set his concerns on record, Smith ended with the curious, and perhaps rather mischievous comment: 'The discoverers were to be congratulated on providing a new and interesting problem, such as would eventually provoke an ingenious solution'.[126]

Eoanthropus dawsoni: 1915

By 1915, *Eoanthropus dawsoni* had become a worldwide celebrity. No less than three books, each one placing Piltdown man centre stage, appeared in print: *The Antiquity of Man* by Arthur Keith, *Ancient Hunters* by William Sollas and *Diversions of a Naturalist* by Ray Lankester. A fourth book, *The Earliest Englishman*, authored by none other than Arthur Smith Woodward, was well into the planning stage, some chapters apparently having been completed,[127] before the project was shelved (it finally appeared in 1948, four years after

Woodward's death). 1915 was also the year that the an oil painting depicting the 'main protagonists' of the Piltdown discovery and subsequent debate, and entitled *A Discussion of the Piltdown Skull*, was unveiled at the Royal Academy in London (**86**).

The *Discussion*, painted by John Cooke, was an artistic interpretation of a meeting held on 11 August 1913 at the Royal College of Surgeons. To the left of centre is a reconstruction of the Piltdown skull, lying on the table with comparative human and chimpanzee remains surrounding it. Arthur Keith, conservator of the Hunterian Museum at the Royal College of Surgeons, sits impassively before the skull in a laboratory coat, callipers in hand. Behind his right shoulder stands Grafton Elliot Smith, Professor of Anatomy at Manchester University, his right arm extended, hand pointing to the cranium of *Eoanthropus* as if suggesting an amendment in anatomical detail. To his right hover Arthur Swayne Underwood (seated), Professor of Dental Surgery at King's College, London and (standing) Frank Orwell Barlow, technical assistant in the Geology Department of the British Museum (Natural History). Sitting on Keith's immediate left, craning to get a better view, are William Plane Pycraft, osteolo-

86 *Piltdown I: the 1915 painting* A discussion of the Piltdown Skull *by John Cooke. Seated from left are Arthur Swayne Underwood, Arthur Keith (in lab coat), William Plane Pycraft and Edwin Ray Lankester. Standing from left are Frank Orwell Barlow, Grafton Elliot Smith, Charles Darwin (in wall painting), Charles Dawson and Arthur Smith Woodward*

gist in the Department of Zoology at the British Museum (Natural History) and Edwin Ray Lankester, formerly Director of the British Museum (Natural History) and Keeper of Zoology. Standing behind Pycraft and Lankester, to the left of Keith, are Charles Dawson and Arthur Smith Woodward, then Keeper of Geology at the British Museum (Natural History). Woodward and Dawson appear united and calm, as if watching the unfolding debate with mild, almost paternal interest; the elder statesmen of the Piltdown story. The positioning of both men takes further significance when one considers what lies just behind the tableaux, for there, on the back wall of the studio, hangs a framed portrait of Charles Darwin, the father of evolutionary science. Dawson is standing in such a way that his features directly impinge upon the background portrait, as if, by discovering Piltdown man, he is being acknowledged by Darwin as his heir and successor.

Although the protagonists in the *Discussion* are neatly divided into two opposing camps, facing each other across Keith's scientific analysis, the overall effect is one of undeniable unity. To those who viewed the painting in May 1915, it must have felt that all the scientists engaged in the debate were, with minor arguments aside, in general agreement as to the nature, interpretation and significance of *Eoanthropus dawsoni*. Unfortunately, as with most things in real life, things were not that simple. In fact 1915 was not a good year for Dawson's 'Man of the Dawn', for he was now to come under sustained attack from the United States of America.

Late in 1915, Gerrit S. Miller Jnr, a mammologist at the United States National Museum of Natural History (Smithsonian Institution), published a study on 'The Jaw of Piltdown Man' in the pages of the *Smithsonian Miscellaneous Collections*. The article provided a detailed comparative analysis of chimpanzee, gorilla and orang-utan mandibles, Miller observing that his work 'convinces me that, on the basis of the evidence furnished by the Piltdown fossils, and by the characteristics of all the men, apes, and monkeys now known, a single individual cannot be supposed to have carried this jaw and skull'.[128] The mandible and cranium of *Eoanthropus dawsoni* were, in Miller's view, totally incompatible with one another, for:

> In order to believe that all the fragments came from a single individual it is necessary to assume the existence of a primate differing from all other known members of the order by combining a braincase and nasal bones possessing the exact characters of a genus belonging to one family, with a mandible, two lower molars, and an upper canine possessing the exact characters of a genus belonging to another.[129]

Whilst agreeing that the deposition of such a cranium and jaw 'within a few feet of each other' did raise some interesting contextual issues, Miller concluded that 'until the discovery of further material it seems proper to treat the case as a purely zoological problem by referring each set of fragments to the genus which its characteristics demand'.[130] Miller, therefore, proposed the restriction of *Eoanthropus dawsoni* to the cranium (which itself could perhaps more plausibly be reassigned to the genus *Homo*), whilst the ape-like lower jaw suggested the presence of a 'British Pleistocene chimpanzee' which should be accorded the name *Pan vetus*.[131] A number of prominent American and British scientists agreed with Miller's rather persuasive arguments, their new heresy becoming known as 'dualism' (in that they believed that *Eoanthropus* represented a composite of two very different animals). Arthur Woodward, champion of the 'monoist' view, quite naturally did not agree. In December 1915, he wrote to Charles Dawson with some feeling concerning this new perspective on his cherished 'Dawn Man':

> I have just sent you the latest ROT from the U.S.A., by an enthusiastic but light-headed friend of mine in Washington. I am surprised that the Smithsonian will publish such nonsense.[132]

Woodward and Dawson must have watched the new debate over the perceived authenticity of *Eoanthropus* with some extra interest, for both men already possessed evidence that the association of human cranium and ape-like mandible at Piltdown was not a 'one off'. In January 1915, Dawson had written to Woodward with the exciting news that he believed he had discovered remains of a second *Eoanthropus* from the gravels around Barkham Manor.[133] The first find comprised 'a fragment of the left side of the frontal bone with portion of the orbit and root of nose' whilst a 'a new molar tooth' was retrieved in July of the same year.[134] The exact provenance of these new artefacts never seems to have been firmly established by Woodward, though the discovery has been credited with the name of Sheffield Park man (or 'Piltdown II': see next chapter). Neither Woodward nor Dawson officially announced the new discovery, which would have effectively silenced the increasing number of dualistic critics in 1915, though they may have initially hoped to have done so at the December meeting of the Geological Society in London. Dawson was, however, by the winter of 1915, in the first stages of the illness that would eventually kill him. Woodward's son was also gravely ill, with appendicitis complicated by post-operative thrombosis.[135] 'Piltdown II' was not formally presented until February 1917.

Other than his discovery of a possible second *Eoanthropus* at Sheffield Park, Dawson does not appear to have spent much of his time undertaking fieldwork in 1915. His academic interest in the significance of the Barkham Manor finds, however, did not diminish, and in February of that year he presented a paper, based on his Sussex work, at a joint meeting of the Royal Anthropological Institute and the Prehistoric Society of East Anglia in London. The presentation, entitled 'Sussex Ouse Valley Cultures', was intended as a damning indictment of 'eoliths', the 'stones of the dawn' which had polarised scientific debate throughout the early years of the twentieth century. Some academics viewed the eolith as the earliest form of humanly worked tool, whilst others saw them as the product of natural breakage. Dawson had already confessed to being in the latter group, his paper to the *Hastings and East Sussex Naturalist* confirming that 'much work remains to be done' in the study of the eolith before he could more readily believe in them.[136] By 1915, however, Dawson had made up his mind, observing that:

> a great deal of error may be created regarding supposed implements of human workmanship from early gravels and horizons, by the adoption of unscientific methods of collection and exhibition on an occasion like this.[137]

Eoliths were, Dawson stated, entirely natural, deriving from the sort of fractures that one could find in any prismatic material. To prove the hypothesis, Dawson illustrated his lecture with a dramatic practical demonstration of the flaking properties of starch. Taking a bag of starch models, stained with chromium to make it appear similar to the Barkham Manor flint, Dawson proceeded to vigorously shake and sit upon the bag, successfully managing to replicate 'all the well-known eolith shapes'.[138] Dawson's paper was never published, but the immediate reaction to it, at least from the supporters of eoliths, appears to have been overtly hostile, Dawson later confiding to Woodward that he had received 'abusive letters about 'starch', especially from Lewis Abbott who seems specially annoyed!'[139]

Eoanthropus dawsoni: 1916–38

In the absence of 'Piltdown II' (Sheffield Park man) from the academic debate, the arguments concerning the possible 'dualistic' nature of the human skull and ape-like jaw rumbled on through 1916 and 1917, becoming increasingly acrimonious in the process. Arthur Keith was dismissive of Miller's arguments, noting the dentition of *Eoanthropus* was 'as unlike chimpanzee teeth as teeth can be'.[140] William Pycraft was far more damning of Miller, commenting that his conclusions:

> are based on assumptions such as would never be made had he not committed the initial mistake of overlooking the fact that these remains – which, by the way, he has never seen – are of extreme antiquity, and hence are to be measured by standards of the palaeontologist rather than the anthropologist. This unfortunate lack of the right perspective has caused him to overlook some of the most significant features of these remains, and

has absolutely warped his judgement in regard to the relative values of the likeness between these fragments and the skulls of the chimpanzee which he has so woefully misread.[141]

Reading Pycraft's words, William King Gregory, vertebrate palaeontologist at the American Museum of Natural History, swiftly wrote to Miller, offering his support in defence of the disgusting 'lawyer-like, hectoring tactics' of the British osteologist.[142] As the battle lines between 'dualists' and 'monoists' hardened, Arthur Woodward decided it was time to bring Piltdown II, the 'Last Great' find that Charles Dawson had made at, or near, Sheffield Park into the glare of public attention (see next chapter).

Woodward had quietly held on to Dawson's Sheffield Park *Eoanthropus* since he had first been alerted to the discovery in January 1915. Part of his delay in reporting was due, as noted below, to the circumstances of the war then raging across the globe, the complications of his job and the deteriorating health of both Dawson and Woodward's own son Cyril. Woodward was also keen to establish the nature and circumstances of the discovery for himself, before producing an official report. To this end Woodward and Grafton Elliot Smith had spent at least two weeks in the summer of 1916 attempting to investigate Dawson's new find.[143] and conducting the last 'official' season of excavations at Barkham Manor.[144]

The 1916 season at Barkham Manor was, in the absence of Dawson who was by then gravely ill, somewhat disappointing. The overall strategy for the renewed programme of excavation is not entirely clear, Woodward noting only that the work was conducted 'round the margin of the area previously explored'.[145] Presumably old spoil heaps were re-examined and new ones generated. Areas close to where earlier spectacular finds, such as the elephant femur of 1914, were extended in the hope of recovering additional remains. Unfortunately, as Woodward later noted in his presentation to the Geological Society in February 1917 (which in any case was more concerned with the Sheffield Park discovery made by Dawson two years before):

> Although so much material was carefully examined, neither bones nor teeth were met with. The only noteworthy find was a battered nodule of black flint, which occurred in a rather sandy patch of the dark-brown gravel resting immediately on the basal layer. This specimen, which is conspicuously different from the other flints and very little stained, may have been used by man as a hammer-stone.[146]

Despite the singular failure of the 1916 programme of investigation, and the sad death of Charles Dawson in August of that year, Woodward's presentation of the Piltdown II remains from Sheffield Park generated considerable renewed enthusiasm for *Eoanthropus dawsoni*. Woodward, inspired by the hope of finding more precious evidence of the 'Earliest Englishman', continued to excavate at Piltdown for many years, even moving to Sussex following his retirement from the British Museum (Natural History) in 1924. Rather sadly, no additional remains of *Eoanthropus* were ever found. Later, Woodward was able to compress the results of his final twenty-one years of fieldwork at Barkham Manor into a single paragraph:

> After Mr Dawson's death, in 1916, I was able to open a series of pits along the other side of the hedge in a field adjacent to the original pit. There I was helped at times by Professor (afterwards Sir Grafton) Elliot Smith, Prof. W.T. Gordon, Prof. Barclay Smith, and others. We began close to the spot where the skull was found, and worked in both directions from this place. Progress was slow because the overlying loam was deeper than that on the other side of the hedge, though the gravel was not reduced in thickness. Our efforts, however, were all in vain. We found nothing of interest in the gravel, and it was evident that we were outside the range of the eddy which brought the scientific treasure to its resting-place.[147]

In fact the only artefact worth commenting on from two decades of excavation at the site was a 'pot-boiler' or piece of fire-cracked flint, which labourers working for the new owner of the Manor, David Kerr, found in the gravel 'at a spot nearer the farmyard'.[148] Perhaps understandably, given the paucity of remains recovered from Piltdown between 1916 and 1937, Woodward made much of this heat-cracked flint nodule, observing that, assuming it were contemporary with the earlier discoveries, it proved *Eoanthropus* must have been 'accustomed to heat or boil water'.[149] The flint had, Woodward hypothesised, first been:

> heated in the fire and then dropped quickly into the water one after another until the water was sufficiently hot. The strong heating and the sudden cooling of the flint cause it to be reddened and crackled to the centre, and eventually, after short use, to break to pieces.[150]

The discovery of charcoal, from an unspecified area within the grounds of Barkham Manor 'which Mr W.N. Edwards tells me are from oak'[151], seemed to imply that *Eoanthropus* had indeed been master of fire.

The termination of work at Barkham Manor led Woodward to propose the creation of a more permanent monument to the first discovery of *Eoanthropus* skull at Piltdown. A sandstone monolith, paid for by public subscription and inscribed with a dedication to 'Mr Charles Dawson FSA' was duly erected at the site on 23 July 1938, being unveiled by Woodward and Arthur Keith (who had long since buried whatever disagreements they had had over the reconstruction of Dawson's 'Dawn Man').

Eoanthropus dawsoni: **1944 and after**

Arthur Smith Woodward, champion of *Eoanthropus dawsoni* for over thirty years, died at his home at Hill Place, Haywards Heath in Sussex on the morning of Saturday 2 September 1944. The day before, despite his advancing illness, he had dictated the closing sentences of his book *The Earliest Englishman*, to his wife Maude. The first pieces of the book, dealing with the discovery of Piltdown man, had actually been written in or around 1916, but the pressures of work at the British Museum (Natural History) meant that Woodward had never found time to complete the text. With the closure of all excavation at Barkham Manor, where he had searched in vain for more traces of the elusive *Eoanthropus*, Woodward at last returned to the unfinished manuscript. In 1948, four years after his death, the book was finally published.

Arthur Keith, the anatomist who had clashed with both Woodward and Dawson early on in the history of Piltdown, wrote the Foreword to *The Earliest Englishman*, at the request of Maude Woodward. He and Arthur Woodward had patched up their differences many years before, Woodward even asking Keith to say a few words at the official unveiling of the memorial to Dawson set up on the road to Barkham Manor in 1938, an honour which Keith confessed touched him deeply.[152] The Foreword to the new book was brief, but full of praise for the recently deceased scientist. On the subject of *Eoanthropus dawsoni* itself, Keith noted that 'The Piltdown enigma is still far from a final solution'.[153] There were, Keith continued, some who still doubted the authenticity of the man from Barkham Manor, though he remained convinced that 'no theory of human evolution can be regarded as satisfactory unless the revelations of Piltdown are taken into account'.[154] Remembering the difficulties that he and others had faced in reconstructing the remains of *Eoanthropus dawsoni*, Keith ended with a comment which, in retrospect, has a curiously prophetic ring: 'how many other surprises may be in store for us before we reach a final settlement?'[155]

At the time Keith was writing his Foreword, *Eoanthropus dawsoni* had become a bit of an anthropological problem. The results of excavations the world over had made him:

> a most awkward and perplexing element in the fossil record of the *Hominidae*, being entirely out of conformity both in its strange mixture of morphological characters and its time sequence with all the palaeontological evidence of human evolution available from other parts of the world.[156]

Increasing numbers of fossil discoveries had, by the late 1940s, made many scientists unsure of where to place Dawson's 'Man of the Dawn' in the tree of human evolution. The features that most clearly defined *Eoanthropus*, namely its ape-like jaw and teeth (all with unusual patterns of wear) attached to a human forehead, were patently not present elsewhere. All the evidence accumulated since 1916 indicated that a human jaw, supporting human-like teeth, was a remarkably early feature in the development of *Homo*, whereas forehead and brain seemed to have changed more gradually. In short, Piltdown was an embarrassment.

The death of Arthur Smith Woodward in 1944 meant that the fossil remains of *Eoanthropus dawsoni* held by the British Museum (Natural History), were no longer untouchable. Woodward had been convinced of the authenticity of Piltdown man, but others felt less sure. In the decades since the first fossil remains had been unearthed at Barkham Manor, a range of analytical procedures and dating techniques, all unthought-of in the early years of the twentieth century, had been developed. Given the controversy that still raged around *Eoanthropus*, the British Museum (Natural History) authorised the first in what was to prove a veritable battery of scientific tests to be conducted upon Dawson's 'Man of the Dawn'.

The fluorine dating test was the first to be conducted. Fluorine is present in all ground waters, usually in extremely small quantities. As it is absorbed by both bone and dentine, the fluorine content of any skeletal remains buried in permeable ground such as gravel, should theoretically increase with time. Any bone added to a natural deposit of permeable ground (in the form of a grave or other deliberate interment), will naturally possess considerably *less* fluorine than any bone material set down when the deposit was originally formed. At Piltdown, it had repeatedly been suggested by Woodward and Dawson that the gravels containing *Eoanthropus dawsoni* were part of 'a flood deposit which might have been formed during a single storm'.[157] The fluorine content of the constituent parts of *Eoanthropus*, as well as all the animals found with him, should, if contemporary, therefore be broadly similar. Of course, fluorine testing does not provide an accurate measurement of the age of a particular sample, but can be used to indicate the relative date of specimens which occur at the same site, or which have been deposited under similar conditions. In 1949, Kenneth Oakley applied the, still relatively new, fluorine test to the skeletal remains recovered from Barkham Manor. The results were rather startling.

All the bone samples analysed showed a greater range of fluorine than would be expected from a single, contemporary assemblage.

> The animal remains of undoubted Lower Pleistocene age all showed high fluorine-content, while those of later Pleistocene age in the same bed showed a much lower fluorine-content. All the remains of Eoanthropus – and some 20 micro-samples were analysed – showed extremely little fluorine. It is evident that fluorine has been deficient in the Piltdown ground-water since the gravel accumulated; but nevertheless the test has shown conclusively that none of the bones and teeth attributed to Eoanthropus belongs to the Lower Pleistocene group. The jawbone and associated brain-case are contemporaneous. It is probable that they date from the time of final settling of the gravel,

which from physiographic and other evidence is now considered to be not earlier than the last interglacial period.[158]

If Piltdown man had lived and died no earlier 'than the last interglacial', then he could be no older, Oakley believed, than '100,000 years'.[159] This estimate was nothing like the antiquity that Piltdown was previously thought to have been. *Eoanthropus dawsoni* now looked less like a distant ancestor of the human race and more like a curious genetic 'throw-back'. If Oakley's thoughts concerning the proposed date of Piltdown man appeared controversial, at least his observations on the compatibility of the *Eoanthropine* jaw and skull satisfied those who still believed that the remains represented the constituent parts of a single individual – 'it is still open to anatomists to argue about the naturalness of the association of an ape-like mandible with a typically human braincase, but in the light of the new dating evidence it appears more probable that they belong to the same creature'.[160]

Despite this, the dualist view concerning the perceived disparity of the cranium and mandible, continued unabated. Ashley Montagu, in the pages of the *American Journal of Physical Anthropology* for 1951, remained concerned that the 'extraordinarily thick' Piltdown cranium was wholly incompatible with the 'remarkably thin' jaw:

> in no known skull of any of the anthropomorpha, extinct or extant, indeed in no known primate, does there exist a disparity of this kind between the thickness of the cranial bones and the thickness of the mandible. When the cranial bones are thick the mandible is also thick and massive; when the cranial bones are moderately developed in thickness so is the mandible. Indeed, in the moderately thick-skulled gorilla the mandible is massive, while among the moderately thick-skulled australopithecines the thickness and massiveness of the mandible may be... simply enormous. On such morphological grounds, therefore, it would seem highly improbable that the gracile mandible found with the Piltdown cranium bones belonged to the same individual.[161]

The debate appeared no closer to resolution.

In July 1953, following a conference in London on 'Research on Fossil Hominidae in Africa', Joseph Weiner, a Reader in Physical Anthropology at Oxford University, returned home, a private discussion that he had had concerning the Piltdown remains having left his mind racing. The skull and jaw recovered from Barkham Manor, Weiner began to realise, presented a number of unusual and largely unresolved problems.

> Thinking it all over again, I realised with astonishment that while there were in fact only the two possible 'natural' theories, i.e. that Piltdown man

was in fact the composite man-ape of Woodward's interpretation, or that two distinct creatures, fossil man and fossil ape, had been found side by side, neither of the 'natural' explanations was at all satisfactory.[162]

The matter was complicated by Dawson's discovery of 'Piltdown II' at Sheffield Park in 1915 (see next chapter), for here there was evidence of a second human cranium associated with ape-like teeth. If the association of skull and jaw at Piltdown I (Barkham Manor) *had* been the result of coincidence, surely that coincidence could not have been repeated elsewhere? Could, Weiner hypothesised, the jaw from Piltdown I have been modern?

> Immediately strong objections loomed up. To say the jaw was modern implied that the fluorine analysis had been inaccurate or that the published results must be in some way compatible with modern bone recently buried. In effect this would imply that the most reasonable interpretation of the results had been in error. That difficulty was dwarfed at once by a far more serious objection. The teeth were almost unanimously acknowledged to possess features quite unprecedented in modern apes – the flat wear of the molars and the curious type of wear of the canine had never been matched in an ape's mandible. A modern jaw with flat worn molars and uniquely worn-down eye tooth? That would mean only one thing: deliberately ground-down teeth. Immediately this summoned up a devastating corollary – the equally deliberate placing of the jaw in the pit.[163]

After considering the serious implications of this new hypothesis, Weiner communicated his theory to his professor at Oxford, Wilfred Edward Le Gros Clark. Convinced that something was amiss, Le Gros Clark telephoned Kenneth Oakley, instigator of the earlier fluorine tests, to ask, as sensitively as possible, whether the Piltdown mandible could conceivably have been fraudulent. As Weiner was later to recall, Oakley called back the same day to report that 'he was utterly convinced that artificial abrasion had been applied' to the teeth.[164] The three men decided that, though the British Museum (Natural History) should 'be actively involved' in the exposure of Piltdown man, until a detailed analysis had been completed, the story should be kept secret.[165]

The tests on *Eoanthropus dawsoni* that followed pursued four main areas of investigation: the abrasion on the teeth; a retesting of the fluorine content; measurement of organic content; and the surface staining. By late October 1953 the results of the analysis proved inarguable: Piltdown man was indeed a hoax. *Eoanthropus dawsoni* was not only dead; he had never lived. The three main protagonists in the exposure, Weiner, Oakley and Le Gros Clark, compiled a paper entitled simply 'The Solution of the Piltdown Problem', which on 20 November was swiftly circulated to the press.

The results of Weiner, Oakley and Le Gros Clark's study was both conclusive and damning (**87**, **88**, **89** & **90**). Examining the evidence for the molar teeth preserved in the mandible of *Eoanthropus dawsoni*, the team cited eight points of blatant forgery:

(1) The occlusal surfaces (particularly of M2) are planed down over almost their whole extent to a flatness which is much more even than that normally produced by natural wear.
(2) The borders of the flat occlusal surfaces – particularly the lateral borders – are sharp-cut and show no evidence of the bevelling which is usually produced by natural wear.
(3) The centre of the talonid basin in M2 is unworn, and is bounded by a sharp-cut and unbevelled border of the planed surface of the crown. This appearance would be produced by artificial abrasion but would not be expected in natural wear.

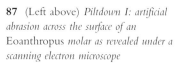

87 (Left above) *Piltdown I: artificial abrasion across the surface of an* Eoanthropus *molar as revealed under a scanning electron microscope*

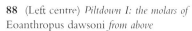

88 (Left centre) *Piltdown I: the molars of* Eoanthropus dawsoni *from above*

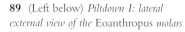

89 (Left below) *Piltdown I: lateral external view of the* Eoanthropus *molars*

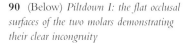

90 (Below) *Piltdown I: the flat occlusal surfaces of the two molars demonstrating their clear incongruity*

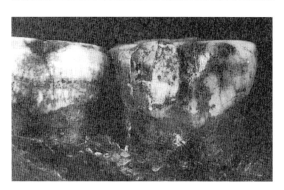

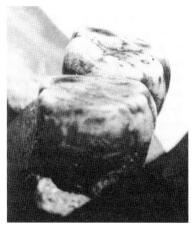

(4) The surface of the areas of dentine exposed on the antero-medial cusps of the two molars is quite flat and flush with the surrounding enamel, instead of forming a depression as would be expected in natural wear.

(5) In both molars much more dentine has been exposed on the antero-internal than the antero-external cusps. But in the course of natural attrition the lateral cusps of lower molar teeth are normally worn down more rapidly (and thus usually show a greater exposure of dentine) than the medial cusps.

(6) The degree of wear in the two molars, M1 and M2, is most identical. But in early stages of natural attrition M1 is commonly (though not always) more severely worn than M2.

(7) The planes of the flat occlusal surfaces of the two molars are not congruous, i.e. they do not fit together to form a uniform contour. Unless the teeth have been displaced from their natural position after death (for which there is no evidence), this incongruity is difficult to explain by natural wear.

(8) Inspection of the isolated molar tooth (referred to the specimen called Piltdown II) with a binocular microscope shows that the occlusal surface of the enamel has been finely scratched, as though by an abrasive.[166]

With regard to the single canine found by Teilhard de Chardin in 1913, four separate, but no less damning, pieces of evidence were cited:

(1) The mode of wear of this tooth is unlike that found normally either in ape or human canines, for the abraded surface has exposed the dentine over the entire lingual surface from medial to distal border and at one point actually reaches the apex of the pulp cavity.

(2) The condition of the apex of the root, and the wide and open pulp cavity seen in an X-ray photograph (**91**), indicate fairly certainly that the canine was still incompletely erupted or had only just recently completed its eruption. But this would be incompatible with the severe attrition of the crown if the latter were naturally produced.

(3) X-ray examination shows no evidence of the deposition of secondary dentine (with a constriction of the pulp cavity) which might be expected if the severe abrasion of the lingual surface of the crown were the result of natural attrition.

(4) The abraded surface of the crown shows fine vertically disposed scratches (as seen under a binocular microscope) which suggest the application of an abrasive.[167]

The team then went on to review the evidence of the fluorine test, which Oakley himself had applied in 1949, and which appeared to suggest that jaw and mandible had both been contemporary.

The fluorine method as applied in 1949 (and reported in full in 1950) served well enough to establish that neither the Piltdown cranium nor the mandible was Lower Pleistocene. It did not distinguish (nor at that time was it intended to distinguish) Upper Pleistocene from later material. The rate of fluorination at this site has probably not been high enough to give a clear separation between Upper Pleistocene and, say, Early Post-glacial bones. Moreover the method of analysis used in 1949 was accurate only within rather wide limits when applied to samples weighing less than 10 milligrams, with the consequence that even the difference between the fluorine contents of fossil and modern specimens was obscured where the samples were of that order of magnitude. Improvements in technique have since led to greater accuracy in estimating small amounts of fluorine, and it therefore seemed worth while submitting further samples of the critical Piltdown specimens for analysis in the Government Laboratory. The new estimations, based mainly on larger samples, were made by Mr C.F.M. Fryd. The following summary of the results leaves no doubt that, whereas the Piltdown cranium may well be Upper Pleistocene as claimed in 1950, the mandible, canine tooth and isolated molar are quite modern.[168]

With regard to the testing of organic content in the Piltdown remains, the team noted that:

extensive chemical studies of bones from early occupation sites in North America... have shown that in bones preserved under broadly the same conditions the nitrogen of their protein (ossein) is lost at a relatively slow, and on an average almost uniformly declining, rate. Thus, N[itrogen]-analysis, used with discretion, can be an important supplement to F[luorine]-analysis, and also for the relative dating of specimens too recent to be within the range of the fluorine method.[169]

Using a new method of estimating nitrogen quantity in the bones of *Eoanthropus*, the team concluded that:

the Piltdown mandible, canine and isolated molar [of Piltdown II: see next chapter] are modern. The possibility that the Piltdown specimens were steeped in a gelatinous preservative has been borne in mind; if this had been the explanation of their nitrogen-content, the cranial bones which are porous would have shown more nitrogen than the highly compact dentine of the teeth; whereas the reverse is true.[170]

The final piece of evidence confirming the extent of the forgery came from the surface of the Piltdown remains. The canine, found by Teilhard de Chardin in 1913 was first to be examined, its surface colour being shown to be, not the 'ferruginous' coat that Dawson and Woodward had claimed,[171] but 'a tough, flexible paint-like substance, insoluble in the common organic solvents, and with only a small ash-content'.[172] Beneath the paint, the 'extreme whiteness of the dentine' demonstrated the 'essential modernity of the canine'.

The *Eoanthropus* mandible was next, the team noting that on first appearance its 'reddish-brown colour' closely matched that of the cranium. However,

> whereas the cranial fragments are all deeply stained (up to 8 per cent of iron) throughout their thickness, the iron staining of the mandible is quite superficial. A small surface sample analysed in 1949 contained 7 per cent iron, but, when in the course of our re-examination this bone was drilled more deeply, the sample obtained was lighter in colour and contained only 2-3 per cent of iron. The difference in iron staining is thus also in keeping with the other evidence that the jaw and the cranium are not naturally associated.[173]

In conclusion, Weiner, Oakley and Le Gros Clark stated:

> From the evidence which we have obtained, it is now clear that the distinguished palaeontologists and archaeologists who took part in the excavations at Piltdown were the victims of a most elaborate and carefully prepared hoax. Let it be said, however, in exoneration of those who have assumed the Piltdown fragments to belong to a single individual, or who, having examined the original specimens, either regarded the mandible and canine as those of a fossil ape or else assumed (tacitly or explicitly) that the problem was not capable of solution on the available evidence, that the faking of the mandible and canine is so extraordinarily skilful, and the perpetuation of the hoax appears to have been so entirely unscrupulous and inexplicable, as to find no parallel in the history of palaeontology discovery.[174]

Analysis of the Piltdown remains did not, however, cease with the exposure of the fraud. Further revelations concerning the extent of the forgery came to light in 1955, Weiner, Le Gros Clark, Oakley, Claringbull, Hey, Edmunds, Bowie, Davidson, Fryd, Baynes-Cope, Werner and Plesters publishing the results of their new survey in the *Bulletin of the British Museum (Natural History) Geology*. In the introduction to the paper, Gavin de Beer, Director of the British Museum (Natural History), summarised the new set of revelations:

> The mandible has been shown by further anatomical and X-ray evidence to be almost certainly that of an immature orang-utan (**92**); that it is entirely recent has been confirmed by a number of microchemical tests, as well as by the electron-microscope demonstration of organic (collagen) fibres; the black coating on the canine tooth, originally assumed to be an iron

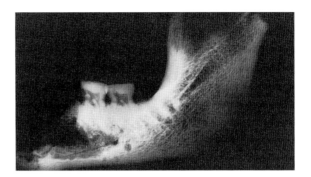

91 *Piltdown I: an X-ray of the mandible showing the unmineralised nature of the bone and the long, ape-like roots of the molars*

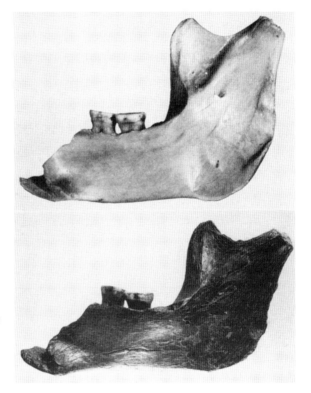

92 *Piltdown I: the mandible of* Eoanthropus *(bottom) shown for comparison with that of a modern female orang-utan (top). The orang-utan specimen has been deliberately broken, and its molars abraded, in order to simulate the Piltdown jaw*

encrustation, is a paint (probably Vandyke brown); the so-called turbinal bone is shown by its texture not to be a turbinal bone at all, but thin fragments of probably non-human limb-bone; all the associated flint implements have been artificially iron-stained (**93**); the bone implement was shaped by a steel knife (**94**); the whole of the associated fauna must have been 'planted', and it is concluded from radioactivity tests and fluorine analysis that some of the specimens are of foreign origin. The human skull fragments and some of the fossil animal bones are partly replaced by gypsum, the result of their treatment with iron sulphate to produce a colour matching that of the gravel. Not one of the Piltdown finds genuinely came from Piltdown.[175]

93 (Left) *Piltdown I: the artificially stained palaeoliths 'unearthed' from Barkham Manor. The second flint from the right is palaeolith E.606 found by Teilhard de Chardin, whilst the specimen at the extreme right was retrieved from the collection of Harry Morris*

94 (Right) *Piltdown I: the worked end of the elephant-bone tool which has been shaped with a steel knife*

Following these new exposures, it may appear surprising that the investigation team did not attempt to supply an absolute date, such as may be achieved through radiocarbon dating, for any of the Piltdown bones. Radiocarbon (or carbon-14) dating is a method of scientifically assessing the age of something that was once alive. All living organisms contain carbon, a proportion of which is radioactive isotope carbon-14. When an animal or plant dies, it stops absorbing carbon-14 and the quantity present within the organism slowly starts to decay. As this rate of decay is theoretically known, the relative concentration of carbon-14 within a sample of bone or charcoal can be measured and an estimate of the date of death can be made.

When the initial testing of the Piltdown bone was undertaken between 1953 and 1955, the possibility of determining an absolute date was not considered as, in order to supply the 2gm of carbon then required by fledgling radiocarbon laboratories, such a procedure 'would have involved total destruction of the specimens'.[176] The steady improvement of radiocarbon dating techniques over the following four years meant that, by 1959, a determination of age could be made using significantly smaller quantities of bone. Accordingly, samples from the mandible and skull of the Barkham Manor *Eoanthropus* were submitted for dating, the results confirming that the specimens were certainly not as old as had previously been suggested.

Cranial fragments from the Barkham Manor gravel pit were dated to 620±100 (GrN-2203), which may be calibrated at 95.4 per cent probability to having an origin somewhere between AD 1210 and 1480. The orang-utan mandible was also assessed at this time, producing a date of 500±100 (GrN-2204), which may be calibrated at 95.4 per cent probability to between AD 1290 and 1640. These results suggested that:

the Piltdown skull (human) is Post-Pleistocene, probably less than 800 years old; and that the Piltdown mandible (orang-utan) is younger rather than older, although possibly several centuries old. It is shown that these findings are not inconsistent with the skull being in 'sub-fossil' condition whereas the mandible (of very different origin) has the preservation of 'recent' bone.[177]

In the late 1980s, a second sample from the Barkham Manor jaw was processed, together with a new sample from the human cranium recovered by Charles Dawson from Sheffield Park (referred to as 'Piltdown II').[178] The new radiocarbon determination for the mandible was given at 90±120 (OxA-1395), which may be calibrated at 95.4 per cent probability to between 1630 and AD 1960. The obvious discrepancy between the two dates provided for the same mandible has never been satisfactorily explained, though the new determination would, the investigation team noted, 'accommodate a postu-lated 19th-century date' for the piece as well as the original suggestion that it may be derived from a 'museum collection'.[179]

Conclusions

Issues of complicity in the Piltdown forgery are far more complex than any of the other discoveries so far catalogued and discussed within the context of this book. This is due, in no small part, to the plethora of theories, counter-theories, suggestions and accusations that have surrounded the Piltdown story since the hoax was first publicly exposed in 1953. Attempting to wade through and assess each and every accusation can be a laborious and thoroughly unrewarding task. Every person who visited the site during the course of the 1912 excavations, every scientist who commented upon the Piltdown remains, everyone whom Dawson and Woodward knew or came into contact with on a daily basis and pretty much any person living within a ten-mile radius of the gravel pit could conceivably be implicated in the hoax.

Many people have indeed been accused of generating the fraud that was *Eoanthropus dawsoni*, often on the flimsiest of evidence. Most prominent of these names in recent years has been that of Sir Arthur Keith, anatomist and conser-vator of the Hunterian Museum of the Royal College of Surgeons. The case against Keith, set out in exhaustive detail by Frank Spencer in his book *Piltdown: a scientific forgery*, seems to rest primarily upon the fact that, when interviewed by Weiner in 1953, some forty years after the event, the anatomist found it difficult to remember the nature of his relationship with Dawson or of the exact timing of important meetings. The case against Keith, which is lacking in anything but the most circumstantial of detail, has been brilliantly dissected by Philip Tobias (1992) and John Evangelist Walsh (1996)[180] and it seems pointless to go over the same ground again here. The biggest mystery in the whole case of Arthur Keith is quite how such a spurious accusation was, given the almost total absence of objective data, ever seriously considered in the first place.

If the case against Arthur Keith is flimsy, then that made against William Johnson Sollas, Oxford University Professor of Geology, is simply laughable. Here the accusation centres upon the ultimately unprovable belief that Sollas hated Arthur Woodward and that he had, at some stage in his career, been in possession of both a packet of potassium chromate and apes' teeth. The charge was made by James Archibald Douglas, a retired Oxford University professor who had once been Sollas' assistant. Douglas, then aged ninety-three, had recorded his allegations onto a tape which, following his death in 1978, was played back to an unsuspecting (not to say largely unbelieving) audience.[181] Accusations made against Grafton Elliot Smith (Professor of Anatomy at Manchester University [182]), William Ruskin Butterfield,[183] Lewis Abbott,[184] Samuel Allinson Woodhead [185] and John Hewitt (Professor of Chemistry at Queen Mary College, London University)[186] are also highly dubious and have already been effectively discredited.[187]

A recent series of accusations have been made against Martin Hinton, who at the time of the Piltdown 'discoveries' was a part-time volunteer cataloguing and examining fossil rodents, though he later rose to become Deputy Keeper in the Zoology Department of the British Museum (Natural History). The central thrust of the case is that a canvas trunk bearing Hinton's initials and containing 'assorted bones' of unspecified origin, some of which had been chemically treated, was 'found' in the attic of the Natural History Museum.[188] These bones prove nothing more than somebody at the museum, possibly Hinton himself, was at some point experimenting in ways to replicate the artificial staining of the Piltdown bone, presumably in order to expose the fraud. To make an accusation solely upon such flimsy, unsupported evidence is amazing. That anyone believed it is even more incredible. For Hinton (and the other characters mentioned above for that matter) to have been the Piltdown forger, he (and they) would have required not just a trunk full of stained bones, but full, unfettered access to the Barkham Manor site. The careful placement of all the fabricated pieces of the fraud, not to say their successful recovery, would have demanded:

> the forger's repeated presence on the scene as digging progressed during more than two years, the three summers in which the finds were made. But in the period 1912-1914, Hinton was never at the Piltdown pit, certainly not during excavations.[189]

As long as ill thought out and poorly conceived accusations such as those made against the likes of Hinton, Butterfield, Keith, Abbott, Woodhead, Hewitt, Sollas, Smith et al. continue to be made, then a full and proper resolution to the Piltdown question will never be possible.

Accusations of conspiracy have not just been made against *named* individuals, however, a large number of theories have recently centred around a mysterious individual who was spotted by Mabel Kenward, daughter of Robert Kenward the chief tenant of Barkham Manor in 1912:

> one evening, early evening, I saw this tall man come up, not even up the drive, but across the fields – must have gotten over the hedges and ditches even to get there... and he walked to the pit and started scratching about... so I said excuse me are you an authorised searcher?... he didn't say one word... off he went the same way across the fields... he was dressed in an ordinary grey suit but he had gum boots on and he was very tall... a man in his forties.[190]

Unfortunately, this mysterious grey-suited man could literally be anyone; an innocent walker, a curious trespasser or the hoaxer himself. J. Combridge [191] inferred, on what appears to be very little evidence, that the figure was John Lewis, Dawson's collaborator at the Lavant Caves and Hastings Castle, whilst Ronald Millar suggested that it was 'one of the little Teilhards, six feet five inches and not a day over thirty-six'.[192] Ian Langham and Frank Spencer however, believed that Kenward had in fact identified Arthur Keith engaged on a 'clandestine visit' to the pit as 'her general description of the mysterious interloper fitted Keith perfectly'.[193]

Of course, none of these claims concerning the identity of an anonymous 'grey-suited man' really require serious consideration, far less the 'reliable witness' to the excavation who claimed to have seen 'Prussian soldiers goose-stepping about the pit in breast-plates and spiked helmets'.[194] A devious plot no doubt organised by the German command to blackmail Charles Dawson into revealing some of his brother Trevor's secrets at Metro-Vickers and Maxims. For the purposes of clarity (not to say common sense), in this conclusion to Piltdown I will examine only those individuals who, having been in someway accused of complicity in the deception, clearly possessed a regular association with both the site and those engaged in the primary stages of the excavation.

The first time that the general public heard about the Piltdown fake was via the media. The London *Times*, one of the quickest off the press, outlined the conclusions of Weiner, Oakley and Le Gros Clark concerning the forgery, adding ruefully that 'the authors of the article do not identify the perpetrator of this fraud – but 'Who did it?' is a question many will ask'.[195] In the absence of a statement from the British Museum, who at this time were more interested in the mechanics of the deception and not the identity of its perpetrator, *The Times* naturally leapt to its own conclusions. Charles Dawson was, the paper reminded its readers, the discoverer of the skull and it was he who first drew people's attention to it. Sir Arthur Woodward, 'an authority of international reputation and unassailable integrity' then joined Dawson's search for more pieces of skull, as did Father P. Teilhard de Chardin, 'an eminent French scholar'.[196]

> Thus two witnesses of the highest character either found, or helped to find, the bones now known to be spurious, and it is hard to resist the conclusion that the jaw and tooth had been put there, by some third person, in order that they might be so unimpeachably discovered.[197]

The implications of this were, in the view of the unidentified *Times* Museum Correspondent, both inevitable and wholly inescapable: 'If that third person were to prove to be Charles Dawson, it would be but one more instance of desire for fame (since money was certainly not here the object) leading a scholar into dishonesty'.[198] Others disagreed. Within two days of the report, the pages of London's *Daily Herald* printed a reply from Trevor Dawson's son and two daughters stating that their uncle 'was not the type of man to hoax anybody... if anyone suggests he was a party to the hoax we shall certainly do something about it to clear his name'.[199]

The implications of the letter were clear enough. Further unfounded accusations against Charles Dawson FGS., FSA. would be met with legal action. Captain F.J.M. Postlethwaite, Dawson's stepson, also wrote a strenuous denial to *The Times*, refuting the insinuations made by the paper on 21 November:

> Charles Dawson was an unassuming and thoroughly honest man and very painstaking, as when he wrote *The History of Hastings Castle*, entailing years of research. From an early age he was interested in flint implements and fossils, uncovering the bones of some saurian near Hastings. He exercised his great general knowledge in many ways, discovering natural gas at Heathfield and becoming an authority on Sussex iron. His hobbies extended in many directions, but it is doubtful whether he could be described as a great expert in any single subject. Until the discovery at Piltdown he did not display any particular interest in skulls, human or otherwise, and so far as I know had none in his possession. To suggest that he had the knowledge and the skill to break an ape's jawbone in exactly the right place, to pare the teeth to ensure a perfect fit to the upper skull and to disguise the whole in such a manner as to deceive his partner, a scientist of international repute, would surely be absurd, and personally I am doubtful whether he ever had the opportunity of doing so.[200]

In Postlethwaite's view the whole Piltdown incident had been manufactured by an unscrupulous and unnamed 'other'.

> No – Charles Dawson was at all times far too honest and faithful to his research to have been accessory to any faking whatsoever. He was himself

duped, and from statements appearing in the Press such is evidently the opinion of those who knew him well, some of whom are scientists of repute.[201]

Though Postlethwaite failed to identify the perpetrator of the fraud who had so cynically 'duped' his stepfather, his comments, together with the continued failure of the British Museum (Natural History) at this time to name names, helped foster the belief that the story was only part of a larger scientific conspiracy: that those working in the British Museum knew who was responsible, but were in some way 'protecting their own'. Dawson was, of course, an outsider to the scientific establishment, he was an amateur in the field of antiquarian and geological research and, therefore, an easy target. The feeling was being generated that there was another person, just lurking on the sidelines, who had been manipulating circumstances for their own devious ends: but who?

Matters were unfortunately not helped by the much-awaited publication of Joseph Weiner's findings in his book *The Piltdown Forgery*, the first serious analysis of the whole affair designed for both the general public and the scientific community. The evidence, as discussed by Weiner, clearly pointed towards Charles Dawson, but Weiner unfortunately held back from firmly naming him as chief conspirator. Perhaps he was mindful of the legal action already threatened by the surviving members of Dawson's family. Perhaps he simply felt that the evidence would speak for itself, observing that:

> If Dawson was an innocent victim, a dupe from the start to finish, we should have to accept a reconstruction of his behaviour which would include a number of very remarkable episodes, for in many ways, as we have learnt, his actions coincide so surprisingly well with those of the perpetrator.[202]

Weiner also hints at alternative scenarios where Dawson may have been the victim of a hoax, or was acting, unwillingly or otherwise, on behalf of another. Much of this supposition is effectively dismissed throughout the course of the book, but although Weiner contends that it is difficult to disassociate Dawson from key aspects of the hoax, his conclusion ends on a decidedly ambiguous note:

> It is true that of the evidence which throws so much suspicion on him [Dawson], part is derived from his own papers and letters, and that most of the information which has come to us indirectly has not gone uncorroborated, but none of it furnishes the positive and final proof of his responsibility. So long as the weight of circumstantial evidence is insufficient to prove beyond all reasonable doubt that it was Dawson himself who set the deception going by 'planting' the pieces of brain-case, our verdict

as to the authorship must rest on suspicion and not proof. In the circumstances we withhold from Dawson's the one alternative possibility, remote
though it seems, but which we cannot altogether disprove: that he might,
after all, have been implicated in a 'joke', perhaps not even his own, which
went too far? Would it not be fairer to one who cannot speak for himself
to let it go at that?[203]

Unfortunately the ambiguity of Weiner's 'final' statement did little to stem the
flow of speculation over the authorship of the Piltdown fraud. The theory that
the whole affair had been only part of a 'greater conspiracy' was one which
was certainly becoming popular in the mid-1950s, being fuelled by the publication of *The Piltdown Fantasy* by Francis Vere (real name Francis Bannister)[204]
in 1955. Vere believed that the first discoveries at Barkham Manor had been
real enough, but that individuals who knew Dawson and to whom he had
mentioned the discovery:

> decided to play a trick on him. Whoever they were they had the material
> at hand and the ability to fake it. There was not much material unearthed
> after all – a few teeth of Stegodon, Mastodon, Hippopotamus, beaver and
> horse, the base of a deer's antler and the proximal end of the metatarsal of
> the same beast: the shaped thigh-bone of an elephant (found under the
> hedge), and about a dozen eoliths and flint implements – the scourings of
> a collection easily purchasable.[205]

In Vere's mind the whole affair was a 'joke' that misfired badly:

> if your object is to make fools of people it is a little disappointing to find them
> turned into popular heroes. Surely then, the hoaxer should have given the
> show away himself, That would not have been so easy as it sounds. In the first
> place, he would be giving himself away, destroying his anonymity, which the
> discovery of the trick would have preserved. He may have been so situated –
> have held such a position or gained such a reputation – that a confession from
> him would have caused him great harm in reputation or in career.[206]

The 'joke gone awry' theory, which was later used to implicate Teilhard de
Chardin in the forgery,[207] is not terribly convincing, especially given the
amount of planning, organisation and co-ordination of resources that went
into the hoax over a period lasting at least eight years. Why prolong the joke
for such a lengthy period? What was it really intended to expose and why was
the punch line never revealed? Nevertheless, such concerns have not prevented
others from intimating that the whole Piltdown affair was a piece of harmless
fun that got out of hand. Perhaps the reason that the elephant tool looked so
much like a cricket bat,[208] was precisely because somebody thought that the

joke had gone on long enough and wanted to end the fun with something that simply could not be taken seriously:

> perhaps the hoax – definitely not a forgery – was nothing personal, not directed at Dawson or Woodward. Perhaps it was just fun but a deadly kind of fun that takes no prisoners, mockery or ridicule aimed at that nation of pebble hunters on this side of the English Channel.[209]

The evidence, such as it stands, for Piltdown I does not, however, suggest such a directionless, gentle piece of 'mockery' intended to embarrass British palaeontology. The logistics and strategy of *Eoanthropus dawsoni* suggests that, if Teilhard de Chardin had been involved, that he was planning something altogether more serious.

Early in 1954, Robert Essex, a biology teacher who had been working at Uckfield Grammar School at the time of the Piltdown discoveries, appeared at the British Museum (Natural History), desperate to tell his version of the Piltdown forgery. Kenneth Oakley and Wilfred Edwards, Keeper of Geology, duly conducted an interview, though Edwards was later to confide in Weiner that he felt that Essex's evidence was 'elaborate surmise', the schoolmaster being 'pretty hopeless on dates'.[210] Despite the museum team's initial misgivings, certain aspects of the story were certainly rather intriguing, though Weiner chose to exclude them from his final summing-up in *The Piltdown Forgery* (1955).

Essex pinned all his suspicions upon the French cleric Teilhard de Chardin, especially concerning the peculiar nature of the elephant-bone tool, or 'cricket bat' recovered during the 1914 season. One event particularly stuck in Essex's mind: a discussion between Charles Dawson, John Montgomery, Essex and 'one or two interested "outsiders"' held outside Dawson's Uckfield office, something which he later related in a letter to Weiner.

> Charles Dawson remarked that he couldn't remember seeing anything quite like the 'sixteen inch bat'... 'But I have', said John Montgomery. 'Oh!' said Dawson, 'Where?' 'In the Dordogne', said J.M. Dawson's eyebrows went up and he looked round to see where Teilhard was standing and for a few seconds seemed deep in thought – From that position he suddenly swung back and apologised for his lapse – then said he must get back to work.[211]

Convenient though it may be for some to accuse Teilhard de Chardin, it is clear that he cannot have been the mastermind behind *Eoanthropus dawsoni* as he was simply not in the country when certain key 'discoveries' were made at Piltdown. His chance finding of the elephant molar and single canine tooth may seem spectacularly fortuitous, but not if these finds had been deliberately planted for him in order to add his authenticity, whilst simultaneously attracting attention away from the real forger.

What then of Dawson's friend and colleague at Piltdown: Arthur Smith Woodward? (**95**) The investigating team co-ordinated by the British Museum (Natural History) was keen to avoid pointing the finger of suspicion directly at Woodward. Certainly Woodward benefited academically from the Piltdown discoveries, the site launching him onto the world stage and international recognition, but was this proof enough of his complicity? Possible involvement in the fraud could explain Woodward's reluctance to quiz Dawson over the exact details of the first finding of *Eoanthropus*, as well as his failure to observe the simpler aspects of the forgery, such artificial abrasion on the teeth of Piltdown man and the modern cut marks across the business end of the elephant femur. Woodward's fruitless continuation of the Barkham Manor excavations for a further twenty-one years after Dawson's death, however, must surely argue against his involvement (unless he planned two decades of unproductive work purely to throw subsequent investigators off the scent). In retrospect, Arthur Smith Woodward's only provable crime in the case of Piltdown man was his gullibility and culpability: he believed Dawson implicitly and never asked the crucial questions which could so easily have undermined *Eoanthropus dawsoni* very early on.

This brings us back to Charles Dawson (**96**). Defenders of the solicitor from Uckfield have at times stated their firm belief that he had somehow been coerced into generating the forgery. After his investigations of 1953 were complete however, Joseph Weiner noted that to the existence of a possible blackmailer 'there is no trail, other than conjecture'.[212] Some have thought that Dawson had been specifically targeted by an enemy, for he had certainly made no friends in the Sussex Archaeological Society over his purchase of Castle Lodge in 1904. If there had been a manipulator of events operating clandestinely 'behind the scenes' at Barkham Manor, then this individual possessed an 'omnipotence not to be despised of Mephistopheles himself' Weiner observed rather wryly, for:

> he has Dawson under the closest surveillance for very many years... In two features he is outstanding – his amazingly intimate and detailed knowledge of Dawson's interests and affairs and his complete grasp of the geological, evolutionary, archaeological, and faunistic potentialities of both Piltdown sites... his professionalism is well attested also in his ability to obtain and fashion the animal and human fossils and recent bones needed for the great design. His acquaintance with Dawson's movements and inquiries is uncanny... having conceived his plan, he has unrestricted access to Barkham Manor and makes his 'plant', always certain that the victim will take the bait. His access to the pit is so unquestioned that in his wait of three or four years, while he is preparing the jaw and other fabrications, he can arrange for the rather rare animal teeth and a few other pieces to be safely recovered by Dawson. With an uncanny prescience, he holds back the jaw from him throughout all those years until the climax, the British Museum's participation.[213]

95 *Piltdown I: Arthur Smith Woodward (left) and the Uckfield photographer John Frisby (right) standing by the edge of the Barkham Manor gravel pit in the summer of 1912*

96 *Piltdown I: Working at the Barkham Manor gravel pit in the summer of 1912. This photograph, taken by John Frisby, shows Charles Dawson (bending over with geological hammer), Arthur Smith Woodward (seated with sieve) and Woodward's son Cyril (standing behind Dawson). This shot was used as the basis for Frisby's famous postcard 'Searching for the Piltdown Man' (see **11**), in which Cyril was subtly removed*

In short, Dawson *cannot* have been innocent of the Piltdown hoax. From the start to the finish of the affair, he is implicated at every single stage. He was, without exception, the only person present at each and every discovery at both Barkham Manor and the subsequent sites (see below); indeed some of the 'finds' were made whilst he was working *by himself*. He is the only common factor in all of the elements of the story. He, together with Arthur Smith Woodward, are the only people to have significantly benefited, in academic terms at least, from the discovery of *Eoanthropus*, though it must be said that as Keeper of Geology at the British Museum (Natural History), Woodward's academic standing was, in 1912, already quite high. Which ever way you look at the evidence, Dawson is there.

If we accept that Dawson cannot in any way be disassociated with the fraud, then we encounter more prosaic problems concerning his involvement, the first of which is a question of basic resources. Did Dawson possess easy access to the raw materials necessary to generate the hoax in the first place? Some have doubted that a 'mere country solicitor' would have had neither the time to perpetrate the fraud, nor the opportunity to acquire certain key ingredients. Time does not appear to have been a problem, for the quantity of publications, exhibitions, displays, excavations, surveys and lectures that we know Dawson organised, belies the suggestion that he had little time off from work to feed his antiquarian habit. Quite how his schedule at Dawson and Hart operated is unclear, though it may have been that Dawson's partner there, George Hart, later to become 'Official Solicitor of England',[214] shouldered most of the burden. Perhaps Dawson was simply a workaholic who never had time for normal 'everyday' activities.

As concerns the means to acquire the raw materials necessary to furnish the fraud, Weiner was quick to observe that a man such as Dawson would in fact have no difficulty at all in procuring 'unusual' items such as an ape-mandible for:

> then, as now [1955], they could be bought from, or through, a local taxi-dermist, or, if not, then easily enough from one of the famous London firms. One would almost certainly go to Gerrard's in Camden Town, who have been established in this business... since 1860. Anyone who has ever worked in a museum would know of the firm. Mr Gerrard tells me that unmatched jaws and other odd bones were probably easier to come by in the years before World War I than now. Before the blitz... blotted out their premises, once a month one could attend a 'taxidermists' auction in the rooms of Stevens in King Street, and a collector could hope to pick up an enormous variety of specimens and bones. Odd bits of the skeleton, such as teeth and mandibles, were cheap enough in those days. Ape and jaw bones could be easily come by and many geologists had them.[215]

But did Dawson? There is no record of him ever having collected 'ape bones' at any time in his archaeological or palaeontological career, but then if he had been the forger he would certainly have covered his tracks. Other local antiquarians of the period, such as the jeweller William James Lewis Abbott, were certainly in possession of chimpanzee remains,[216] but that of course opens the enquiry up to almost every amateur archaeologist in the area.

One piece of evidence, albeit circumstantial, is, however, worth noting here. Joseph Weiner, during a visit to Lewes made before 17 August 1953, interviewed 'Drs Nicholl Jnr and Snr' the then owners of Castle Lodge, the former family home of Charles and Helene Dawson. Weiner hoped to obtain supporting data concerning the acquisition of the Lodge by the Dawsons in 1904. He may also have hoped that potential evidence linking Dawson with the Piltdown hoax, in the form of correspondence, notebooks, artefact or possibly even chemical residue, may have come to light within the house following the demise of Helene in 1917. Weiner later observed, in a letter to Le Gros Clark, that during the course of the interview there occurred 'one episode of the most fantastic and exciting kind'.[217] At one point, Dr Nicholl Jnr:

> suddenly said that he remembered as a boy of 8 that while the floor in the back dining room was being relaid for dry rot 'two monkey skulls were found under the floor'. You can imagine that this was startling indeed, yet on the following day no one else could be found to corroborate it. Neither Nicholl senior, the old nurse, the gardener, nor even the foreman who had done the work 20 years ago, but it may have happened while the family was away and there was a locum who, Nicholl Jnr. thought, may have actually had the skulls. The locum is now in Transjordania and although I shall write to him, this now seems a slender hope.[218]

A tantalising if ultimately ephemeral lead. Whether Weiner was able to contact the peripatetic locum, is not recorded; certainly no 'monkey skulls' were ever produced in evidence to support the tale. Weiner did, however, receive some independent corroboration of the story from Lady Maude Woodward, Arthur Woodward's widow, who was interviewed by Wilfred Norman Edwards, then Keeper of Geology at the British Museum (Natural History) in January 1954. Edwards recorded that Lady Woodward confirmed to him that:

> a successor who occupied C[harles] D[awson]'s house had occasion to take up some floor boards and that a skeleton (said to be an ape) was found underneath. Lady Woodward had recently talked to Miss Kenward about this, and the latter remembered the story.[219]

Quite how (and why) Lady Woodward and Mabel Kenward, daughter of Robert Kenward, the tenant of Barkham Manor, should have reason to remember this story, whilst the owner of Castle Lodge, Dr Nicholls Snr, did not, cannot be satisfactorily explained. Given that the tale of 'monkeys beneath the floorboards' had not, by January 1954, fully been made public may however provide it with some authenticity. When a reporter from the London *Daily Mail* followed the story up early the next year, the details of the discovery had unfortunately changed somewhat, the find being described as having been made 'in a cavity in a wall behind "wainscoting near the window bay"'.[220] The basics of the story as related by 'Dr Nicholls Jnr to Weiner could, of course, be a false memory, or the exaggerated recollection of a young boy. One thing is clear however: as Weiner's interview with Nicholls was conducted in August 1953, a full three months *before* the revelation of fraud at Piltdown was made, we can discount possible conflation with newspaper reports of doctored skulls and faked chimpanzee mandibles.

As the prime mover behind the Piltdown hoax, Dawson would have found many of the basic building blocks necessary to accomplish the forgery readily to hand in Sussex. Dawson was a co-founder, in 1889, of the Hastings and St Leonards Museum Association and also a member of the Museum Committee, in charge of the acquisition of antiquarian artefacts (such as Blackmore's flint collection)[221] and historical documents. The museum itself regularly proved to be the ideal display case for Dawson's own collection of antiquarian curiosities, which eventually occupied a section all of its own.[222] Whilst performing his legal role, as partner in Dawson and Hart, Dawson found himself acting as solicitor to a number of prominent Sussex antiquarian collectors, and was able to catalogue a variety of materials bequeathed or otherwise donated to Hastings Museum throughout the 1890s and early 1900s. One such assemblage was the Brassey Collection, comprising a diverse set of materials brought back to England by Lord and Lady Brassey 'after several round the world voyages on their steam yacht'. Interestingly enough, the Brassey's yacht, *The Sunbeam* 'visited Malta, Crete and Sarawak, North Borneo amongst many other ports. These happen to be the chemically identified provenances of the associated Piltdown animal fossils, and the orang-utan jawbone'.[223]

By the 1890s, Dawson was even conducting his own excavations in and around Hastings Castle, an early phase of which was reported to have produced a 'great haul' of artefacts.[224] In addition to all this, we know that Dawson was purchasing materials from local dealers (such as the Hastings Mace bought from a pawnbroker's 'somewhere in Kent').[225] We should also not forget that Dawson claimed to be in contact with all the workmen in his area 'who might make accidental discoveries',[226] such contacts allegedly helping him to collect the 'Sussex Loops' and 'Toad in a Hole' from Brighton. A man such as Dawson would, had he the mind to, certainly be in an excellent position to accumulate the necessary specimens for any number of frauds, forgeries and deceptions.

A further, perhaps more specific lead, presents itself. John Clements, writing to the magazine *Current Archaeology* in 1997, observed that the 'thickened cranium' of Piltdown I may have had its origins within the town of Hastings itself. In 1858, Mayor Alderman Thomas Ross was excavating on East

Hill in Hastings, looking for a Roman lighthouse, but in reality finding 'a group of sixty graves'.[227] At least one of the skulls, apparently part of a sixth-century grave deposit, was unusual, being 'upwards of seven sixteenth's of an inch thick'. This, and other relics from the cemetery, remained in Ross' not inconsiderable private collection. Clements noted that, interestingly enough, 'Charles Dawson acted as solicitor for Ross after his death, inheriting some of his collection'.[228] A reopening of Ross' trench 'backfilled with many bones' occurred in 1902 during the building of East Cliff railway, itself a popular tourist attraction for many years after, whilst in 1912 'drainage works by the Borough engineers near the upper cliff railway station uncovered two more unusually thick skulls, and two rather thin ones'.[229]

Of course this is all surmise, it does not represent conclusive proof of where the 'thickened' human cranium of Piltdown I originated, and neither for that matter is it meant to be. It does, however, serve to demonstrate that an early archaeologist, or amateur interested in antiquarian pursuits, could in the early years of the twentieth century easily accumulate the basic human skeletal remains necessary for the fraud.

Easier to acquire from Dawson's perspective would have been flint tools, or 'palaeoliths' supposedly recovered from Barkham Manor. Despite claims to the contrary, only four or five 'palaeoliths' were ever produced by Dawson in evidence for the workmanship of *Eoanthropus*.[230] Any fieldworker worth his salt could gather such material up from the ploughed fields of southern England, and, in the early years of the late nineteenth and early twentieth centuries, many private antiquarian lithic assemblages were known to exist.[231] Dawson himself had no mean collection of worked flint, including serrated blades, spears and polished axes and flints from Denmark, flakes from Birling Gap near Eastbourne and various arrowheads from North America.[232] Some of this material was passed on to Hastings Museum after his death. A complete listing of the Dawson lithics, as held by Hastings Museum, interestingly shows that Dawson also possessed 'four modern copies of flint implements, made by Flint Jack',[233] a famous nineteenth-century fabricator of prehistoric-looking flint tools.

The Barkham Manor lithics, though repeatedly referred to as 'palaeoliths', inferring an early date for their use, are more likely to represent unfinished stages in Neolithic flint axe manufacture. Many flint mines are known to have existed along the chalk ridge of the South Downs during Neolithic times (*c*.4200 BC – 2500 BC), concentrating in areas such as Cissbury, Harrow Hill and Blackpatch Hill behind modern-day Worthing. A walk across these hills today will reveal large numbers of struck flints, in rabbit burrows, molehills and plough ruts, the by-product of prehistoric mining and flint-shaping activities. When these sites were first scientifically examined, in the mid-nineteenth to early twentieth century, many 'roughouts', the unfinished residue of Neolithic axe manufacture, were actually believed to represent finished examples of *Palaeolithic* workmanship. The association of Palaeolithic tools with obvious signs of deep mining, led a number of prominent scholars to suggest that flint mines were not Neolithic, but were thousands of years older, dating to the earliest phases of human occupation in the British Isles.[234] The Barkham Mills flint certainly fits more comfortably within a Neolithic lithic assemblage than anything yet recorded from the British Palaeolithic. The flints' artificially stained surface, apparently conducted in order to disguise their origin (from the white chalk not the brown gravels of Piltdown),[235] further increases the likelihood that they represent Neolithic artefacts, not the product of early human tool manufacture.

The staining of the Barkham 'palaeoliths' is 'surprisingly superficial',[236] their white, chalky patina having been effectively disguised by an application of bichromate solution of the sort that Dawson used to 'harden' the Piltdown bone.[237] Of course the lithics did not require artificial hardening, and so the use of chromium here can only have been in order to disguise the surface colour of the material as 'flint nodules with white cortex do not occur naturally in the Piltdown district'.[238] Dawson is, as far as can be ascertained, the only person to have used bichromate solution on the Piltdown artefacts (see below), Woodward commenting on the fact on a number of occasions.[239]

There is a curious piece of evidence relating to the Piltdown 'palaeoliths' which appears to directly identify the hand of the forger. In the autumn of 1953, Joseph Weiner heard from an interviewee that a certain Harry Morris, 'a bank clerk and keen amateur archaeologist', had once believed the Barkham Manor flints to be fraudulent.[240] Having somehow acquired one of the flint 'palaeoliths', Morris had become convinced that something was wrong, voicing his concerns in a series short written statements. Unfortunately, Morris had since died though a 'large cabinet of flints', apparently containing the Piltdown artefact, had been bequeathed to his friend A.P. Pollard. Pollard, not being an avid collector of such things, eventually exchanged the cabinet with Frederick Wood for a collection of bird eggs. Wood died shortly after, but Pollard believed that his wife lived in the village of Ditchling, to the north of Brighton. It looked to Weiner that this was going to prove to be another frustratingly intangible lead, but Mrs Wood was finally traced and, yes the cabinet remained in her possession.[241]

The elusive Piltdown flint that Morris had somehow obtained from Charles Dawson (**97**) proved more interesting than Weiner could have hoped. The artefact, which was identical in lithology to those recorded by Dawson, was 'somewhat quadrangular in outline' with evidence of battering.[242] Directly onto the surface of the flint, Morris had written 'Stained by C. Dawson with intent to defraud (all) – H.M.'.[243] On a small note accompanying the piece Morris had added the comment: 'Stained with permanganate of potash and exchanged by D. for my most valued specimen! – H.M.'.[244] A third note, this time written on a small piece of photographic backing, continued:

97 *Piltdown I: the Morris palaeolith*

> Judging from an overheard conversation there is every reason to suppose that the canine tooth found at Pdown was imported from France! I challenge the S[outh] K[ensington] Museum authorities to test the implements of the same patina as this stone which the impostor Dawson says were 'excavated from the Pit!' They will be found [to] be white if hydrochlorate [sic] acid be applied – H.M. Truth will out.[245]

In pencil, across the ink-written note, Morris had added 'Watch C. Dawson. Kind regards'.[246] The reference to the canine tooth having been 'imported from France' appears to be an accusation against Teilhard de Chardin who found the piece during the 1913 season, though the context of the 'overhead conversation' is left infuriatingly vague. A fourth and final note reads:

> Dawson's Farce: 'Let not light see my black and deep desires. The eye wink at the hand; yet let that be. Which the eye fears when it is done – to see!' Macbeth Act I, 3.[247]

Weiner did not at first know what to make of these extraordinary accusations. The first issue to resolve was when they had been written, for Morris did not date any of the comments, though their tone and content suggested that they had been compiled between 1913 and 1916.[248] Morris mentioned that he had obtained the palaeolith by exchanging it for 'my most valued specimen' (presumably another flint). This would seem to imply a date very early on in the investigation of Barkham Manor, as, following the involvement of Arthur Smith Woodward and the British Museum (Natural History) in the summer of 1912, all artefacts derived from the Piltdown dig went directly to South Kensington. The comment 'Watch C. Dawson', scribbled over the top of the third note, further implies a *living* Dawson, so its addition cannot have been any later than Autumn 1916. Whatever the exact date of their writing, it was clear that the notes predated any formal accusation against either Dawson or the authenticity of the Piltdown assemblage.

Any queries concerning the authenticity of the Morris flint (as a 'genuine fake') were dispelled by the application of dilute hydrochloric which, just as Morris intimated it would, dissolved away the yellow brown stain 'leaving a pale yellowish or greyish white surface'.[249] Morris' challenge on the third note to the 'authorities' of the British Museum (Natural History) to 'test the implements of the same patina as this stone' was accepted, hydrochloric acid similarly dissolving the artificial brown stain of the three palaeoliths in their custody. Morris had been wrong in one respect, however; the staining had been caused not by 'permanganate of potash', but by the application of bichromate solution (as per the animal bone, cranium and mandible of *Eoanthropus*).

Three questions remained unanswered: how had Morris become aware of the fraud, why had he not disseminated his evidence and to whom was he writing with his plea to 'Watch C. Dawson'? A.P. Pollard believed that Morris had first discovered the deception because, as an expert on the area 'he knew from the geological formation of the gravel at Piltdown that it was *not* Palaeolithic or pre-P[alaeolithic] but transitional between P[alaeolithic] and Neolithic'.[250]

Having obtained the necessary flint from Dawson (quite how the Uckfield solicitor was persuaded to part with such a valuable item is never established – perhaps the exchange was only at first a temporary loan?), Morris was then 'utterly convinced that some deception had been carried out'.[251] That he only seems to have conveyed his convictions to 'his close friend Major R.A. Marriott' and later to Pollard, perhaps belies the fact that, by 1912, Dawson was held in great esteem by archaeologists, anthropologists, geologists and palaeontologists alike. He was, furthermore, a renowned solicitor and pillar of local society (despite falling out with the Sussex Archaeological Society). For Morris to attack Dawson, by announcing that the Piltdown flints were fraudulent, would be to attack all the eminent academics and scientists who were becoming increasingly involved in the *Eoanthropus* debate.

It is possible that word of Morris' accusations reached the ears of the American vertebrate palaeontologist William King Gregory, for it is he who noted that unnamed individuals had suggested that Piltdown was 'a deliberate hoax'.[252] It is, however, important to point out here that Morris seems only to have believed the Piltdown flints to be fraudulent; we have no evidence to suggest that he similarly thought the skull and mandible of *Eoanthropus* to be. As a 'whistle-blower', Morris was, furthermore, in something of a quandary, for he was an ardent supporter of 'eoliths', the crudely broken flints that some thought to be the earliest evidence of human handiwork. Dawson, as we have already seen, publicly (and convincingly) announced his disbelief concerning authenticity of eoliths at a joint meeting of the Royal Anthropological Institute and the Prehistoric Society of East Anglia in February 1915. This ensured that Morris was, in Weiner's belief:

palpably caught in a dilemma. He nourished (in private) these serious accusations of fraudulent dealing, and we may be sure that he would ardently wish to see the faked palaeoliths swept away in favour of his eoliths... but to denounce the flint [palaeolith] implements must bring the whole of the Piltdown remains into disrepute. And the continued existence of Piltdown man was vital to Morris. For no better evidence of the human workmanship and the genuine antiquity of the 'eolith' could be imagined than Piltdown man himself.[253]

Certainly Morris clung on to his belief that eoliths were a genuine product of early human endeavour, so much so that, in his latter years, he appeared a 'cranky and heterodox protagonist of a half-forgotten theory',[254] a point later remembered by Arthur Keith when he recalled his view that Morris had turned sour 'because of scepticism'.[255]

Were the eoliths recovered with the remains of *Eoanthropus* in 1912 and 1913 a genuine part of the forger's master-plan (designed to show the range of Piltdown man's capabilities) or were they really naturally broken flints that just happened to be located in the gravel? The eoliths' brown surface staining certainly did not appear to be artificial and, unlike that of the palaeoliths, was not affected by the application of hydrochloric acid.[256] Dawson was largely sceptical of the artefacts from the start of the investigation,[257] something which may further indicate that they were never intended to be part of the hoax. Even if they were, it is possible that Dawson decided to remove them from the inquiry at a very early stage. This would have had a double benefit: demonstrating his objectivity (in not accepting every artefact from the gravel as genuine) and also providing him with a useful defence against Morris, should the bank clerk ever decided to 'go public' with his story of fraudulent palaeoliths.

Dawson must have been aware that the loss of an artificially stained palaeolith to Morris was something that could jeopardise the whole project (which again brings us to ask why Dawson agreed to exchange it with Morris' 'most valued specimen' – whatever that was). If Morris appeared to be thinking of using the flint in evidence against Dawson, he may well have thought twice after Dawson's extravagant paper to the Royal Anthropological Institute in February 1915. To reveal Dawson's flint then would undoubtedly have reflected badly on Morris, making it look as if he were a sore loser, seeking a form of retribution over his persecutor (as many seemed to believe anyway). Ridiculing the eoliths in such an emphatic (not to say public) way would probably also have gratified Dawson immensely, certainly his letters to Woodward after the presentation seem almost proud of how he has upset the eolithophiles.[258] Morris' rather cryptic comment concerning the possible importation of the Piltdown canine 'from France', need not detain us long here. It is possible that Morris may simply have been suggesting a provenance for the piece, or it may have been intended as a way of indirectly accusing Teilhard de Chardin, its finder in 1913, of complicity in the fraud.

Having accepted that Dawson certainly possessed the *means* to generate the Piltdown hoax, did he similarly posses the *opportunity* to execute it? Was he a sufficiently competent chemist; did he possess the knowledge or facilities required to successfully fabricate the data; was it possible that he was in the right place at the right time to plant the forged artefacts in order to allay suspicion and convince other members of the excavation team that the discoveries were genuine? The skills of the Piltdown forger have been elevated by some writers to near mythical status. Surely Dawson, as a country solicitor, could not have 'had the knowledge and the skill to break an ape's jawbone in exactly the right place, to pare the teeth to ensure a perfect fit to the upper skull and to disguise the whole in such a manner as to deceive his partner, a scientist of international repute'.[259] The belief that the hoaxer must have been an international expert in many fields, a man combining sharply honed academic capabilities and practical skills, is, when one re-examines the evidence, fundamentally flawed. The forger may appear at first glance:

> to possess the abilities of an expert palaeontologist and geologist, as well as to be highly adept in chemistry, human anatomy, and dentistry; yet this would certainly be an uncritical and exaggerated assessment of his qualities. Without doubt the key to all his accomplishments lies in a solid palaeontological background or training... with his palaeontological knowledge, the perpetrator would realise... the potential significance of an apparently Lower Pleistocene or Upper Pliocene gravel deposit. His experience would tell him at once with what kind of animal fauna to stock this horizon. He would be aware of the relatively simple archaeological succession recognised in 1908, and therefore would know the likely tools to expect in his gravel deposit. The idea of a possible ape-like man at this period would be a completely familiar notion to any well-versed palaeontologist. For such a man, well experienced in handling fossil mammalian material, little specialised knowledge of human anatomy would be required for putting into operation his great plan.[260]

Those who seek to defend Dawson on the basis of his poor scientific knowledge or limited intellectual prowess, do him a great disservice. Dawson was a man:

> possessed of a mental capacity characterised by unusual breadth and quickness, when his interests were engaged he became a lightening assimilator of knowledge, both as to concept and detail. Within the limited framework of the moment, and under the pressure of necessity and concentrated effort, he could actually become more expert, more

proficient for the time needed than the leading authorities on whatever topic was in question.[261]

He lectured, presented papers, organised exhibitions and published articles on subjects as diverse as palaeontology, archaeology, ethnography, anthropology, chemistry, mineralogy, anatomy, history (both human and natural), heraldry, photography, lithics, ceramics, metallurgy, entomology, biology, aerodynamics and physics. He was a true scholar; a jack of all trades and master of most. As a forger he had the knack of being able to identify just what material the various 'experts in the field' required in order to support their theories. He could identify the transitional phase or 'missing link' in most subject areas and 'discover' what academics had long thought really ought to be there. In short, he gave people what they wanted.

What about the facilities necessary to perpetrate the Piltdown hoax? Where did Dawson create *Eoanthropus*? A clue may be given by various contacts who approached the British Museum (Natural History) following the initial exposure of the fraud. One such letter, emphatically linking Charles Dawson to the forgery, was received by the Keeper of Geology from a Captain Guy St Barbe. Joseph Weiner and his assistant, Geoffrey Harrison, duly conducted a formal interview with St Barbe at his St Alban's home on 4 January 1954. Key in the recollection of St Barbe were a series of unannounced visits to Dawson's Uckfield office.

> B[arbe] described how extremely frightened Dawson was when B surprised him in his office staining bones. There were perhaps 20 dishes, 6 inches in diameter, full of brownish liquid. Dawson, when he had calmed down, explained that he was interested in staining bones... on a second occasion B came into Dawson's office and found he was staining flints and stones. He remembers saying to D that he could not believe that flint would take up much stain.[262]

Later, St Barbe discussed these incidents with Major Reginald Marriott and the two agreed that they 'believed Dawson was 'salting the mine''. Twenty-three days later, on 27 January, Barbe was again interviewed, this time by Kenneth Oakley, and provided slightly more detail concerning the incidents in Dawson's Uckfield office:

> D[awson] was surprised in his office on three occasions. First by B[arbe] who noted a strong smell as of a chemist shop and several dishes containing dark-coloured fluid, in some of which bones were being boiled. Second by Marriott who also noticed bones being boiled in dark fluid. Third by B again when D was apparently boiling flints. D was very agitated and explained that he was experimenting with a view to finding out how bones

and flints become stained. He said on one occasion, 'I'm trying iodine'. His agitation was very obvious on each occasion. B was not expected in D's office on either of these occasions, when he 'burst in', because he was in the habit of calling upon him on the spur of the moment in regard to matters concerning his estate.[263]

On the timing of these 'three occasions', St Barbe was imprecise, though he felt that '1910 was the earliest possible year during which this could have happened'.[264] Then he recalled Dawson having shown him, on one of the visits, a cast of the skull as reconstructed by Woodward, 'therefore it must have been later than 1912' interposed Oakley.[265]

What was Dawson doing exactly? St Barbe could not provide exact details of what sort of bone was being stained, nor whether these pieces had certainly derived from Piltdown, precise details being difficult to remember after the passing of some forty years. Of course, the intimation was that here Dawson had been 'caught in the act' of forgery. If Dawson had been using his own solicitor's office as a form of secret laboratory, it would appear strange that he did not possess 'sense enough to lock the door when working',[266] but then would he expect a sudden, unannounced visit of the sort perpetrated by St Barbe? Who is to say that the temptation to work on scientific experiments in his office, away from the pressures and demands of home, was not an irresistible one? In any case, we have, by Dawson's own admission, details concerning just such extracurricular activities.

On 3 July, for instance, shortly after recovering a piece of human cranium from a new site at Barcombe Mills (see below), Dawson wrote to Woodward:

> Will you get Barlow to give us the recipe for gelatinising, as the bone looks
> in a bad way and may go wrong in drying. I have got a saucepan and gas
> stove at Uckfield.[267]

The passage is of particular interest when St Barbe's testimony is recalled, for here Dawson is being particularly open about his experiments and where they were conducted (quite when he found time to pursue legal matters is left unclear). That Dawson also chemically treated a number (if not all) of the Piltdown fossils is also readily apparent, for, on 4 August 1913, Dawson wrote again to Woodward, this time to request some more of 'Barlow's hardening solution', adding 'I think it is made of spirit and shellac, but I am quite out of it, and want some for that bit of grinder (*Elephas*) in the matrix'.[268]

That Woodward was aware of the extent of Dawson's treatment of the Piltdown bone assemblage is evident from his later comments in *The Earliest Englishman* where he notes that the skull bones:

are all hardened and stained brown by oxide of iron, but none of them has lost its original shape during fossilisation, or by crushing in the gravel. The colour of the pieces which were first discovered was altered a little by Mr Dawson when he dipped them in a solution of bi-chromate of potash in the mistaken idea that this would harden them.[269]

Woodward apparently accepted Dawson's reasons for conducting the treatment, though he observed that it did not really affect the hardness of the bone, merely that it 'affected the colour to a minor degree'.[270] What neither Woodward, nor any of the other scientists corralled to make comment upon the Piltdown bone ever seemed to question however, was why Dawson had felt it necessary to subject certain of the Barkham Manor flints to the same level of treatment. Flint is a stone which, in hardness and durability, is second only to diamond. It does not require any form of artificial hardening in order to ensure long-term preservation.

Soaking in a 'solution of bi-chromate of potash' was, incidentally, not the only way of introducing artificial colour to specimens which Dawson 'confessed' to Woodward. On 23 April 1913, Dawson had written to his friend, casually observing that he had been:

> trying an experiment with it [a cast of the Piltdown I skull] by duplicating the parts of the skull and jaw on each side in a slightly different shade of brown. I have done this in water-colour which rubs off easily. I like it better this way because it helps the uninitiated. I have got three different shades for the real, the restored, and the hypothetical. It does not look as if it had ever been restored.[271]

The use of paint to generate realistic shades of brown to the plaster cast of Piltdown I assumes a rather different light when one remembers the single canine recovered by Teilhard de Chardin at Barkham Manor in 1913. Unlike the bulk of the fossil remains discovered at the site, the canine had been artificially stained with 'bitumen earth containing iron oxide, in all probability the well-known paint – Vandyke brown'.[272] Furthermore, Weiner later noted, 'the reddish brown stain on the occlusal or chewing surface (like that on the molars) is probably also a ferruginous earth pigment applied as an oil paint (e.g. red sienna)'.[273] The differential form of artificial staining that the canine was subjected to could, Weiner explained, have been due to the fact that:

> the staining of fresh teeth by means of iron with or without chromium is, in our experience, by no means easy. To get a good fossil appearance, there was probably no other recourse than to use paint.[274]

Dawson, of course, speaks only of using 'water-colour' not oils, and his observations to Woodward (perhaps understandably) refer only to treatments applied to the plaster replica. Nevertheless, the use of paints by the Uckfield solicitor in order to simulate the 'genuine' colours of the Piltdown bone fragments is certainly intriguing.

If the application of bichromate solution by Dawson to the Piltdown bone had indeed been entirely innocent, we are faced with a rather interesting, not to say worrying, observation. The first finds of bone at Barkham Manor were passed on to Woodward only after an unspecified, but presumably rather lengthy, period of time. Whilst in his possession, Dawson evidently treated these artefacts in order to 'harden' them. The artefacts retrieved during the course of the 1912-4 excavations, such as the mandible and canine, were, however, not entrusted to Dawson's care, but were taken almost immediately back by Woodward to the British Museum (Natural History) in London. The fact that the jaw had been chemically treated in the same way as the earlier finds means that either Woodward or the technicians at the museum themselves used bichromate solution (unlikely given Woodward's understanding that it did not affect the hardness of the samples, only their colour), or that they were chemically treated *before being planted* at Barkham Manor. Here, the treatments conducted by Dawson on the cranial fragments *exactly* match those that the forger conducted upon the Piltdown mandible, being conducted 'only as a necessary part of the deliberate matching of the jaw of a modem ape with the mineralised cranial fragments'.[275]

Although Woodward himself presents an entirely innocent explanation of the use of bichromate by Dawson, the evidence compiled by Joseph Weiner appears damning.

> Of the miscellaneous remains brought to Woodward, the perpetrator used chromium on all except the five cranial pieces, for these Dawson had by some coincidence already so treated. And, again, while Dawson dealt with the occipital, parietal, and temporal bones of Piltdown I in this way, the unknown perpetrator did just the same to the frontal bone of the same skull which came to light in 1915. If Dawson's activities were innocent, they turned out at the same time to be quite complimentary to those of the culprit. The iron-staining emphasises this strange conformity. Where Dawson had super-added the chromate 'mistakenly for hardening', the perpetrator had done this deliberately as part of the staining of the fossils which needed no hardening – for example Stegodon, hippo and flint E.606.[276]

We are left with a 'niggling' doubt concerning the treatment of the Piltdown bone assemblage for, if Dawson *had* been the 'perpetrator' (as intimated by Weiner), why would he have confessed use of chemicals such as bichromate to

Woodward in the first place? Surely this would have been akin to a confession? Of course we do not know *when* Woodward first became aware of Dawson's chemical experiments (his letters of 3 July and 4 August 1913 providing the first suggestion of using an artificial 'hardening solution'),[277] and neither do we know *how*. It is possible that Woodward became aware of the treatments only after tests conducted by himself or one of his colleagues at the British Museum (Natural History). Perhaps he received a 'tip-off' from elsewhere. Either way, Dawson would undoubtedly have been keen to quickly explain that the treatment was designed purely to harden the bone samples, and not for any other alternative purpose.

Chemical treatment aside, would the Piltdown forger have been able to successfully 'plant' his fraudulent artefacts at Barkham Manor without arousing the suspicion of his colleagues and associates? The answer here is: 'almost certainly'. If no one is suspecting a hoax, it is doubtful that anyone would have had the presence of mind to question the authenticity of any 'discovery'. Given the diverse range of finds made over the seven-year period between 1908 and 1915, we must plausibly assume that the hoaxer was present at all times to ensure that any given object was securely placed and reasonably recovered. As suspicion would have been aroused if only one person had discovered all of the important bone, tooth or flint artefacts at Piltdown, the hoaxer would need to make sure that any given piece was set down where it might reasonably be 'found' by another member of the team. If this failed, leaving the forger no option but to 'find' the artefact himself, then he would need to ensure that sufficient independent witnesses were present in order to verify the authenticity of the find. There was, as has already been noted, only one constant throughout the entire catalogue of Piltdown discoveries: Charles Dawson.

If Dawson was indeed the mastermind behind Piltdown, then the vagueness with which Dawson relates the initial phases (not to say dates) of the skull's discovery by two unnamed workmen, as well as the inexplicable gap of 'several years' between the first piece of cranium and the 'left supra-orbital border' in 1911, become understandable, for the skull was never in the ground in the first place. It also helps explain the glaring inconsistencies in Dawson's stories of the workmen destroying the skull, despite being asked to 'keep a look out' for interesting finds and their remembrance of Dawson's request over a period of 'some eight or nine years', as well as the surprise Dawson recalls in hearing that 'some men *were then actually digging* a gravel pit', despite the fact that he must have passed them to gain access to Barkham Manor in the first place. These were all made up to provide a plausible background story for the discovering of the cranium.

In such a context, the initial 'coco-nut discovery story', with two labourers breaking up the Piltdown skull into small fragments, was a masterstroke. Destruction at the hands of a modern workman meant that in order to recover more pieces of the ancient cranium, any future exploration would first have to search the many spoil heaps around the gravel pit, into which forged pieces of *Eoanthropus* could safely be introduced without fear of displaying obvious intrusion. To attempt to place such pieces in the ground within an *in situ* context would not only be very difficult, but would also be dangerous, potentially creating a recovery scenario that was patently fraudulent. Obvious 'plants' needed to be avoided at all costs.

The ape-like mandible 'found' in 1912 was an absolutely crucial find for *Eoanthropus dawsoni*, but its sheer size probably created a specific problem for the Piltdown forger. The piece:

> was much too large an object, too bulkily obvious, to allow it to be found lying on the surface in a spoil heap. Even to have reached the spoil heap it would supposedly have come out of the ground on Hargreaves' shovel, and in that case the workman himself, or someone nearby, could have been expected to notice it rather quickly. The possibility of damage by a probing shovel had also to be avoided. For those reasons, and to achieve its maximum impact of authenticity, the supremely important jawbone had to be found *in situ* in the pit, or appear as if it had.[278]

The realisation that the prized find simply *had* to be found embedded in the gravel as if undisturbed created problems of its own, for to simulate such ground conditions sufficient to fool a member of the excavation team (be it Dawson, Woodward or Hargreaves) into thinking they were digging into virgin soil would be impossible. Here the forger was presented with one of two possible solutions to the quandary. First they could bury the piece (difficult in itself without attracting attention) and get someone unfamiliar with the complexities of the gravel to commence excavation over the area. Certainly there were many inexperienced volunteer helpers visiting the excavations during the course of the 1912 season, but would any of them really have been entrusted with the removal of soil in a sensitive and untested part of the trench? Strangely enough the answer to this, on at least one occasion, was 'yes'. On 12 July the following year a field visit to Piltdown for geologists and their families was organised by Dawson and Woodward. A photograph of the event (**98**) shows a confused mass of people, crowding into and around the excavated area (presumably causing damage to the site in the process), whilst a reporter from the *Sussex Daily News* observed that 'taking advantage of the extended halt many of the party proceeded to carry on excavations, but no more skulls or indications of their presence were discovered'.[279] Such chaotic disturbance to the site would not, however, be what the Piltdown forger required if sensitive evidence were to be successfully recovered. The geological field visit does, rather thankfully, appear to have been the exception, most of the volunteer help at Barkham Manor having been directed to the inspection of spoil heaps and the sieving of freshly excavated gravel, rather than heavy labour.[280]

98 *Piltdown I: a rather chaotic visit to Barkham Manor by the Geologists' Association on 12 July 1913*

The second option available to the forger with regard to the recovery of the ape-like jaw was to actually 'find' the piece themselves. To do so may, quite naturally, attract some suspicion, especially if they had already recovered a great many other finds from the site, but the advantage was that the hoaxer would not actually have to plant the find in the gravel or in some way disguise its presence there. All they had to do was to convincingly provide the impression that it had indeed been *in situ* and, to this end, an independent (and unwitting) witness would, therefore, be required. Thus the circumstances of the 'discovery', dislodged by Dawson's vigorous picking at the supposedly undisturbed gravel bed, can be explained:

> on a warm evening after an afternoon's vain search, Mr Dawson was exploring some untouched remnants of the original gravel at the bottom of the pit, when *we both* saw half of the human lower jaw fly out in front of the pick-shaped end of the hammer which he was using. Thus was recovered the most remarkable portion of the fossil which we were collecting. It had evidently been missed by the workmen because the little patch of gravel in which it occurred was covered with water at the time of year when they reached it.[281]

Dawson himself made the discovery, making him the only real candidate for the imposture. Any other experienced excavator working in an area where a forged artefact such as the ape-like jaw had deliberately been planted, would surely have been aware that that the gravels were not 'undisturbed' (even if the area was, or had previously been, covered in water).

In 1913, all the main discussions concerning *Eoanthropus dawsoni* were focussing upon the interpretation of the original skull and the nature of the 'missing canine'. This is something that the hoaxer cannot plausibly have envisaged beforehand, but it was one which he endeavoured to resolve in dramatic style. Again, suspicion would inevitably fall upon Dawson if he had discovered the elusive canine, his eagle eyes had already spotted the faked 'human nasal bones' in the disturbed gravel earlier in August,[282] and so to add authenticity, the artefact needed to be found by another. Whilst Dawson and Woodward continued the excavation of the pit (their usual hired help Venus Hargreaves was not on site that day), Teilhard de Chardin was asked if he would not mind unsuspecting the 'rain-washed gravel spread' of the old spoil heaps. To aid in the inspection, the spoil had been 'mapped out in squares', presumably with the aid of string 'and minutely examined section by section'.[283] Unsurprisingly, perhaps, within a small amount of time Teilhard had recovered the canine.

No one appeared, at least in public, to be at all surprised that the new tooth appeared to match *exactly* the canine predicted by Woodward in the original plaster cast of *Eoanthropus*; nor did anyone comment on the fortuitous way in which it 'only turned up when it was clear that the experts had decided what it would look like'.[284] The tooth was just another dramatic find from the Piltdown gravels, albeit one which confirmed Woodward's hypothesis at the expense of his critics. A similar experience was to occur with Piltdown II at the site of Sheffield Park (see next chapter).

The worked elephant femur, discovered close to the end of the 1915 excavation season, was the last daring hoax of the Barkham Manor investigations; it was also the one to elicit most suspicion and disbelief from the members of the Geological Society to whom it was presented in December 1914. This time it was Woodward who spotted the artefact, or to be precise it was Woodward that saw 'some small splinters of bone' following their disruption by Venus Hargreaves' mattock.[285] Again, the object in question had not been lying *in situ* within the gravel, but 'about a foot below the surface, in dark vegetable soil, beneath the hedge which bounds the gravel-pit'.[286] This detail is crucial for, although the size of the object (even when broken into two pieces) ensured that the bone could not easily be transported onto site in a bag or jacket pocket without attracting the attention of another member of the team, its surroundings, the loose dark earth 'beneath the hedge' means that its safe insertion into subsoil could be achieved without arising suspicion that the ground had been disturbed in recent times. In fact the bluff was further helped by the observation that 'the soil left not the slightest stain on the specimen, which was covered with firmly-adherent pale-yellow sandy clay, closely similar to that of the flint-bearing layer at the bottom of the gravel'.[287]

It was therefore likely that the implement could not have been at its place of discovery for very long, probably having been 'thrown there by the workmen with the other useless debris when they were digging gravel from the adjacent hole'.[288] This was a perfect place for the artefact to be found, sealed enough below the level of the hedge, but disturbed enough by the labourers so as to deflect attention away from the original context of the artefact. Curiously, with regard to the 'disruption by labourers' hypothesis, no one thought to ask why, if the diggers had been offered payment for every artefact recovered, did they not spot an elephant femur, albeit one cut into a strange shape? Why did they toss it aside and bury it beneath a hedge? The first part of the femur being so rudely exposed to the air then taken from the pit to be washed; 'Mr Dawson accordingly grubbed with his fingers in the earth around the spot where the broken end had lain, and soon pulled out the rest of the bone'.[289] No doubt in the process of 'grubbing around', Dawson also managed to obliterate all evidence as to the situation, position and exact context of the bone prior to first contact with Hargreaves' mattock.

In all this postulated activity, Dawson's presence at the pit would never have been questioned. As discoverer and co-director of the project, as well as friends of both the landowner and tenant (not to say steward of the Manor of Barkham) he could come and go as he pleased. Certainly, any unannounced appearance at the pit would occasion no alarm nor spark any concerns from the tenant, Robert Kenward. His office in Uckfield was only a mere hour's walk away and Dawson was often seen in the vicinity conducting both business and his antiquarian hobby.

One last 'case against' ought to be considered here, if only for complete-ness sake. The accusation against the physician and world-famous novelist Sir Arthur Conan Doyle was first set out by John Winslow in an article entitled 'The Perpetrator at Piltdown' published in the journal *Science*.[290] Curious though it seemed to many at the time, Winslow was convinced that Doyle had not only been involved in the hoax, but had also been the mastermind behind it. Doyle, wrote Winslow, 'was a man who loved hoaxes, adventure, danger; a writer gifted at manipulating complex plots; and perhaps most important of all, one who bore a grudge against the British scientific establishment'.[291]

The 'grudge' that Winslow so pointedly referred to, allegedly arose from Doyle's belief in spiritualism and his anger at those who sought to somehow discredit it. One such critic of the spiritualist movement was Edwin Ray Lankester, a former Director of the British Museum (Natural History) and Keeper of Zoology, who at the end of the nineteenth century had exposed the American medium Henry Slade and forced him to leave England 'as expedi-tiously as he could'.[292] Though not adverse to 'outing' obvious frauds, Doyle, Winslow argued, was keen to ensure that spiritualism itself avoided wholesale condemnation. Lankester, however, was a clear and present danger to the survival of the movement and Doyle, Winslow reasoned, felt that the only way he could successfully silence his enemy was to 'reverse the tables' by generating a scientific fraud the like of which had never been seen before. Piltdown man would therefore prove to be the undoing of Lankester and the other men and women of science whom Doyle considered to be 'his adversaries'.[293]

The attacks upon Winslow, following the publication of his article, came thick and fast.[294] Few people could believe that Doyle, the creator of Sherlock Holmes, one of the most famous literary characters of all time, could seriously have been behind the Piltdown fraud. Outlandish though Winslow's claim first appeared, however, there were a number of unsettling aspects contained within the main accusation that deserved deeper consideration. First among these was the motive, already alluded to. Winslow was at pains to relate the anger that Doyle felt with regard to Lankester's attacks on the spiritualist movement; but was such anger real and, if it were, would it really have provoked Doyle to the length of generating a complex scientific hoax?

It seems hard to credit that Doyle would have been that well disposed towards Lankester following the affair of Henry Slade, but, by the time that Piltdown man first appeared on the scene in 1912, any differences between the two men appear to have dissipated. John Walsh, in his book *Unravelling Piltdown*, notes that by 1912:

> no longer enemies, they had actually become good friends, and it was in the pages of Lankester's book *Extinct Animals*, published in 1906, that Doyle found much of the inspiration for his *Lost World* novel. In acknowledgement of this debt, he even offered the scientist a generous salute in his narrative.[295]

Walsh provides one further damning piece of evidence which helps to destroy the central thesis behind Winslow's belief that it was the attack on the spiritualist movement that had first inspired Doyle to generate Piltdown at some point before 1908: Doyle, by his own admission, did not convert to the 'spiritualist cause' until 1916,[296] some eight years *after* Dawson allegedly recovered the first pieces of *Eoanthropus* skull.

Furthermore why, if it *were* conceivably possible to prove Doyle's involvement in the fraud, did the author never reveal the punch line and shame his scientific tormentors? Winslow suggested that he had on a number of occasions tried to do just this, the whittled elephant femur found at Piltdown representing something that Doyle had deliberately placed there because 'as he was an expert cricketer who had played on some of the country's top teams, what could be better than to place a cricket bat 'in the hands' of Piltdown man?'[297] The world of science, however, failed to take the bait. Doyle then planted Piltdown II at Sheffield Park, in an attempt to 'strain the credulity' of those engaged in researching the early human who, apparently, would not be able to believe in the existence of two well-preserved sets of remains.[298] Again science failed to see the joke, leaving Doyle apparently 'exasperated'.[299] This is, of course, all pure supposition, Winslow failing to produce any clear evidence with regard to motive that could be used to support his argument that Doyle had masterminded the forgery.

Two further aspects of Winslow's accusation do, however, deserve further scrutiny. First, Doyle was indeed acquainted with both Charles Dawson and Arthur Woodward, the author's home at Windlesham in Crowborough, lying close to the 'scene of the crime' at Barkham Manor. Secondly, and perhaps more interestingly, Doyle's novel *The Lost World*, a story of a scientific party coming face to face with fearsome dinosaurs and a savage race of 'ape-men' was first serialised in 1912, the very year of Piltdown man's first announcement to the world. This aspect alone suggested to Winslow that both novel and hoax had perhaps developed together, the novel containing the clues necessary to expose the fraud and therefore debunk the myth.[300]

Many investigators into the Piltdown story have noted the apparent coincidence of timing between Doyle's *Lost World*, complete with its tribes of hairy ape-men, and the first announcement of Piltdown man. Given that Doyle lived relatively close to the site and was known to both Dawson and Woodward has further convinced many that there must somewhere be a link; that even if Doyle had not conceived the fraud, that he must somehow have been aware of it and hoped to expose it in the pages of his novel. Certainly the publication of Doyle's book so close to the announcement of Dawson's discovery does appear fortuitous and may hint that the author knew more about the forgery than he ever let on. When one considers the exact chronology and sequence of events surrounding both the book and the skull, as well as the relationship between Doyle and Dawson, however, a new and more interesting scenario presents itself.

That Arthur Conan Doyle knew Charles Dawson is clear enough, but the exact circumstances behind their friendship remain vague. Their first confirmed meeting occurred in 1911, a point established by correspondence surviving in the archives of the Natural History Museum,[301] though they may well have met as early as 1909, following an inquiry made by Doyle to Arthur Woodward concerning a number of possible dinosaur footprints discovered near Crowborough. Woodward alerted Dawson and asked if it were possible to visit Doyle and ascertain exactly what it was that he had found. Dawson responded that:

> I am interested in what you say about Crowborough and the footprints... I shall be very pleased to make Sir A. Conan Doyle's acquaintance. If I am in Crowborough first I will call on him or if he comes to Lewes I hope he will come and see me.[302]

By November 1911 the Doyles and the Dawsons were on sufficiently good terms for Charles and Helenc to be invited to Windlesham for lunch.[303] After the meal Dawson examined a number of Doyle's supposed fossil discoveries. Unfortunately the 'great fossil' that Doyle was most enthusiastic about proved to be 'a mere concretion of oxide of iron and sand', though the discovery of a Neolithic arrowhead 'in view of us all' apparently saved the day.[304] Given the context of the day, it seems inescapable that Doyle must at some point have mentioned his novel *The Lost World*, the writing of which he had by then completed. What Dawson made of the book we do not know though he later recorded in a letter to Arthur Woodward, following an inquiry by Woodward concerning *The Lost World*, that:

> Yes, C. Doyle is writing a sort of Jules Verne book on some wonderful plateau in S. America with a lake which somehow got isolated from 'Oolitic' times and contained old the [sic] fauna and flora of that period, and was visited by the usual 'Professor'. I hope someone has sorted out his fossils for him![305]

Interestingly, this is the same letter that Dawson first announced, rather casually, to Woodward of the first discovery of 'a human (?) skull' from the Piltdown gravels. Though the publication of Doyle's finished novel did not occur until Autumn 1912, it was serialised in the *Strand* magazine from April of that year, two months after Dawson had appraised Woodward of its contents.

Now, if we take Dawson at his word, the first discovery of human remains at Piltdown occurred 'several years' before the autumn of 1911, when a fragment of the 'frontal region' of *Eoanthropus*' skull was recovered by him 'among the rain-washed spoil heaps' of the Barkham Manor gravel pit.[306] The exact chronology concerning the earlier discovery of flints and the 'unusually thick human parietal bone',[307] or 'coco-nut', is frustratingly vague, though most modern writers place the event as occurring in 1908.[308] Of course we only have Dawson's word concerning the accidental exposure of the first skull piece by workmen on the Barkham Manor estate, and the time lag between discovery and reporting has an uncanny resemblance to the circumstances surrounding the Beauport Park Statuette,[309] Blackmore's Stone Axe,[310] the Bexhill Boat[311], the Uckfield Horseshoe,[312] the Pevensey Brick[313] and the Toad in a Hole.[314] The first objective piece of evidence concerning the existence of the Piltdown remains comes from Dawson's letter to Arthur Woodward dated 14 February 1912. Before this date, as far as it may be ascertained, Dawson confided his discovery to no other person, not even his wife Helene.

As Dawson was clearly the mastermind behind the creation of *Eoanthropus*, we cannot logically accept anything that he tells us concerning the find prior to 14 February 1912 as being in any way truthful. The date 1908 provides for Piltdown, just as it did for Pevensey, Bexhill and Beauport Park, a significant time lag between the initial recovery of an artefact and its eventual reporting (nearly five years for the Pevensey Brick, five years for the Bexhill Boat and a full ten years for the Beauport Statuette) in order to help obscure the provenance and circumstances of discovery. Anyone trying, in 1912, to record the *exact* details of when, where and how the first pieces of human skull of Piltdown man were found, would have to rely solely upon Dawson's testimony, the original 'workmen' of the story having long since disappeared.

As the first confirmation by Dawson of the existence of human remains at Piltdown occurred as late as February 1912, it is apparent that against the sequence of events established in most works on the hoax, it is Doyle's novel that claims precedence over *Eoanthropus*. Clearly Doyle was inspired in part by his own surroundings, many fossils including his own 'discoveries' had been made from the Sussex Weald, and by those whom he had recently corresponded (for example Professor Summerlee in *The Lost World* has a more than passing resemblance to Arthur Woodward),[315] but his savage 'ape-men' appear to possess few, if any, of the traits associated with *Eoanthropus dawsoni*. Doyle's lost race of missing links have ape-like skulls, 'thick and heavy brows' and, rather crucially, 'curved, sharp canine teeth',[316] unlike the early human recovered from the gravels of Barkham Manor.

If anything then, the curious coincidence between the appearance of *The Lost World* and Dawson's *Eoanthropus* can be explained in that the inspiration for the creation of the Piltdown hoax came from the pre-publication manuscript of Doyle's novel, and not the other way around. Dawson, whilst searching for 'the big 'find' which never seems to come along',[317] presumably listened to the details of Doyle's novel at the Windlesham lunch in November 1911 with glee. Here was the basis for the 'big find'; the discovery that would launch him from local to international academic recognition. All he had to do, if he were to successfully remove suspicion that Doyle's novel had pre-eminence over his find, was to push the initial date of *Eoanthropus*' discovery back to 1908.

It has been suggested on a number of occasions that Charles Dawson could not have been working on the Piltdown forgery alone; that the skills involved were way beyond those usually associated with a solicitor and amateur antiquarian. Dawson, as we have seen, was no ordinary amateur; he was, as noted above, a self-professed expert in archaeology, palaeontology, photography, chemistry, biology, physics, mineralogy, anatomy, anthropology, ethnography, lithics, ceramics, metallurgy, natural history, human history, numismatics, heraldry, languages (ancient and modern), entomology and aerodynamics. Despite such obvious experience and detailed knowledge of a variety of diverse subjects, rumours of an accomplice persist in Piltdown-related literature. Some claim that he must have had a willing friend in the British Museum or perhaps he knew of a scientist on the take. Possibly it was an academic on the first faltering steps of their career, desperate to make a discovery that would make their name, or perhaps it was a fellow amateur enthusiast with a grudge against the establishment?

A series of co-conspirators in the Piltdown deception have been publicly outed since the exposure of the fraud in 1953, but few of the accusations have, on closer inspection, any real basis in fact. Most of the theories concerning potential collaboration concentrate solely upon Piltdown, as if this were a 'one-off' event; a single lapse in Dawson's otherwise spotless academic career. We have seen, however, that Piltdown was not unique amongst Dawson's catalogue of Sussex discoveries; it was by no means a 'one-off', more the culmination of his life's work.

12

PILTDOWN II AND III

Few people are today aware that the remains recovered from Barkham Manor (constituting the main Piltdown 'discovery') were in fact only one of three separate finds of *Eoanthropus dawsoni* recovered in the immediate area of Piltdown prior to 1916. The two additional discoveries, characterised here as 'Barcombe Mills man' (Piltdown III) and 'Sheffield Park man' (Piltdown II), are usually not discussed in any great detail when the circumstances surrounding Piltdown are considered, though their relationship to the 'great hoax' are pivotal. For the purposes of this discussion, though these additional sites are treated under separate headings as per all earlier discoveries made by Charles Dawson, the nature of both and their relationship to the main Piltdown site at Barkham Manor, means that neither can truly be considered in objective isolation.

Barcombe Mills Man (Piltdown III)

On 3 July 1913, Charles Dawson wrote a letter to his friend Arthur Woodward claiming to have made another spectacular discovery at Piltdown. The letter stated that Dawson had found nothing less than fragments of a second prehistoric human, but this time the remains were not from Barkham Manor, but from a site nearby:

> I have picked up the frontal part of a human skull this evening on a ploughed field covered with flint gravel. It's a new place, a long way from Piltdown, and the gravel lies 50 feet below level of Piltdown, and about 40 to 50 feet above the present river Ouse. It is not a thick skull but it may be a descendant of *Eoanthropus*. The brow ridge is slight at the edge, but full and prominent over the nose. It was coming on dark and raining when I left the place but I have marked the spot.[1]

Quite what Woodward made of this new find is not known. According to Dawson's correspondence, Woodward had a chance to inspect the 'bit of skull' on a visit he made to Uckfield on Friday 4 July, though Dawson pre-warned him with the words 'don't expect anything sensational'.[2]

Certainly he and Dawson must have discussed the new find at length, and Woodward had more than enough time to inspect the alleged findspot during the 1913 and 1914 excavation seasons at Barkham Manor. Strange then that the discovery of a human cranium so close to Piltdown both geographically and morphologically, was never formally reported upon by either Dawson or Woodward, though both could easily have noted it at any one of their Geological Society presentations. Beyond Dawson's letter to Woodward, we do not know how he felt about the presence of human remains at this new locale, or indeed whether he ever conducted further fieldwork there.

The details concerning the provenance of the new discoveries and the information concerning their discovery are vague, even by Dawson's standards. It is, however, assumed that, though Dawson does not name the site in his letter of July 1913, the finds were probably made at, or close to, Barcombe Mills. The reason for believing this is that following Dawson's death in 1916, Arthur Woodward specifically asked his widow Helene if he may examine all skeletal material in her husband's private collection prior to the public auction.[3] On 7 January 1917, Helene wrote to Woodward: 'I have not yet come across pieces of skull answering to y[ou]r description but as I am putting everything of that nature into a cupboard you will have a wide assortment from which to choose'.[4]

There was evidently something in the collection that bothered Woodward and which he particularly needed to acquire. In late January 1917, a selection of bones derived from Dawson's collection was delivered by Frederick Du Cane Goodman to Woodward's London office, apparently at the request of Helene.[5] This selection, which was mostly cranial, comprised 'a large part of the frontal bone, a fragment of what may have been part of a right parietal, a pair of zygomatic bones which do not in any way fit the frontal, and a mandibular right second molar tooth'.[6] Woodward, who compiled the accession details for the British Museum (Natural History), noted that the material had derived from the 'Pleistocene gravel in [a] field on top of [a] hill above Barcombe Mills railway station'.[7] In addition to the fragments of skull was a single canine tooth, 'very chimpanzee-like in form',[8] which had apparently been found in 1915. Woodward was uncertain as to the derivation of the piece, noting in the accessions register that it had probably come from the same place as the skull, though he added the proviso '(not certain)'.[9]

Information concerning the provenance of these pieces, vague though it is, can only have been supplied by Charles Dawson, possibly as a note accompanying the artefacts. From the surviving correspondence, it would appear possible that Woodward and Dawson visited the Barcombe Mills site together as early as late April 1913.[10] Dawson had certainly been examining the area around Barcombe towards the end of 1912, a letter from him to Woodward dated 9 November 1912 observing:

> We [Dawson, Edgar Willett and Edwin Lankester] went in the plough fields
> both there [Barkham Manor] and at Barcombe Mills. I found a very early-
> looking implement in the middle of the plough field adjoining our gravel
> pit and Willett found another in the plough at Barcombe Mills.[11]

Nowhere, unfortunately, is there any specific information as to exactly where
the Barcombe Mills bone was found and under what circumstances, the 'spot'
marked by Dawson never being accurately plotted. Only once was there an
outside record of the site, this being from the pen of Father Pierre Teilhard de
Chardin. In 1953, following the exposure of the Piltdown hoax, Teilhard
wrote, in reply to a query from Kenneth Oakley concerning the discovery of
'Piltdown II' (Sheffield Park man), that:

> as far as the fragments of Piltdown Locality 2 are concerned, it must be
> observed that Dawson never tried to emphasise them particularly, although
> (if I am correct) these specimens were announced after the finds in Locality
> 1 were complete. He just brought me to the site of Locality 2 and explained
> [to] me that he had found the isolated molar and the small pieces of skull
> in the heaps of rubble and pebbles raked at the surface of the field.[12]

What made the investigation team initially confused concerning this aspect of
Teilhard's Piltdown testimony, was that he claimed to have been taken to
'Locality 2', which both Oakley and Weiner assumed was Sheffield Park, in the
summer of 1913, and yet Dawson did not report the finds from here until 1915.[13]
Of course, Dawson *had* reported the discovery of 'the frontal part of a human
skull' from Barcombe Mills to Woodward in a letter dated 3 July 1913 (see
above), a find apparently made 'on a ploughed field covered with flint gravel'.[14]
The correlation of dates, cranial pieces and (apparently) recently ploughed fields
makes it seem clear that it was to Barcombe Mills that Dawson took Teilhard in
the summer of 1913, not Sheffield Park. The passing of time, when combined
with the broad similarity of both assemblages, would undoubtedly have clouded
the issue in the priest's mind, creating confusion over the two locations.

Beyond the scanty detail in the accessions register of the British Museum
(Natural History), Woodward never made a formal report on the Barcombe
Mills assemblage. Given the apparent urgency with which he had retrieved the
cranial fragments from Helene Dawson early in 1917, it does appear somewhat
strange that he chose not to publicly disclose the find. Perhaps, given a preliminary analysis of the bone, he came to the decision that this was not after all
part of another *Eoanthropus*, merely 'a recent skull of no particular scientific
value'.[15] There was certainly nothing morphologically distinctive about the
pieces of bone (least of all their thickness), which, although they appeared to
have derived from at least two individuals, were largely 'indistinguishable from
modern bones'.[16] In fact the only aspect of the Barcombe Mills bone which in

any way resembled that from Piltdown was their 'somewhat similar brown colour'.[17] With Woodward's enthusiasm concerning the Barcombe Mills assemblage apparently on the wane, the material was put into the stores of the British Museum (Natural History), where in lay forgotten.

In 1949, the South African palaeontologist Robert Broom and the American anatomist Ashley Montagu rediscovered, retrieved and reanalysed the Barcombe Mills bone assemblage.[18] Believing that the pieces recovered constituted the remains of at least three individuals, Broom concluded that all three were certainly 'antique' and 'probably belong to one species *Eoanthropus dawsoni*'.[19] Montagu was not so convinced.[20] The rediscovery of the Barcombe Mills site, at a time when the weight of academic opinion was increasingly shifting away from Piltdown man, proved rather awkward. Why had there been no previous discussion of either the site or the remains recovered there? Why, if the pieces really had first been noted in 1913, did neither Dawson nor Woodward explore the area in more detail? Why did Woodward, who spent much of the final twenty-eight years of his life fruitlessly digging at Barkham Manor looking for more evidence of *Eoanthropus dawsoni*, not dig at Barcombe Mills instead?

The Barcombe Mills bone assemblage was subjected to scientific analysis, in order to ascertain its place in the world. In 1955, a collective of scientists led by Joseph Weiner, Wilfred Le Gros Clark and Kenneth Oakley were able to confidently assert that 'all these fragments have been artificially iron-stained, by the sulphate process, but unaided by a chromium compound'.[21] Furthermore 'their negligibly low fluorine content and their high nitrogen content show them to be almost certainly modern'.[22]

The Barcombe Mills assemblage was a clear piece of modern forgery. It was, however, more than just a simple fraud revealed by science, but also a rather significant piece in the whole Piltdown puzzle, for:

> These fragments from Barcombe Mills have been subjected to a very remarkable chemical treatment, so remarkable that it was the staining which they underwent which threw so much light on the iron-staining used so extensively by the forger. These Barcombe Mills pieces have adhering to them some gravelly matrix mixed with a little soil, and this material is also of a dark brown colour. Like that of the bones, the colour is attributable to artificial iron-staining, and in both cases the iron salt used was an acid sulphate, which formed gypsum as a by-product. The matrix provides undeniable evidence that this iron-staining was deliberate, for the matrix contains, in addition to iron oxide, traces of ammonium sulphate, never known to occur in nature and indicating without doubt that the staining was produced by the use of iron alum, which is ferric ammonium sulphate, and which, like the combination of chromate and ferrous salts, is an efficient and recognised method of depositing an iron salt. The

artificiality of the gypsum in the bone is confirmed completely by the virtual lack of sulphate in the gravels and loam in the river terraces at Barcombe Mills. The higher terrace is an extension of that at Barkham Manor and there, too, the absence of sulphate contrasts with the cranial fragments (Piltdown I).[23]

Dawson, as has already been noted in the preceding chapter, was not adverse to chemically treating the bone assemblage recovered from Piltdown. Much of this treatment, the solicitor readily confessed to Woodward (in letters dated 3 July and 4 August 1913),[24] was in order to 'harden' and therefore preserve the samples. Once again, though such chemical treatment could have been entirely innocent, we are faced with the 'remarkable coincidence' that the forger of the Barcombe Mills bone should also 'have occasion to use the same salt extensively'.[25]

Barcombe Mills Man: conclusions

Our list of suspects for the creation of the Barcombe Mills assemblage is, of necessity, a small one and one which, quite naturally, is closely linked to that already discussed for Barkham Manor (Piltdown I).

First suspicion must naturally fall upon Charles Dawson, the discoverer of Barcombe Mills man. We do not possess any detail concerning the circumstances surrounding the 'discovery', other than at least one of the cranial pieces was found on or shortly before 3 July 1913, whilst the tooth was retrieved possibly as late as 1915. We furthermore do not know whether Dawson was working alone or with others when he claimed to have made the discovery. The presence of additional persons in the examination of the field, as on 9 November 1912 when Dawson had been accompanied by Edgar Willett and Edwin Lankester,[26] could of course divert suspicion away from Dawson. Additional people provided additional motives for fraud as well as ample opportunities to plant artefacts within the area of Dawson's planned search. Dawson's letter of 3 July to Woodward, where he first announced the find, implies that he had been working alone ('*I have picked up* the frontal part of a human skull'),[27] but this alone is by no means conclusive.

Joseph Weiner, in his analysis of the chemical treatment of the Barcombe Mills assemblage, noted that 'one treatment involved in the staining, the bichromate, was certainly known to Dawson',[28] and of course Dawson had, as noted in the previous chapter, already confessed to having experimented with a variety of staining methods. Even if Dawson had been an innocent victim in the affair, then his possession of the Barcombe Mills bone assemblage, which had been so obviously 'treated in the same fashion as the material from Barkham Manor and Sheffield Park'[29] would seem, on the face of it, a rather massive coincidence.

If Dawson *had* himself been duped by another into believing that he had found the remains of another *Eoanthropus*, then that mysterious 'other' would have to have been both clever and devious. To fool Dawson into thinking his find was genuine, a forger would have to plant the pieces of cranium, and later the single tooth, in places where they could guarantee that Dawson would subsequently see them. To successfully accomplish this, the hoaxer would have required either a huge amount of luck, for the fields at Barcombe Mills are large and leaving the 'finds' at random within them would have been a massive gamble, or be thoroughly convinced that they knew *exactly* where Dawson would later be searching. The forger would also have to have planted the cranial pieces only a short time before Dawson's search got underway, for leaving the bone exposed to the elements for any length of time would almost certainly result in their loss.

A case could be made for making Father Marie-Joseph Pierre Teilhard de Chardin this mysterious forger attempting to dupe Charles Dawson. Teilhard was, as noted in the previous chapter, responsible for at least two of the more spectacular finds at Barkham Manor, and we know, by his own admission, that he visited Barcombe Mills with Dawson in the summer of 1913. Teilhard could, if implicated in the creation of the first *Eoanthropus*, plausibly made the second to help confirm the nature and interpretation of the speculative early human. If he did, then it is not clear how he could have made sufficient time from the Hastings seminary, where he was based, to plant the finds in areas where he could be 100 per cent sure that Dawson would later examine. As noted above, if Dawson was the innocent victim in the Barcombe Mills case, then the real forger, in order to successfully plant the bone and be sure that Dawson would find it, must have been at Barcombe Mills only a very short time (possibly no more than days) before the arrival of the Uckfield solicitor. In this Teilhard has a useful alibi, for he was in France from July 1912 to the August of 1913;[30] Teilhard had been out of the country for a whole year *before* Dawson made his first discovery at Barcombe Mills. His absence from the site, and indeed from England, at key points such as this in the Piltdown story precludes Teilhard from being the mastermind behind the hoax, though it could still be argued, perhaps with little real conviction, that he worked with another, perhaps even Dawson himself, to orchestrate proceedings and to make the forgery appear genuine.

It is, of course, possible to point the finger of suspicion at Arthur Woodward. Woodward's theories concerning the antiquity of Piltdown I, as well as the association of jaw and skull (which many in the scientific community still doubted were part of the same individual), would certainly have benefited in 1913 from the discovery of a second *Eoanthropus* so close to the site of the first. The desire to confirm the status of Piltdown man, as well as hinting at a viable population of *Eoanthropoids*, would certainly have provided a plausible motive for the hoax, but could Woodward have achieved this alone? As noted above, in order to successfully dupe Dawson into believing that he had indeed found a second

Eoanthropus, any speculative forger would have to have planted the pieces of cranium and the single tooth in a place where they could be sure that the solicitor would find them. Such clandestine activity would have to rely either on a huge amount of luck or precise and detailed knowledge of exactly *where* in Barcombe Mills Dawson would be working.

What can we make of Woodward's reluctance to discuss the Barcombe Mills material? Even if he had not been convinced of the antiquity of the skull fragments, as Robert Broom has suggested,[31] surely their geographical proximity to the main site at Barkham Manor (and the fact that both appeared to sit on the same level of gravel deposit) was reason enough to at least mention the discovery, even if only in passing? The strangely similar 'brown colour' of two assemblages was certainly of sufficient interest to warrant consideration, as was the alleged association of a 'chimpanzee-like' canine molar. Dawson must have shown Woodward the site of his second discovery of human remains at Barcombe (we know that he certainly showed Teilhard) and the two men would certainly, at some point during the 1913 or 1914 excavation seasons, have discussed the potential significance of the find. Dawson's reporting of at least one 'early-looking' flint implement from the fields at Barcombe Mills in November 1913 was also sufficiently intriguing, pointing perhaps to a second area of early human activity, and yet still Woodward said nothing. Perhaps he wanted to examine the Barcombe Mills site in greater detail before coming to any definitive conclusion, though he would certainly have had more than enough time to do this following Dawson's death in 1916. Perhaps he was cautious because he could not exactly remember *where* the second assemblage had been found in the Barcombe gravels. Perhaps he was suspicious of their authenticity. Perhaps he was himself the forger.

If Woodward was in someway implicated in the Barcombe Mills forgery, it is far more likely, given the considerations above, that he was working in concert with another, and that this 'other' can only plausibly have been Dawson himself. With the bogus cranial fragments successfully created by the two men, Dawson could then write to Woodward, outlining the details of his 'discovery', safe in the knowledge that he was creating a plausible origin for the finds, not to say an alibi for his friend. An insiders knowledge of the dubious origins of the Barcombe Mills bone could also explain Woodward's urgency to retrieve the 'finds' from Dawson's private collection, following the solicitor's death, from the hands of his widow Helene. Leaving the forgeries in Lewes where they could be found by another could of course link Woodward to the greater hoax, something which he simply could not allow. If, however, Woodward had snatched the tooth and cranial fragments from Helene Dawson in order to obscure any trace of his hand in the forgery, why did he then enter them into the British Museum (Natural History) accessions register? No one else was, to this date, aware of the existence of the material from Barcombe Mills (only Teilhard appears to have later remembered the site but his recollection was sketchy). Woodward, if he were indeed implicated in the creation of the Barcombe Mills forgery, could simply have disposed of the bone without a whiff of suspicion. Instead, leaving them to languish in the museum archive until their almost inevitable retrieval, would be akin to a game of academic Russian roulette.

Given the details of the 'discovery' and its immediate aftermath, the only convincing candidate for the imposture is Charles Dawson, though his apparent motive for the fraud, as well as his public silence concerning its discovery, have yet to be explained. What is clear is that the suggestion of a second *Eoanthropus* at Barcombe Mills, some distance from Piltdown I, would have strengthened the case for the original find being genuine, something which, in 1913, was still by no means certain. Having generated the second find at Barcombe Mills, why did Dawson appear to have done nothing substantive with it? That he reported the discovery to Woodward (on 3 July 1912) is on record, though we do not, unfortunately, know how Woodward reacted to the news. Perhaps he urged Dawson to keep the find a secret, until a better understanding of the Barcombe Mills gravels could be ascertained. Perhaps Woodward was not convinced that the Barcombe cranium was in any way similar to that of Piltdown I and felt that its disclosure would only 'muddy the waters' of the earlier find. Perhaps he was simply not convinced about the antiquity of this new cranium.

Whatever Woodward's response, Dawson did not move any further with the Barcombe Mills discovery, and does not appear to have discussed it either publicly or privately (though he seems to have shown Teilhard the alleged findspot in the summer of 1913). John Evangelist Walsh has recently suggested that though the Barcombe Mills find was central to the whole hoax, providing the much-needed evidence for a second *Eoanthropus*, the reason for shelving it was that by the summer of 1913, the debate surrounding Dawson's discovery had suddenly taken a different turn.

> when, unexpectedly, the dispute over the form of the [Piltdown] canine, as reconstructed by Woodward, claimed the spotlight, matters quickly altered. Taking advantage of the new development, Dawson was able on the instant to change direction, settling Barcombe Mills aside temporarily in favour of the controversial tooth.[32]

The 'discovery' of a single 'chimpanzee-like' canine molar, possibly as late as 1915, in the same general area of the Barcombe Mills skull fragments, *may* therefore have been generated by Dawson, following the finding of the Barkham Manor canine a year before. Such a find would certainly have redrawn Woodward's attention to the alternative site at Barcombe Mills, helping to convince him of its importance. Whatever the nature of the alleged 'discoveries', Dawson certainly kept them safely stored in his private collection at Castle Lodge in Lewes. Having established *when* the bone had first been found (3 July 1913) and obtained a witness (Teilhard) as to *where* they had been found, all Dawson had to do was to wait until such time that the material was

required, at which point it could be 'dusted off' and thrust into the full glare of academic attention. Dawson's death in 1916, it could be argued, abruptly terminated this particular aspect of the forgery, leaving Woodward unsure as to the true significance of the Barcombe Mills site.

Sheffield Park Man (Piltdown II)

The story of 'Sheffield Park man', or 'Piltdown II' as it came to appear in the literature, has a curiously similar echo to that of Barcombe Mills. Early in January 1915, Dawson, who had widened the area of his search for *Eoanthropus dawsoni* away from the main trenches at Barkham Manor, wrote excitedly to Woodward with news of a brand new discovery:

> I believe we are in luck again! I have got a fragment of the left side of the frontal bone with portion of the orbit and root of nose. Its outline is nearly the same as your original restoration and being another individual the difference is very slight.
>
> There is no supra-orbital foramen and hardly any supercilliary ridge. The orbital border ends abruptly in the centre with a sort of tubercle, and between it and the nose there is a groove or depression three quarters of an inch in length. The section is just like Pycraft's model section and there are indications of a frontal suture. The wall of the left sinus shows as a shallow depression in the section. The tables are thin and the diploe very thick. The general thickness seems to me to correspond to the right parietal of *Eoanthropus*.
>
> The weather has been awful, but I shall have another search before the plough comes along. I enclose rough sketches made from pencil outlines. When is Elliot Smith likely to be in town? I will bring it up as soon as I can get away.
>
> P.S. The outer surface is very rough, but the general colour and condition much the same as *Eoanthropus*. The forehead is quite angelic![33]

Six months later, on 30 July 1915, Dawson wrote again to Woodward with a further tantalising reference to the new discovery:

> I have got a new molar tooth (Eoanthropus) with the new series. But it is just the same as the others as to wear. It is a first or second right m[olar]. The roots broken.[34]

Woodward's replies to Dawson's letters remain unknown, though he must presumably have been elated. There could be no doubt about it; Dawson was referring to the new discovery of a second *Eoanthropus*, somewhere close to the original site at Barkham Manor. Whether or not Woodward recalled Dawson's earlier claims to have recovered a potential 'descendant of *Eoanthropus*' at Barcombe Mills in July of 1913 [35] is unknown, but the scientist must have felt, as with Barcombe before, to advise caution until the full nature and circumstances of the discovery could be gauged.

When Woodward was finally able to inspect and examine the new bone, at some stage after Dawson's death in 1916, all doubts concerning the genetic affiliation of the skeletal remains were dispelled. The first fragment of cranium recovered was:

> part of the supra-orbital region of a right frontal bone adjacent to the middle line. It is in exactly the same mineralised condition as the original skull of *Eoanthropus*, and deeply stained with iron-oxide. It is also similarly thickened, exhibiting the characteristic very fine diploe with comparatively thin outer and inner table of dense bone. It provides a portion that was absent in the first specimen, its upper end approaching within a few millimetres the level of the anterior broken edge of the left frontal in the latter, while its lower portion now leaves only about 2cm. of the supra-orbital border unknown. [36]

The smaller cranial fragment recovered by Dawson proved to be:

> part of an occipital bone, which is also well fossilised, but seems to have been weathered since it was derived from the gravel. Though still stout, it is thinner than the corresponding bone of Eoanthropus from Piltdown. [37]

In conclusion, Woodward felt that the skull demonstrated that:

> the muscles of the neck must have extended farther up the occiput than is usually the case. Such an upward extension of the neck-muscles is already known in Neanderthal man, where it is supposed to be correlated with the support of a heavy face; and it may be that in still earlier man the condition was variable, perhaps even different in the male and in the female. If this were so, there would be no reason to hesitate in referring the fragment now described to *Eoanthropus dawsoni*. [38]

The single ape-like tooth that Dawson reported on 30 July 1915:

> is a left first lower molar agreeing very closely with that of the original specimen of *Eoanthropus dawsoni*, but more obliquely worn by mastication. It is equally well fossilised, and stained brown with oxide of iron in the usual manner. [39]

As with Barcombe Mills before it, neither Dawson nor Woodward immediately 'went public' about the 1915 discoveries. In retrospect this seems strange

for, unlike the assemblage retrieved from Barcombe Mills, these new pieces clearly matched the remains of *Eoanthropus* already recovered from Barkham Manor. In fact the finding of a second 'Man of the Dawn' was precisely what both Woodward and Dawson had long been hoping for, especially as significant elements within the scientific community had recently cast doubt as to the authenticity of *Eoanthropus*. Any suspicion that the human cranium and ape-like jaw from Barkham Manor had been accidentally paired within the Piltdown gravels would, once and for all, be blown away by the new discovery, for the chances of such associations occurring twice were astronomical. *Eoanthropus dawsoni* was a genuine ancestor of the modern human, and the bones from Dawson's new findspot would conclusively prove it.

Woodward's most detailed description concerning both the circumstances and the location of the new site, came in a formal presentation to the Geological Society on 28 February 1917 and later published in their *Quarterly Journal*. Here Woodward noted that:

> One large field, about 2 miles from the Piltdown pit, had especially attracted Mr Dawson's attention, and he and I examined it several times without success during the spring and autumn of 1914. When, however, in the course of farming, the stones had been raked off the ground and brought together into heaps. Mr Dawson was able to search the material more satisfactorily; and early in 1915 he was so fortunate as to find here two well-fossilised pieces of human skull and a molar tooth, which he immediately recognised as belonging to at least one more individual of *Eoanthropus dawsoni*. Shortly afterwards, in the same gravel, a friend met with part of the lower molar of an indeterminable species of rhinoceros, as highly mineralised as the specimens previously found at Piltdown itself.[40]

It is worth pointing out here that although Woodward asserts that he and Dawson 'examined' the area of the new find 'several times',[41] nowhere does he acknowledge that he had visited the place at, or even shortly after, Dawson's discovery of the skull and tooth. This point was later confirmed in a private letter to Ales Hrdlicka, Curator of Physical Anthropology at the United States National Museum of Natural History in Washington, dated 26 October 1926, where Woodward, having discussed the remains of 'Piltdown II', confessed that Dawson had 'told me that he found them on the Sheffield Park Estate, but he would not tell me the exact place – I can only infer from other information that I have'.[42]

In a letter to Osborne White, quoted in White's book *The Geology of the Country near Lewes*,[43] Woodward suggested that the likely findspot of 'Piltdown II' was Netherall Farm, though as Walsh has pointed out,[44] this may have been solely due to the fact that, as with Barkham Manor, the Netherall Farm was the property of George Maryon-Wilson, under the stewardship of Dawson. Doubts concerning the exact provenance of the second *Eoanthropus* meant that Woodward was ultimately unable to continue Dawson's examination of the alternative site in and around the Sheffield Park estate (all of his later work at Piltdown appears to have concentrated around the area of the main trenches at Barkham Manor). When Woodward finally compiled the data surrounding Piltdown man for his book *The Earliest Englishman*, Piltdown II was confined to nothing more than a footnote, the site itself being briefly dismissed as 'a patch of gravel about two miles away from the original spot'.[45]

One further curious aspect of Woodward's 1917 presentation is the 'friend' (presumably of Dawson) who 'met with part of the lower molar of an indeterminable species of rhinoceros'.[46] This information must have derived from Dawson himself, perhaps anecdotally, otherwise Woodward, presumably, would have been more precise. It is possible that the mysterious 'friend' was Edgar Willett, a retired administrator of anaesthetics at the Alexandra Hospital for Children and St Bartholomew's Hospital in London and long-time associate of Dawson, who lived in Crawley. Willett certainly accompanied Dawson on a number of field visits in the area of Barkham Manor and Barcombe Mills,[47] though his main function appears to have been unofficial driver for both Dawson and Woodward.[48] The 'friend' could also have been Edwin Ray Lankester, former Director of the British Museum (Natural History) and Keeper of Zoology, who is also known to have accompanied Dawson on field excursions. Lankester also appears to have been given advanced notice of the Sheffield Park find, for he was, in his 1915 book *Diversions of a Naturalist*, able to insert a footnote concerning the 'recent discovery... of a second skull' at Piltdown.[49] If someone of Lankester's stature *had* found the rhinoceros molar, then Dawson would certainly have been mentioned it (and Woodward remembered it). Whatever the case, the 'unnamed friend' certainly has the ring of a Dawson story, the lack of detail surrounding the finder mirroring with the general vagueness that often accompanied discoveries made by the Uckfield solicitor.

The presentation that Woodward made to the Geological Society on 28 February 1917 was less triumphal than it could have been, probably because of the war, but Woodward's summing-up was pretty conclusive.

> From the new facts now described it seems reasonable to conclude that *Eoanthropus dawsoni* will eventually prove to be as definite and distinct a form of early Man as was at first supposed; for the occurrence of the same type of frontal bone with the same type of lower molar in two separate localities adds to the probability that they belonged to one and the same species.[50]

A second presentation, made by Grafton Elliot Smith, then discussed the evidence supplied from an 'endocranial cast' of the new *Eoanthropus*. Smith noted that although only a small area of the inner surface survived for the right side of the frontal bone,

it is of interest and importance because it sheds some light upon a part of the endocranial cast of which nothing was known before. Moreover, it is a part of the cast, the frontal pole, the form of which is of peculiar significance in the study of the features of early Man.[51]

Exact analogies for the recorded features of the new *Eoanthropus* were difficult to find in modern skull casts, Smith observed, though similarities could be detected in Neanderthal casts.

> If these tentative suggestions are justified, this small fragment affords further corroboration of the opinion that I expressed with reference to the endocranial cast of the Piltdown skull; namely, that it presents features which are more distinctly primitive and ape-like than those of any other member of the human family at present available for examination.[52]

Anyone who had previously doubted that the cranium and mandible recovered from Barkham Manor (Piltdown I) were in any way connected, must, it was now abundantly clear, eat humble pie. Few speakers rose to question either Woodward or Smith following their lectures, and those that did broadly agreed with the comments made. Arthur Keith, previously an opponent of Woodward's concerning the reconstruction of *Eoanthropus dawsoni* (even to the point of renaming it *Homo piltdownensis*: see previous chapter), commented that:

> these further Piltdown 'finds' established beyond any doubt that *Eoanthropus* was a very clearly-differentiated type of being – in his opinion a truly human type. He agreed with Dr Smith Woodward and Mr Pycraft that the lower molar now found and the original mandible and teeth must be ascribed to Eoanthropus, and constituted the characteristic features of the type.[53]

Edwin Ray Lankester further congratulated Woodward:

> on the gradual addition, by his patient work and that of the late Mr Charles Dawson, of new bits to our knowledge of the Piltdown man. He pointed out that it was a possibility – although highly improbable – that the piece of the frontal bone and also the molar tooth now described belonged to the same individual as that represented by the imperfect skull and lower jaw already known. But this was not true of the fragment of the occipital bone, since the region corresponding to this fragment was present in the imperfect skull now in the Natural History Museum. The present 'find' therefore makes it impossible to regard the Piltdown man as an isolated abnormal individual. The fragments hitherto found must be referred to two, and possibly to three or even four individuals.[54]

The remainder of Woodward's presentation, concerning the results of the 1916 summer season, which had unfortunately been conducted without Dawson who was by then was entering the final stage of his illness, were not overly commented upon. The work had proved disappointing. True, Woodward and Grafton Elliot Smith had further confirmed the extent of the Piltdown gravel, suggesting that the deposit was 'a shingle-bank which may have accumulated within a comparatively short space of time',[55] but the artefactual remains were sparse. 'Neither bones nor teeth were met with', Woodward commented sadly, the only 'noteworthy' find from the whole two week season being:

> a battered nodule of black flint, which occurred in a rather sandy patch of the dark-brown gravel resting immediately on the basal layer. This specimen, which is conspicuously different from the other flints and very little stained, may have been used by man as a hammer-stone. It measures nearly 13 centimetres in length by 9.5 cm. in width, and about 7.5 cm. in maximum thickness. The largest face, which is almost flat, has been produced by coarse flaking, and bears marks of much battering round the edge, especially at one angle. The opposite large face is covered for the greater part by the original crust of the flint-nodule, but is strongly battered along the two cross-ridges and one connecting edge, from which lateral flakes have been struck. Where not thus flaked the periphery of the flint is also covered with the original crust. Like the later undoubted hammer-stones, therefore, this flint has been used mainly on two opposite faces; but it appears to owe its present form merely to use, not to any original intentional shaping. All the edges are remarkably sharp, and the black facets bear scarcely any patina. [56]

Still, the undoubted 'hammer stone' did imply prehistoric workmanship, suggesting that *Eoanthropus* had been capable of manufacturing, designing and shaping flint tools. Not everyone was convinced, however, that the artefact was in any way associated with Piltdown man, such hammer stones being relatively commonplace throughout all periods of prehistory and from all areas of the county. Following the presentation, Mr W. Dale, previously a critic of the worked elephant femur recovered during the 1914 season, observed that the patination evident on the hammer stone suggested that:

> it had probably sunk down from a higher level and was of newer date. At a previous meeting on the same subject, Palaeolithic implements had been shown which were of the deep-ochreous colour of the bones.[57]

Having conclusively proved both the existence and authenticity of *Eoanthropus dawsoni*, effectively silencing any doubters, Sheffield Park man (or 'Piltdown II') quietly sank back into obscurity. Even Woodward himself preferred to limit discussion of the second *Eoanthropus*, mentioning it only once in his book *The Earliest Englishman*,[58] and then only in extremely vague terms. Interestingly, it was the very 'obscurity' of such a vital and important component of the entire *Eoanthropus* story, that first led Joseph Weiner to investigate the whole Piltdown assemblage. Later Weiner was to record that, at the dinner of the 1953 Congress of Palaeontologists, Kenneth Oakley of the British Museum (Natural History), commented that there was no record as to the exact spot that 'Piltdown II' had been found. Weiner was amazed because:

> the second group of finds had done so much to convince many people that the first Piltdown man was by no means an isolated phenomenon. One had imagined that if it were ever thought worthwhile it would be possible to go and excavate the second site. Now it appeared that this had never been done because the second site could not be located... This small puzzle turned my thoughts to the larger Piltdown conundrum.[59]

Subsequent detailed analysis of the Sheffield Park remains confirmed Weiner's worst fears. First, the wear pattern on the canine molar found by Dawson in July 1915 was revealed, under a binocular microscope, to have been 'finely scratched, as though by an abrasive'.[60] Such scratching, or grinding, across the biting surface of the tooth had clearly been applied post-mortem. Detailed examination of the frontal and occipital fragments of Sheffield Park man, found by Dawson in January of 1915, revealed that they, like the 'artificially hardened' bone from Barkham Manor, contained 'small amounts of chromate'.[61] Far more disconcerting, however, was the observation hat the frontal piece of the Piltdown II cranium could, anatomically, have formed part of the *same skull* recovered from Barkham Manor, as:

> in colour and in its content of nitrogen and fluorine it resembles the first occipital of Piltdown I rather than that of Piltdown II. Just as the isolated molar almost certainly comes from the Piltdown mandible, it seems only too likely that this frontal fragment originally belonged to the cranium of Piltdown I.[62]

Such a conclusion was potentially explosive, for the investigation team were suggesting that the right frontal piece of the second *Eoanthropus* skull had orig- inally formed part of the first. The reason that Piltdown I and II therefore appeared 'similarly thickened',[63] was because they were indeed from *the same skull*. In order to test this hypothesis, a sample of the Sheffield Park cranium was submitted for radiocarbon dating in 1987. The results, processed by the Oxford Radiocarbon Accelerator Unit, provided a date range for the Piltdown II cranium of 970 ± 140 (OxA-1394), which may be calibrated (at 95.4 per cent probability) as between AD 750 and 1300. The statistical differences between this determination and that provided for the Barkham Manor cranium I in the late 1950s (AD 1210 – 1480) appeared to suggest that the pieces were in fact from 'two distinct individuals'.[64] However, given that the Oxford Radiocarbon Accelerator Unit also supplied a date for the Piltdown I mandible which was similarly at odds with the sample dated in the late 1950s (see previous chapter), the likelihood remains that both the Piltdown I and II crania were originally from the same individual: someone who had died at some point during the early medieval period.

Prior to deposition at Barkham Manor, the skull that formed the basis for Piltdown I must, therefore, have been deliberately broken, selected pieces being used for the first site. A single, unused fragment of the right frontal from this broken skull could then have been put to one side for later use at Sheffield Park, where it was placed with a piece of occipital bone from a second, more 'normal' (and possibly modern) skull. The inclusion of a rhinoceros tooth in the assemblage, as with the mammalian remains recovered from Barkham Manor, hinted at a Pliocene date for this second example of *Eoanthropus dawsoni*.[65]

Sheffield Park Man: conclusions

The list of suspects associated with the Sheffield Park forgery is small and, perhaps unsurprisingly, rather familiar. This is due primarily to the fact that the perpetrator of Piltdown II is so clearly implicated with the Barkham Manor fraud, the cranial fragments from both having ultimately derived from the same source. Father Marie-Joseph Pierre Teilhard de Chardin has at times been implicated in the Piltdown II deception,[66] but it is clear that he was out of the country when certain key discoveries were made at Barkham Manor.[67] His involvement in the fabrication and planting of the Sheffield Park 'finds' must further be in question due to the priest's involvement, from March 1915, in the Great War as a 'stretcher-bearer attached to an artillery regiment'.[68] He would not have had the time, let alone the desire, to orchestrate the fabrication of archaic human remains in Sussex whilst embroiled in one of the worst conflicts ever known. Arthur Keith has also been suspected of involvement in the Piltdown II fraud,[69] but the evidence presented is inconclusive and unconvincing, ultimately boiling down to the fact that Spencer was convinced of Keith's guilt at Barkham Manor (itself unproven).

The case against Arthur Woodward has a bit more substance to it, but ultimately hinges upon the non-disclosure of Piltdown II until early 1917, two years after its discovery, combined with his reluctance to accurately locate the findspot. If the new discovery was indeed so crucial, why had Woodward not mentioned it to anyone sooner? The timing could have been critical here for, in 1915, not only was Britain involved in a catastrophic European war, public attention quite rightly being drawn towards the ever increasing number of casualties resulting from the conflict, but also Charles Dawson himself was becoming gravely ill. Quite when the first symptoms of his illness became manifest, is not known, but certainly by the autumn of 1915 he was clearly unwell.[70] Throughout the spring of 1916, Dawson rested at home in Lewes, being put on a course of serum injections.[71] After a brief spell back at work, presumably trying to tie-up loose ends, he returned home, dying early on 10 August. Little of his correspondence with Woodward survives from this period, certainly nothing related to the discovery of material from the second site, but it is possible that both men were planning to withhold from any formal announcement until either Dawson recovered or that a more detailed survey of the new site could be undertaken. Unfortunately, given Dawson's deteriorating health, no new survey was ever undertaken.

A further possibility to explain Woodward's initial reluctance to announce Dawson's discovery presents itself: he simply did not know *where*, exactly, the new finds had been made. When Dawson found material at Barcombe Mills, he was able to show Teilhard de Chardin and, as far as we can ascertain, Woodward himself, the site. Such a luxury may not have been possible for Sheffield Park. Even without Dawson's illness, both men were very busy, and the pressure of their professional lives, especially given the context of the First World War, may not have permitted time to explore the Sussex countryside in detail together. Add to this the fact that Woodward's son Cyril was, in late 1915, recovering from appendicitis 'complicated by post-operative thrombosis',[72] then Woodward's time would indeed have been precious.

Given the perceived importance of the new find, as well as its close proximity to London where Woodward worked, it would however seem surprising, in the months following January 1915, that Woodward could not have found at least a day, say in the spring of 1916, to spare in order to investigate the location of the second *Eoanthropus*. Even if he could not find the time, both Woodward and Grafton Elliot Smith managed to spend at least two weeks during the summer excavating at Barkham Manor (with little result).[73] That they accomplished this without visiting Dawson, who was by then bedbound, would seem highly unlikely. Yet the possibility that Woodward did not know precisely *where* the site of Dawson's second great discovery at Piltdown had been made, especially if Dawson had not been able to take him there in person, could help to explain both his delay in its reporting, as well as the vagueness with which he later referred to it.

Later evidence does appear to confirm the idea that it was Woodward's lack of certainty concerning the provenance of the Sheffield Park finds that resulted in his delay in reporting them. In 1954, following the initial exposure of the Piltdown I fraud, Joseph Weiner interviewed Lady Maud Smith Woodward concerning the nature of her late husband's relationship with Charles Dawson. During the conversation, Lady Woodward confirmed that Dawson 'would not give details of the exact spot' of Piltdown II, despite her husband being 'most anxious about it'. Specifically Lady Woodward observed that the nature of Dawson's illness made the 'enquiries fruitless' and though Woodward had 'spent much time searching' for site II, he never managed to pin it down. At this point Lady Woodward confided that the search had, at least partially, been conducted to allay certain fears that her husband had concerning the nature of the 'discovery' as:

> it seemed to her that her husband regarded site II as something that D[awson] had imagined; it 'existed in Dawson's imagination'. She knew that D. was rather queer in his last illness.[74]

Despite the vagaries of provenance, there can be no doubt that Woodward certainly gained from the Sheffield Park discovery, for the second *Eoanthropus* helped authenticate the first, whilst simultaneously, and effectively, destroying all academic opposition. The death of Dawson late in 1916, although both unexpected and unfortunate, would also have ensured that Woodward received the full recognition and acknowledgement of the scientific community without having to share any of the glory. This, rather cynical, hypothesis, is perhaps undermined by the observation that Woodward was not slow to praise Dawson throughout his presentation to the Geological Society, seeing that he received full credit for the discovery. Of course, it could be possible to argue that such praise was a 'smokescreen', designed to extricate Woodward from the suggestion that he may have been involved in the initial phases of discovery. In such a scenario, Woodward's rather lengthy attempts to find an origin for Piltdown II would however require some explanation. In failing to provide anything but a vague provenance for the second *Eoanthropus* in the final published report, Woodward only drew attention to the inadequacy of its recovery.

Charles Dawson, as discoverer of the second site, must be chief suspect in the Sheffield Park forgery. His complicity in the Piltdown I forgery at Barkham Manor (see previous chapter) leaves little doubt that he *must* somehow have been involved in Piltdown II, for whoever broke apart the skull used in the first site also seeded pieces of the same skeleton at Sheffield Park. Dawson's failure to record the exact circumstances surrounding the Sheffield Park discovery are at best frustrating, at worst an indication of his guilt. Failure to adequately record the findspot, or communicate the provenance to Woodward, could of course be excused by Dawson's illness, the first stages of which may have been manifest by the spring of 1915, were it not for the fact that he had also been similarly vague at both Barkham Manor and Barcombe Mills. As with the Barcombe Mills discovery, we cannot be sure whether the solicitor was working by himself or with others at Sheffield Park, though the implication of the letters that he sent to Woodward [75] was that he was working alone. Only the rhinoceros tooth appears to have been found by another, and this by an unnamed 'friend' of either Dawson or Woodward.[76]

To claim that Dawson was in any way unaware of the fraud at Sheffield Park, that he was a dupe at the mercy of another, still anonymous forger, requires special pleading. If he had been wholly innocent of the forgery, then the story he told Woodward concerning the discovery of the second *Eoanthropus* must be true; and yet the nature of their finding proves that this cannot have been the case. To fool a man of Dawson's antiquarian experience into believing the artefacts were genuine, the real forger must have planted the pieces of skull and ape-like canine in an area where they could be certain that Dawson would later be closely investigating. The finds would have to have been clearly visible on the surface, no mean feat given the ground conditions of a ploughed field (as anyone who has undertaken a surface collection survey can testify), and all without attracting Dawson's suspicion. As previously stated, in order to achieve this operation successfully, the fraudster would have to be on site at Sheffield Park only days (possibly only hours) before the solicitor arrived. Leaving the bone out at the mercy of the elements would be too big a gamble. Furthermore, if the planted artefacts were not recovered during the course of the survey, then the forger would himself have to rediscover and retrieve all pieces of bone and plant them somewhere else for Dawson to find. All this effort and to what end? If the fraudster hoped to expose Dawson or Woodward to ridicule, then the plan backfired, for all Sheffield Park did was to finally confirm the status of both *Eoanthropoids* and the man who found them. With Dawson as the forger, the nature and details concerning the hoax become far easier to explain for the finds were never in the ground to start with.

In retrospect, Arthur Smith Woodward's only crime in the case of Sheffield Park was his culpability. He desperately needed Piltdown II in order to deflect and neutralise the growing attacks on *Eoanthropus dawsoni*. He delayed the public reporting of the second 'Man of the Dawn' whilst he investigated the circumstances surrounding its discovery. By February 1917 he had had enough, and finally revealed Dawson's last 'great find' to the world and, in doing so:

> he placed himself and his reputation squarely and shamelessly in the breach... If he had rejected the Sheffield Park bones, or reserved judgement on them, if he had been more forthright and honest about their uncertain background, Piltdown man would soon have lost its place in the evolutionary argument. Persistent doubts and objections as to the linkage of jaw and cranium [from Piltdown I], growing from the outset, would eventually have carried the day.[77]

By 1917, of course, five years after first becoming embroiled in the story of Piltdown man, Arthur Smith Woodward could not afford to loose his precious *Eoanthropus*.

13

A BRIEF HISTORY OF CRIME

It has become apparent, through a case by case analysis of all of Charles Dawson's major antiquarian finds, looking at both the composition and circumstances of each, and publications, that all was not as it outwardly appeared (**99**). Of the discoveries listed here, at least thirty-three are clear fakes: *Plagiaulax dawsoni* I, II and III; the shadow figures of Hastings Castle; Stephen Blackmore's hafted stone axe and the accompanying flint assemblage; the Bexhill Boat; both of the Pevensey Bricks; the Lavant Cave artefact assemblage; the Beauport Park Statuette; the Bulverhythe Hammer; the Chinese Vase; the Brighton 'Toad in a Hole'; the English Channel sea serpents; the Piltdown cranium; the Piltdown mandible and teeth; the single Piltdown canine; the Piltdown nasal bones; the Piltdown beaver jaw; the Piltdown beaver incisor; the Piltdown hippopotamus molar; the Piltdown elephant molar; the Piltdown rhinoceros premolar; the Piltdown palaeoliths; the Piltdown elephant bone tool; the Piltdown mastodon molar; the Piltdown deer antler; the Piltdown horse molar; the Barcombe Mills cranium; the Barcombe Mills canine; the Sheffield Park cranium; the Sheffield Park canine; the Sheffield Park rhinoceros molar. The chief (and sometimes *only*) suspect in each of these cases is none other than Charles Dawson himself.

In addition to these, we may cite the Uckfield Horseshoe, the Lewes Prick Spur and the standard mount from the St Leonards bronze hoard as fakes probably generated by Charles Dawson, and the 'Arabic' Anvil, the Beauport Park Axe and the Piltdown 'eoliths' as possible fakes with a clear association with Dawson. The Herstmonceux Fireback, the Chiddingly Dog Gate, the Bermondsey Abbey Curfew, the Hastings Mace and the Sussex Loops may also be appended to the list as unusual items, albeit ones with no obvious associated trace of fraudulent activity. With regard to Dawson's publications, we can note that the only written article that is clearly plagiarised is the manuscript 'On the persistence of a Thirteenth Dorsal Vertebra in Certain Human Races'. Papers on 'Dene Holes', Sussex iron, pottery and glass and the 'Red Hills of Essex' are, together with the two-volume study the *History of Hastings Castle: the Castlery, Rape and Battle of Hastings, to which is added a History of the Collegiate Church within the Castle, and its Prebends*, all essentially compilations of other people's work. Furthermore, the Hastings Rarities (all 542 specimens), the

Maresfield Map and the Ashburnham Dial are all clearly fraudulent, though it has not been possible to prove a definite link with Charles Dawson as perpetrator. The incidence of natural gas at Heathfield appears entirely genuine, Dawson being in the right place at the right time to deliver a formal report. The Castle Lodge incident implies grave professional misconduct, though no formal charge against Dawson was ever made.

Possible accomplices

During the course of his antiquarian career, Dawson rarely worked alone. When he collected fossils from the Hastings area during the 1880s, it was with Samuel Beckles. When he found the remains of *Plagiaulax dawsoni* in 1911 and *Eoanthropus dawsoni* between 1911 and 1912, it was in collaboration with Teilhard de Chardin and Arthur Woodward. The Lavant Caves and the subterranean tunnels beneath Hastings Castle were both cleared and recorded with the active help of John Lewis. Those who were not present at the time certain discoveries were made, such as Richard Lydekker, Augustus Wollaston Franks, Arthur Keith and Grafton Elliot Smith, were quickly involved (and therefore implicated) as experts keen to voice an opinion. If at any stage of his career Dawson did in fact possess a co-conspirator, is it possible that such an accomplice to forgery may be found within such a list of eminent colleagues?

99 *A Brief History of Crime: material from the archive of Hastings Museum and Art Gallery including, from top right, the skull of Piltdown I, the prick spur from Lewes Castle, the Beauport Park Statuette, the Pevensey Brick, the Bulverhythe Hammer and various documents and letters from the Dawson Collection*

Arthur Smith Woodward is perhaps the most obvious candidate for co-conspirator, for he was intimately involved in Dawson's earliest traceable fraud, the teeth of *Plagiaulax dawsoni*, as well as being co-director of the excavations and survey at Piltdown. As we have seen, however, though Woodward was clearly involved in both these deceptions, his role appears to have been little more than academic dupe. His failure to spot flagrant pieces of forgery in the blatantly artificial wear patterns in the teeth of both *Plagiaulax* and *Eoanthropus*, the steel cut marks in the Piltdown elephant-bone tool and the chemical staining of the entire Piltdown bone and flint assemblage is unforgivable, but he appears to have been totally taken in by Dawson's 'discoveries'. *Eoanthropus*, and to some extent *Plagiaulax*, fitted his theories concerning human and animal evolution perfectly and he never seems (at least publicly) to have questioned their authenticity. That he went to his grave defending his friend and colleague Charles Dawson, is clear enough from the pages of his posthumously published book *The Earliest Englishman*; his final twenty-one years of fruitless excavation at Barkham Manor an attempt perhaps to vindicate Dawson and prove that *Eoanthropus* was genuine.

Marie-Joseph Pierre Teilhard de Chardin is someone whom, like Arthur Woodward, was intimately associated with Dawson's discovery of *Plagiaulax dawsoni* and *Eoanthropus dawsoni*, but he was not in Britain when Dawson found his first forged *Plagiaulax* and neither was he during the final stages of Piltdown I, II or III. Teilhard, like Woodward, was another dupe; an expert brought in to witness the discovery of certain fabricated items, thus increasing their perceived authenticity. The same can be said for Samuel Allinson Woodhead who accompanied Dawson in his early phases of artefact retrieval at Piltdown in 1912 and 1913 [1] and who conducted the first scientific analysis of a fragment of *Eoanthropus* cranium, analysed the chemical composition of chalk for Dawson's article on dene holes, examined pottery for his article on Sussex iron and pottery and conducted tests on the Heathfield gas. Woodhead was, in other words, Dawson's 'tame scientist', a colleague who worked with the Uckfield solicitor, providing valuable background information, but who was, ultimately, unaware of any fraud.

As Charles' wife, Helene Dawson must understandably come under some form of suspicion regarding the string of forgeries now attributed to the Uckfield solicitor. Surely she must have been aware of her husband's nefarious activities? How could he have generated artefacts such as those recovered from Piltdown, Pevensey and Beauport Park, without her knowledge? Surely something would have given him away? Unfortunately, we know very little about Helene Dawson, other than she was, by all accounts, a loving and devoted partner. How extensively she shared her husband's interests in matters antiquarian, however, is unclear. She does not seem to have accompanied him on any of his major expeditions, and was certainly never present at Piltdown when any of the 'discoveries' were made. It is possible that Dawson kept this side of his life secret from her. His interests in all things historical, archaeological, geological and palaeontological were well known, and must have kept him busy for long periods of time,

time enough perhaps to devise and generate forgeries without the merest hint of suspicion from his friends and family.

What little is known about Dawson's private life seems to confirm this hypothesis. Joseph Weiner, writing forty years after Charles Dawson's death, observed that:

> He told his wife little of his Piltdown doings. He was extremely secretive about his excursions, as Mrs Dawson told a friend and lamented again after his death, for she felt that at the end he had had some important information he wanted to pass on.[2]

Confirmation of such 'secretive' behaviour may perhaps be glimpsed in the details of a dinner party held at the Dawson's family home of Castle Lodge, in or around the autumn of 1911. Guests that evening were Mr and Mrs Clarke, long-time friends of the Dawson's. After dinner Charles Dawson asked Mr Clarke if he would accompany him to the cellar as there was something he would like him to see,

> to which Mrs Dawson said something to the effect that she did not know what was going on. He would not let her into the secret. 'I sometimes think he is a Dr Crippen'.[3]

Helene Dawson, referring to Hawley Harvey Crippen, a convicted murder who disposed of his wife's remains beneath their house, was undoubtedly gently mocking her husband and, from what we know of Dawson, he would no doubt have laughed along. Nevertheless, an 'off the cuff' comment such as this could well have made him feel rather uneasy.

Following Dawson's death in 1916, Helene, herself quite ill, sold much of her husband's collection to Hastings Museum, passing those artefacts associated with Piltdown on to Arthur Woodward. What remained of Charles Dawson's own private papers, which may have helped identify any potential collaborator in fraud, were destroyed in 1917,[4] by which time Helene herself had passed away. There is nothing in the story of Piltdown, nor indeed in any of the 'discoveries' made by Dawson in the thirty years before, that in any way implicates Helene as co-conspirator. This particular side to his otherwise public life, Dawson appears to have kept very private indeed.

Of all the people involved with Charles Dawson, Henry Willett is possibly one of whom the least is known within Piltdown-related literature. Willett (1823-1903) was a wealthy Brighton-based collector of fossils, rocks, paintings, porcelain and general curios and a keen advocate of public involvement and awareness. He is credited as being the main impetus in the creation of Brighton Museum and Art Gallery (between 1901 and 1903), following substantial donations from his own private collections, to the people and council of the town. Many of his ceramics and paintings remain on display in Brighton Museum whilst the bulk of his fossil collection was given to Brighton's Booth Museum of Natural History.

Willett's name is of course associated with at least two of Dawson's more strange 'discoveries': the Chinese *hu* and the 'Toad in a Hole', whilst he is also credited in Dawson's articles on Sussex pottery[5] and appears to have been the primary discoverer of natural gas at Heathfield.[6] The bronze ritual vase, or *hu*, was presented by Willett to the British Museum in 1885 (Dawson arrived with a similar bronze a year later). Willett claimed that the vessel had been found 'in the Dane John (donjon) at Canterbury'.[7] Sixteen years later, in 1901, Willett presented Brighton Museum with the petrified 'Toad in a Hole', allegedly on Dawson's behalf.[8]

Given his interests as a collector and his involvement in public projects (such as the creation of a Brighton Emigration Society to help people move to Canada), Willett seems an unlikely suspect for archaeological fraud. Unlike Dawson, he never aspired to be a great antiquarian and never seems to have specifically craved academic acknowledgement. His donation of the 'Toad in a Hole' to the Booth Museum of Natural History in Brighton seems, on the face of it, entirely innocent, for many specimens of the natural world were donated by him to the town in the final years of his life. How he actually came by the find in the first place is not explained, but it is clear that he did not gain materially from the object, however, temporarily it was in his possession. In no way can Willett be associated with the discovery or early reporting of the 'Toad in a Hole', all academic recognition having gone to Dawson as the 'discoverer' and chief reporter of the find. It is likely that in this instance Dawson passed the artefact to Willett with the specific and express hope of it being donated to the Brighton-based Natural History Museum.

The *hu* however is a different matter. As has already been noted, the date of the vase (fourth or fifth century BC) is at odds with its alleged provenance, the medieval 'Dane John' of Canterbury, making it somewhat unlikely (though not altogether impossible) that the artefact was ever really found there. There were, furthermore, no known nineteenth-century archaeological investigations within this area of medieval Canterbury, so how the bronze came to be 'found' has yet to be explained. How Willett came into possession of the artefact in the first place is also unclear, though as an avid collector he could easily (and plausibly) have purchased the item from a dealer in antiquities who supplied him with a spurious provenance. Dawson's later donation of a similar vessel to the British Museum could also been seen in such a light: Dawson himself being the innocent victim of an unscrupulous salesperson, rather than the actual instigator of an archaeological hoax.

An alternative explanation presents itself, however. It is possible (though ultimately unprovable) that Dawson was in receipt of a spectacular artefact (in this case a bronze vase from China) which he hoped to show came from a highly unusual source (here medieval Kent). To do this successfully he would need to create an atmosphere where no suspicion would arise concerning his 'find'. As with the forged Roman bricks from Pevensey, Dawson would require a dupe, someone with no obvious links to himself, who could make a similar find first. Such subterfuge certainly later worked well for Dawson at Pevensey, the brick 'found' in Louis Salzman's excavations helping to authenticate Dawson's artefact, whilst his more complete piece helped confirm the first in 'a sort of inverse camouflage'.[9] A second, broadly similar Chinese vase complete with dubious provenance could therefore be passed to Willett (possibly via an intermediate) safe in the knowledge that, as a trusted and well-respected collector, such a donation to the British Museum would not be questioned. All suspicion defused, Dawson could then present his piece. In such a scenario, Willett would be no more guilty of forgery than Salzman had been at Pevensey: he was, for Dawson, just the right man at the right time to unknowingly complete a particular piece of deception.

Of all the characters listed so far, John Lewis would appear, on the face of it, to be a prime suspect for the role of co-conspirator, for he was associated with at least two of Dawson's early excavations: at Lavant and Hastings Castle. He was also, as we have seen, clearly the author of the fraudulent Maresfield Map and the infamous Ashburnham Dial, both of which have been linked to Dawson. He also seems to have accompanied the solicitor in the exploration of dene holes, or underground caverns, somewhere in the Brighton area during the 1890s [10] and collaborated with Dawson in the accumulation of material for the latter's study into 'Sussex Ironwork and Pottery'.[11] Closer examination of Lewis, however, raises certain doubts as to the solidity of such an accusation.

Little is really known about John Lewis. His certificate of candidature for election to fellowship of the Society of Antiquaries in 1896, following his collaboration with Dawson at Hastings and Lavant, notes his occupation as 'retired CE, formerly in the service of the Indian Government', his qualification being as a result of 'archaeological research in India and England'.[12] The exact nature of his earlier work is unknown, though John Sawyer, writing on the excavation of the Lavant Caves, notes that Lewis had previously 'done some good work in the same line, especially in India'.[13] The term 'CE' in Lewis' application has been understood to have been an abbreviation for civil engineer. John Combridge has observed that 'a John Lewis' was 'employed as a permanent way inspector on the civil engineering staff of the North, and East, Bengal State Railways [and] appears to have continued in service there until 1893'.[14]

It would seem likely that the two Lewis' were in reality the same, especially as 1893, the year that the Lewis employed by 'the North, and East, Bengal State Railways' retired, was also the same year that the John Lewis 'formerly in the service of the Indian Government' came to work in the Lavant Caves with Charles Dawson. Dawson later thanked Lewis for providing plans of the Heathfield gas borings, so perhaps, in the capacity of 'CE' Lewis had already put his experience on the Indian railway to work in a similar field on his return to England.[15] If he was, indeed, an experienced civil engineer, then Lewis would certainly have been an invaluable asset to Dawson in his clearance and subsequent recording of both the Hastings 'dungeon' and the Lavant 'caves'.

At Lavant, it has already been noted that the bizarre collection of artefacts assembled there could best be explained as having been 'smuggled into the Caves in somebody's pocket and planted in the soft chalk debris by a person with free access to the Caves'.[16] A case could be made for this deception against anyone with unfettered access to the caves, be they the directors Dawson and Lewis, the team of (largely unnamed) workmen, the landowner, tenant farmers, shepherds or visitors to the site during the course of the 1893-4 excavation. Dawson is, of course, the prime suspect, as he gained materially from the caves through plaudits from a number of important antiquarian groups; but then so too did Lewis, Lavant being one of the sites that helped both men achieve fellowship of the Society of Antiquaries. Either Lewis or Dawson could, therefore, be held accountable for the deception, though only Dawson would conceivably have been collecting British antiquities long enough to be able to call upon the diverse range of archaeological material necessary to 'salt the mine'.

Dawson and Lewis could, of course, have been working in unison, both hoping that by making the Lavant Caves appear more impressive than it really was, they would increase their chances of academic recognition. The scale of the deception may however argue against such a scenario: if both men were working in concord, surely they could have generated something on a far grander scale? All the artefacts were, as Downes has observed, small enough to secrete within a pocket. Such illicit transportation of objects would only be necessary if the person organising the fraud felt that they were under some form of supervision. If the site directors had been working together here, it would have been unnecessary to 'smuggle' anything in, for they could easily have provided a mutual alibi or organised diversions for the workmen, as and when required. The workmen would almost certainly have been supervised, making their involvement in any deception likely to have employed 'smuggling tactics'. But, as has already been noted, the workforce themselves were unlikely to have been in a position where they could have acquired such special finds in the first place. The smuggling of discrete objects into the Lavant Caves would only make sense if one of the directors was generating the fraud without the knowledge of the other.

During the excavation of the Hastings Castle 'dungeon', it is clear that it is Lewis, not Dawson, who adds a note of caution concerning the rock face 'discoloration' in the main gallery of the north-eastern tunnel. Lewis did not observe the staining, as is made clear in the final publication.[17] Although the Revd Marshall observed the oily marks in the late 1870s, only Dawson claimed to have seen the shadows in human outline. Crucially it is only Dawson who was able to interpret the stains (apparently on the basis of a visit made when he was only eight years old), and it was Dawson alone who provided the rather curious sketch for inclusion within the *Sussex Archaeological Collections*. Although Lewis worked in close collaboration with Dawson at both Lavant and Hastings, it would, therefore, appear unlikely that he was involved in deception at either site.

The case of the Maresfield Map and of the Ashburnham Dial may, however, suggest that Lewis was not above generating frauds of his own. Both items are, as has been frequently observed, clearly not original antiquities, the drawing of both clearly belonging to the hand of Lewis, the civil engineer from India. That the scenes engraved on the face of the Ashburnham Dial were designed by him is not in dispute (see chapter 12), but what is unclear is the purpose for which they were created.

Since the exposure of Piltdown, the Ashburnham Dial has been treated as a similar piece of blatant forgery designed to fool the scientific establishment. The fact that the dial had at some stage belonged to Charles Dawson, may however be something of a 'red herring', for Dawson never made use of the artefact in any of his exhibitions, displays, lectures or publications. He never, as far as it is possible to ascertain, even appears to have publicly acknowledged the existence of the artefact, which was one of the few items not passed to Hastings Museum after his death in 1916. This could of course imply that Dawson was here the victim of a hoax, rather than its creator. He and Lewis had a serious quarrel at some point in 1911, effectively ending their friendship.[18] Perhaps this disagreement provided a motive for Lewis to perpetrate the clock face deception in the hope of undermining Dawson's academic credibility.[19] Many of the scenes depicted on the dial were, however, directly copied from an engraving of 1773 by Richard Earlom (itself derived from a 1772 painting by Joseph Wright entitled *The Iron Forge*) which had already been reproduced by Dawson in his article on Sussex ironwork.[20] If Lewis had been intending to create a believable hoax, why would he have used images already well known to both Dawson and the greater antiquarian community?

It is possible that Dawson and Lewis worked together on the creation of the clock design. Perhaps Dawson, implicated in the manufacture of fraudulent objects since the 'discovery' of *Plagiaulax dawsoni* in 1891, wished to create an artefact that would help advance certain theories concerning the manufacture of Wealden iron. Having persuaded Lewis to engrave the nineteenth-century clock face, perhaps the two men fell out, leaving Dawson unable to use the artefact for fear of being blackmailed or exposed. Alternatively, the piece could have been engraved by Lewis as a keepsake, gift or memento of past work to his excavation colleague and (pre-1911) friend. It could conceivably have begun life as a present to Dawson 'on the occasion of his marriage in 1905'.[21] As the dial was not given to Hastings Museum by Dawson's widow Helene, it may well have possessed some special significance to either her or her husband. As a personal gift, Dawson would certainly never have included the item in his collection of antiquities, and would never have attempted to display or exhibit it.

The Maresfield Map provides us with a different situation entirely, for here we have a fraudulent item, clearly drawn by Lewis and credited to Dawson (for having 'made it'), published in the *Sussex Archaeological Collections*.[22] The map as reproduced, however, is no clever attempt at forgery, for it contains many fatal errors, omissions, inconsistencies and anachronisms. Some of the errors furthermore appear so deliberate (the misspelling of the word 'Hundred', for example, has been highlighted by the positioning of an arrow-like blot which points directly to the mistake), that it is almost as if the forger *wanted* to be found out.

Having noted the catalogue of errors contained within the Maresfield Map, we have to question the inclusion of the caption, which expressly states that the image was 'made by C. Dawson'.[23] As noted in chapter 12, there is no reason why, in 1912, Dawson should be sending anything to the Sussex Archaeological Society for inclusion within their annual *Collections*. He had, by all accounts, fallen out with the county Society rather spectacularly in 1904, ostensibly over the sale of Castle Lodge which had left the organisation homeless. Similarly, following their eviction from Castle Lodge, why would anyone in the Society consider publishing anything even remotely connected to Dawson (Piltdown itself, after all, was never acknowledged or referred to in the pages of the *Sussex Archaeological Collections*). Editor of the *Collections* from 1909, till his retirement in 1958, was Louis Salzman who, after both the Castle Lodge incident and the Pevensey Bricks affair, was certainly no friend of the solicitor from Uckfield.

We also have to consider why the illustration of the Maresfield ironworkings should appear at all with W.V. Crake's article of 1912, there being no explicit reference to it (or to any other figure) in the published text. In fact Crake's article stands well without the inclusion of the map (in fact the article appears to have been written as if it were intended to be unillustrated). Why then was the figure published at all in a journal whose members and editorial board were, let us not forget, hostile towards Dawson?

Perhaps it is Piltdown itself that provides the key here. As both Heal [24] and Combridge [25] have noted, the name 'Piltdown' occupies a prominent place on the Maresfield Map, a geographical impossibility made possible by the 'compression of the scale on the left of the map, to approximately one quarter of that on the right'.[26] 'Piltdown' therefore assumes an important and obvious part of the map, something which gains significance when one considers the timing of publication. The 1912 edition of the *Sussex Archaeological Collections*, containing the offending plan of the Maresfield Forge, came out in the spring of 1913, a mere three months after the Piltdown discoveries had officially been announced to the world. If, as seems likely, the map was a last-minute addition to an existing article (hence its incompatibility and lack of clear association with the published text), the prominence of the name 'Piltdown' combined with the sheer quantity of obvious anachronisms is intriguing. Add to this the authorship of the map by

John Lewis (who by 1911 had fallen out with the Uckfield solicitor), and the clear attempt to link the hoax with Dawson, then something rather more devious than the 'careless fraud' suggested by P.B.S. Andrews [27] and Philip Howard [28] may at last be glimpsed.

Here then, it is suggested that the Maresfield Map was not just 'any old' forgery, another one designed to fool the archaeological establishment; rather it was a clever attempt to point the finger of suspicion at both Dawson and his latest discovery at Piltdown. The Maresfield Map is therefore a subtle attempt at whistle-blowing. Perhaps Lewis had, during his time working with Dawson, become aware that there was something not altogether above board concerning the activities of his erstwhile colleague. The discoveries 'made' within the Lavant Caves could first have triggered his suspicion. Perhaps Dawson's interpretation of the Hastings Castle wall shadows, followed by his purchase of Castle Lodge, generated further doubt in Lewis' mind. The unearthing of apparently early human remains at Piltdown may finally have tipped the balance against the solicitor and Lewis planned to create something which was so full of errors, that it could not possibly be accepted as being genuine.

By crediting this blatant hoax to Dawson, Lewis would presumably have hoped that more people would see the amateur antiquarian for what he was. By placing the name 'Piltdown' so centrally in the map, as well as repeatedly using the word 'forge' throughout the drawing, Lewis was perhaps further hoping to plant seeds of doubt regarding Dawson's latest discovery in the public mind. What we have, therefore, is a map of the 'Maresfield *Forgery*', Salzman, as editor of the *Sussex Archaeological Collections* in 1912-3, would probably have supported Lewis' actions for we have evidence not only of his intense dislike of Dawson, but also of his satirical wit. By 1910, Salzman had little reason to like Dawson: if the whole Castle Lodge incident had not been enough, he also believed that the solicitor had been responsible for a spoiling campaign against his candidacy for election to the Society of Antiquaries, an act itself a result of Salzman's poor review of Dawson's book the *History of Hastings Castle*. That Dawson did indeed bear a grudge was something allegedly confirmed to Salzman by John Lewis himself.[29]

Dawson must have been shaken by the publication of the Maresfield Map. In 1913, he was still a member of the Sussex Archaeological Society, and so would have received the annual journal containing the offending map. It must have been abundantly apparent to him that, not only was there significant doubt concerning his latest discovery within the Sussex Society, but also that his colleague John Lewis and, by implication, Louis Salzman, were both 'in on his secret'. Dawson never publicly denied involvement in the map, even though the accompanying caption clearly stated that he had made it, but then why should he? To deny the map would only be drawing further attention to it and to Piltdown. Even if he had made himself heard, who in the Sussex Archaeological Society would have listened? Given the situation following the eviction of the

Society from Castle Lodge in 1904, it is unlikely that there would ever have been either an apology or retraction within the pages of the *Collections*.

What is really curious about the whole Maresfield Map incident is that, despite its obviously fraudulent origins, no one publicly questioned its authenticity. When, in 1974, Lieutenant-Colonel P.B.S. Andrews commented that the map was 'wholly fictitious',[30] Phillip Howard declared in the pages of the New York *Times* that the missing link connecting Charles Dawson to the Piltdown hoax had finally been made. The Maresfield Map was the 'smoking gun' 'positively identifying Dawson's hand in forgery'.[31] This, of course, appears to have been Lewis' intention all along, but the exposure occurred some sixty years too late to help explode the myth of Piltdown man.

In 1915 John Lewis resigned his prestigious position as a fellow of the Society of Antiquaries.[32] His reasons for doing so are not recorded, though it is tempting to suggest that it was in part as a protest against the Society's full and total acceptance of Dawson's 'discovery'. Despite his best efforts, *Eoanthropus dawsoni* was to survive for another thirty-eight years.

An Alternative Timeline

At the start of this book, Charles Dawson was introduced as a great antiquarian, amateur geologist, well-respected solicitor and all-round pillar of the community. He was all these things and more. He was also a first-rate forger, fraudster, fabricator, hoaxer, manipulator, trickster and liar. This side of his life, perhaps understandably, he kept rigidly separate from his professional duties. It was also kept secret from all who knew him, including his friends, colleagues, brothers, wife, stepchildren and other relatives. He was indeed a veritable Jekyll and Hyde. Given what has already been discussed, here would appear to be a suitable place to review and briefly reassess the 'discoveries' of J. Charles Dawson, presenting an alternative version of the life and works of the 'Wizard of Sussex'.

Charles Dawson spent his early years growing up in St Leonards on Sea, exploring cliffs and quarries in search of fossils and geological specimens. He was enrolled into the Gosport Royal Academy to complete his education and, unlike his younger brothers Hugh Leyland and Arthur Trevor Dawson, eventually followed his father into the legal profession. How Charles viewed his brothers we do not know, for none of the correspondence that might have helped us has survived. Perhaps he envied Hugh and Trevor for their access to a university education and later successful careers in the Church and military respectively. Perhaps he did not care. Certainly there is no evidence of a family rift or of deep-seated resentment or hatred. As far as can be told, the brothers got on well and supported one another in their chosen careers.

In 1880, Charles, then aged only sixteen, began to work for F.A. Langhams Solicitors. His interest in the local geology of East Sussex remained unabated, however, and soon he was filling his free time with fossil hunting. Many of his fossil expeditions were conducted with the distinguished geologist Samuel H. Beckles F.R.S. Together with Beckles, Dawson amassed a considerable collection of fossil specimens, which he donated to the British Museum (Natural History) in 1884. Pleased by his regular contributions, the museum conferred upon Dawson the title 'honorary collector'. In 1885, aged only twenty-one, Dawson was elected a fellow of the Geological Society. In 1889 Dawson co-founded the Hastings and St Leonards Museum Association. By 1890 he was working with James Langham in F.A. Langhams' branch office in the East Sussex town of Uckfield.

At some stage, however, Charles Dawson changed his ambition. Perhaps the time spent fossil hunting in the quarries of East Sussex was simply not producing sufficient rewards; perhaps the process was simply taking too long; perhaps he craved greater academic recognition? For whatever reason, in 1891 Charles Dawson made the decision to gently manipulate existing geological data. He created a fraud.

Doctoring a plagiaulacoid tooth, possibly derived from the extensive collection of his late colleague Samuel Beckles (which he was helping the British Museum to catalogue), Dawson filed down the crown, eroding much of the enamel in the process, and created a wholly new species. The first of many 'missing links' or transitional forms that were to play such a prominent part of his antiquarian career. It was a basic and fairly clumsy fraud, but no one doubted its authenticity. Arthur Smith Woodward, to whom Dawson forwarded the tooth, enthusiastically named the new creature *Plagiaulax dawsoni* in honour of its 'finder'. Dawson's path to infamy had begun.

In the years that followed 1891, Dawson sporadically continued his fossil hunting, but his main interest now derived from the antiquities of man. He began his own archaeological examination of Castle Hill in Hastings and, in 1892, joined the Sussex Archaeological Society, becoming honorary local secretary for Uckfield. As a solicitor, Dawson also found himself acting as on behalf of a number of prominent antiquarian collectors who had bequeathed their materials to Hastings Museum. Dawson soon became a member of the Hastings Museum Committee, in charge of the acquisition of historical documents. In 1893, his first archaeological publication detailed the extraordinary discoveries of Stephen Blackmore, a shepherd who lived near Eastbourne. Blackmore's greatest find was that of a Neolithic stone axe, still in its wooden haft. Neither the haft, nor the flints, nor even Blackmore's sketch of the original find existed in the form that Dawson was to publish them, his elaborate description, given the passage of time and vagueness of reporting, being impossible to verify. The description of the Bexhill Boat, Dawson's second archaeological publication, also related to the 'discovery', many years before, of an unusual artefact. In neither the case of the Bexhill Boat or Blackmore's axe was there a real, quantifiable object which anyone else could examine. Both reports were cleverly generated from an almost total absence of hard data.

The year 1893 was also the year of the Beauport Statuette. Presented to Augustus Wollaston Franks, Keeper of Roman and Medieval antiquities at the British Museum and President of the Society of Antiquaries, the statuette was clearly Roman in style, Dawson claiming it to be the earliest example of cast iron in Europe. The artefact was presented before the Society of Antiquities and, though it received a rocky ride from some members of the audience, Dawson was later able to verify its authenticity as a genuine piece of cast iron. Unfortunately, its authenticity as a Roman find was not so clear, the object being a modern copy of an ancient original. Whether Dawson manufactured the statuette himself, or merely doctored a modern item, is unknown, but he made the most of it in a number of prominent exhibitions on ancient ironworking.

In 1893 Dawson also represented the Society at the fifth Congress of Archaeological Societies and began co-directing the excavation of the subterranean passageways of the Lavant Caves near Chichester. His colleague in this was John Lewis, a retired civil engineer recently returned from India. Lewis was an experienced surveyor and draughtsman, an ideal companion in the work that was to follow. Lewis was also, at this stage, unaware that his colleague was planning to make the caves a little more spectacular than they really were.

The deception played out in the Lavant Caves was simple enough, for the medieval chalk quarry was devoid of most things other than rubble. Dawson simply introduced a variety of artefacts such as worked flint, chalk and antler, which suggested that the caves had begun life as a Neolithic flint mine. The addition of later 'finds' gave the site a currency greater than any other known flint mine, having being reused in the Roman and later medieval periods as a store and refuge. All the finds brought into the caves were small and could easily be hidden in coat or trouser pockets, to be securely hidden in the unexcavated piles of chalk debris that littered the floor. A series of presentations on the importance of the caves followed, but a publication was never forthcoming.

At Hastings the deception of 1894 was, of necessity, a little different. The subterranean tunnels here were clearly medieval, so the inclusion of 'early finds' would appear incongruous. The main tunnel beneath the castle had been emptied some years previously, though the passage to the south remained choked with debris. The tunnels were cleared and excellently recorded in John Lewis' drawings and the photographs of Charles Dawson. Both men debated the possible function of the tunnels as possible store, refuge or prison, in the final publication. Though the scope for fraud here was not great, Dawson managed to include an interpretative sketch of a series of 'shadow markings' that he had seen many years previously, on one of the walls. Both clearly implied the former presence of manacled human figures, increasing the likelihood of the tunnels having once been a dungeon. Lewis could not see the markings so clearly and conjectured that the amorphous greasy stains could be fraudulent.

In 1895, in recognition of his hard work and amazing discoveries at Lavant and Hastings, combined with his ever-increasing collection of archaeological curiosities, Charles Dawson was elected a fellow of the Society of Antiquaries of London. Now, as Charles Dawson FGS, FSA, his interests changed again. He continued to procure archaeological objects, Hastings Museum and the Sussex Archaeological Society proving to be the ideal showcase for his ever expanding collections. In 1901 Dawson was present at the founding of the Sussex Record Society, a sister group to the Archaeological Society, founded to research, curate and publish historical documents relating to the county. By 1902 Dawson had become a full member of the Record Society's Council.

Dawson now set his sights on a fellowship of the Royal Society, and he began to write extensively on all aspects of Sussex history (human and natural) and archaeology, especially its ironwork, pottery, glass and resources of natural gas. He studied ancient dene holes, reanalysed the Bayeux Tapestry and produced the definite study of Hastings Castle. All these works were hastily compiled using extensive amounts of earlier writers' work in the form of extended passages. Dawson defended his actions by stating he wanted the original records to speak for themselves, but in reality he was desperate to get his name attached to as many publications (covering a variety of diverse subjects) as possible.

By this time Dawson no longer required the help of the Sussex Archaeological Society, most of his new 'discoveries' being sent directly to either the British Museum or Hastings Museum and Art Gallery. What he did need, however, was an elegant townhouse which would best reflect his status as premier antiquarian of his generation. Using his influence, profession and position in the Society, Dawson managed to purchase the Society's headquarters, Castle Lodge, and promptly evicted the organisation in the spring of 1903.

Apart from a vast array of curious archaeological finds, derived from a variety of unnamed local sources, which Dawson continued to display in Hastings Museum, his only major find of the period was the Pevensey Brick. This brick, which complemented a fragmentary piece recovered from the excavation trench of the Sussex Archaeological Society, conclusively demonstrated one of the last pieces of official garrisoning strengthening completed by the Roman state in Britain. Both bricks were forged, in all probability by Dawson himself.

With the fellowship of the Royal Society in his sights, Dawson also started to investigate the more unorthodox aspects of the natural world. Examples of the 'unnatural' which caught his interest included a toad petrified inside a flint nodule (which he presented to Brighton Museum), the English Channel sea serpents, the presence of 'incipient horns' in cart horses, a new species of human (possessing a Thirteenth Dorsal Vertebra), and a strange cross between the goldfish and the carp. Dawson reinvigorated his interests in palaeontology at this time, finding more faked teeth of *Plagiaulax dawsoni* and, working with

100 *Charles Dawson in the background at Piltdown in the summer of 1912. Arthur Smith Woodward and his son Cyril are closer to the camera*

a number of amateur geologists from France, discovered the remains of at least two more unique mammals.

In March 1909 Dawson wrote to his friend Arthur Woodward complaining that he was 'waiting for the big "find" which never seems to come along'.[33] A little while later, inspired by a meeting with the local author Arthur Conan Doyle, Dawson conceived his greatest hoax yet, one that would surely gain him a fellowship of the Royal Society and undoubtedly earn him a knighthood, just like the one his younger brother Trevor already possessed. Piltdown man was on his way.

Eoanthropus dawsoni, in his various incarnations at Barkham Manor, Barcombe Mills and Sheffield Park, generated academic interest like no other discovery before it. Using the skills honed over the previous decades (such as the filing of *Plagiaulax* teeth and the whittling of the Bulverhythe fossilised antler with a steel knife), Charles Dawson gave British palaeontology what it had craved for so long: a British ancestor, a missing link from the home counties. The world's media was ecstatic, their headlines speaking of nothing else. In fact it would appear highly likely that, despite his outward signs of irritation, it was Dawson himself that leaked information to the press. Advance media attention certainly generated plenty of free publicity for Piltdown man, helping establish him as a world celebrity. Dawson's place in posterity was assured. A painting unveiled at the Royal Academy in 1915 shows him at the peak of his academic achievements, standing amidst the greatest scientific minds of Edwardian England with Charles Darwin, father of evolutionary science, sitting contentedly in the background (**86**).

Charles Dawson FGS, FSA, never received his knighthood, though many others associated with the Piltdown 'find' were to. He was never elected to the Royal Society. He died in 1916 before receiving such great honours. This leaves us with perhaps the greatest conundrum of the whole story for, had he obtained his fellowship and become Sir Charles Dawson, would his amazing 'discoveries' have come to an end? Were the spectacular finds constituting Piltdown I, II and III sufficient, or would more evidence relating to *Eoanthropus dawsoni* have come to light? Where could the solicitor from Uckfield have gone from there? Surely new, ever more spectacular 'finds' would have increased the suspicion of those in the Sussex Archaeological Society (such as John Lewis, Harry Morris and Louis Salzman), and yet I cannot imagine Charles Dawson ever having voluntarily retired (**100**).

POSTSCRIPT

A drive along the A272 in East Sussex takes you on a pleasantly winding stretch of tarmac fringing the southern margins of the Ashdown Forest. The villages encountered along this road appear peaceful and picturesque; the views across the sandy heathland are sometimes breathtaking. As the road heads east from Newick to Maresfield, however, a number of unsuspecting drivers have over the years been brought to a sudden halt by an unexpected encounter with a road sign (**101**). The sign in question is a small white rectangle edged in black. Supported by two grey poles, it stands less than a metre high on the eastbound edge of the A road, about a kilometre east from Newick. Eight simple letters are neatly arranged across the centre of the white rectangle, spelling a single name: PILTDOWN.

Strange how the name of a pleasant though quietly unremarkable collection of Sussex hamlets has become so ingrained in the human psyche. Piltdown has today become synonymous with frauds, hoaxes and conspiracy theories the world over. For most people, though the exact details surrounding the discovery of *Eoanthropus dawsoni* have faded, the legacy of the hoax has become more potent than ever. Every time a fraud or hoax is exposed, it is referred to as 'a new Piltdown'. There have been innumerable television and radio programmes, as well as countless books and articles and a seemingly never-ending stream of Internet websites. The public appetite for the fraud seems insatiable. Given such a context, the small road sign alerting drivers to the boundary of an otherwise unassuming East Sussex village seems wholly incongruous.

The route from Newick into modern Piltdown is largely unremarkable: some well tended trees; a hedge or two; a few wooden fences protecting houses set back from the road; a scattering of telegraph poles. Approach from Maresfield in the west and you could be excused for driving straight through without realising, for here the old sign, emblazoned with the county symbol, is today so heavily splattered with mud that it is scarcely legible. Piltdown seems almost embarrassed by its famous past. Once in the village, there are no obvious monuments, signs or display boards commenting on the 'discovery' of 1912. Nothing out of the ordinary, certainly nothing to alert you to the fact that you are entering what was, on two separate occasions during the twentieth century, the most famous place on planet Earth.

Today, the only aspect of the village that gives the game away is the pub; a small but undeniably attractive white-painted building advertising a welcoming mixture of home-cooked lunches, à la carte dinners, bed and breakfast and real ale. The blood red sign outside depicts a bleached, almost human-like skull (**102**). A single eye stares out through knotted sockets, its jaw locked in an unsettlingly toothy grin.

The pub used to be known as the Lamb. It had its identity altered in the 1920s, following the increase in tourism to the site of Europe's earliest human ancestor. There was, in the wake of the 1953 exposure, serious talk in the village of changing the name back, but thankfully common sense prevailed and the 'Man' survived.

Heading east from the pub, a minor road heading south is signposted to Isfield, a golf course and Barkham Manor vineyard. If you follow the road, past Piltdown pond, you end up, via a brown tourist sign, at the impressive iron gates of Barkham Manor. There is no regular public access to the manor today, but, behind the gates, a series of coppiced trees can be seen flanking the long approach to the house (**103**), just as they did in the photographs of 1912 and '13. Somewhere in the middle distance lies a now backfilled gravel pit, once the centre of attention for the world's press. Next to it a single sandstone monolith stands, forgotten and somewhat forlorn, within the modern hedgerow. Despite the covering of lichen, it is still just possible to read the inscription carved into the face of the stone:

> 'Here in the old river gravel Mr Charles Dawson FSA,
> found the fossil skull of Piltdown man 1912-1913.'

No one has thought of either removing or correcting the stone.

Further afield in Sussex, there is little evidence either to the existence of 'Piltdown man' or even to Charles Dawson himself. The firm of solicitors that Dawson took over in 1900, and which he was later to partner with George Hart,

101 *Piltdown: the western approach from the A272 in 2003*

102 *The Piltdown man in 2003*

103 *The road to Barkham Manor in 2003*

104 *St John Sub Castro in 2003*

105 *The last resting place of Charles and Helene Dawson. St John Sub Castro Churchyard, Lewes, East Sussex, Autumn 2003*

still occupies an office in Uckfield High Street and retains the name of Dawson Hart. Despite the exposure of the Piltdown forgery in November 1953, the solicitor's waiting room still displays a replica of the Piltdown skull, the only place in Britain where any trace of *Eoanthropus dawsoni* may still be regularly inspected.

In Hastings, there is little evidence of the Dawson Loans Collection. Some of the metal artefacts recovered from the Hastings Castle excavations, together with the extant pieces of the hoard from St Leonards on Sea, may still be seen upstairs in the excellent Town Hall Museum, securely nestled within the old town. The remainder of the collection, however, which includes the Beauport Park Statuette, the 'Arabic' Anvil, the Bulverhythe Hammer and the curfew from Bermondsey Abbey, are held unseen, in the store of Hastings Museum and Art Gallery. The fall-out from the 1953 exposure was so great that anything associated with Charles Dawson has been swiftly and permanently spirited away.

To the east of Hastings, the A259 and A27 wind their way across the county, past the solid stone and brick walls of Pevensey Roman fortress, towards the picturesque market town of Lewes. Here, Castle Lodge, the Dawson family home from 1904 to 1917, sits majestically between the Norman castle and the imposing fourteenth-century barbican gatehouse. The Lodge is still a private house, though its exterior has remained largely unaltered from the time that the Dawsons were in residence. Across the road, the Sussex Archaeological Society still own Barbican House, the property they found following their sudden eviction at Dawson's hands in 1904. The sixteenth-century timber-framed house contains a rather splendid museum and library, although, just as Joseph Weiner discovered in the early 1950s, no trace of either Dawson or of his discoveries may be found here.

A short walk through the flint-faced barbican, past the bowls club and the grassy slopes of Brack Mount, and you emerge out by the former line of Lewes town wall with its views across to Mount Harry (where Simon de Montfort defeated Henry III in 1264). Descending the hill, the early nineteenth-century religious splendour of St John Sub Castro rises before you (**104**). Walk up the narrow passage by the side of the church, squeezing through the rusty iron gate, and you enter the impossibly romantic setting of the now redundant cemetery. Here amidst the ivy, trees and cold stone, your attention is automatically drawn to an impressive nineteenth-century obelisk commemorating Russian prisoners from the Crimean War. Close by, however, a simply decorated headstone in the shape of a cross lies by the side of the little-used path (**105**). The now faded lettering preserved across the base of the stone records that this is the final resting place for the mortal remains of Charles Dawson FSA, and his wife Helene. Sadly, as with the lichen-covered monolith on the road to Barkham Manor, most visitors pass by without sparing a second glance.

APPENDIX I
THE LAVANT CAVES

List of objects found in the Lavant Caves 1893-4 as summarised by H. Dixon Hewitt in 1955 (Downes archive: Sussex Archaeological Society).

LABEL DESCRIPTION	REMARKS AND COMMENTS
Flint core	Flint is all typical Downland or 'Cissbury-type' white such as can be found within a few yards of the caves
Flint flake	Found by Mr Lawrence
Flint scraper	
Worked flint	
Worked flint	
Worked flint	Large flake; very slight secondary work
Carbonised wheat	Should be examined by an expert to ascertain date of cultivation
Portions of human teeth	One molar, one canine (?), the latter broken. Apparently well worn
Weight	Lead. Roughly conical with hole at the top
Broken bowl of Samian ware	Good ornamental ware. Portion of potter's name stamped inside
Portion of earthenware vessel	Black. Probably Romano-British
Piece of green glass	Portion of a bowl of the well known 'pillar-moulded' type
Portion of tine of the red deer	Only about 4in or 5in long. Not identifiable as a pick
Bone scoop made from the shank bone of a sheep	Very similar to one in 'Bygones Section' of Thetford Museum, known to be made by a man known to my mother (born at Blackheath, S.E. *c.*1846 or '47) and described as an 'apple-corer'. Probably not much over 100 years old
Bronze bangle	Composed of wire strands and the other solid, but engraved to resemble wire strands
Bronze bangle	Solid, but engraved to resemble wire strands
Copper mask or boss	Probably forming the terminal to the handle of a vase. Allcroft calls it a small mask of a Roman face
The top of some small bronze vessel	Probably for oil, for use after the bath
Ornamental jet bead	'Melon' type. Large. About 1in diameter
Bronze tube	Blowpipe?
Terracotta lamp	With conventional design of a toad upon it
Right and left arms of a bronze statuette	Holding a vase and a bunch of grapes respectively. Probably belonging to a figure of the infant Bacchus
Portion of earthenware tile	With impression of human finger
Bronze buckle	

Curious copper badge	Thought to be Masonic or belonging to some trade guild. Found about a yard deep below the debris of the cave near the door by workman Hammond. It was then corroded but he cleaned it before giving it up
Tesserae for composing a mosaic	Apparently a grey stone. These seem to indicate the presence of a house near the cavern. They may have been used for counters in a game
Portion of a bracelet	Probably formerly enamelled
Chalk lamp	Triangular in shape with distinct lip channel. Not like Grimes Graves lamps which are half round in shape at top
Cast of ancient lamp	Original fell to pieces. Red material, more or less spoon-shaped. Probably original colour is imitated
Rounded water-worn flint	Probably brought from seashore and perhaps used as a game
Rounded water-worn flint	
Rounded water-worn rock crystal	Crystal somewhat damaged. Material unlikely to be found on Sussex coast
Piece of amber	Much water-worn. Probably brought from seashore. Sand drift. In pieces. Probably spilt since finding
Small bronze pin	Probably formally enamelled
Bronze needle	3 and a quarter inches
Bone pin	Broken. Largest of three. Could be easily repaired
Bone pin	
Bone pin	
Bronze pin	Of Celtic form
Lozenge-shaped silver pendant	Composed of beaded strands with round bosses. Debased silver
Bronze arrow-shaped ornament	Traces of gilding
Bronze arrow-shaped ornament	Traces of gilding
Bronze pendant or amulet	Traces of enamel
Lead seal or tally	Broken. Wool tally?
Lead seal or tally	Wool tally?
Lead seal or tally	Wool tally?
Lead seal or tally	Wool tally?
Fragments of pseudo-Samian pottery	Mentioned by Sawyer and repeated by Allcroft. But as these are linked with the fragment of Samian in both lists, this may be a cautious preliminary verdict on item, labelled as one broken bowl of Samian ware
Georgian halfpenny	Mentioned by Allcroft alone
Charcoal	Mentioned by Allcroft, but not likely to have been preserved
A few small bones	Mentioned by Allcroft, may be a comment on human teeth from an early report. Allcroft says one tooth, while Clinch has 'fragments of human teeth', which is more correct

APPENDIX II
THE DAWSON LOANS COLLECTION

List of objects lent to Hastings Museum by the late Charles Dawson Esq. FGS, FSA. (Reproduced with permission of Hastings Museum and Art Gallery).

1. Four modern copies of flint implements made by 'Flint Jack'
2. Three shell implements. Barbados
3. Obsidian core (Mexico)
4. Stone implement (modern) hafted with fur
5. Eight arrowheads of various substances. North America
6. Jade flayer. New Zealand
7. Jade axe, hafted with gum. Australia
8. Three jade axes, New Zealand
9. Jade chisel. New Zealand
10. Jade ornament (pierced at one end). New Zealand
11. Flint implement with serrated edges. Denmark
12. Flint implement, knife-shaped, with serrated edges. Denmark
13. Six flint spearheads. Denmark
14. Five polished flint axes. Denmark
15. Flint axe. Denmark
16. Two pointed implements of bone. East Dean
17. Pointed implement of bone. Birling Gap
18. Two bone implements (showing tool marks)
19. Bone implement, pierced at broad end. East Dean
20. Flint implements. Birling Gap
21. Two spindle whorls. Beachy Head
22. Portion of red deer antler, pierced in middle. Bulverhythe
23. Bronze palstave, broken across. Marina
24. Two bronze palstaves. Marina
25. Portion (cutting edge) of bronze palstave. Marina
26. A wedge-shaped piece of bronze
27. Bronze implement, broken across
28. Socketed bronze object. Marina
29. Iron boss
30. Portion of rush-candle holder
31. Medieval bronze key from Hastings Castle
32. Four iron keys from Hastings Castle
33. Three iron-socketed spearheads from Castle Hill
34. Iron axe head found in a slag heap at Beauport
35. Two iron prick spurs from Castle Hill
36. Prick spur from Lewes Castle
37. Seven fragments of iron knives and one almost complete iron knife from Castle Hill

38. Part of an ancient iron nail
39. Earthenware ewer found in St Clement's Caves, Hastings
40. Two small Bellarmine jugs found at Brede, Sussex
41. Sixteen plaster casts of medals, two silver medals and one bronze medal commemorating the defeat of the English and Dutch fleets at the Battle of Beachy Head, 1670. French
42. Medieval horseshoe from Uckfield
43. Framed copy of plan of Beachy Head
44. Lithograph. Hastings from the East Hill. Drawn from nature and on stone by A. Agloo; printed by C. Hullmandel. Published by G. Wooll, Printseller, High Street, Hastings, November 1823
45. Plaster cast of a fireback depicting the burning of Sussex martyrs
46. A curfew
47. A small statuette of cast iron from the slag heaps at Beauport. Roman
48. A flask of Sussex glass from Beckley
49. Four pieces of Sussex pottery a) vase of classical shape with spiral bands of slip b) flowerpot similar ware to above c) bread pot dark brown richly glazed d) jar
50. A spring gun
51. Two coins found in Hastings Castle 10 October 1908
52. A small anvil dated 1515
53. A framed enlarged photograph of Hastings Castle from the East
54. A framed enlarged photograph of a section of the Bayeux Tapestry depicting Normans throwing up a rampart at Hastings
55. Two chalk moulds probably used for impressing cakes or gingerbread
56. Two photographs, framed, of lightening at Hastings taken by cameras placed one mile apart, and showing the same flashes
57. A pair of wrought-iron andirons with ratchets and spit-hooks (one hook broken), and cressets
58. Casts (40) of Anglo Saxon and Norman coins of the Hastings mint
59. Casts (9) of seals of the Counts of Eu (Lords of the Rape of Hastings), and of the Dean of the Church of St Mary at Hastings
60. Casts (10) of seals of the Dukes of Brittany (Lords of the Rape of Hastings)
61. A seventeenth-century deed chest
62. Mace ('oar-mace') of the Hastings water-bailiff

NOTES

Preface

1. Millar 1998, 65

Chapter 1

1. Woodward 1916, 479
2. Quoted in Walsh 1996, 55
3. Walsh 1996, 56
4. Walsh 1996, xvi
5. Woodward 1916, 477
6. Costello 1985, 168
7. Woodward 1916, 477
8. Walsh 1996, 189-190; Miller 2002, n25
9. Weiner 1955, 84
10. Dawson Hart 2000
11. Downes 1956, 9
12. Weiner 1955, 84; Spencer 1990a, 152-3
13. Teilhard correspodence quoted in Spencer 1990b, 23
14. Downes 1956, 11
15. *Ibid.*
16. Weiner 1955, 175
17. Woodward 1916, 477
18. Spencer 1990a, 152
19. Spencer 190, 1
20. Walsh 1990, 183-4
21. Woodward 1916, 478
22. Woodward 1911, 280; Millar 1998, 20
23. www.hastings.gov.uk
24. Downes 1956, 14
25. *Ibid.*
26. Clements 1997, 277
27. Downes 1956, 14
28. Downes 1956, 15
29. Allcroft 1916, 69; Weiner 1955, 86-7
30. Weiner 1955, 182: Walsh 1996, 170
31. Walsh 1996, 183
32. Downes 1956, 16
33. Dawson 1903
34. Dawson 1905
35. Dawson 1898

36. Dawson 1907
37. Dawson 1909
38. Dawson 1907
39. Dawson 1897; 1898
40. Weiner 1955, 178
41. Ray 1909, 189-92
42. Weiner 1955, 180-1
43. Weiner 1955, 181
44. *Sussex Archaeological Collections* 1904, xiv-v
45. Weiner 1955, 174-5
46. Salzman 1946, 38
47. Downes 1956, 189-90
48. Teilhard correspondence quoted in Spencer 1990b, 23
49. Weiner 1955, 175
50. Salzman 1946, 38
51. Weiner 1955, 175
52. Weiner 1955, 1
53. Weiner 1955, 169-70
54. Weiner 1955, 170
55. Spencer 1990a, 222-3
56. Walsh 1996, 54
57. Walsh 1996, 56
58. Woodward 1916, 477
59. Woodward 1916, 479
60. Keith 1916, 265
61. *Sussex Daily News* 18 August 1916
62. Keith 1938, 197
63. Spencer 1990, 191, 195
64. Oakley and Hoskins 1949
65. Weiner 1955, 26
66. Weiner 1955, 203
67. *The Times* 23 November 1953
68. Vere 1955, 87
69. Essex 1955, 95
70. *Ibid.*
71. Vere 1955, 87
72. Costello 1985, 168
73. Walsh 1996, 178
74. Walsh 1996, 182
75. Downes 1956, 1-2

Chapter 2

1. Woodward 1916, 478
2. Woodward 1891, 585
3. Woodward 1891, 586
4. *Ibid.*
5. *Ibid.*
6. *Ibid.*
7. Woodward 1911, 278
8. *Ibid.*
9. Woodward 1911, 279
10. Woodward 1911, 280
11. Clemens 1963
12. Simpson 1928, 2
13. Clemens 1963, 56
14. Clemens 1963, 58
15. Woodward 1911, 278
16. Spencer 1990a, 137-8
17. Woodward 1891, 586
18. Weiner 1955, 68-9; Downes 1956, 80-1
19. Woodward 1891, 586
20. e.g. Essex 1955; Vere 1959; Thompson 1968; Bowden 1977; Gould 1980; Booher 1986; Millar 1998
21. Woodward 1911, 280
22. Woodward 1916, 477
23. Downes 1956, 80
24. 1916, 478

Chapter 3

1. Allcroft 1916, 74
2. 1916, 69
3. Allcroft 1916, 69
4. Clinch 190x, 326-7
5. 1916, 68-9
6. Allcroft 1916, 69
7. Downes 1956, 15
8. Sawyer 1893, 22
9. Clinch 1905, 326
10. Sawyer 1893, 22
11. Downes 1956, 119
12. 1.2 and 1.5m: Allcroft 1916, 69-71
13. Quoted in McCann 1997, 311

14. Downes correspondence 14 May 1955, Barbican House Museum
15. Allcroft 1916, 71
16. Downes1956, 132
17. e.g. Allcroft 1916, 73-4; Curwen 128, 81
18. Downes 1956, 120
19. Downes private correspondence of 14 May 1955, Barbican House Museum archive
20. Allcroft 1916, 74
21. Curwen 1928, 81
22. National Monuments Record No. 245589
23. Downes Papers, 14 May 1955: Barbican House Museum Lewes
24. e.g. Allcroft 1916, 69; Downes 1956,122
25. Allcroft 1916, 71; Curwen 1928, 81
26. Dawson and Lewis 1896, 230
27. Dawson and Lewis 1896, 231
28. Dawson and Lewis 1896, 226
29. *Ibid.*
30. *Ibid.*
31. Dawson and Lewis 1896, 228
32. Dawson and Lewis 1896, 229
33. Dawson and Lewis 1896, 228-9
34. Dawson and Lewis 1896, 232
35. *Ibid.*
36. *Ibid.*
37. 1896, 232
38. Dawson and Lewis 1896, 232-3
39. 1896, 77
40. 1896, 232

41. Dawson and Lewis 1896, 230
42. *Sussex Archaeological Collections* 1904, xiv-v
43. Weiner 1955, 174-5
44. Salzman 1946, 38
45. Weiner 1955, 175
46. Walsh 1996, 83
47. Downes 1956, 189
48. *Ibid.*
49. Downes 1956, 190
50. 1956, 191

Chapter 4

1. Dawson 1894a, 97
2. 1894a, 98
3. Dawson 1894a, 98
4. *Ibid.*
5. Combridge 1981, 220
6. Walsh 1996, 179
7. Dawson 1894a, 98
8. Evans 1897, 154
9. Heal 1980, 222-3
10. Heal 1980, 223
11. Downes 1956, 112
12. Dawson 1894b, 161
13. *Ibid.*
14. Dawson 1894b, 162
15. Dawson 1894b, 161
16. *Ibid.*
17. Dawson 1894b, 161-2
18. Dawson 1894b, 162
19. Dawson 1894b, 162-3
20. Dawson 1894b, 163
21. *Ibid.*
22. *Ibid.*
23. *Southern Weekly News* 21 January 1888, quoted in Walsh 1996, 180
24. *Southern Weekly News* 21 January 1888, quoted in Walsh 1996, 248 n179
25. Walsh 1996, 248-9, n179

Chapter 5

1. Downes 1956, 219
2. Downes 1956, 217
3. Dawson 1903, 33-5
4. Downes 1956, 195
5. Walsh 1996, 170
6. Downes 1956, 193
7. Downes 1956, 193-4
8. Rock 1879, 169
9. e.g. Straker 1931, 38-47

10. Downes 1956, 195
11. Roberts-Austen quoted in Downes 1956, 195
12. Read 1893, 359
13. Read 1893, 360
14. Smith in Read 1893, 360
15. Murray in Read 1893, 360
16. Evans in Read 1893, 360
17. Dawson correspondence preserved in the Downes Archive: Sussex Archaeological Society
18. *Ibid.*
19. Rock 1879, 169
20. Rock 1879, 170
21. Dawson correspondence preserved in the Downes Archive: Sussex Archaeological Society
22. Dawson 1903a, 4-5
23. Dawson 1903a, 4
24. Dawson 1903a, 5
25. Downes 1956, 199
26. Straker 1931, 337
27. Cathy Walings pers. Com. 2003
28. Downes 1956, 174
29. Downes 1956, 201
30. Straker 1931, 337
31. Walsh 1996, 176-7
32. Downes 1956, 208
33. Dawson 1903, 24
34. Holland 1896, 203; Dawson 1903, 23
35. Dawson 1903, 23
36. Downes 1956, 221
37. Dawson 1903, 24
38. Downes 1956, 220
39. Dawson 1903, 19
40. Dawson 1903, 47-52
41. Dawson 1903, plate 8l and 8m
42. 1903, 20
43. Dawson 1903, plate 8m
44. Beetlestone 1926, 222
45. 1926, 222
46. Dawson 1903, 34
47. Dawson 1903, 25
48. Holland 1896, 202
49. Dawson 1903, 34
50. Downes 1956, 225
51. *Ibid.*
52. *Ibid.*
53. Downes 1956, 226
54. Downes 1956, 218

55. Downes 1956, 189
56. Dawson quoted in Downes 1956, 217
57. Downes 1956, 217; Jones 1990, 96
58. Quoted in Downes 1956, 218
59. Downes 1956, 218
60. Downes 1956, 218-9
61. Downes 1956, 219
62. Dawson quoted in Downes 1956, 329
63. Downes 1956, 329
64. 1956, 229-30
65. 1956, 330
66. Downes 1956, 330
67. Quoted in Downes 1956, 330
68. Quoted in Downes 1956, 330
69. Downes 1956, 330-1
70. Downes 1956, 223
71. *Ibid.*
72. *Ibid.*
73. *Ibid.*
74. *Ibid.*
75. Hastings Museum Dawson Loan Collection, S260
76. Dawson 1903a, 4-5
77. Quoted in Downes 1956, 222
78. Downes 1956, 222
79. Downes 1956, 223

Chapter 6

1. Clinch 1905, 328
2. Clinch 1905, 327
3. *Ibid.*
4. Clinch 1905, 227-8
5. Clinch 1905, 328
6. Downes 195X, 328
7. Downes 195X, 329
8. Weiner 1954, 56
9. Clinch 1905, 330
10. *Ibid.*
11. 1905, 327
12. Clinch 1905, plate facing page 330
13. Dawson 1909, 8
14. Grinsell 1931, 62
15. Anon.1935, 466
16. Anon.1935, 467
17. Rowlands 1976, 269
18. Downes 1956, 333
19. Anon.1935, 466-7
20. Downes 1956, 333
21. 1976, 269
22. Dawson quoted in Downes 1956, 334

23. Woodward 1916, 477
24. Downes 1956, 335
25. Jones 1990, 94-5
26. Jones 1990, 95
27. Downes 195x, 336
28. Downes 1956, 336
29. *Ibid.*
30. *Ibid.*
31. Watson quoted in Downes 1956, 336
32. *Ibid.*
33. Jones 1990, 99
34. *Ibid.*

Chapter 7

1. Dawson 1907, 410
2. *Against Eutropius* I, 391-3 quoted in Ireland 1986, 163
3. *On the Consulship of Stilicho* II, 247-55 quoted in Ireland 1986, 163
4. Dawson 1907, 411
5. *Ibid.*
6. *Ibid.*
7. Dawson 1907, 412
8. Dawson 1907, 411
9. Salzman 1908, 112
10. Dawson 1907, 411
11. Peacock 1973, 138
12. *Ibid.*
13. Dawson 1907, 411
14. 1908, 112
15. Peacock 1973, 139
16. Baines 1997, 5
17. Peacock 1973, 139
18. Peacock 1973, 140
19. Salzman 1908, 112-3
20. Salzman 1908, 180
21. 1908, 112
22. Salzman 1908, 112
23. Dawson 1907, 411
24. *Ibid.*
25. Baines 1997, 5-6
26. Baines 1997, 6

Chapter 8

1. Dawson 1898, 294
2. Sawyer 1893, 22; Combridge 1981, 221
3. Dawson 1898, 293
4. Dawson 1898, 295
5. *Ibid.*
6. Dawson 1898, 297
7. Dawson 1898, 302
8. Holmes 1898, 195
9. Dawson 1903a, 1-31

10. (59):1903a, 33-62
11. Dawson 1903b, 49
12. Dawson 1905, 8
13. Dawson 1903a, 12
14. e.g. Straker 1931, vii-viii
15. Downes 1956, 246
16. Weiner 1955, 182
17. 1956, 229-46
18. Walsh 1996, 185-6
19. Dawson 1907, 253
20. Walsh 1996, 187
21. Dawson correspondence 10 July 1910 as quoted in Spencer 1990b, 10
22. Dawson 1909a, v
23. *Ibid.*
24. Dawson 1909a, v-vi
25. Dawson 1909a, vi-vii
26. Dawson 1909a, vii
27. Dawson 1909, viii-ix
28. Dawson 1909a, viii
29. Dawson 1909a, ix
30. e.g. Weiner 1955, 85
31. *Sussex Archaeological Collections* 1910, 282
32. Vere 1955, 100-1
33. Vere 1955, 101
34. Weiner 1955, 177
35. Downes 1956, appendix B21-5
36. Blinderman 1986, 111
37. Miles 1994, 358
38. Weiner 1955, 188
39. Weiner correspondence quoted in Spencer 1990b, 216-7
40. Miles 1994, 358
41. Miles 1994, 364
42. *Ibid.*
43. *Ibid.*
44. Miles 194, 370
45. Dawson 1911, 128
46. *Ibid.*
47. *Ibid.*
48. Dawson 1911, 128-9
49. Dawson 1911, 132
50. *Ibid.*
51. Quoted in Walsh 1996, 187
52. Dawson 1909a, v

Chapter 9

1. Hastings Museum Dawson Loan Collection: Accession No. L1220
2. Spencer 1990b, 6

3. Weiner 1955, 180
4. Spencer 1990b, 4-14
5. Woodward 1916, 479
6. Spencer 1990b, 103
7. Dawson 1898, 564
8. *Ibid.*
9. Dawson 1897, 150
10. Downes 1956, 86
11. Dawson 1898, 564
12. Dawson 1897, 150
13. Dawson 1897, 151
14. Dawson 1898, 566
15. Downes 1996, 188
16. Hewitt in Dawson 1898, 572-4
17. Dawson 1898, 574
18. Dawson correspondence quoted in Spencer 1990b, 4
19. e.g.Walsh 1996, 188
20. Weiner 1955, 180
21. Woodward 1916, 477
22. Weiner 1955,180
23. Weiner 1955, 180; Jones 1990, 94
24. Weiner 1955, 180
25. Quoted in Welfare and Fairley 1980, 205
26. Welfare and Fairley 1980, 205
27. Welfare and Young 1980, 206
28. Jones 1990, 95
29. *Ibid.*
30. Quoted in Walsh 1996, 195-6
31. Quoted in Walsh 1996, 196
32. Quoted in Welfare and Fairley 1980, 77
33. Jones, *The Times* Saturday 20 October 1883
34. e.g. Sewell, 9 January 1893; Russell, 10 January 1893 and Huxley, 12 January 1893
35. Walsh 1996, 196
36. Welfare and Fairley 1980, 113-5
37. Weiner 1955, 180-1
38. Dawson correspondence quoted in Spencer 1990b, 22
39. Spencer 1990a, 239
40. Spencer 1990b, 22
41. Keith 1915, 63
42. Weiner 1955, 180
43. Spencer 1990a, 195
44. 1990b, 22

45. Walsh 1996, 167
46. Nicholson and Ferguson-Lees 1962, 299
47. Nicholson and Ferguson-Lees 1962, 322
48. Anon. 1962, 281
49. *Ibid.*
50. Nicholson and Ferguson-Lees 1962, 321
51. Bristow quoted in Harrison 19xx, 38
52. Quoted in Harrison 19xx, 38
53. Nicholson and Ferguson-Lees 1962, 318
54. *Ibid.*
55. *Ibid.*
56. Bristow correspondence quoted in Nicholson and Ferguson-Lees 1962, 329
57. Nicholson and Ferguson-Lees 1962, 299
58. Harrison 1968, 42; Marchant 1997, 123
59. Harrison 1968, 42
60. Marchant 1997, 123
61. *Ibid.*
62. Nicholson and Ferguson-Lees 1962, 332-3
63. Weiner 1955, 175

Chapter 10

1. Crake 1912
2. Straker 1931, 401
3. Andrews 1974, 165
4. Howard 1974
5. Andrews 1974, 167
6. Andrews 1974, 166
7. Howard 1974
8. Crake 1912, 279
9. Combridge 1977; 1981
10. Combridge 1981, 220
11. Weiner 1955, 169-76
12. Andrews 1974, 165
13. Clinch 1905, 326-7
14. Dawson and Lewis 1896
15. Weiner 1955, 179
16. Combridge 1981, 221-2

17. 1974, 166
18. Howard 1974
19. Weiner 1955, 169-76
20. Hayden 1912, 305-6, 309
21. Combridge 1977, 428
22. Jenkins 1921, 26; Straker 1931, 75; Attwill 1952, 43
23. Combridge 1977, 428
24. Winton 1956
25. Downes 1956, 226-7
26. Combridge 1977, 429-31
27. Combridge 1977, 431
28. Combridge 1977, 429
29. 1977, 429
30. Combridge 1977, 429
31. Walsh 1996, 181
32. 1977, 432
33. Combridge 1977, 431-2
34. Dawson 1903, 12
35. e.g. Combridge 1981, 221-2
36. Combridge 1977, 433

Chapter 11

1. Dawson correspondence 14 February 1912 quoted in Spencer 1990, 17
2. *Ibid.*
3. Dawson 1913, 76
4. Millar 1998, 15
5. Walsh 1996, 14
6. Dawson correspondence quoted in Spencer 1990, 18
7. Dawson correspondence quoted in Spencer 1990, 19
8. *Ibid.*
9. Dawson correspondence quoted in Spencer 1990, 20
10. Teilhard correspondence quoted in Spencer 1990b, 20
11. Spencer 1990b, 19
12. Dawson 1913, 76
13. Dawson 1913, 75-6
14. Dawson and Woodward 1913, 117

15. *Ibid.*
16. *Ibid.*
17. Dawson correspondence quoted by Spencer 1990b, 126
18. Weiner 1955, 128
19. 1913, 75
20. Weiner 1955, 128
21. *Ibid.*
22. *The Times* Thursday 19 December 1912
23. e.g. Weiner 1955, 189; Spencer 1990a, 196-7; 1990b 16; Walsh 1996, 27
24. Dawson 1913, 76; Dawson and Woodward 1913, 117
25. Weiner 1955, 128
26. Woodward 1948, 7-8
27. Walsh 1996 214
28. Weiner 1955, 128-9
29. *The Times* 19 December 1912
30. Dawson and Woodward 1913, 120
31. Walsh 1996, 213-4
32. Dawson 1913, 75: [my italics]
33. Woodward 1948, 8
34. Dawson correspondence quoted in Spencer 1990, 20
35. Woodward 1948, 9
36. Spencer 1990a, 158
37. Teilhard correspondence quoted in Spencer 1990b, 23
38. *Ibid.*
39. Dawson 1913, 77
40. Woodward 1948, 8-9
41. Dawson and Woodward 1913, 117-8
42. Woodward 1948, 8
43. Dawson and Woodward 1913, 121-2
44. Woodward 1948, 10-11
45. Walsh 1996, 226, n19
46. Dawson 1913, 77
47. correspondence quoted in Spencer 1990b, 23
48. Woodward 1948, 10
49. Possibly Saturday the 23rd: Walsh 1996, 226 n19
50. Dawson and Woodward 1913, 121
51. Dawson 1913, 77

52. Dawson and Woodward 1913, 121
53. Woodward 1948, 10
54. Dawson and Woodward 1913, 121
55. Dawson and Woodward 1913, 122
56. *Ibid.*
57. Dawson 1913, 82
58. Dawson and Woodward 1913, 122
59. Dawson and Woodward 1913, 121
60. *Ibid.*
61. *Manchester Guardian* 21 November 1912
62. Spencer 1990a, 48-9
63. *Saturday Review* 21 December 1912
64. Dawson and Woodward 1913, 132-5
65. Dawson and Woodward 1913, 135-7
66. Smith in Dawson and Woodward 1913, 147
67. Dawson and Woodward 1913, 123
68. *Ibid.*
69. Keith 1925, 505
70. Dawkins in Dawson and Woodward 1913, 148-9
71. Reid in Dawson and Woodward 1913, 150
72. Keith in Dawson and Woodward 1913, 148
73. Newton in Dawson and Woodward 1913, 151
74. Dawson and Woodward 1913, 151
75. Keith in Dawson and Woodward 1913, 148
76. Waterson in Dawson and Woodward 1913, 150
77. Woodward 1948, 9
78. Maryon-Wilson correspondence quoted in Spencer 1990b, 49
79. Dawson correspondence quoted in Spencer 1990b, 50
80. *Ibid.*
81. Maryon-Wilson correspondence quoted in Spencer 1990b, 52
82. Spencer 1990a, 57
83. Keith 1915, 345
84. *The Times* 12 August

1913
85. *The Times* 14 August 1913
86. *Ibid.*
87. Dawson correspondence quoted in Spencer 1990b, 76-7)
88. *Daily Express* 15 August 1913)
89. Dawson and Woodward 1914, 82
90. Dawson and Woodward 1914, 84
91. Dawson and Woodward 1914, 84-5
92. Dawson and Woodward 1914, 85
93. *Ibid.*
94. *Ibid.*
95. Teilhard correspondence quoted in Spencer 1990b, 79-80
96. Dawson and Woodward 1914, 85
97. Woodward 1948, 11-12
98. Teilhard correspondence quoted in Spencer 1990b, 80
99. *Daily Express* 3 September 1913
100. *Dawson Correspondence* quoted in Spencer 1990b, 79
101. Spencer 1990a, 69
102. Spencer 1990a, 70-76; Walsh 1996, 44-7
103. Smith correspondence 8 April 1914 quoted in Spencer 1990b, 106
104. Keith 1950, 327
105. Gregory 1914, 190
106. *Ibid.*
107. Woodward 1948, 12
108. Woodward 1948, 44
109. Dawson and Woodward 1915, 133
110. *Ibid.*
111. Woodward 1948, 44-8
112. Dawson and Woodward 1915, 147
113. Woodward 1948, 44
114. Woodward 1948, 46
115. Dawson and Woodward 1915, 146
116. Dawson and Woodward 1915, 147
117. Woodward 1948, 47
118. Dawson and Woodward 1915, 147
119. Lawrence and Warren

in Dawson and Woodward 1915, 148-9
120. Waren in Dawson and Woodward 1915, 148
121. Dale in Dawson and Woodward 1915, 148
122. Kennard in Dawson and Woodward 1915, 149
123. *Ibid.*
124. Smith in Dawson and Woodward 1915, 148
125. *Ibid.*
126. *Ibid.*
127. e.g. Walsh 1996, 50-1
128. Miller 1915, 2
129. Miller 1915, 18
130. Miller 115, 19
131. Miller 1915, 19
132. Woodward correspondence quoted in Spencer 1990b, 134
133. Dawson correspondence quoted in Spencer 1990b, 119
134. Dawson correspondence quoted in Spencer 1990b, 128
135. Spencer 1990a, 105
136. Dawson 1913, 82
137. Dawson unpublished notes quoted in Spencer 1990a, 89
138. Weiner 1955, 183
139. Dawson correspondence quoted in Spencer 1990b, 123
140. Keith 1917, 82
141. Pycraft 1917, 390-1
142. Gregory correspondence quoted in Spencer 1990b, 145
143. Woodward correspondence quoted in Spencer 1990b, 239
144. Woodward 1917
145. Woodward 1917, 1
146. Woodward 1917, 2
147. Woodward 1948, 13
148. *Ibid.*
149. Woodward 1948, 50
150. Woodward 1948, 50-51
151. Woodward 1948, 51
152. Keith 1948, xii
153. 1948, xii
154. Keith 1948, xii
155. Keith 1948, xiii
156. Weiner *et al.* 1953, 146
157. Woodward 1948, 20

158. Oakley 1949, 2
159. *Ibid.*
160. Oakley 1949, 2
161. Montague 1951 464-5
162. Weiner 1955, 27-8
163. Weiner 1955, 29-30
164. Harrison 1983, 47
165. Spencer 1990a, 137
166. Weiner *et al.* 1953, 142
167. Weiner *et al.* 1953, 142-3
168. Weiner *et al.* 1953, 143
169. *Ibid.*
170. Weiner *et al.* 1953, 144
171. 1914, 87
172. Weiner *et al.* 1953, 144
173. Weiner *et al.* 1953, 145
174. *Ibid.*
175. de Beer in Weiner *et al.* 1955, 228
176. De Vries and Oakley 1959, 224
177. De Vries and Oakley 1959, 226
178. Spencer and Stringer 1989, 210
179. *Ibid.*
180. 1996, 149-68
181. Halstead 1978; Blinderman 1986, 183-5
182. Millar 1974
183. Librarian of Hastings Museum: van Esbroeck 1972
184. Jeweller: Blinderman 1986
185. Public Analyst for East Sussex & Hove
186. Costello 1985; 1986
187. Spencer 1990a, 165-82; Walsh 1996, 93-106
188. Gardiner 1996
189. Walsh 1996, 260
190. Quoted in Spencer 1990, 238
191. 1981, 222
192. Millar 1998, 73
193. Spencer 1990, 238
194. Millar 1998, 73
195. *The Times* 21 November 1953
196. *Ibid.*
197. *Ibid.*
198. *Ibid.*
199. *Daily Herald* 23 November 1953
200. *The Times* 23 November 1953
201. *Ibid.*
202. Weiner 1955, 195
203. Weiner 1955, 203-4

204. Spencer 1990, 239
205. Vere 1955, 79
206. *Ibid.*
207. Gould 1980, 28
208. c.f. Smith in Dawson and Woodward 1915, 148
209. Millar 1998, 73
210. Edwards quoted in Spencer 1990a, 150
211. Essex correspondence quoted in Spencer 1990b, 241
212. 1955, 200
213. Weiner 1955, 200-1
214. Blinderman 1986, 101
215. Weiner 1955, 109
216. *Ibid.*
217. Weiner correspondence quoted in Spencer 1990b, 216
218. *Ibid.*
219. Edwards correspondence quoted in Spencer 1990b, 234
220. *Daily Mail* 6 January 1955 quoted in Walsh 1996, 235
221. Dawson 1894a, 97
222. Downes 1956, 14
223. Clement 1997, 277
224. Downes 1956, 14
225. Downes 1956, 330
226. Woodward 1916, 477
227. Clements 1997, 277
228. 1997, 277
229. Clements 1997, 277
230. Weiner 1955, 59
231. e.g.Dawson 1894a
232. Hastings Museum Dawson Loan Collection MSS
233. *Ibid.*
234. Russell 2000, 22-5
235. Weiner 1955, 157
236. *Ibid.*
237. Weiner 1955, 196
238. Weiner 1955, 157
239. e.g.1948, 59
240. Weiner 1955, 155
241. Weiner 1955, 155-6
242. Weiner 1955, 156
243. Quoted in Weiner 1955, 156
244. *Ibid.*
245. Quoted in Spencer 1990b, 218
246. Quoted in Weiner 1955, 158
247. Quoted in Spencer 1990b, 218
248. Weiner correspon-

dence quoted in Spencer 1990b, 217
24. Weiner 1955, 157
250. Pollard correspondence quoted in Spencer 1990b, 231
251. Weiner 1955, 155
252. Gregory 1914, 190
253. Weiner 1955, 160
254. Weiner 1955, 161
255. Keith correspondence quoted in Spencer 1990b, 222
256. Weiner 1955, 157
257. e.g.Dawson 1913, 82
258. Dawson correspondence quoted in Spencer 19090b, 122-3, 125, 126-8
259. J.M. Postlethwaite, *The Times* 23 November 1953
260. Weiner 1955, 112-3
261. Walsh 1996, 192
262. Weiner Manuscript quoted in Spencer 1990b, 229
263. Weiner Manuscript quoted in Spencer 1990b, 235
264. *Ibid.*
265. *Ibid.*
266. Walsh 1996, 91
267. Dawson correspondence as quoted in Spencer 1990b, 71
268. Dawson correspondence quoted in Spencer 1990b, 76
269. Woodward 1948, 59
270. Weiner 1955, 126
271. Dawson correspondence quoted in Spencer 1990b, 69
272. Weiner 1955, 41
273. Weiner 1955, 42
274. Weiner 1955, 77
275. Weiner *et al.* 1953, 145
276. Weiner 1955, 196
277. Quoted in Spencer 1990b, 71 and 76
278. Walsh 1996, 202-3
279. *Sussex Daily News* 14 July 1913
280. e.g.Walsh 1996, 41
281. Woodward 1948, 11
282. Dawson and Woodward 1914, 85
283. *Ibid.*

284. Weiner 1955, 115
285. Woodward 1948, 44
286. Dawson and Woodward 1915, 133
287. *Ibid.*
288. *Ibid.*
289. Woodward 1948, 44
290. Winslow 1983
291. Winslow 1983, 34
292. Winslow 1983, 41
293. *Ibid.*
294. Walsh 1996, 109-11
295. Walsh 1996, 126
296. Walsh 1996, 127
297. Winslow 1983, 42
298. Winslow 1983, 42-3
299. Winslow 1983, 43
300. Winslow 1983, 39
301. Spencer 1990b, 13-14
302. Dawson correspondence 26 May 1909, quoted in Spencer 1990
303. Spencer 1990, 14
304. Dawson correspondence 30 November 1911 quoted in Spencer 1990, 14
305. Dawson correspondence 14 February 1912, quoted in Spencer 1990, 17
306. Dawson and Woodward 1913a, 118
307. Dawson and Woodward 1913a, 117
308. e.g. Spencer 1990b, 16
309. Dawson 1903, XX
310. Dawson 1894a, 98
311. Dawson 1894b, 161
312. Dawson 1903, 23
313. Dawson 1907, 411
314. Weiner 1955, 180
315. Walsh 1996, 117-8
316. Doyle 1912, 142
317. Dawson correspondence 28 March 1909 as quoted in Spencer 1990, 4

Chapter 12

1. Dawson correspondence quoted in Spencer 1990b, 70
2. Dawson correspondence 3 July 1913 quoted in Spencer 1990b, 71

3. Weiner 1955, 150-1
4. Quoted in Spencer 1990b, 143
5. Spencer 1990b, 143
6. Montagu 1971, 212
7. Woodward quoted in Spencer 1990b, 143
8. Montagu 1971, 212
9. Woodward quoted in Spencer 1990b, 143-4
10. Dawson correspondence quoted in Spencer 1990b, 69
11. Dawson correspondence quoted by Spencer 1990b, 28
12. Teilhard correspondence quoted in Spencer 1990b, 212
13. Spencer 1990a, 182-7
14. Dawson correspondence quoted in Spencer 1990b, 70
15. Broom 1949 quoted in Spencer 1990b,188
16. Weiner 1955, 151
17. Ibid.
18. Weiner 1955, 151; Spencer 1990a, 153
19. Broom quoted in Spencer 1990b, 187
20. Montagu 1951b
21. Weiner et al. 1955, 262
22. Weiner 1955, 151
23. Weiner 1955, 152
24. As quoted in Spencer 1990b, 71 and 76
25. Weiner 1955, 149
26. Dawson correspondence quoted by Spencer 1990b, 28
27. Dawson correspondence quoted in Spencer 1990b, 70

28. Weiner 1955, 153
29. Spencer 1990a, 153
30. Walsh 1996, 137
31. 1949 quoted in Spencer 1990b, 188
32. Walsh 1996, 211
33. Dawson correspondence quoted in Spencer 1990b, 119
34. Dawson correspondence quoted in Spencer 1990b, 128
35. Dawson correspondence quoted in Spencer 1990b, 70
36. Woodward 1917, 3
37. Woodward 1917, 4
38. Ibid.
39. Woodward 1917, 5
40. Woodward 1917, 3
41. Ibid.
42. Quoted in Spencer 1990b, 163)
43. 1926, 67
44. 1996, 231
45. Woodward 1948, 65
46. Woodward 1917, 3
47. e.g. Dawson correspondence quoted by Spencer 1990b, 28
48. e.g.Weiner 1955, 87
49. Lankester 1915, 284
50. Woodward 1917, 6
51. Smith 1917, 7
52. Smith 1917, 8
53. Keith in Woodward 1917, 10
54. Lankester in Woodward 1917, 10
55. Woodward 1917, 1
56. Woodward 1917, 2-3
57. Dale in Woodward 1917, 10
58. 1948, 65
59. Weiner 1955, 27

60. Weiner et al. 1953, 142
61. Weiner et al. 1953, 145
62. Ibid.
63. Woodward 1917, 3
64. Spencer and Stringer 1989, 210
65. Weiner 1955, 75
66. e.g. Essex 1955; Vere 1959; Bowden 1977; Gould 1980; Booher 1986; Millar 1998
67. Walsh 1996, 137
68. Boule correspondence quoted by Spencer 1990b, 123
69. Most notably by Spencer 1990a, 208
70. Spencer 1990a, 222-3; Walsh 1996, 54-8
71. Walsh 1996, 54
72. Spencer 1990b, 130
73. Woodward 1917
74. Woodward correspondence quoted in Spencer 1990b, 239
75. Dawson correspondence quoted in Spencer 1990b, 119 and 128
76. Woodward 1917, 3
77. Walsh 1996, 218

Chapter 13

1. Weiner 1955, 194-5
2. Weiner 1956, 188
3. Clarke interview 1954 quoted in Spencer 1990b, 242
4. Weiner 1956, 188
5. e.g.Dawson 1903a, 30
6. Dawson 1898, 564
7. Jones 1990, 94-5

8. Jones 1990, 94
9. Baines 1997, 6
10. Dawson 1898, 293
11. Dawson 1903a, 12
12. Combridge 1981, 221
13. Sawyer 1893, 22
14. 1981, 221
15. Downes 1956, 86
16. Downes Papers, 14 May 1955: Barbican House Museum Lewes
17. Dawson and Lewis 1896, 232
18. Weiner 195x, xx
19. Combridge 1981, 221-2
20. Dawson 1903, 12; Combridge 1977, 431-2
21. Combridge 1977, 433
22. Crake 1912
23. Crake 1912
24. 1980, 225
25. 1981, 221
26. Combridge 1981, 221
27. P.B.S. Andrews 1974
28. Philip Howard (1974)
29. Spencer 1990b, 234-5
30. 1974, 165
31. Howard 1974
32. Combridge 1981, 221
33. Dawson correspondence quoted in Spencer 1990b, 4

BIBLIOGRAPHY

The best starting point for anyone new to the subject of Piltdown man is the excellent online 'A mostly complete Piltdown man Bibliography', compiled and regularly updated by Tom Turritin, which at time of publication can be found at www.talkorigins.org/faqs/piltdown. Other extensive online resources can be found on the Piltdown man homepage: www.home.tiac.net/~cri/piltdown/piltdown.html, which is compiled by Richard Harter and on the Clark University 'Piltdown Plot Project' at www.clarku.edu/ ~piltdown/pp_map.html.

Allcroft, H.A., 'Some Earthworks of West Sussex' (1916) in *Sussex Archaeological Collections* 58, pp.65-90.

Andrews, P., 'Piltdown Man' (1953) in *Time and Tide* 12, pp.1,646-7.

– ,'A Fictitious Purported Historical Map' (1974) in *Sussex Archaeological Collections* 112, pp.165-7.

Anon., 'A Bronze Age Problem' (1953) in *Antiquaries Journal* 15, pp.466-7.

Ashmore, M., 'Fraud by Numbers: Quantitative Rhetoric in the Piltdown Forgery Discovery' (1995) in *South Atlantic Quarterly* 94, pp.591-618.

Baines, J., *Historic Hastings* (Cinque Port Press: St Leonards-on-sea, 1995).

– ,'Charles Dawson: The Saga Continues' (1997) in *Hastings Area Archaeological Research Group Journal* May, pp.5-6.

Beetlestone, C., 1 'A Sussex Fireback' (1926) in *Sussex Archaeological Collections* 67, pp.221-2.

Blinderman, C., 'The Curious Case of Nebraska Man' (1985) in *Science* 85, pp.46-9.

– , *The Piltdown Inquest* (Prometheus Books: New York, 1986).

Boaz, N., 'History of American Paleoanthropological Research on Early Hominidae, 1925-1980' (1981) in *American Journal of Physical Anthropology* 56, pp.397-405.

– , 'The Piltdown Inquest' (1987) in *American Journal of Physical Anthropology* 74, pp.545-6.

Booher, H., 'Science fraud at Piltdown: The amateur and the priest' (1986) in *Antioch Review* 44, pp.389-407.

Boswell, R., 'Skull-diggery at Piltdown' (1963) in *Baker Street Journal* 13, pp.150-5.

Bowden, M., *Ape-Men – Fact or Fallacy?* (Sovereign Publications: Bromley, 1977).

Bowler, P., *Theories of Human Evolution: A Century of Debate, 1844-1944* (Johns Hopkins University Press: Baltimore, 1986).

Broad, W. and Wade, N., *Betrayers of the Truth* (Simon and Schuster: New York, 1982).

Burkitt, M., 'Obituaries of the Piltdown Remains' (1955) in *Nature* 175, p.569.

Carr, J., *The Life of Arthur Conan Doyle* (Harper: New York, 1949).

Chamberlain, A., 'The Piltdown 'forgery'' (1968) in *New Scientist* 40, p.516.

Chippindale, C., 'Piltdown: Who Dunnit? Who Cares?' (1990) in *Science* 250, pp.1,162-3.

Clark, W., 'The Exposure of the Piltdown Forgery' (1955a) in *Proceedings of the Royal Institution of Great Britain* 36, pp.138-51.

– ,'The Exposure of the Piltdown Forgery' (1955b) in *Nature* 175, pp.973-4.

Clements, J., 'Piltdown Man again' (1997a) in *Current Archaeology* 13, p.277.

– , 'Reviewing Piltdown: The Hastings Connection' (1997b) in *Hastings Area Archaeological Research Group Journal* December, pp.8-10.

Clermont, N., 'On the Piltdown Joker and Accomplice: A French Connection?' (1992) in *Current Anthropology* 33, p.587.

Clinch, G., 'Early Man' (1905a) in W. Page (ed.), *The Victoria History of the County of Sussex: Volume 1.* (James Street: Haymarket, 1905) pp.309-332.

– , 'Ancient Earthworks' (1905b) in W. Page (ed.), *The Victoria History of the County of Sussex: Volume 1.* (James Street: Haymarket, 1905) pp.453-80.

Cohen, D., 'Is there a missing link?' (1965) in *Science Digest* 58, pp.96-7.

Cole, S., *Counterfeit* (John Murray: London, 1955).

Combridge, J., 'A Georgian Dial with Edwardian Scenic Engravings' (1977 Beeching/Ashburnham) in *Antiquarian Horology* 10, pp.428-38.

– ,'Charles Dawson and John Lewis' (1981) in *Antiquity* 55, pp.220-2.

Costello, P., 'Teilhard and the Piltdown hoax' (1981a) in *Antiquity* 55, pp.58-9.

– , 'Piltdown Puzzle' (1981b) in *New Scientist* 91, p.823.

– , 'The Piltdown hoax reconsidered' (1985) in *Antiquity* 59, pp.167-73.

– , 'The Piltdown hoax: beyond the Hewitt connection' (1986) in *Antiquity* 60, pp.145-7.

Cox, D., 'Piltdown debate: not so elementary' (1983) in *Science* 83, pp.18-20.

Crake, W., 'A Notice of the Maresfield Forge in 1608' (1912) in *Sussex Archaeological Collections* 55, pp.278-83.

Curwen, E., 'The Lavant Caves, Chichester' (1928) in *Sussex Notes and Queries* 2, p.81.

Daniel, G., 'Piltdown and Professor Hewitt' (1986) in *Antiquity* 60, pp.59-60.

Dawson, C., 'Neolithic Flint Weapon in a Wooden Haft' (1894a) in *Sussex Archaeological Collections* 39, pp.96-8.

– , 'Ancient Boat found at Bexhill' (1894b) in *Sussex Archaeological Collections* 39, pp.161-3.

– , 'Note on the Seals of the Barons and of the Bailiffs of Hastings' (1896) in *Sussex Archaeological Collections* 40, pp.261-4.

– , 'Discovery of a Large Supply of Natural Gas' (1897) in *Nature* 57, pp.150-1.

– , 'On the Discovery of Natural Gas in East Sussex' (1898a) in *Quarterly Journal of the Geological Society of London* 54, pp.564-74.

– , 'Ancient and Modern Dene Holes' (1898b) in *Geological Magazine* 5, pp.293-302.

– , *List of Wealden and Purbeck-Wealden Fossils*, Brighton and Hove Natural History and Philosophical Society (Southern Publishing Co.: Brighton, 1898c).

– , 'Sussex Ironwork and Pottery' (1903a) in *Sussex Archaeological Collections* 46, pp.1-62.

– , 'Sussex Pottery: a new Classification' (1903b) in *Antiquary* 39, pp.47-9.

– , 'Old Sussex Glass: its Origin and Decline' (1905) in *Antiquary* 41, pp.8-11.

– , 'Note on some Inscribed Bricks from Pevensey' (1907a) in *Proceedings of the Society of Antiquaries* 21, pp.411-13.

– , 'The Bayeux Tapestry in the hands of the Restorers' (1907b) in *Antiquary* 43, pp.253-8, 288-92.

– , *History of Hastings Castle* (Constable: London, 1910).

– , 'The Red Hills of the Essex Marshes' (1911) in *Antiquary* 47, pp.128-32.

– , 'The Piltdown Skull' (1913) in *Hastings and East Sussex Naturalist*, pp.73-82.

– , 'The Piltdown Skull' (1915) in *Hastings and East Sussex Naturalist*, pp.182-4.

Dawson, C. and Lewis, J., 'Description and Remarks on the Dungeon Cells at Hastings Castle' (1896) in *Sussex Archaeological Collections* 40, pp.222-35.

Dawson, C. and Woodward, A., 'On the Discovery of a Palaeolithic Human Skull' (1913) in *Quarterly Journal of the Geological Society of London* 69, pp.117-51.

– , 'Supplementary note on the Discovery of a Palaeolithic Human Skull and Mandible at Piltdown (Sussex)' (1914) in *Quarterly Journal of the Geological Society of London* 70, pp.82-93.

– , 'On a Bone Implement from Piltdown' (1915) in *Quarterly Journal of the Geological Society of London* 71, pp.144-9.

de Beer, G., 'Proposed Rejection of the Generic and Specific Names Published for the so-called Piltdown Man' (1955) in *Bulletin of Zoological Nomenclature* 11, pp.171-2.

Dempster, W., 'Something up Dawson's sleeve?' (1996) in *Nature* 382, p.202.

de Vries, H. and Oakley, K., 'Radiocarbon Dating of the Piltdown Skull and Jaw' (1959) in *Nature* 184, pp.224-6.

Dodson, E., 'Was Pierre Teilhard de Chardin a Co-conspirator at Piltdown?' (1981) in *Teilhard Review* 16, pp.16-21.

Downes, R., *Charles Dawson on Trial (a study in archaeology)* (Unpublished manuscript. Sussex Archaeological Society, Lewes, 1956).

Durrenberger, E., 'More about Holmes and the Piltdown Problem' (1965) in *Baker Street Journal* 15, pp.28-31.

Eiseley, L., 'The Piltdown Forgery' (1956) in *American Journal of Physical Anthropology* 14, pp.124-6.

Elliott, D. and Pilot, R., 'Baker Street meets Piltdown Man' (1996) in *Baker Street Journal* 46, pp.13-28.

Essex, R., 'The Piltdown Plot: A Hoax That Grew' (1977) in *Kent and Sussex Journal* July-September 1955, pp.94-5.

Fuller, B. and Turner, B., *Bygone Uckfield* (Phillimore & Co. Ltd: Chichester, 1988).

Garner-Howe, V., 'Piltdown' (1997) in *Current Archaeology* 13, p.277.

Gee, H., 'Box of bones 'clinches' identity of Piltdown palaeontology hoaxer' (1996) in *Nature* 381, pp.261-2.

Godfrey, W., *Lewes: The Official Guide to the Historic County Town* (W.E. Baxter Ltd: Lewes, 1977)

Gould, S., 'Piltdown Revisited' (1979) in *Natural History* 88, pp.86-97.

– , 'The Piltdown Conspiracy' (1980) in *Natural History* 89, pp.8-28.

– , *Hen's Teeth and Horse's Toes* (Norton & Co.: New York, 1983).

Grigson, C., 'Missing links in the Piltdown fraud' (1990) in *New Scientist* 125, pp.55-8.

Grigson, Caroline, 'Comments' (1992) in *Current Anthropology* 33.3, pp.265-6.

Guy, J., *Castles in Sussex* (Phillimore & Co. Ltd: Chichester, 1984).

Halstead, L., 'New light on the Piltdown hoax?' (1978) in *Nature* 276, pp.11-3.

Hammond, M., 'A Framework of Plausibility for an Anthropological Forgery: The Piltdown Case' (1979) in *Anthropology* 3, pp.47-58.

Harrison, G., 'J.S. Weiner and the exposure of the Piltdown forgery' (1983) in *Antiquity* 57, pp.46-8.

Harrison, J., *Bristol and the Hastings Rarities Affair* (G.A. Butler Ltd. Hastings, 1968).

Heal, V., 'Further light on Charles Dawson' (1980) in *Antiquity* 54, pp.222-5.

Holden, E., 'The Lavant Caves' (1981) in *Sussex Archaeological Society Newsletter* 34, p.244.

Hoskins, C. and Fryd, C., 'The Determination of Fluorine in Piltdown and Related Fossils' (1955) in *Journal of Applied Chemistry* 5, pp.85-7.

Hollands, S., 'The Extinct Iron Industry of the Weald of Sussex' (1896) in *Antiquary* 32, pp.198-206.

Hrdlicka, A., 'The Most Ancient Skeletal Remains of Man' (1914) in *Smithsonian Annual Report*, pp.491-519.

– , 'The Piltdown Jaw' (1922) in *American Journal of Physical Anthropology* 5, pp.337-47.

– , 'The Skeletal Remains of Early Man' (1930) in *Smithsonian Miscellaneous Collections* 83, pp.65-90.

Jones, M. (ed.), *Fake? The Art of Deception* (British Museum Publications: London, 1990).

Keith, A., 'The Piltdown Skull' (1913) in *Nature* 92, pp.197-9.

– , 'The Reconstruction of Fossil Human Skulls' (1914) in *Journal of the Royal Anthropological Institute* 44, pp.12-31.

– , *The Antiquity of Man* (Norgate: London, 1915).

– , *New Discoveries Relating to the Antiquity of Man* (Norgate: London, 1931).

– , 'A Resurvey of the Anatomical Features of the Piltdown Skull' (1938) in *Journal of Anatomy* 75, pp.155-85, 234-54.

– , *An Autobiography* (Watts: London, 1950).

Langham, I., 'The Piltdown hoax' (1979) in *Nature* 277, p.170.

– , 'Sherlock Holmes, Circumstantial Evidence and Piltdown Man' (1984) in *Physical Anthropology News* 3, pp.1-4.

Lankester, E., *Diversions of a Naturalist* (Methuen: London, 1915).

Leaky, L., *By the Evidence (Memoirs)* (Harcourt: New York, 1974).

Lowenstein, J. Molleson, T. and Washburn, S., 'Piltdown jaw confirmed as orang' (1982) in *Nature* 299, p.294.

Lower, M., 'Iron Works of the County of Sussex' (1849) in *Sussex Archaeological Collections* 2, pp.169-81.

Lukas, M. and Lukas, E., *Teilhard: a Biography* (Doubleday: New York, 1977).

– , 'The haunting' (1983) in *Antiquity* 57, pp.7-11.

Lyell, C., *The Antiquity of Man* (Murray: London, 1863).

Lyne, W., 'The Significance of the Radiographs of the Piltdown Teeth' (1916) in *Proceedings of the Royal Society of Medicine* 9, pp.33-6.

Marston, A., 'Comments on 'The Solution of the Piltdown Problem'' (1954) in *Proceedings of the Royal Society of Medicine* 47, pp.100-2.

McCann, T., 'Charles Dawson and the Lavant Caves' (1981) in *Sussex Archaeological Society Newsletter* 33, p.234.

McCurdy, G., 'Significance of the Piltdown Skull' (1913) in *American Journal of Science* 35, pp.312-20.

Miles, P., The Piltdown Man and the Norman Conquest: Working Volumes and Printer's Copy (1993) for Charles Dawson's *The History of Hastings Castle. Studies in Bibliography* 46, pp.357-70.

Millar, R., *The Piltdown Men* (Gollancz: London, 1972).

Millar, R., *The Piltdown Mystery: the Story behind the World's Greatest Archaeological Hoax* (S.B. Publications: Seaford, 1998).

Miller, G., 'The Jaw of Piltdown Man' (1915) in *Smithsonian Miscellaneous Collections* 65, pp.1-31.

– , 'The Piltdown Jaw' (1918) in *American Journal of Physical Anthropology* 1, pp.25-52.

– , 'The Piltdown Problem' (1920) in *American Journal of Physical Anthropology* 3, pp.585-6.

Moir, J., 'The Piltdown Skull' (1914) in *Antiquary* 50, pp.21-3.

Montagu, M., 'The Piltdown Nasal Turbinate and Bone Implements: Some Questions' (1954) in *Science* 119, pp.884-6.

– , *An Introduction to Physical Anthropology* (third edition) (Thomas Books: Springfield, 1960).

Musty, J., 'Dawson Reprieved? Piltdown and XRF' (1996) in *Current Archaeology* 13, p.226.

Nelder, J., 'A Statistical Examination of the Hastings Rarities' (1962) in *British Birds* 55, pp.283-98.

Nicholson, E. and Ferguson-Lees, J., 'The Hastings Rarities' (1962) in *British Birds* 55, pp.299-345.

Oakley, K., 'Analytical Methods of Dating Bones' (1955) in *Advancement of Science* 12, pp.3-8.

– , 'Artificial Thickening of Bone and the Piltdown Skull' (1960) in *Nature* 187, p.174.

– , 'The Piltdown problem reconsidered' (1976) in *Antiquity* 50, pp.9-13.

Oakley, K. and de Vries, H., 'Radiocarbon dating of the Piltdown Skull and Jaw' (1959) in *Nature* 184, pp.224-6.

Oakley, K. and Hoskins, C., 'New Evidence of the Antiquity of Piltdown Man' (1950) in *Nature* 165, pp.379-82.

Oakley, K. and Weiner, J., 'Chemical Examination of the Piltdown Implements' (1953) in *Nature* 172, p.110.

Osborn, H., *Men of the Old Stone Age* (Scribner: New York, 1915).

– , 'The Dawn Man of Piltdown' (1921) in *Natural History* 21, pp.577-90.

– , *Man Rises to Parnassus* (Princeton: New Jersey, 1928).

Page, W. (ed.), *The Victoria History of the County of Sussex: Volume 1* (James Street: Haymarket, 1905).

Peacock, D., 'Forged brick-stamps from Pevensey' (1973) in *Antiquity* 47, pp.138-40.

Pycraft, W., 'The Jaw of Piltdown Man' (1917) in *Scientific Progress* 11, pp.389-409.

Ray, J., 'Skeleton found near Eastbourne' (1909) in *Sussex Archaeological Collections* 52, pp.189-92.

Reid, C., 'Geology' (1905) in W. Page (ed.), *The Victoria History of the County of Sussex: Volume 1* (James Street: Haymarket, 1905) pp.1-26.

Rock, J., 'Ancient Cinder Heaps in East Sussex' (1879) in *Sussex Archaeological Collections* 29, pp.167-80.

Rosen, D., 'The jilting of Athene' (1968) in *New Scientist* 39, pp.497-500.

Rowlands, M., *The Organisation of Middle Bronze Age Metalworking* (British Archaeological Reports 31, 1976).

Russell, M., 'Of Flint Mines and Fossil Men: the Lavant Caves Deception' (1999) in *Oxford Journal of Archaeology* 19, pp.497-500.

– , *Flint Mines in Neolithic Britain* (Tempus: Stroud, 2000).

Salzman, L., 'Excavations at Pevensey 1906-7' (1908) in *Sussex Archaeological Collections* 51, pp.99-114.

– , 'A History of the Sussex Archaeological Society' (1946) in *Sussex Archaeological Collections* 85, pp.2-76.

Smith, G., 'The Piltdown Skull' (1913) in *Nature* 92, pp.267-8.

– , 'On the Exact Determination of the Median Plane of the Piltdown Skull' (1914) in *Quarterly Journal of the Geological Society of London* 70, pp.93-4.

– , 'Primitive Man' (1917) in *Proceedings of the British Academy* 7, pp.1-50.

– , *The Evolution of Man* (Humphry: London, 1924)

– , 'The Reconstruction of the Piltdown Skull' (1925) in *Proceedings of the Anatomical Society* 59, pp.38-40.

– , *The Search for Man's Ancestors* (Watts: London, 1931).

Smoker, B., 'Piltdown again' (1997) in *Current Archaeology* 13, p.358.

Sollas, W., *Ancient Hunters and their Modern Representatives* (Macmillan: London, 1915).

Spencer, F., *Piltdown: A Scientific Forgery* (Oxford University Press: New York, 1990a)

– , *The Piltdown Papers: 1908-1955* (Oxford University Pres: New York, 1990b)

Straker, E., *Wealden Iron* (Bell: London, 1931).

Straus, W., 'The Great Piltdown Hoax' (1954) in *Science* 119, pp.265-9.

Thackeray, J., 'On the Piltdown Joker and Accomplice: A French Connection?' (1992) in *Current Anthropology* 33, pp.587-9.

Tobias, P., 'Piltdown: An Appraisal of the Case against Sir Arthur Keith' (1992) in *Current Anthropology* 33, pp.277-93.

– , 'On Piltdown: The French Connection Revisited' (1993) in *Current Anthropology* 34, pp.65-7.

Underwood, A., 'The Piltdown Skull' (1913) in *British Dental Journal* 56, pp.650-2.

Vere, F., *The Piltdown Fantasy* (Cassell: London, 1955).

Vere, Francis, *Lessons of Piltdown: A Study in Scientific Enthusiasm at Piltdown, Java and Peking* (The Evolution Protest Movement: London, 1959).

Wade, N., 'Voice from the Dead Names New Suspect for Piltdown Hoax' (1978) in *Science* 202, p.1,062.

Walsh, J., *Unravelling Piltdown: The Science Fraud of the Century and Its Solution* (Random House: New York, 1996).

Washburn, S., 'The Piltdown Hoax' (1953) in *American Anthropologist* 55, pp.759-62.

– , 'The Piltdown Hoax: Piltdown 2' (1979) in *Science* 203 (March 9) pp.955-8.

Weiner, J., *The Piltdown Forgery* (Oxford University Press: London, 1955).

– , 'The Evolutionary Taxonomy of the Hominidae in the Light of the Piltdown Investigation' (1960) in *Men and Cultures, Selected Papers of the Fifth International Congress of Anthropological and Ethnological Sciences, Philadelphia, September 1-9, 1956* by A. Wallace (ed.) (University of Philadelphia Press: Philadelphia) pp.741-52.

– , 'Piltdown hoax: new light' (1979) in *Nature* 277, p.10.

Weiner, J. and Oakley, K., 'The Piltdown Fraud: Available Evidence Reviewed' (1954) *American Journal of Physical Anthropology* 12, pp.1-7.

Weiner, J. Oakley, K. and Clark, W., 'The Solution of the Piltdown Problem' (1953) in *Bulletin of the British Museum (Natural History) Geology* 2, pp.139-46.

Weiner, J., Clark, W., Oakley, K., Claringbull, G., Hey, M., Edmunds, F., Bowie, S., Davidson, C., Fryd, C., Baynes-Cope, A., Werner, A. and Plesters, R., 'Further Contributions to the Solution of the Piltdown Problem' (1955) in *Bulletin of the British Museum (Natural History) Geology* 2, pp.225-87.

Welfare, S. and Fairley, J., *Mysterious World* (Collins: London, 1980).

Wilson, D., *Atoms of Time Past* (Penguin: London, 1975).

Winslow, J. and Meyer, A., 'The Perpetrator at Piltdown' (1983) in *Science* 83, pp.33-43.

Winton, W., 'The Piltdown Clock' (1956) in *The British Steelmaker* October 1956, pp.292-3.

Woodward, A., 'On a Mammalian Tooth from the Wealden Formation at Hastings' (1891) in *Proceedings of the Zoological Society of London* 24, pp.585-6.

– , 'On Some Mammalian Teeth from the Wealden of Hastings' (1911) *Quarterly Journal of the Geological Society of London* 67, pp.278-81.

– , 'Note on the Piltdown Man' (1913) in *Geological Magazine* 10, pp.433-4.

– , 'Charles Dawson Obituary' (1916) in *Geological Magazine* 13, pp.477-9.

– , 'Fourth Note on the Piltdown Gravel, with Evidence of a Second Skull of *Eoanthropus dawsoni*' (1917) in *Quarterly Journal of the Geological Society of London* 73, pp.1-10.

– , 'The Second Piltdown Skull' (1933) in *Nature* 5, p.86.

– , 'Recent Progress in the Study of Ancient Man' (1935) in *Report of the British Association for the Advancement of Science*, pp.129-42.

– , 'Geographical Distribution of Early Man' (1944) in *Geological Magazine* 81, pp.49-57.

– , *The Earliest Englishman* (Watts: London, 1948).

Zuckerman, S., 'A new clue to the real Piltdown forger?' (1990) in *New Scientist* 128, p.16

INDEX

Abbott, Lewis 26, 139, 155, 186, 200, 209
Abergavenny, Marquess of 48
Allcroft, Hadrian 33-34, 36, 38
American Museum of Natural History 178, 184, 187, 241
Anderida 98
Andrews, P. B. S 141-4, 259, 260
'Arabic' Anvil 81-84, 250, 269, **39**, **40**
Arabic Numerals 82
Arcadius 97
Arctic Circle 124
Ashburnham 144, 146
Ashburnham Dial 144-8, 250, 255, 257
Ashdown Forest 266
Atkinson, J. C. 121

Bagshot de la Bere of Buxted, Basil 12
Baines, John Mainwairing 80-1, 84, 102, 107, 118-9
Bannister, Francis 138, 204
Barbe, Guy St 217-8
Barbican House, Lewes 17, 269-70
Barcombe Mills 20, 231-9
Barkham Manor 22, 152-230, 267, 270, **103**
Barlow, Frank Orwell 183-4, 218, **86**
Battle 91
Bayeux Tapestry 15, 58, 77, 106, 113-4, 123, 263, **61**
Beauport Park Axe 84-5, 250
Beauport Park Statuette 15, 61-70, 84, 139, 228-9, 250, 262, 269, **30**

Beckles, Samuel 13, 28, 32, 251, 261
Beeching Family 146
Beeching, Thomas 146
Beetlestone, Charles 72
Bennett, F. J. 111
Bermondsey Abbey Curfew 78-80, 250, 269, **37**, **38**
Berry, William 93-4
Bexhill Boat 52, 55-60, 139, 228, 250, 261-2
Birmingham University 67, 112
Blackmore, Stephen 51-4
Blackmore's Stone Axe 51-4, 210, 228, 250, 261-2
Blackrock 93
Blinderman, Charles 119
Bodleian Library 117-8
Booth Museum of Natural History 127, 128, 149, 200, 254
Brassey Institute 114, 86, 91
Brassey, Lord & Lady 210
Brightling 109, **56**
Brighton 93, 94, 108, 125, 253
Brighton & Hove Natural History & Philosophical Society 126, 128
Bristow, George 137-40, **67**, **68**
British Museum 15, 25, 63-4, 69, 71, 77, 85, 94, 96, 100-1, 117, 128, 254, 263
British Museum (Natural History) 13, 23, 28, 32, 124, 133, 166, 171-2, 149, 200, 203, 213-4, 220, 233, 254, 261
British Ornithologists Club 137

Broom, Robert 234, 237
Bruce-Mitford, Rupert 77,85
Buckland, Willliam 127
Budgen, Mr 144
Bulverhythe Hammer 86-9, 139, 250, 264, 269, **41**, **42**
Burbridge, J. 126-7, 128
Burlington House, London 19, 166
Butterfield, William 25
Butterfield, William Ruskin 200

Canterbury 94-5, 254
Castle Hill, Hastings 14, 261
Castle Lodge 13, 16-7, 48-50, 77, 78, 106, 118, 132, 143, 144, 206, 209-210, 238, 251, 253, 258, 259, 260, 263, 269-70 **4**, **26**, **27**
Chichester 61
Chichester, Lord 42, 117
Chiddingly Dog Gate 73-6, 250, **34**, **35**
Chinese Vase 94-6, 250, 254-5
Cinque Ports 80-1
Cissbury 37, 41
Clark, Wilfred le Gros 24, 192-3, 201
Clarke, Ernest 48, 151, 253
Clarke, G. T. 117
Claudian 98
Clements, John 210-11
Clinch, George 34, 36, 86-7, 89, 90, 92
Colonial Williamsburg Foundation 144-5
Combridge, John 143, 146, 147, 201, 255
Cooke, John 183
Costello, Peter 26
Crake, W. V. 64-5, 66, 143, 258

Cretaceous 29, 132
Crippen, Hanley Harvey 253
Cromwell, Oliver 72
Crowborough 149-227
Curwen, Elliot 38

Dacre Family 72
Dacre, Elizabeth 72
Dacre, Francis 72
Dacre, Thomas 72
Daily Express 173, 177
Dale, W. 182, 244
Damon Company 172, **77**
Darwin, Charles 166, 183-4, 265, **86**
Dawkins, William Boyd 170
Dawson (nee Postlethwaite), Helene 12-13, 18, 84, 106, 209, 227, 228, 232, 233, 237, 252-3, 257, 270 **105**
Dawson Hart & Co. 12, 20, 106, 208, 210, 267-9
Dawson, Arthur Trevor 11, 12, 13, 201, 260, 264
Dawson, Charles **1**, **3**, **11**, **72**, **73**, **74**, **86**, **96**, **100**, **105**
'Arabic' Anvil 84
Ashburnham Dial 147-8
Beauport Park Axe 85
Bermondsey Abbey Curfew 79-80
Chiddingly Dog Gate 75-6
Chinese Vase 96
Collaborators 229-30, 251-60
Creator of Blackmore's Stone Axe 53-4
Creator of the Bulverhythe Hammer 88-9

Creator of Uckfield Horseshoe 72
Death 20, 187
Early Days 10-13, 260-1
Eviction of Sussex Archaeological Society 15-7, 48-9
Forger of Pevensey Brick 106-7
Forger of Piltdown I 24-7, 202-5, 206-25
Forger of Piltdown II 248-9
Forger of Piltdown III 235-6, 238-9
Forger of *Plagiaulax dawsoni* 31, 32
Fossil Hunting 13-14, 261
Fraudster at Beauport Park 68-70
Fraudster at Castle Lodge 49-50
Fraudster at Hastings Castle 47-8
Fraudster at Lavant Caves 38, 40-1
Funeral 20-1, **9**
Geological Society 13, 132, 261
Hastings Mace 81
Hastings Rarities 138-40
Herstmonceux Fire Back 73
Illness 20, 185, 187, 247, 248
Lewes Prick Spur 78
Maresfield Map 142-4
Royal Society 124, 133, 135, 177-8, 262, 264, 265
Sea Serpent 131-2
Society of Antiquaries 15, 108, 132, 256, 263
St Leonards Bronze Hoard 92-3
Staining of Samples 186, 212-3, 217-29, 235
Suspected Plagiariser 121-3, 135
Sussex Archaeological Society 14-7, 19-20, 261, 263

Sussex Loops 94
Thirteenth Dorsal Vertebra 134-5
Toad in a Hole 128
Wizard of Sussex 10, 107, 260
Dawson, Hugh 10
Dawson, Hugh Leyland 11, 20, 260
Dene Holes 108-11, 121, 122-3, 250, 252, 263, 265, **56, 57**
Dieppe 129
Dipridon Valdensis 14, 29, 32, **13**
Discussion of the Piltdown Skull 183-4, 264-5, **86**
Douglas, James Archibald 200
Dover 81, 94-95, 98
Downes, Robert 7, 27, 36, 38, 49-50, 54, 67, 68, 71, 72, 75-6, 77, 79, 81, 83, 84, 85, 87, 9`, 95-6, 112, 118-9, 123, 145
Doyle, Arthur Conan 25, 149, 225-9, 264

Earlom, Richard 147, 257
East Dean 51
Edwards, Wilfred 188, 205, 209
Eoanthropus dawsoni 19, 23, 157-230, **7, 8**
Essex Field Club 110-1, 121
Essex, Robert 25, 205
Evans, John 53, 64

Ferguson-Lees, J. 137-8
Fleming, S.J. 102
Flint Jack 211
Flint Mines 37-8, 39-40, 211-2
Forester, Thomas 120
Franks, Augustus Wollaston 15, 61, 68, 69, 71, 251, 261
Frisby, John **79, 95**
Fryd, C.F.M. 195, 196
Fuller of Heathfield 74, 75-6

Geological Society 13, 19, 68, 125, 126, 132,

153, 155, 166, 185, 224, 232, 242-3, 248, 261
Goodman, Frederick du Cane 232
Goodwood House 36-7, 40
Gordon, Alexander 37
Gordon, W.T. 188
Greenwell, William 37, 41
Gregory, William King 178, 187, 214
Grimes Graves 37, 41
Grimm, S.M. 117
Grose, Francis 117

Hadrian 64-5, 68
Han Dynasty 95
Hargreaves, Venus 25, 158, 174, 222, 224-5, **72, 73, 74**
Harrison, Geoffrey 138, 217
Harrison, J. Park 37
Hart, George 12, 208, 267, **3**
Hastings 11, 12, 13, 14, 28-9, 78, 80, 81, 91, 135-40, 119, 151, 154, 177, 202
Hastings 'Dungeons' 41-8, 251, 256-7, 259, 262, **18, 19, 20, 21, 22, 23, 24**
Hastings and St Leonards Museum Association 14, 18, 51, 54, 64, 210, 261
Hastings Castle 14, 15, 41-8, 52, 61, 76-7, 106, 114, 143, 210, 250, 255, 263, 269, **18, 19, 20, 21, 22, 23, 24, 61, 62, 63, 64**
Hastings Mace 80-1, 210, 250
Hastings Museum 14, 18, 61, 64, 67, 81, 84, 102, 138, 143, 147, 148, 211, 253, 257, 261, 263, 269, 273-4, **6**
Hastings Natural History Society 18, 143
Hastings Rarities 135-40, 250, **67, 68**
Hayden, Arthur 144
Haywards Heath 189

Heal, Veryan 53
Heathery Burn Cave 87
Heathfield 15, 124-6, 202, 250, 252
Herbert, William 117-20, 123, **65**
Herstmonceux Fire Back 72-3, 250, **33**
Hewitt, H. Dixon 36, 38
Hewitt, John 26, 125, 200
Hinton, Martin 26, 200
History of Hastings Castle 46, 114-20, 123, 250, 263,
HMS Daedalus 130, 131
HMS St. Vincent 130, 131
Hollands, Sidney 71, 74-6, **32, 35**
Holmes, Sherlock 226
Holmes, T.V. 110-1
Homo heidelbergensis 149-50
Homo keithii 173
Homo neanderthalensis 150, 240, 243
Homo piltdownensis 172-3, 176, 243
Homo sapiens 150
Honorius 97-8, 102, 105, 107
Howard, Philip 141, 259, 260
Howlett, B. 117
Hrdlicka, Ales 241
Huggins, Arthur 48
Hythe 81

Iguanodon dawsoni 14, 28, 124
Inuit 133
Isfield 267
Isted, Joseph 126, 128

Joicey, James 12
Jones, W. Gore 130

Keith, Arthur 21, 22, 25, 133-4, 135, 170-1, 172-3, 177-8, 182, 183, 186, 188, 189, 199-200, 201, 215, 243, 246, 251, **86**
Kelener, Dr. 66
Kennard, A.S. 182
Kenward, Mabel 201, 209-10

Kenward, Robert (Junior) **73**

Kenward, Robert (Senior) 157, 201, 209, 225, **72**

Lambert, James 117

Lane Fox, Augustus 37, 41

Langham, Ian 201

Langham, James 261

Langhams, F.A. 11-2, 68, 260

Lankester, Ray 182-3, 184, 225-6, 233, 235, 242, 243

Lardner, Dr. 112

Lavant Caves 14, 33-41, 52, 143, 250, 251, 255, 256, 259, 262, 271-2, **15**, **16**, **17**

Laver, Henry 121

Lawrence, G.F. 182

le Double, A. F. 134

Lepidotus mantelli 13, 28, 124

Lewes 13, 20, 70, 71, 94, 102, 111, 126, 143, 269, **9**

Lewes Bowls Club 78, 270

Lewes Castle 16, 48, 76-7, 269, **4**, **26**, **27**

Lewes Prick Spur 76-8, 250, **36**

Lewis, John 14, 33-48, 52, 77, 109, 110, 112-3, 125, 143-4, 147-8, 201, 251, 255-60, 262, 265, **28**, **29**, **56**, **57**, **60**, **69**, **70**

Loch Ness 131-2

London 79-80, 91, 93

London – Brighton Railway 125-6

London University 125

Longstone 91

Lycopidotus teilhardi 14

Lydekker, Richard 14, 251

M'Quhae, Peter 130

Manchester Guardian 19, 166, 177

Manchester University 127, 168, 170, 177, 183

Marchant, Rex 138-9

Maresfield 142, 266

Maresfield Map 141-4, 250, 255, 257, 258-60, **69**

Marriott, R.A. 214, 217

Marshall, E. 42, 45-6, 47, 256

Maryon-Wilson, George 157, 171-2, 241

Mennell, F.P. 182

Merritt, William 65-6, 68-9, 84

Metro-Vickers and Maxims Ltd. 17, 201

Miles, Peter 119-20, 123

Millar, Ronald 201

Miller, Gerrit. S. (Junior) 184-5, 186-7

Mitchdean Cliffs 51, 53, 54

Montagu, Ashley 191, 234

Montgomery, John 205

Morris, Harry 20, 178, 212-4, 265

Morrogh, H. 67

Mount Harry 270

Mr 'X' 24, 26, 27

Multituberculata 28-32

Murray, A.S. 63

Natural Gas 15, 124-6, 251, 252, 254

Natural History Museum (See British Museum (Natural History))

'Nessie' 131-2

Netherall Farm 241

Newhaven 129

Newick 266

Newman, E. 61

Newton, Edwin 171

Nicholl, Dr. (Junior) 209-10

Nicholl, Dr. (Senior) 209-10

Nicholl, M.J. 137

Nicholson, E. 137-8

Niedermayer, R.A. 49-50

North and East Bengal State Railways 255-6

Nye, Thomas 126-7

Oakley, Kenneth 24, 89, 190-1, 192, 194, 201, 205, 217-8, 233, 245

Oxford University 102, 217-8, 233, 245

Pan vetus 185

Peacock, David 100, 102-3

Pelletier, Felix 29, 149

Pevensey Bricks 97-107, 228, 250, 255, 263, **46**, **47**, **48**, **49**, **50**, **51**, **52**, **53**, **54**, **55**

Pevensey Castle 15, 97-107, 139, 269, **46**, **47**, **48**, **49**, **50**, **51**, **52**, **53**, **54**, **55**, **58**

Phosphorescent Bullets 15

Piltdown I 17, 18-20, 23-7, 30, 133, 134, 139, 144, 149-230, 250, 252, 258-9, 264-5, 266-7, **7**, **8**, **12**, **71**, **72**, **73**, **74**, **75**, **76**, **77**, **78**, **79**, **80**, **81**, **82**, **83**, **84**, **85**, **86**, **87**, **88**, **89**, **90**, **91**, **92**, **93**, **94**, **95**, **96**, **97**, **98**, **101**, **102**

Age 23, 168-7, 190-1, 198-9, 246

Brain Capacity 18-19, 23, 172-3

Discovery of Canine 175-6, 224

Discovery of Cranium 151, 152-6, 221

Discovery of Elephant Femur 179-81, 224,

Discovery of Jaw 161-2, 222

Discovery of Nasal Bones 174-5, 224

Dualists versus Monoists 185, 186-7, 191

Elephant Femur 179-82, 197, 204-5, 224, **84**, **85**, **94**

Eoliths 164-5, 174, 185-6, 214-5, 250

Excavations after Dawson's Death 23, 188, 189

Flourine Testing 23, 190-1, 192, 194-5

Geological Reserve 23

Hammerstone 187, 244

Media Storm 19, 264

Monolith 22, 188, 189, 267, 270, **10**

Organic Content 192-4, 195

Palaeoliths 164-5, 211-2, **93**

'Pot Boiler' 188

Radiocarbon Dating 198-9, 246

Staining 192-4, 195-6, 200, 212-3, **93**

Wear Patterns on Teeth 192-5, **87**, **88**, **89**, **90**

Witness Section 23

Piltdown II (Sheffield Park Man) 186, 187-8, 224, 226, 233, 239-49, 250, 264-5

Announcement 185, 187, 240-1, 246-7, 248

Dating 199, 245-6

Discovery 185, 192, 241

Match with Piltdown I 245-6

Molar 194, 195

Provenance 185, 241-2, 245, 247-8

Staining 245

Wear Patterns on Teeth 194, 245

Piltdown III (Barcombe Mills Man) 218, 231-9, 250, 264-5

Discovery 231-2, 235

Provenance 232-3

Staining 234-5

Plagiaulax dawsoni 14, 28-32, 124, 250, 251, 252, 257, 261, 263-4, **13**

Pleistocene 168-9, 170-1, 181, 190-1, 195, 199, 216, 232

Plesiosaur 132

Pliocene 168-9, 170-1, 181, 216, 246

Pollard, A.P. 212-3

Portsmouth 130

Postlethwaite, F.J.M. 12, 17, 24-5, 202-3

Postlethwaite, Gladys 12

Postlethwaite, Helene (See Dawson, Helene)

Prehistoric Society of East Anglia 185, 214

Pycraft, William Plane 183-4, 186-7, 239, 243, **86**

Ray, John 15
Read, Charles Hercules 63-4, 69
Red Hills Exploration Committee 121
Red Hills of Essex 120-1, 122-3, 250
Reid, Clement 170
Richmond, Duke of 34-5, 40
Rines, Robert 132
Roberts-Austen, W.C. 63, 66
Rock, James 62-3, 64-5, 68-9
Rolleston, George 37
Romney 81
Ross, Alderman Thomas 210-1
Rowlands, M. 92
Royal Anthropological Society 134, 185, 214
Royal College of Surgeons 133-4, 172, 183
Royal Commission on the Historical Monuments of England 38
Royal Society 124, 133, 135, 177-8, 263, 264, 265

Salaginella dawsoni 14, 28
Salzman, Louis 16-17, 48, 100-7, 255, 258, 259, 265
Sandwich 81
Sargent, Henry 151
Saunders, John 67
Sawyer, John 34, 35
Schettensack, Otto 150
Sea Serpents 15, 129-32, 250, 263
Sheffield Park (See also Piltdown II) 20, 233, 239-49
Slade, Henry 225-6
Smith, A.H. 63-4, 65, 66
Smith, Barclay 188

Smith, Grafton Elliot 26, 168, 177-8, 183, 187-8, 200, 239, 242-3, 244, 247, 251, 86
Smith, Reginald 182
Smith, Treave 111
Society of Antiquaries 14, 15, 61, 63, 64, 66, 69, 76-8, 84, 93, 97, 106, 107, 124, 132, 143-4, 255, 256, 259, 260, 261, 263
Sollas, William 26, 182, 200
South East Union of Scientific Societies 125
Southampton University 102
Spencer, Frank 134-5, 199-200, 201, 246
Spokes, S. 20
SS Manche 129, 131, 132
St Leonards Bronze Hoard 89-93, 250, 269, 43, 44
St Leonards on Sea 10, 89, 90, 92, 137, 138, 260
St John Sub Castro 20, 270, 9, 104, 105
Stilicho 98
Stopes, H. 121
Straker, Ernest 66-7
Sussex Archaeological Society 14-7, 19-20, 33, 34, 41, 48, 50, 51, 61, 72, 73, 84, 100-7, 108, 118, 132, 143, 206, 214, 258, 259, 261, 263, 265, 269-70
Sussex Daily News 34
Sussex Ironwork 111-4, 122-3, 250, 255, 263
Sussex Loops 93-4, 210, 250, 45
Sussex Record Society 15, 263
Swanage 32

Teilhard de Chardin, Marie-Joseph Pierre 14, 17, 25, 29, 31-2, 151, 157-61, 174-7, 195-6, 201, 202, 204, 205, 213, 216, 219, 224, 233, 236, 237, 238, 246, 247, 251, 252
The Times, London 19, 118, 130, 137, 153, 155, 173, 201, 202
The Times, New York 19, 141, 260
Thirteenth Dorsal Vertebra 133-5, 250, 263
Tindall, Plumpton 37
Toad in a Hole 126-8, 132, 210, 228, 250, 254, 263, 66
Tobias, Philip 199
Topley, William 112-3
Treagus, Jack 127
Trevor Family 72

Uckfield 12, 17, 20, 21, 48, 49, 70-2, 106, 108, 119-20, 149, 217, 225, 231, 261, 269, 2, 3
Uckfield Horseshoe 70-2, 228, 250, 31, 32
Underwood, Arthur Swayne 183-4, 86
University of Heidelberg 150

Vere, Francis (See also Bannister, Francis) 25, 26, 138, 204
Victoria County History of Sussex 34-5, 89, 92, 100
Visigoths 97

Walsh, John Evangelist 26-7, 58-9, 68, 113, 114, 131, 155, 199, 226, 238
Warren, S.H. 182
Waterson, David 171
Watson, White 127

Watson, William 95
Webb, Mr. 58-60
Weiner, Joseph 19-20, 23-4, 48, 113, 118, 127, 134, 143, 153, 154, 191-2, 199, 201, 203-4, 205, 206, 208-9, 212-3, 214, 220, 233, 235, 245, 247-8, 253, 270
Wells Cathedral 82
Westfield 65
White, Osborne 241
Willett, Edgar 233, 235, 242
Willett, Ernest 37
Willett, Henry 94-5, 96, 124-5, 127, 253-5
Winslow, John 225-7
Wood, Frederick 212
Woodhead, Samuel Allinson 26, 125, 126, 151, 152, 155, 165-6, 200, 252
Woodward, Arthur Smith 20-1, 22, 25, 28-32, 94, 124, 126, 129, 130, 131-2, 133-4, 135, 149, 150, 151, 153-230, 231-49, 251, 252, 253, 261, 264, 10, 11, 72, 73, 74, 86, 95, 96, 100
Woodward, Cyril 185, 187, 247, 79, 96, 100
Woodward, Maude 174-5, 189, 209-10, 247-8
Worthing 93
Wright, Joseph 112, 147, 257, 60
Wyndham, Mary 36

Young, Jessie 55-60

Zeppelins 15
Zoological Society of London 28